International Relations

THEORIES AND EVIDENCE

Michael P. Sullivan

The University of Arizona

PRENTICE-HALL, INC., ENGLEWOOD CLIFFS, NEW JERSEY

Library of Congress Cataloging in Publication Data

SULLIVAN, MICHAEL P
   International relations.

   Includes bibliographical references and index.
   1. International relations. I. Title.
JX1391.S85   327   75-43541
ISBN 0-13-473470-X

Printed in the United States of America

10 9 8 7 6 5 4 3 2 1

PRENTICE-HALL INTERNATIONAL, INC., LONDON
PRENTICE-HALL OF AUSTRALIA, PTY. LIMITED, SYDNEY
PRENTICE-HALL OF CANADA, LTD., TORONTO
PRENTICE-HALL OF INDIA PRIVATE LIMITED, NEW DELHI
PRENTICE-HALL OF JAPAN, INC., TOKYO
PRENTICE-HALL OF SOUTHEAST ASIA PTE. LTD., SINGAPORE

To My Mother

Contents

Preface

ix

chapter 1   International Behavior and Theories
of International Relations

1

INTRODUCTION   THE BEHAVIOR OF NATIONS
THEORIES OF INTERNATIONAL BEHAVIOR
THEORIES, EXPLANATION, AND EVIDENCE   DISPUTES   CONCLUSION

part I   *Man and the State*

19

chapter 2   Man and His Images

23

INSTINCT   PERSONALITY   IMAGE THEORIES
CONCLUSIONS AND IMPLICATIONS

v

chapter 3   Decision-Making

66

DECISION-MAKING MODELS   THEORIES OF DECISION PROCESSES   CONCLUSION

chapter 4   National Attribute Theory: Domestic Sources of Foreign Policy

102

CONTEMPORARY EMPIRICAL ANALYSIS   SIZE AND DEVELOPMENT
TYPE OF GOVERNMENT   SOCIAL AND POLITICAL STABILITY
MULTIPLE ATTRIBUTES   CONCLUSION

part II   *The International System: System Dynamics*

143

chapter 5   Power and Rank: Distance and Systems

155

POWER   TWO CONCEPTIONS OF POWER   POWER THEORY
POWER AS DISTANCE   POWER AS SYSTEM   RANK AND STATUS THEORIES
MEASUREMENT   POWER ANALYSIS   CONCLUSION

chapter 6   Integration, Distance, and Balance Theories

207

INTEGRATION   INTEGRATION: DEFINITION AND MEASUREMENT   DISTANCE
STRUCTURAL BALANCE THEORY   MEASUREMENT
DISTANCE AND INTEGRATION: EMPIRICAL LINKAGES   BALANCE AS DISTANCE
CONCLUSION

chapter 7   The Bargaining Approach
to International Politics

252

BEHAVIOR AS BARGAINING: THE GAME OF INTERNATIONAL POLITICS
THEORETICAL CONSIDERATIONS
DETERRENCE, BRINKMANSHIP, AND COMMITMENT   BARGAINING MODELS
MEASUREMENT   COGNITIVE MODELS   STIMULUS-RESPONSE MODEL
LEARNING MODELS   CONCLUSION

chapter 8   Multivariate Approaches

301

MULTIVARIATE: SINGLE LEVEL   CROSS-LEVEL ANALYSIS   CONCLUSION

part III   *Conclusion*

327

appendix   Methodological Problems and Issues

343

INTRODUCTION   A. STATISTICAL ANALYSIS
A1. DATA DISTRIBUTIONS: OUTLIERS   A2. AGGREGATION
A3. NONRANDOMNESS AND STRENGTH OF RELATIONSHIP
A4. ERRORS IN PREDICTION: RESIDUALS   B. OPERATIONAL INDICATORS
C. FACTOR ANALYSIS   D. TIME SERIES ANALYSIS   E. RESEARCH DESIGN

Name Index

377

Subject Index

380

Preface

Academic disciplines, regardless of area, focus, or content, undergo constant change, and the study of international relations is no exception. During the past generation there has been a shift in some quarters of the discipline from historical-descriptive research toward a greater emphasis on explicit theory formulation and the testing of specific hypotheses with empirical, quantified data. I do not believe, as some do, that this change constitutes a revolution as significant as the transition from Newtonian to quantum physics—or that it heralds the dawn of a new day in international relations research. The change is more of degree than of kind, but nonetheless it has spawned interest in a different style of research and a different way of understanding international behavior.

Change is a slow process, and it takes a long time for new scholarship to permeate professional journals into specialized books and finally into more comprehensive analyses of entire fields. This book attempts to achieve three goals. First, the central focus of the book is on theory formulation. It concentrates on questions concerning international behavior that can be cast in theoretical terms and that can be answered through tests of specific hypotheses. Thus, the chapter headings reflect what I consider to be the most general ways that we understand international behavior.

Second, these theories for explaining international behavior are, of necessity, linked concretely to the empirical research that has emerged in the past generation. Too often students are presented with what appear to be a myriad of approaches to international relations. They are bombarded with research efforts—in the form of journal articles or readings —that they have no way of placing within larger theoretical or substantive issues. As a result, research in international relations often appears to be fragmented and disorganized, lacking central themes or questions; each researcher seems to go his merry way. To remedy this, I have tied individual research efforts to broader theoretical and substantive questions, which have long been of great concern to scholars and practitioners.

Third, the book shows how international relations research can be viewed as a cumulative body of knowledge. Although many may be dissatisfied with exactly what and how much we do know about international relations, the remedy for that discontent is not to give up, but rather to try to organize the complexity. This book questions the time-worn truism that international relations is too complex, that "too much" is going on and "too many" variables are involved to ever allow a real understanding. Of course everything is complex, to one degree or another, and the task is not to bemoan that fact but to grapple with it.

Two standard approaches eschewed in this book are (1) presenting the student with only one theory of explaining international behavior—such as the traditional "power" or "national interest" frameworks—and forcing that one theory to fit all international behavior; or (2) asserting that only by considering *all* possible approaches, merely piling them one on top of another, can the student truly understand a given event or behavior. Both methods have serious drawbacks, the first because no one theory or approach can possibly explain *all* international behavior, and the second because it provides the student with a false sense of understanding, relieving him of the more difficult task of assessing many possible explanations. To get a better grip on this complexity, the student must realize that just as there are different theories to explain international behavior, likewise there are many different types and levels of behavior. Some approaches only have validity when applied to certain behavior: the task is to link the appropriate explanation to the type of behavior it can account for. By doing this, some of the surface complexity fades in importance, for we can then separate out the domains of behavior the respective theories can account for, and no one theory is given the impossible task of accounting for all international behavior.

In sum, I have tried in this book to bring a coherence to the study of international relations that I do not think exists at the present time. International relations is certainly complex, but it is not hopelessly so, and one way to fathom that complexity is through a rigorous concern for theory formulation and testing. As noted, this book does not present one approach, nor any "new" approach, nor does it simply leave many approaches at the student's disposal, implying that he can pick and choose. Understanding the complexity of international relations goes beyond that, and this book establishes what I feel are the primary parameters to begin that task.

No book can be completed in a vacuum. In the present case, I gratefully acknowledge the careful analysis of the entire manuscript by Kal Holsti, Fred Sondermann, and Thomas Volgy. Thomas Sullivan read almost every chapter and provided very helpful criticisms. Others who read portions of the manuscript were also generous and helpful with their comments: Gail Bernstein, Andres Onate, R. J. Rummel, Lawrence Scaff, Mitchell A. Seligson, and William Hoth. Discussions with John Schwarz, Edward J. Williams, and John Sullivan were very valuable. I must also thank the Department of Political Science at the University of Arizona, as well as the University of Arizona Computer Center and the Institute of Government Research at the University of Arizona for providing research and computer assistance. Belinda Gallardo, Linda Garcia, Jane Bakos, Jeanne Marshall, and Janet Griffing all provided yeomanly secretarial skills.

In addition to intellectual assistance, Gail Bernstein's unflagging optimism and prodding provided the spiritual wherewithal to keep this project going in what appeared to be its darkest hours. To Don and Harriet Davis, I owe a real debt of gratitude for having generously provided the essential physical surroundings in which to work.

chapter 1 International Behavior and Theories of International Relations

Introduction

This book is about theories of international relations and the evidence that supports or contradicts these theories. Its primary concern, therefore, is with international behavior in its multiple forms and how to explain it. "Theory" and "explanation" are two sides of the same coin. Theory is a crucial and necessary element in understanding international behavior; explanation is inextricably a part of understanding. This introductory chapter discusses what exactly the international behavior is that we are trying to explain, and how theories are essential to those explanations. It also describes some rules of evidence to be used as criteria for evaluating explanations, as well as several disputes that surround the different methods of understanding international behavior.

The Behavior of Nations

The concept "international behavior" is not one simple entity. The primary emphasis of scholars, diplomats, and journalists has, of course, focused on war: what causes war, what nations will most likely be involved in war, how war can be ended. Behaviors below the level of war are nonetheless of the same general type: what states are more likely to use threats, which ones are more likely to sever relations with other nations, which are more likely to vote with one another in the United Nations. International behavior also concerns which states are going to join together in alliances—and how long the alliances will last.

But war, conflict, threats, voting, alliances represent only a handful of potential behaviors on the part of. nation-states. To speak of the "behavior of nations" is to refer to a broad spectrum of international conduct. Though it is ultimately an individual that acts in the international arena, we make use here of a shorthand abstraction by referring to the behavior of "nations." In recent years this perspective has been under attack for not taking into account behavior that occurs in international politics but is not performed by a specific nation-state. We retain the shorthand of the "behavior of nations" for two reasons. First, it is still true that most important behavior in international politics remains the behavior of nations. Second, the theories used to explain that behavior can—with few exceptions—be used to explain international behavior by groups or by individuals not designated as nations.

Just as international behavior can take many different forms—war, alliances as already mentioned—likewise each of the forms itself can be viewed at different "levels." War, for example, can mean a specific war such as the Chaco War, the Korean War, or the Vietnam War. Or, it can be broadened to mean the totality of war in the international system, that is, the amount of warfare conducted across long periods of time irrespective of which nations are involved. In the case of specific wars, the analyst's concern might be over the decision in each case to go to war: who made the decision, why did they make the decision to go to war rather than remain at peace, why did they make it at that particular point in time. In the case of war in the international system, the analyst's concern might be on what large-scale elements in the world—famine, instability, the global "power structure"—cause varying levels of war at different times.

It is much easier, of course, to concentrate on smaller, day-to-day events in considering the behavior of nations. The crisis-oriented daily newspapers foster this outlook by dealing primarily with the events of the day, and by paying much less attention to the larger picture. Day-to-day events are interesting and important, but they are not the sole concern of the theorist of international behavior. The "I-was-there-when-the-decision-was-made" memoir relates only one type of international behavior. It represents only one of many perspectives. The behavior involved in the "close-up" view may be different—for analytical reasons—than the behavior involved in the long-range view, and therefore the theories used to explain those behaviors may be different.

The Cuban Missile Crisis of 1962 serves as a good illustration. From one perspective, the crisis was a series of decisions. The Soviet Union decided to put missiles on Cuba; shortly after that the United States, discovering them, decided to place a quarantine around the island. The Soviets then made their decision to remove the missiles. An analyst could be concerned primarily with the three decisions; each one can be considered an international "behavior." From another perspective, however, the crisis was only one in a long series of events between the United States and the Soviet Union. An analyst might, for instance, deal with the fluctuations in "hostility" between East and West during the Cold War, the missile crisis being only one among many zigs and zags in East-West relations. Different theories, therefore, might account for (1) the increased hostility between the United States and the Soviet Union in October, 1962, (2) for such hostility having occurred in the Carribean, or (3) for a quarantine being imposed rather than an invasion conducted to remove the missiles. The Chaco War between Bolivia and Paraguay is another illustration. It was a specific war between two states. At the same time, it can be viewed as only one of many that occurred in the twentieth century, and from that perspective the "behavior" becomes not a specific war but part of the trend of war throughout the century. Both perspectives are dealing with "war," but they view that behavior differently, and therefore different theories may be involved in explaining them.

One widely used distinction that is often called upon in assessing international behavior should be discarded at this point, namely, that there is a difference between international relations and foreign policy. International relations are usually seen as the interaction of two or more states, and foreign policy as the "foreign" action of one nation. For certain purposes that distinction may be helpful, but it is unnecessary here because both encompass a kind of behavior, and behavior is what we are interested in, regardless of whether it is "foreign" (only one nation acting) or "international" (more than one nation acting).

To be sure, all studies of international relations focus in one way or another on the behavior of nations. That focus has been made quite explicit here, however, and for several reasons. First, many of the disputes over how to explain international politics derive from talking about different kinds of behavior; some analysts will discuss *decisions* to go to war whereas others will discuss *trends* in warlike activity. Many of the disputes can be settled by specifying what behavior is under examination. Second, and more important, certain international behaviors simply cannot be accounted for by some theories; in other words, the domain of all theories is not the same, and theories should be linked only to behavior they can explain. Finally, in focusing constantly on the behavior of nations, one is prevented from being sidetracked into the definitional disputes so characteristic of scholars. To ask "What is the balance of power between China and India?" is meaningless for present concerns unless it can be shown that "balance of power" relates in some way to the behavior of China, India, or some other nation.

One further point: the fact that behavior is the focus of our analysis means that behavior *varies*. If man were always at peace and aggression never occurred, there would be no variation and, therefore, nothing to explain. The very fact that behavior varies—that sometimes man is at war and sometimes at peace, that sometimes China is at war and sometimes at peace, that some states form alliances and others do not—prompts the development of theories. Our greatest attention will be on war, conflict, or aggressive behavior for the primary reason that most analysts have been concerned with that type of behavior. War is not our exclusive concern, but it is the central one, not because of a fascination with it but because of an earnest desire to see it eradicated.

Theories of International Behavior

Americans have a propensity for the "facts," to brush aside ideologies, abstractions, and interpretations to get at "reality." American "pragmatism" is no doubt a corollary of this characteristic. Students complain that by studying theories of international relations they remove themselves from the real world of facts. Such thinking represents a misconception of how humans think or organize their ideas about their environment.

To place things in perspective, several distinctions should be introduced concerning types of theories so that the term "theory" as used here can be evaluated. There are several generally recognized kinds of theories. First, "normative" theory *prescribes* how people *ought* to act or how things *ought* to be, usually on the basis of some sort of moral prescription. People should obey laws because that is the "just" and "right" thing to do. A democratic system is the best political system because it allows individual choice and prohibits tyranny by a minority, and that is "good." Nation-states should "balance" one another in power because no one state will then become dominant. Based on assumptions that are viewed as empirically sound, normative theory nonetheless is concerned with prescribing what ought to be.

A second kind of theory might be labeled "intuitive." To have a "hunch" about something is to have an intuitive theory about it. Most people have pet theories about crime, for instance ("Anyone who steals does so because they are evil, that's my theory''), but they are rarely interested in testing their intuitive theories against reality.

A third kind of theory—and the one which we shall employ—is "causal." It is an empirical theory which posits that some phenomenon is dependent on some other phenomenon: the first *causes* the second. All theories are in some respect causal, but the emphasis with empirical causal theory is not on simply stating an idea but in confirming or disconfirming it, on testing it against reality. James Caporaso and Alan Pelowski's notion of "politics" is an illustration of a causal theory. "In one sense," they note, "politics as a practical concern is one big quasi-experimental laboratory," because behind all legislation, reform movements, and political stratagems (and here it is important to include *international* political stratagems) "lies a guess (hypothesis) concerning the impact each will have. Politics . . . implicitly introduces the notion that altering X (or a series of Xs) will change Y (or a series of Ys)."[1] In other words, introducing a "reformed" local government system (X) will, hypothetically, cause the elimination of graft and corruption (Y). Establishment of international organizations such as the League of Nations or the United Nations (X) will serve to eliminate, or at least decrease, the incidence of war (Y). Increases in interaction between nations on a personal level (cultural- or student-exchange programs) (X) will bring about a reduction in possible levels of hostility between those interacting (Y). In each case, we wish to see the *effect* of one *variable* upon another *variable*.

Pet theories often have causal inferences implicit, but they are rarely tested. Causal empirical theory always implies that a theory must be tested. Once tested and shown to be correct, it is then to be accepted as accurate until at some future time another test proves it to be wrong. The retort, "Well, that's just *your theory*," implying that the hypothesis is still in the realm of the make-believe, cannot be made against causal theories that have been tested and confirmed.

One important caveat, and one often made concerning empirical studies in the social sciences, is that the presence of a statistical correlation between two variables does not necessarily imply a causal relationship between them. However, causal inferences can often be drawn from such correlations, particularly if a time lag is involved and if other variables are shown *not* to be related to the behavior in question. Moreover, while the dictum "Correlation does not equal causation" is true and should be

[1] James Caporaso and Alan L. Pelowski, "Economic and Political Integration in Europe: A Quasi-Experimental Analysis," *American Political Science Review* 65 (June, 1971), p. 419.

kept in mind, it nonetheless applies equally well to studies not utilizing specific correlation techniques.

Theories are also distinguished in several other ways. A theory can be either "deductive" or "inductive," and its "range" can be either high, middle, or low. Deductive theory is derived from abstract, general axioms or assumptions. Inductive theory, on the other hand, is formulated from facts or data with little regard or attention given to any general assumptions. An assumption such as "all Latin people are hotheaded" might be the basis of a deductive theory concerning the differing foreign policies of Latin and non-Latin countries. Inductive theory, on the other hand, would not make any assumptions about "hotheadedness," but would simply watch the way in which Latin states behave and then from that behavior formulate a general proposition. No theory, however, is either completely deductive or completely inductive.

The distinction between high, middle, and low range theory refers to the spectrum of phenomena that the theory covers. If a theory, for instance, can account for why China invaded India in 1962, it would be considered a low-range theory compared with one that could account for why similar aggressive acts occurred in fifty other situations. The latter, in turn, would be a middle-range theory compared with one that could account for *all* acts of aggression in international politics.

But why this emphasis on theory? Because theories organize complex information by categorizing it, relating it to other information, and using it to provide predictions. To cross the street in the face of an oncoming car, for instance, is irrational unless that onrushing car and its driver are placed into certain categories, related to other categories, and predictions drawn from that relationship. We know (or assume) that the vast majority of people are rational; that most cities provide for pedestrian rights-of-way; that for the driver not to stop would cause him great grief, including possibly court cases. Therefore, one concludes, the driver will stop, and one feels safe in crossing in front of him or her.

This illustration involves two axioms and a hypothesis. The first axiom is that drivers are rational, an axiom most would agree with most of the time. The second axiom, roughly labeled "system constraints," suggests that the social system within which the driver operates is free to take sanctions against him and will do so in certain situations. The hypothesis is that one behavioral variable—walking into the intersection —will cause a second variable to occur, namely the oncoming driver will slow down. This theory might be called a stimulus-response theory or a decision-making theory, but the label is unimportant for the moment. The important point is that each time one walks across the street it is not an entirely new and unique situation. Though it will never be *exactly* the same as the preceding crossing (speed of car, name of street, time of day will all change), nonetheless those differences will not necessarily and automatically alter the predictions. In spite of the changes that do occur, the theory still allows one to operate in many situations. (At times, of course, when the situation changes drastically—such as trying to cross a street in New York City—then that specific theory breaks down, and a new one must be used involving taxi drivers.)

To use an illustration from international relations, many scholars have puzzled over the thaw in Chinese-American relations which began roughly about 1971. Some argued the Chinese feared the Soviets, prompting closer ties with the United States; others saw the end of the Cultural Revolution allowing Chinese leaders to once again undertake friendly foreign ventures because their internal stability was secure; still others argued that internal dove elements attained leadership in China, changing the nation's foreign policy. Each explanation is not dependent on the Chinese-American situation, for each is based on broad-gauged theories that can be applied to any country, any similar situation, at any time. Each is based on patterned behavior. The first theory suggests a country threatened by another country will align with a third country to protect itself. The second asserts that internal unrest explains why a country behaves in certain ways in foreign affairs. The third theory rests on notions of the effect of differing elites on the make-up of a nation's foreign policy: To know how a country will act in foreign affairs, look at who runs it.

Nonuniqueness or patterned behavior is, therefore, a crucial assumption underlying theory, though it is not one that is universally agreed to. Albert Hirschman, for example, contends that the historian is concerned only with the uniqueness of historical situations, that "large-scale social change (is) a unique, nonrepeatable, and *ex ante* highly improbable complex of events," and consequently the search for "laws of change" is bound to be frustrated. Yet he admits that history contains lessons for those who study it.[2] The extrapolation of lessons from past historical events, however, can only be done by recognizing that the events are similar—at least to some degree. Despite his protestations, Hirschman in fact agrees with that premise. He argues that John Womack's book on *Zapata and the Mexican Revolution*,[3] although using no paradigms, provides not only understanding for the Mexican Revolution, "but of peasant revolutions everywhere."[4] But the jump from the Mexican Revo-

---

2 Albert O. Hirschman, "The Search for Paradigms As a Hindrance to Understanding," *World Politics* 22 (April, 1970), p. 343.

3 John Womack, *Zapata and the Mexican Revolution* (New York: Alfred A. Knopf, 1969).

4 Hirschman, "Search for Paradigms," p. 331.

lution to peasant revolutions "everywhere" can only be made by assuming that peasant revolutions, despite their differences, have some similarities.

The assumption that one can operate *without* theories or frameworks is what David Hackett Fischer calls the Baconian fallacy. It

consists in the idea that a historian can operate without the aid of preconceived questions, hypotheses, ideas, assumptions, theories, paradigms, postulates, prejudices, presumptions, or general propositions of any kind. He is supposed to go a-wandering in the dark forest of the past, gathering facts like nuts and berries, until he has enough to make a general truth.[5]

Fischer cites Fustel de Coulanges's argument that the historian should

carefully observe all the facts, all the institutions, all regulations public or private, all the customs of domestic life, and particularly everything that relates to the possession of land (sic!). He should study all these things with equally careful attention, for he does not know beforehand from which side enlightenment will come to him.[6]

Fischer's point is obvious: Fustel has already loaded his case, for his "theory," although hidden, has stated that for some reason the possession of land is important.

In sum, no one undertakes scholarly research, or even everyday thinking, without some type of theory, paradigm, model, or guiding framework. Even in international affairs, presidents, prime ministers, and secretaries of state do not just deal pragmatically with facts, permitting information from the outside world to randomly impinge on them without interpreting and classifying it. When they act they have predictions in mind, and their predictions derive from theories, whether explicit or not.

In early 1965, for instance, when President Lyndon Johnson decided to begin bombing North Vietnam, he and his advisors may have been working from a theory—perhaps not stated explicitly—that a small and weak country would back down and cease its activities in another small country if it perceived that a large and powerful nation was prepared to defend the third country. *If* that was the operative theory explaining the administration's actions (it is plausible, but note that we present no evidence), then American decision-makers did not just *decide* to bomb; their action was based on predictions derived from a theory about how an opponent was likely to respond. The same decision-makers consistently refused to extend the bombing in North Vietnam to Haiphong

[5] David Hackett Fischer, *Historians' Fallacies: Toward a Logic of Historical Thought* (New York: Harper & Row, 1970), p. 4.

[6] Ibid., p. 6.

and Hanoi. That decision may have been based on predictions about probable responses by both China and the Soviet Union to such action, and how far they would permit the United States to intervene. In that instance the theory might have been: Countries with close political and ideological ties are likely to come to the defense of one another. Such ties might be measured by similar ideologies, trade, and exchange of military and other advisers. Because Condition A existed (North Vietnam was tied by ideology and military aid to China and the Soviet Union), then Condition B (U.S.S.R. and China are likely to come to the defense of North Vietnam if it is seriously threatened) has a high probability of occurring.

But, the critic or skeptic might contend, seven years later President Nixon did decide to bomb Hanoi and Haiphong; furthermore, that action did not produce a response by either the Chinese or the Russians. Neither of these facts can be read, however, as indicating that (1) the Johnson decision-makers did not use theoretical assumptions to arrive at their decision, or (2) that their theories were necessarily incorrect. Rather, the seven years between 1965 and 1972 saw changes in the variables involved, and therefore the predictions of Chinese and Soviet response were different. In both cases, nonetheless, theories were used to arrive at predictions concerning another country's behavior.

Thus, theories are not removed from the facts. To the contrary, theory provides organizing principles and categories into which multiple facts can be fit. Theories relate variables in a causal way, providing—as an ultimate goal—predictions about behavior. To do that, theories must be tested with empirical evidence. They are not merely abstract ideas that remain abstract, or are "proved" by scavenging through history to find examples supporting it, nor merely somebody's "idea" about something. One can argue a theory endlessly, citing isolated facts to "support" it, but that does not constitute confirmation.

This section has presented a very general description of how we view the concept of theory. Its role, however, becomes more complex when we consider evaluating *competing* theories in terms of their ability to explain the same behavior. For example, was it President Nixon's personality or the interaction of his advisers in the decision-making unit that better explains the bombing of Haiphong and Hanoi? For some of the studies presented later, that task of evaluation will be undertaken. At the present time, however, our study of international behavior deals primarily with the testing of single theories or hypotheses, rarely evaluating them against competing theories or hypotheses. Some of the theories will be deductive and some inductive; some will be high range and some very low range. But the common denominator will be the inference of causality. An abbreviated discussion of theory alone, however, can only go so far, for in addition to the different kinds of theories there are also different ways of "explaining" behavior, and different ways of using theory to explain. It is to these questions that we now turn.

Theories, Explanation, and Evidence

"Explaining" an event often seems to be very simple. But there is much more to it than appears on the surface in terms of *true* explanation. One way in which to explain an event is merely to present a *plausible* interpretation, one that seems to make sense and does not contradict any canons of logic. To say that Chinese behavior toward the United States in 1971, friendly compared with earlier years, was caused by fear of the Soviet Union is to posit a *plausible* explanation. It is not the only one, however, nor necessarily the true one.

A second common way in which to explain behavior is to trot out a *series* of plausible reasons, with the inference that one of them singly or all of them combined account for the behavior under investigation. For instance, the Chinese-American détente in 1971 may indeed have been caused by Chinese fear of the Soviet Union, prompting closer ties with the United States. But it might also have been plausibly due to internal developments in China following the tumultuous Cultural Revolution, suggesting that the Chinese elite might have been better able to respond to foreign overtures in a peaceful fashion because they no longer needed foreign enemies to insure their internal stability. Or it might have been due to the ascendancy of the dove elements in Chinese leadership, causing a shift in foreign behavior.

This "series" method is certainly superior to the first because several explanations are offered. Still, there is no way of assessing their accuracy and no way of evaluating among them. For all the reader (or policy-maker) may know, only *one* of the many explanations is actually the accurate one, or one may be more accurate than another. Regardless of whether one or many plausible explanations are put forth, the "evidence" can take two forms. One form produces *no* evidence; the theorist merely relies on the logical plausibility of his explanation—and a vague, commonly agreed-upon assumption that evidence *might* exist supporting the theory. The other form of "evidence" offers an *illustration* in line with the theory.

A third common method of explaining behavior is to *describe* the events under consideration, with the explanation implied in the description. Sang-Woo Rhee illustrates this method with Allen Whiting's well-known analysis of the Chinese intervention in the Korean War.[7] First, Whiting sets out the chronology of events. During the first four months of the war, domestic Chinese propaganda stressed that the battle was the North Koreans' struggle; the Chinese gave no material assistance during that period; seven months after China recognized the North Korean regime, it sent representatives to Pyongyang; Peking then notified the Indian ambassador that the crossing of the 38th Parallel by the United States would bring Chinese intervention; U.S. forces did cross the parallel; and Chinese "volunteers" began crossing the Yalu. From these events, Whiting concludes that "the sequence of Chinese Communist calculations and movements indicates that North Korean territory as such was not the issue. Rather it was the survival of a *de jure* North Korean regime which motivated Chinese Communist entry into the war." [8]

As Rhee points out, however, the events themselves do not explain Chinese behavior; rather, the inferences drawn from them—not made explicit by Whiting—provide the explanation. Whiting argues that the Chinese thought U.S. success would lead it to further "imperialistic" actions elsewhere; this line of reasoning, however, requires a general psychological theory that success in one area automatically whets the appetite for further bold and adventurous moves. The explanation is only inferred by the description. The theoretical propositions are only implicit.

All three methods of explanation are common—and will be used here in certain circumstances—but they nonetheless have serious drawbacks, especially regarding "evidence." The most serious can be termed the rule of "sampling" or "control." For instance, to revert to our earlier example, if China did decide on détente with the United States from fear of the Soviet Union, what evidence would support that theory? One type of evidence might be Chinese statements of hostility toward the Soviet Union. If one finds such a statement in 1971, does that confirm the theory? No, it merely illustrates a correlation between a Chinese statement in 1971 toward the Soviet Union and a changed attitude toward the United States in the same year. Sampling and control might suggest looking at Chinese statements over a long period of time toward the Soviet Union, and toward other countries. Two conditions would have

[7] Sang-Woo Rhee, "China's Cooperation, Conflict and Interaction Behavior: Viewed from Rummel's Field Theoretic Perspective," *Research Report No. 64,* Dimensionality of Nations Project (Honolulu: University of Hawaii, 1973).

[8] Allen S. Whiting, "The Logic of Communist China's Policy: The First Decade," in *China: The Emerging Red Giant,* ed. Devere E. Pentony (San Francisco: Chandler, 1962), pp. 74–75; cited in Rhee, "China's Cooperation," p. 10.

to be satisfied—at a minimum—to offer confirmatory evidence for the theory in question. First, hostile Chinese statements toward the Soviet Union in 1971 would have to be markedly different from what they were in earlier periods. Second, their statements would have to be more markedly different toward the Soviets than toward other countries. Such evidence would constitute some support for the theory. On the other hand, if their statements had been equally hostile toward the Soviet Union for ten years, then why did their behavior change toward the United States in 1971? Second, if their statements toward all countries —large and small, Communist and non-Communist—were just as hostile as those directed at the Soviet Union, then their statements toward the Soviet Union were just part of their overall foreign policy stance. The danger of "illustrating" a theory with selected evidence is that for each illustration supporting it, another can all too often be dredged up showing the opposite.

As opposed to plausibility, the goal of explanation here will be to account for the variation in the behavior of nations. In simplified form, it means accounting for the variation of one variable or behavior (such as Chinese-American détente), by variation in another variable or behavior, (such as Soviet-Chinese hostility). Variation, therefore is the key, for if there is no variation in behavior, nothing needs to be explained. To revert to the example of Chinese détente with the United States, the problem with the plausible explanation—the hostile statement by the Chinese toward the Soviets in the same year of détente with Americans— is that there is variation on only one variable (i.e., détente). In figurative form, the relationship would look like this:

	CHINESE — UNITED STATES BEHAVIOR	
	Détente	No Détente
CHINESE — SOVIET BEHAVIOR Negative	xxx	

While there is variation in Chinese-American behavior, there is no variation in Chinese-Soviet behavior. Therefore we cannot really account for the variation in the former simply by the presence of negative Chinese-Soviet behavior. The following illustration shows how variation in one variable can account for variation in the second.

	CHINESE — UNITED STATES BEHAVIOR	
	Détente	No Détente
CHINESE — SOVIET BEHAVIOR Negative	xxx	
Positive		xxx

Here when Soviet-Chinese behavior is positive, there is no need for China to enter into a détente, but when that shifts to negative—assuming for the moment this signifies fear of the Soviet Union—China enters into détente with the United States. Regardless of the substantive case at hand, variation is central to explanation, and it is theories that suggest logical explanations for that linked variation.

A more general rule regarding evidence concerns the overall carrying out of research. As Patrick Morgan notes, "You must provide others with every chance to demonstrate that you are in error." [9] To do this, the researcher describes as carefully as possible exactly what his evidence is and how he has gone about collecting it. If he has used documents, he indicates how many and which ones. If he cannot use all documents, he "samples"—another rule—so that he has a set of documents that is *representative* of the entire set of documents. But he informs the reader how the sampling was done. Similar rules apply to other evidence, such as trade data, diplomatic exchanges, everyday behavioral interactions between countries, perceptions of national leaders, and so on. Furthermore, any numerical or statistical manipulation performed on the evidence must be noted, because many manipulations contain underlying assumptions that may affect the interpretation of results. The goal is to provide others with the possibility of "replicating" a study in exactly the same way to see if the same results occur.

In sum, in addition to the criterion that a theory must make logical "sense" out of a relationship between one variable and another, explanation also involves following certain "rules of evidence." (An extended discussion of explanation in a statistical sense is given in the appendix, paragraph A.) Explanation is really solving a "puzzle," and that should not be done haphazardly. It involves logical theories in conjunction with empirical evidence.

This discussion of theory and explanation is in no way exhaustive; numerous treatises exist for those interested in pursuing the subject. The intent here has been to suggest that explanation is not as patently easy as it may seem, that there are quite different kinds of explanation, and that here the goal will be to have explanation account empirically for variation. We repeat the caveat: in some instances the nature of the subject or the current state of research means the goal will not be attained, and single case studies—with no exact estimate of the variation—will have to be utilized. Readers are asked only to be aware of the drawbacks of that method, just as they will be cautioned about drawbacks and operational problems in research that more closely adheres to rules governing empirical evidence. Neither method, in other words, is foolproof.

[9] Patrick M. Morgan, *Theories and Approaches to International Politics: What Are We to Think?* (San Ramon, Calif.: Consensus Publishers, 1972), p. 27.

Disputes

The last two sections emphasized a research perspective, and one that is disputed by many. These disputes must be considered for they involve the definition of the field of international relations, the methods to be used, and the questions that should be studied.

Scholars have for decades gone through tortured efforts to define the field of international relations. Is "international relations" different from "international politics"? How do we define an international actor? Where does international economics fit in? The questions are endless and despite reams addressed to them, no one ever seems to be satisfied. The reasons for this are multiple. First, once definitions are proposed, few people pay much attention to them anyway. Second, definitions often arbitrarily and unnecessarily restrict the field of study. Third, the field is constantly undergoing change; [10] scholars of international politics have moved from concern with diplomatic history to international law and organization to the development of high-level, abstract models, and finally—the current focus—to the explicit testing of specific hypotheses with data from the real world of international politics.

Given this situation, strict definitions tend to be nonfunctional. Nonetheless, as a guide one must attempt some assessment of the parameters of the subject. The previous sections should make clear that the study of international politics in the most general sense is here considered to be the explanation of the myriad types of international behavior: wars; invasions; treaty signings; economic negotiations; acts of international organizations; acts of national leaders; trade between countries; and so on. Many will no doubt be dissatisfied with this broad, general definition, but the contention here is that rather than spend time on a nonfunctional definition, the field should be allowed to define itself, as it will in the ensuing chapters.

A second dispute concerns *how* the scholar studies international relations, and relates to the question of explanation already discussed. The dispute is normally between the so-called traditionalists and the so-called behavioralists, and the contrasting positions can be found in the arguments of Hedley Bull and J. David Singer.[11] Bull contends that inter-

[10] Kenneth W. Thompson, "The Study of International Politics: A Survey of Trends and Developments," *Review of Politics* 14, (October, 1952), pp. 433–67; K. J. Holsti, *International Politics: A Framework for Analysis,* 2d ed. (Englewood Cliffs, N.J.: Prentice-Hall, 1972), pp. 6–14.

[11] Hedley Bull, "International Theory: The Case for a Classical Approach," and J. David Singer, "The Incompleat Theorist: Insight Without Evidence," in *Contending Approaches to International Politics,* ed. Klaus Knorr and James N. Rosenau (Princeton: Princeton University Press, 1969).

national relations is too complex to be studied in a "scientific" fashion, that no two international situations are exactly the same, that the important variables cannot be measured in an explicit sense, and that "theories" of international politics—being highly abstract—fail to capture the true substance of international reality. More recently this position has added the contention that scientific or empirical research cannot investigate the "relevant" issues and topics of international relations.

The other side of the debate, argued by Singer, is that despite the complexity in international affairs, there *are* regularities in international behavior, and theories can capture these regularities; that empirical measurement of variables can—and has always been—carried out; and that "scientific" international relations means only that rigorous rules of gathering empirical evidence are necessary so research findings are not dependent on the way the research was done. Needless to say, the approach taken here leans more heavily toward Singer's position. But we would also contend that the debate is in reality a pseudo-debate, for several reasons.

First, "scientific" analysis of international behavior does not imply the establishment of *immutable laws* applying to *all* states at *all* times, nor does it make the untenable assumption that human behavior is somehow "determined" by such laws. Rather, it recognizes that amidst what appear to be very complex and random events, patterns do occur. Second, *all* research involves some form of quantification. Unfortunately, the myth persists that quantification exists only if numbers appear in a table or if the quantification is explicitly stated. Thus, quantification occurs in the use of such hard indicators of "integration" as international trade,[12] in frequency counts of specific words in presidential statements,[13] or by counting interstate visits by heads of state.[14] But *any* time a trade figure is cited, an inference drawn from a presidential speech, or a foreign visit by a national leader is noted, quantification is involved. The distinction, therefore, is not between those who attempt to quantify international political phenomena and those who do not, but rather in terms of *how* the quantification is done, which refers back to the issue of rules of evidence in the last section.

[12] Hayward Alker, Jr., and Donald Puchala, "Trends in Economic Partnership: The North Atlantic Area, 1928–1963," in *Quantitative International Politics: Insights and Evidence*, ed. J. David Singer (New York: The Free Press, 1968).

[13] Michael P. Sullivan, "Symbolic Involvement as a Correlate of Escalation: The Vietnam Case," in *Peace, War, and Numbers*, ed. Bruce Russett (Beverly Hills: Sage Publishing Co., 1972).

[14] Steven Brams, "The Structure of Influence Relationships in the International System," in *International Politics and Foreign Policy: A Reader in Research and Theory*, ed. James Rosenau, rev. ed. (New York: The Free Press, 1969).

Yet a third dispute over research perspectives in the study of international relations resembles the debate over theory: the call in recent years has been for more "substance" in the study of international relations (as opposed to abstract "theories"), with emphasis on the so-called relevant issues that confront mankind in international affairs. Preoccupation with theories and models, it is argued, has forced concentration away from history, reality, and the *substance* of the relevant questions. To some degree this critique has validity: for a period during the 1950s and 1960s an excessive concern for the elaboration of very high-level models dominated the field. Although this overpreoccupation has receded, objections against formal theory-building and testing remain because, it is said, such activity sidetracks attention from the "real" questions. But the previous section has made clear that, whether made explicit or not, *theory* plays a central role in every study of international behavior.

The question of relevance, however, does require elaboration. As often presented, one must decide to be either rigorous and scientific on the one hand, or be concerned with the more relevant issues and current problems on the other, and thereby of necessity give up some of the rigor required of scientific studies. Unfortunately, the term "relevance" suffers from overuse. A recent extended analysis of three "policy-relevant" studies investigated many of the questions surrounding the issue of relevance. It concluded that studies are often called "relevant" because they deal with (1) specific, historical situations or individuals, (2) current "issue-areas" (such as the Vietnam War or Third World problems), or (3) policy recommendations.[15] It was found, however, that the three studies in question presented no recommendations that could be immediately (or even not so immediately) *utilized* by decision-makers; that recommendations did not necessarily flow from the research, but rather constituted a distillation of the thinking of numerous contemporary scholars, policy-makers, and journalists; and that the very design of the research made the conclusions tenuous.

Relevant research is needed, but "relevance" must not be equated with timeliness or with nontheoretical research. Given the difficulty of *truly explaining* international behavior—touched upon already—rigorous research is needed in order to produce findings that can be relevant to policy-makers. We shall attempt in each chapter to tackle the question of the policy relevance of research findings, but the reader is forewarned that we will meet with mixed success. Some variables in international relations are simply *not* manipulable, and those interested in policy relevance must understand that. Moreover, specific policy recommenda-

---

[15] Michael P. Sullivan, "The Question of 'Relevance' in Foreign Policy Studies," *Western Political Quarterly* 26 (June, 1973), pp. 314–24.

tions are extremely difficult to provide without knowledge of the specific task at hand. Nonetheless, some attempt can be made to set out the possible domain within which relevant recommendations might be formulated, as well as those areas that are simply not amenable to such policy advice. The final chapter will propose ways of thinking about current relevant topics in international politics through the use of the theories covered in the chapters that follow.

The question is not, therefore, whether we should be relevant *or* rigorous, relevant *or* scientific, relevant *or* abstract and theoretical. Rather, the issue should be how to conduct rigorous studies that will produce meaningful and relevant results; studies that, by being sound—in that they carefully follow rules of procedure and evidence—will produce carefully formulated and accurate results; and how the use of abstract and theoretical models will allow the generalization of findings from one or two cases to many cases.

Debates over methods and approaches, over whether it is possible to study international politics from a scientific point of view, tend to wither away when each of the disputed elements is analyzed carefully. To undertake "scientific" analyses of international behavior does not suggest that *laws* will be derived that will then make international behavior immutable. It implies only that underlying theories be made explicit, that the drawbacks in "plausible" explanations be recognized, and that, where possible, acknowledged procedures and rules of evidence be followed.

Conclusion

This introduction has set forth the focus of the book, the biases and approach of the author, and several prominent disputes in the field. Of necessity the discussion has brushed over much that is important in each of these areas. One could go on for chapters discussing "theories," "explanation," or the academic debates. The objective here has not been to present an exhaustive examination of the issues, but rather to establish the parameters of the book.

Each chapter sets out a theoretical approach or way of explaining international behavior. It then, rather than merely repeat what others have said, attempts to separate the important issues from the trivial in terms of how they relate to explaining international behavior. Many subsidiary issues (such as definitional disputes) are not considered. Each chapter also presents evidence: what the findings are concerning each approach, how valid they are, how inclusive they are. In most cases, this presentation requires sifting through those research reports, journal articles, and books that provide empirical data to test the various theories. In some instances, especially in Chapter 3 in the discussion on decision-making, the paucity of research demands that we fall back on case studies and large-scale models. Though case studies or biographical histories have definite drawbacks, they often contain a wealth of historical information as well as propositions that may be suitable to more rigorous testing. Concerning the use of empirical evidence, data collected for one purpose may sometimes be used for answering other questions. We should add that the conclusions drawn here may not always agree with those made by the original authors.

A note of caution should be mentioned concerning research in the social sciences. The term "findings" often carries a ring of finality to it; in many cases, however, the ring is false. In some instances, findings will directly contradict other findings; in other cases, questions will occur concerning the evidence used to test the theories. The only path out of either bind is more replication and research, and more—and better— data. The solution for contradictory findings is not to throw up one's hands, but to do more research or do it differently in order to account for the discrepancy. Likewise, the only solution for "bad data" is not "no data," but "better data." The "findings" that follow, therefore, are not cast in bronze. Research never ceases, some of the findings will be confirmed, some may be changed or modified, others may have to be discarded.

International behavior goes on twenty-four hours a day, 365 days a year. Old data are constantly being updated and new data being collected. The true test of a theory is the test of time, and because history continues to unfold there is a never-ending laboratory within which the theories can be tested.

part I   *Man*
and the State

The next three chapters present several different perspectives on international relations involving man and the nation-state as independent variables for understanding behavior in the international system. These approaches are familiar to most, and lengthy introductions are therefore unnecessary.

Briefly, when we talk of *man* as an independent variable we mean that behavior in the international system is due to an individual's desires, goals, perceptions, beliefs, personality, or other elements lumped together under the rubric "individual idiosyncracies." To view the *state* as an independent variable means that the multiple processes referred to as "decision-making" affect a state's international behavior, or that attributes of the state itself move that state toward its behavior in the international system.

It seems fairly safe to say that approaches involving man have probably been the most frequently utilized in explaining international behavior, and for several reasons. First, man, being an egotistical animal, sees himself as the center of the universe, and likes to think he is the cause of events around him. Rare is the individual willing to admit that he is merely tossed about by the "system" he inhabits. Although everyone at one time or another feels "defeated" by the system—the you-can't-fight-city-hall syndrome—on the whole we much more readily see ourselves as independent individuals affecting what is around us. The correctness of this perspective remains to be seen, but man as an inward-looking animal certainly accounts for a great deal of the popularity of explanations based on the individual level.

Second, man sees other individuals in action every day and therefore feels he understands behavior between people. He also feels behavior between nations can't be much different. Most people's lives are very circumscribed: home, family, job, car, school provide the meat of daily existence. Beyond that, most of us find it difficult to conceptualize larger systems, even on a local basis. To move even beyond that to see the international system as an *entity* is fraught with difficulties. Because we *see* individuals every day, we build explanations for their behavior based on them. When contemplating international behavior therefore, the ease of individual-level analysis makes it a natural in accounting for international behavior. Obviously, the "individual level" approach carries a great attraction, for it deals with personalities, idiosyncracies, motivations, and goals, all those very human things we witness every day.

Ultimately, of course, *all* explanations can be brought down to the individual level; that does not mean, however, that we can always explain international relations with individual-level variables. Chapter 3, for instance, deals with decision-making: What processes occur within a decision-making unit that produce certain outcomes? How does the interaction of individuals within a unit produce one decision whereas a different type of interaction produces a different decision? What categories can be used to distinguish among different types of decision-making units—in other words, how do they *vary* in their composition—and how does that variation relate to the variation in decision outcome? Further, how do different views of the decision process provide different explanations of the reason for decisions? Are decisions rationally thought out, or do they just occur? What implications derive from those competing views—or "models"—of decision-making?

Chapter 4, on the other hand, discusses the attributes of nations and how they influence international behavior, not unlike the way in which personality attributes are linked to individual behavior. On the individual level, for instance, authoritarian or schizoid personalities are thought to behave differently from nonauthoritarian and nonschizoid personalities. Similarly, on the national level democratic countries—to use only one type of national attribute as an illustration—may behave much differently in their foreign relations than nondemocratic countries. A nation's behavior is a function of its attributes, even though ultimately the attributes must in some way affect the decision-makers, forcing them to act in specified ways. But the *variation* in behavior occurs on the state level, the point being of course that individuals tend to react similarly to the same national attribute variables.

The progression in the following three chapters is relatively straight-forward. Chapter 2's focus is man; Chapter 3 places the individual within a social, decision-making unit and investigates what happens in that unit and what outside variables affect the unit in what way; Chapter 4 moves more concretely to the level of the state itself.

chapter 2   Man and His Images

A common explanation for international behavior resides on the individual level, with man himself. This chapter presents several approaches linking man to his behavior in the international system: first, theories based on man's instinct; second, the role of personality; and third, the images man has of his environment, and the changes in these images or perceptions.

Instinct

One way in which to explain man's international behavior is to view it as the result of his basic instinctual makeup. As Kenneth Waltz remarks, this assumes that.the "locus of the important causes of war is to be found in the nature and behavior of man." [1] Such explanations run the gamut from basic instinct with no outside connections to frustration-aggression theories, which posit a basic instinctual response mechanism that must be triggered by some outside force.

Waltz cites Spinoza, for instance, who argues that the "end of every act is the self-preservation of the actor," [2] and he notes the conflict

[1] Kenneth Waltz, *Man, the State, and War* (New York: Columbia University Press, 1959), p. 16.

[2] Ibid., p. 22.

between reason and passion. If man could live by his reason alone, he could learn to live side by side with other men with no necessary conflict. His passion, however, directs him "to be first among men" and he then "takes more pride in the harm he has done others than in the good he has done himself." [3] Others, like Augustine, Niebuhr, and Morgenthau, reject this dualism suggested by Spinoza. Yet "despite the differences, the substratum of agreement remains; for each of them deduces political ills from human defects." [4] The basis of Morgenthau's well-known "power theory" resides at this level: Man is born seeking power, and because there exists no authority over him in the international sphere, the use of force and violence results.

Such arguments possess a strong attraction for two reasons. They can be traced back to basic religious premises: The "original sin" of the Catholic religion comes close to the "driving force" in Morgenthau's formulation, or the "will" to do evil over good to one's fellow man. Also, they seemingly cite strong historical evidence to show that man has always been in conflict, and will always resort to war or aggression. Evidence for this reasoning is often taken from the animal kingdom. Robert Ardrey, for instance, concludes from his studies of animals that territorial defense is a dominating, instinctual drive, and that the same type of constant drive exists in man.[5]

For Konrad Lorenz also, aggression is a natural instinct, and helps to preserve the species. Lorenz, though, claims to have found that aggression tends to occur among animals of the same species, which he dubs "intra-specific" aggression. When animals go outside their own species to kill for food, aggression is not taking place, only the desire to preserve territory, to ward off others, and to protect oneself. Annihilation is not the objective.[6]

Although a plausible approach, especially in explaining man's propensity to go to war, the instinct argument nonetheless raises one very serious empirical and logical question concerning, of all things, human history. The argument usually derives from the observation that "man has always been at war." Because he has "always" been at war—a constant—and his instinct has always been present—another constant—the two are popularly joined in a causal sequence. But the empirical statement is incorrect; man has not always been at war.

But, people ask, when has there *never* been a war between men? If

3 Ibid., p. 24.

4 Ibid.

5 Robert Ardrey, *The Territorial Imperative: A Personal Inquiry into the Animal Origins of Property and Nations* (New York: Atheneum, 1966).

6 Konrad Lorenz, *On Aggression* (New York: Harcourt, Brace, & World, 1966).

there has always been some war, then doesn't this satisfy the assumption of a drive or instinct for aggression? Or, pushing the question even further, if man is not actually fighting a war, then he is making preparation for a war, or man is at least always *thinking* about going to war! These statements, of course, change the original theory rather drastically, for they recognize that man at times has *not* fought wars and therefore there is variation in the occurrence and intensity of war. Figure 2-1 illustrates this point by showing the amount of intense international war (measured by nation-months of war underway) from 1816 to 1965, collected by J. David Singer and Melvin Small in their Correlates of War project.[7] There *has* been a great deal of war, but note the vast fluctuations. Instinct theory as usually formulated does not account for that variation. In other words, if instinct is always operative, why does war occur heavily at one point and is relatively nonexistent at another?

At this juncture in the argument, some external variable is usually posited as "bringing out" man's aggressive instinct. However, to rely on a new variable illustrates even further the inability of instinct to account

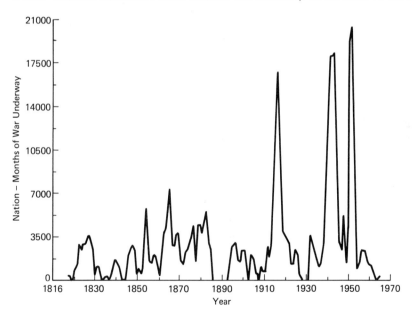

Source: J. David Singer and Melvin Small, *The Wages of War, 1816–1965: A Statistical Handbook* (New York: Wiley, 1972), p. 209.

Figure 2-1.   Annual amount of international war, 1816–1965.

[7] J. David Singer and Melvin Small, *The Wages of War 1816–1965: A Statistical Handbook* (New York: Wiley, 1972).

for variation. If there is some other variable (X), then the equation would read:

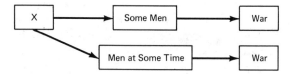

To introduce a new element, however, is quite a bit different from the simplistic reliance on instinct as a sufficient and necessary explanation for aggression. That is, if instinct is constant, then the variation occurs in X, which then becomes the explanation of war.

One other possibility would be the following:

Here again man's instinctual drive does not cause war, nor X, but rather something that exists in "some men" that leads to war. Such reasoning does not disprove an instinctual drive toward aggression; it only demonstrates that it cannot be a *sufficient* cause for aggression, for if instinct is always present it cannot account for the variation in aggression and war. One way out of this impasse is to say that other instincts cause peaceful behavior, and that both instincts operate at different times. The remedy is only partial, however. Something must activate these differing instincts, unless human behavior is completely random, which is hardly a realistic assumption; it is then the activator that becomes the crucial variable in determining which instinct will be followed.

Instinct, therefore, cannot explain variation in state behavior. It may be a background variable "allowing" or "permitting" a specific type of behavior—war or aggression—to occur, but it cannot be considered an important variable accounting for variation in war. Furthermore, as noted, instinct often has implicit religious connotations, which view man's behavior from a moral basis. As such, the above arguments would also conclude that man's behavior in international affairs cannot be accounted for by variables of morality. War does not occur only because there are evil men.

Personality

A somewhat more logically sound theory insists that a national leader's personality affects the foreign policy decisions he makes.

As with instinct, the intuitive and logical plausibility of personality as a determining force make it hard *not* to utilize it. Merely to question the importance of personality, especially in foreign policy decisions, often raises the specter of national leaders as determined robots, acting at the whim of external forces. Despite its attractiveness and plausibility, however, the concrete links between personality and international behavior are small in number, for once the Pandora's box of personality is opened, anything can—and usually does—come out.

Joseph de Rivera admits the difficulty of adequately conceptualizing personality, and of discovering the important personality variables. This dilemma, he says bluntly, stems from "our basic ignorance about many of the dynamics of personality".[8]

Two points stand out. First, to rely on the explanation of personality *implies* a simple, individual-level analysis, when in fact personality theory encompasses a large cluster of variables and very distinct approaches. Second, plausibility in connection with personality does not equate with explanation; the mere presence of one or a series of personality characteristics logically related to behavior does not constitute confirmation of the effect of personality.

In terms of the first observation on personality as an explanation of national behavior, one popular survey of theories of personality presents twelve different types of theories, while another review notes that "one cannot help but be impressed by the diversity of theoretical and methodological orientations" in the field.[9] Freud, for instance, focused on the id, ego, and superego, all unconscious determinants of behavior. William Sheldon's "constitutional" theory related behavior to underlying biological factors, while Raymond Cattell's "factorial" system concentrated on nonphysical traits.[10]

Numerous other personality theories exist, including Allport's psychology of "individuality", Murray's "personology," both concerned with a "humanistic, holistic, and eclectic orientation to the problems involved in developing a science of personality," [11] and Carl Rogers' "self theory." [12] In other words, personality encompasses a broad range of study and even among personality theorists there is much disagreement about the basic dynamics of personality and which approach is

8 Joseph H. de Rivera, *The Psychological Dimension of Foreign Policy* (Columbus, Ohio: Charles E. Merrill, 1968), p. 168.

9 James P. Chaplin and T. S. Krawiec, *Systems and Theories of Personality* (New York: Holt, Rinehart and Winston, 1968), p. 600.

10 Calvin S. Hall and Gardner Lindzey, *Theories of Personality* (New York: Wiley, 1957), pp. 336–77 and 393–413.

11 Chaplin and Krawiec, *Systems and Theories of Personality*, p. 584.

12 Hall and Lindzey, *Theories of Personality*, pp. 467–502.

correct or which cluster of variables or personality characteristics is important.

In terms of the second observation, concerning the "plausibility" of personality hypotheses, we must reiterate that plausibility does not equal explanation. Linking Joseph Stalin's personality characteristics to the existence and perpetuation of the Cold War is no confirmation of personality's effect on international behavior. Likewise, the assertion that Richard Nixon had a competitive, aggressive personality in no way explains the continuation of the Vietnam War during his four years in office.

Hence, on both theoretical as well as research strategy lines, personality presents obstacles as an explanation of international behavior. Even so, much research has been undertaken on the role of personality. The following sections will discuss the psychoanalytic approach to personality, the "personality attribute" or "characteristic" approach, and finally we will explore the issue of what domain personality theories can cover in international politics by using some indirect historical tests of what would happen if personality variables *did* affect international behavior.

PSYCHOANALYTIC APPROACH

Not surprisingly, there are very few psychoanalytic studies of national leaders, primarily because of the difficulty of access to reliable data. Perhaps the most extensively analyzed individual has been President Woodrow Wilson. Alexander and Margaret George, for instance, devoted a full-length study to an analysis of Wilson's life and career from a psychoanalytic perspective. Following Freud and Lasswell, the Georges note that for Wilson, "the basic hypothesis concerning [his] political behavior is that power was for him a compensatory value, a means of restoring the self-esteem damaged in childhood." [13]

The mix of psychoanalytic and "attribute" approaches appears in the Georges' work, however, when they assert that Wilson was plagued by "bottled up" aggressive impulses, and that throughout his public life he needed to purify his exercise of power by taking on tasks only on a moral plane. On American entry into World War I, they note, for instance, Wilson's wish

to transform the war into a great crusade for an ideal peace; his tendency to overrate the efficacy of moral appeals; his inclination to substitute vaguely worded aspirations and general principles for concrete proposals.[14]

[13] Alexander L. George and Margaret George, *Woodrow Wilson and Colonel House: A Personality Study* (New York: Dover Publications, 1964), p. 320.

[14] Ibid., p. 172.

After the war Wilson entered into the debate about the League of Nations with great ferocity, and the Georges argue that Wilson did so because he always needed to do immortal work. "He had always wanted —*needed*—to dominate." [15] The Georges and others who have analyzed Wilson trace much of his adult behavior and personality characteristics to his relationship with his father, an essential element of almost any psychoanalytic perspective on personality.

In spite of the richness of psychoanalytical studies, however, there are several drawbacks. First, of course, is the lack of evidence on most world leaders. This drawback does not apply to Wilson because he was a prolific writer, but it nonetheless does stymie effective analysis. A second and much more important pattern that occurs in the majority of such analyses, however, is that they focus on early developmental processes in personality and the possible way in which these influence later attributes and behavior. There is a lack of connection, however, between such personality constructs and actual foreign policy decisions. The Georges ably categorized Wilson's personality, and were also able to associate—plausibly—these characteristics with one or more of his general foreign policy moves. But that is rare. Psychoanalytical studies, for instance, of Forrestal, Luther, Lenin, Trotsky, and Ghandi [16] may provide insight into important personalities, but that may say little or nothing about the effect of personality on foreign policy behavior. This drawback brings up yet a third problem with such studies, namely the empirical domain. With the exception of Wilson and the possible exception of Hitler, few public officials involved in foreign policy-making have undergone intense scrutiny from this perspective. The "data base," therefore, has been extremely small, with the result that generalizations about the plausibility of personality must be limited. In short, while many interesting insights can be derived from psychoanalytic analyses of national decision-makers, it is something else to tie these analyses or characteristics to foreign policy actions, decisions, or overall trends.

ATTRIBUTES

The unconscious determinants in psychoanalytic theory often relate to elements normally considered to be personality "attributes." It is therefore difficult to separate the two. We do it here merely for purposes of organization, but in full realization that the distinction is partly arti-

[15] Ibid., p. 197.

[16] Arnold A. Rogow, *James Forrestal: A Study of Personality, Politics, and Policy* (New York: Macmillan, 1963); Erik H. Erikson, *Young Man Luther: A Study in Psychoanalysis and History* (New York: Norton, 1962); E. Victor Wolfenstein, *The Revolutionary Personality: Lenin, Trotsky, Gandhi* (Princeton: Princeton University Press, 1967).

ficial. Such personality attributes are characteristic descriptions of personalities, descriptions that carry theoretical import for they are thought to explain resultant behavior. Anthony D'Amato illustrates such personality attributes in terms of dichotomies. [17] The primary dichotomy is "systemic-personalist": the systemic individual views the international system as highly important in determining an individual's behavior, while the personalist individual views the decision-maker as possessing overriding free will to influence the international system. A second dichotomy is "hawk-dove": a hawkish individual tends to rely more frequently on physical aggression or activity to solve a problem, while the dove tends to be reluctant to rely on such behavior. Another well-known dichotomy used to describe personality is "flexibility-rigidity": the flexible individual is more apt than the rigid person to receive and accept new information and ideas.

These attributes are not dissimilar from James Barber's categories of active-passive and positive-negative as applied to U.S. presidents: the first refers to how much energy a president invests in his job of being president and the second to whether the individual actively enjoys—has positive feelings toward—his work as president.[18] Unfortunately, as George has pointed out, explaining a President's behavior from such "character" attributes is very difficult, for while "it is not difficult to find evidence that a subject's character-rooted needs or motives . . . are *expressed* in his behavior," such evidence is nonetheless "a necessary *but insufficient* condition for establishing the *critical causal importance* of those personality factors in the explanation of that behavior." [19] Thus in spite of much intuitive appeal that categories such as Barber's may have, they nonetheless lack a hard operational definition, and fall heir to the problems of personality theories already noted.

These attributes have, however, been linked to *attitudes* about foreign policy and international issues. The so-called F-scale, or measure of authoritarianism, for instance, has as one component "aggressiveness." Individuals scoring high on the authoritarian scale are thought to be generally more aggressive than those scoring low. Scott cites numerous studies indicating a relationship between authoritarianism and attitudes toward various international phenomena, such as nationalism and world-mindedness. Other studies have shown that authoritarian personalities are more likely to approve atomic bombing to stop propaganda coming from Russian ships off-shore, and to score high on scales of jingoism,

[17] Anthony A. D'Amato, "Psychological Constructs in Foreign Policy Prediction," *Journal of Conflict Resolution* 11 (September, 1967), pp. 294–311.

[18] James David Barber, *The Presidential Character: Predicting Performance in the White House* (Englewood Cliffs, N.J.: Prentice-Hall, Inc., 1972), pp. 11–12.

[19] Alexander L. George, "Assessing Presidential Character," *World Politics,* 26 (January, 1974), p. 253, emphasis in original.

isolationist sentiments, and the expectancy of war.[20] Other personality traits have been related to congressmen's attitudes on an internationalism-nationalism scale: the greater the congressman's sense of personal insecurity, for example, the more nationalist his voting record, whereas the more secure he was, the more internationalist his record. Further, the greater his tolerance of ambiguity and the more negative his orientation to people, the more nationalist his voting record.[21]

Charles Hermann and Margaret Hermann used personality attributes as one controlling factor in their simulation of the outbreak of World War I. In one simulation, they matched personality characteristics of their simulation participants with personality traits of the actual decision-makers in 1914, especially along dimensions of dominance, self-acceptance, and self-control. In a second simulation they did not match personalities. The simulation with more closely matched personalities turned out much more similar to the historical situation in 1914. Indeed, that simulation appeared on the verge of war with alliance commitments similar to those of 1914. The perceptions of the simulation participants correlated with decision-makers' perceptions in 1914. Further, hypotheses concerning communication patterns within alliances was supported by the simulation, as they had been supported by communications among the participants in 1914. As the authors note, "correspondence between a simulation and its reference system appears to have been facilitated by closer matching of the personalities of the participant and the historical figure." [22] In neither simulation did actual war break out, although Hermann and Hermann contend that if the personality-matched simulation had been continued for one or two more simulated days, "war would have been declared along lines similar to the historical situation." [23] War did not come to the point of nearly breaking out in the non-personality-matched simulation, but "an alternative actually considered and subsequently excluded by the historical figures" did manifest itself—namely, getting the countries to agree to an international meeting. Thus, although the simulation with matched personalities more closely adhered to the actual 1914 situation, the other simulation likewise exhibited amazing similarities with that historical incident.

In another simulation experiment, the personality attribute of self-

[20] William Scott, "Psychological and Social Correlates of International Images," in *International Behavior: A Social-Psychological Analysis,* ed. Herbert C. Kelman (New York: Holt, Rinehart, and Winston, 1965), p. 90.

[21] James A. Robinson and Richard Snyder, "Decision-Making in International Politics," in *International Behavior,* p. 445.

[22] Charles F. Hermann and Margaret G. Hermann, "An Attempt to Simulate the Outbreak of World War I," in *International Politics and Foreign Policy: A Reader in Research and Theory,* ed. James N. Rosenau, rev. ed. (New York: The Free Press, 1969), p. 636.

[23] Ibid., p. 630.

esteem was found related to the decision to counterattack—instead of delaying a response—once warned of an enemy attack.[24] Decision-makers with low self-esteem were more likely to counterattack on warning rather than delay their response. A second personality variable, however, cognitive complexity, was unrelated to the decision to respond or delay.

Margaret Hermann investigated the personalities of ten world leaders —including Fidel Castro, Charles de Gaulle, Gandhi, Lyndon Johnson, and Nikita Khrushchev—along the dimensions of nationalism, belief in one's ability to exercise control over events, cognitive complexity, and dogmatism.[25] Relating these variables to the leaders' respective foreign policies, she found that the higher the nationalism, the higher the conflict behavior, although this occurred primarily in closed (i.e., authoritarian) nations. Cognitive complexity was positively related to cooperative behavior. A composite personality of low nationalism, high cognitive complexity, less closed-mindedness, and a great belief in the ability to control events tended to be more cooperative than his opposite number —and slightly less likely to initiate action as opposed to merely responding to it.

While the small number of observations (ten) merits caution in generalizing these findings, they nonetheless coincide with what we would expect. Her findings do suggest, however, that the effect of personality on foreign policy was mediated by how much authority the leader held over that policy; when it was great, then personality played a more important role. In addition, the contradiction concerning the role of cognitive complexity between her study and the one conducted by herself, Charles Hermann, and Robert Cantor, suggests that it might be most potent in explaining large-scale trends or levels of foreign policy rather than specific actions. This inference is reinforced in the discussion of the composite personality types—labeled "the participater" and "the independent." The participator would tend to become more actively involved and more interested in the give-and-take of international politics; the independent would be more interested in keeping the nation from interacting with the world, and doing so only on his own terms. Both behaviors represent large-scale trends or levels of foreign policy, as opposed to specific decisions.

[24] Charles F. Hermann, Margaret G. Hermann, and Robert A. Cantor, "Counterattack or Delay: Characteristics Influencing Decision-makers' Responses to the Simulation of an Unidentified Attack," *Journal of Conflict Resolution* 18 (March, 1974), pp. 75–106.

[25] Margaret G. Hermann, "Leader Personality and Foreign Policy Behavior," in *Comparing Foreign Policies: Theories, Findings, and Methods,* ed. James N. Rosenau (New York: Wiley, 1974). Personality characteristics were assessed through content analysis of the leaders' statements; the foreign policy data were taken from the "events data" of the Comparative Research on the Events of Nations (CREON) project.

De Rivera utilized experimental studies on risk-taking behavior to analyze General Douglas MacArthur's decision to land troops at Inchon during the Korean War, arguing that the decision was undoubtedly a function of MacArthur's propensity to take high risks. The landing had been opposed by many of MacArthur's subordinates, and involved a grave risk; failure would have had devastating consequences. On the other hand, success afforded what appeared to be a drastic turning point in the war. De Rivera concludes that MacArthur's decision was at least partly affected by his propensity for risks. Although anecdotal, the linkage is logical, and a rough "correlate" does exist.[26]

The Georges' study of Wilson, already noted, viewed his behavior in foreign affairs as at least partly a function of his childhood deprivation of affection, resulting in his craving for power over others.[27] According to de Rivera, George Kennan offers a slightly different personality explanation. Kennan "explains Wilson's decision to impose harsh terms on Germany as a result of the German attempt to dominate his idealized Russia."[28] In either case, personality obviously does not operate in a vacuum. As de Rivera notes, summarizing the argument made by the Georges concerning Wilson:

When Wilson had a small degree of personal involvement in a task and did not link success with his need for self-esteem, he could be extremely skillful in handling the situation. He could be very flexible, select political goals that were ripe for development, and be both shrewd and inventive in his leadership. It was only when the situation related to his unconscious problems that he became inflexible. . . .

Whenever we know something about an individual's personality, whether it be a comparative measure or a description of some function, and want to predict his behavior, we must take into account the nature of the situation he will be in.[29]

There is, therefore, growing experimental (or simulation) evidence that personality relates to foreign policy behavior, and there is in addition plausible evidence logically relating personality characteristics or attributes to foreign policy decisions. In other words, beyond much doubt personality has *some* effect *some* of the time. The nagging problems of "plausibility" remain, however, and do not settle the question of the "domain" of personality theory. Daniel Druckman, for example, in reviewing a large array of literature on personality, maintains that in

[26] De Rivera, *Psychological Dimension of Foreign Policy*, pp. 175ff.

[27] George and George, *Woodrow Wilson and Colonel House.*

[28] De Rivera, *The Psychological Dimension of Foreign Policy*, p. 198.

[29] Ibid., p. 199.

"complex and highly threatening" negotiating situations, the "negotiators are locked into rigidly defined roles and share a subculture with their opposite numbers. Under these conditions, the effects of personality characteristics have been shown to be minimized." [30]

Moving beyond simulation and experimental case studies, and historical case studies as well, one way in which to attack this domain problem is to ask this question: If different personalities affect foreign policy, do they have a broad effect or a narrow one, and can cases be cited that show personality as *not* having an effect? In a study of the Cold War between 1946 and 1963, William Gamson and Andre Modigliani found four "watersheds" where observable changes in East-West relations (primarily Soviet-American) took place along a positive-negative dimension. None of these shifts occurred when new personalities took over the reins of government, namely when Eisenhower succeeded Truman and Khrushchev succeeded Stalin in 1953 and when Kennedy succeeded Eisenhower in 1961. Although they admit that their watersheds are "neither more nor less obvious than others," nonetheless inspection of Figures 2-2 and 2-3 indicate that their cutting points seem to be more obvious than any others that could be made during the period. Figure 2-2 shows the West's "pattern" of behavior with the corresponding major Soviet actions appearing as C (conciliatory) or R (refractory) across the width of the figure; the reverse is true for Figure 2-3.[31] To illustrate both figures, the first "R" in Figure 2-2 represents Soviet troops marching into Teheran in March, 1946, whereas S-62 is the agreement to the limited test-ban treaty in July, 1963. For the United States, W-7 is Truman's announcement of aid to Greece and Turkey. While these represent specific actions, the patterns listed along the left-hand side of the figures represent the overall pattern of action of the other side *preceding* the major action. The two arrows at the top of each figure indicate the emergence of new leaders on both sides in 1953, and the inauguration of Kennedy in 1961. Figure 2-2 shows the Western "pattern" of behavior as ranging from extremely belligerent to "balanced flexible" from 1946 to late 1950, where it shifts quite clearly to the accommodative part of the scale. In October, 1956, the pattern shifts back up to the middle of the scale, with most behavior ranging between "fairly accommodative" and "fairly belligerent." November, 1962, shows a swing back to accommodative patterns. In the same figure, major Soviet actions are both conciliatory and refractory until November, 1946; the next thirteen out of

[30] Daniel Druckman, *Human Factors in International Negotiations: Social-Psychological Aspects of International Conflict* (Beverly Hills: Sage Publications, 1973), p. 71.

[31] William Gamson and Andre Modigliani, *Untangling the Cold War: A Strategy for Testing Rival Theories* (Boston: Little, Brown, 1971). Details on the figures are in Gamson and Modigliani, Appendix A.

Figure 2-2. Western pattern of action, and major Soviet actions, 1946-1963

Phase of the Cold War

Unit Number*

Western Pattern	Phase I — January, 1946, to October, 1946 (S01–S07)	Phase II — November, 1946, to November, 1950 (S08–S21)	Phase III — December, 1950, to September, 1956 (S22–S37)	Phase IV — October, 1956, to October, 1962 (S38–S60)	Phase V — November, 1962, to November, 1963 (S61–S63)
Extremely belligerent	C R C C	R		C C	
Quite belligerent		R		R	
Fairly belligerent					
Balanced firm	R	R R R R R R R C R R		R C R C R R R	
Balanced	R C		R C	R R R R R	
Balanced flexible		R R	C C C R C	R R R R R R	C
Fairly accommodative			C C C C	R	C
Quite accommodative					
Extremely accommodative		C C			
Inconsistent		R R	R R	C R	C

Key: R = Refractory Soviet response.
 C = Conciliatory Soviet response.
*Read down as S01, S02, . . . S63 as representing Soviet actions.

Source: William A. Gamson and Andre Modigliani, *Untangling the Cold War: A Strategy for Testing Rival Theories*, p. 111. Copyright © 1971 by Little, Brown and Company (Inc.). Reprinted by permission.

35

Figure 2-3. Soviet pattern of action, and major Western actions, 1946-1963

Unit Number*

Soviet pattern	Phase I W01–W07	Phase II W08–W21	Phase III W22–W37	Phase IVa W38–W45	Phase IVb W46–W59	Phase V W60–W62
Extremely belligerent	R	R				
Quite belligerent	R	R		C C	C R R	
Fairly belligerent		R R R R R R			R R R R R R	
Balanced firm		R	R			
Balanced	R R	R R R R	C R R C R R	R R C R	R R R R R R	
Balanced flexible	.		C C		R	C
Fairly accommodative	R R		C C C C C			
Quite accommodative			C	R R	C	C
Extremely accommodative			C			
Inconsistent	R				C	C

Phase I January, 1946, to March, 1947	Phase II April, 1947, to December, 1950	Phase III January, 1951, to September, 1956	Phase IVa October, 1956, to September, 1958	Phase IVb October, 1958, to October, 1962	Phase V November, 1962, to November, 1963

Key: R = Refractory Western response.
　　 C = Conciliatory Western response.
*Read down as W01, W02 . . . W62 as representing Western actions.

Source: From William A. Gamson and Andre Modigliani, *Untangling the Cold War: A Strategy for Testing Rival Theories*, p. 112. Copyright © 1971 by Little, Brown and Company (Inc.). Reprinted by permission.

fourteen major Soviet actions, spanning four years, are all refractory. The period from December, 1950, to September, 1956, however, shows only 25 percent of the major Soviet actions as refractory, while during the following period—the six years from October, 1956, to October, 1962—78 percent of Soviet actions are refractory. The final period shows all three major Soviet actions are conciliatory. The same analysis can be done to Figure 2-3, with Soviet patterns and major Western action with relatively similar results.

Prominent international events such as the Korean War, the Middle East War of 1956, and the Cuban Missile Crisis all seem to "correlate" more closely with the watersheds of large-scale changes in East-West relations during the Cold War than do changes in personality. Even considering the possibility of a time lag, it is unreasonable to think that the shifts that do occur would take, respectively, three and one-half and one and one-half years.

Other indirect evidence also throws light on the limited effect of personality in terms of the domain of behavior it covers. Ole Holsti investigated the differences in perceptions of hostility by nineteen leading decision-makers in 1914 (such as Kaiser Wilhelm, Tsar Nicholas II, and Sir Edward Grey of England). If personality influences such perceptions, we should find differences among the individuals. To the contrary, Holsti found that the variation that did occur depended more on the situation that existed—namely whether the leaders were involved in a crisis or not—than on the individual personality (Table 2-1):

we have accounted for such a high proportion of the variation in perception of hostility that the "unexplained" part which might be attributed to individual differences is extremely small.[32]

Even comparing the decision-makers by country (perhaps cultural differences affect perceptions of hostility) and by role (such as monarch, prime minister, foreign minister, and ambassador) showed that differences in perceptions of hostility were almost entirely accounted for by the different situation—crisis or noncrisis.

Randolph Siverson analyzed the perceptions of five Egyptian and five Israeli leaders during the 1956 Arab-Israeli War, with one individual being the representative at the United Nations and the remaining four labeled as "national" leaders. The one international decision-maker in each country differed very little from the four "national" leaders in their perception of their own country, the enemy, and the United Nations along a good-bad continuum. Although Holsti found the situation of

---

[32] Ole Holsti, "Individual Differences in 'Definition of the Situation,'" *Journal of Conflict Resolution* 14 (September, 1970), p. 305.

Table 2-1.   Effects of Situation, Nation, and Individual Differences on Intensity of Perceived Hostility

	Mean Intensity of Perceived Hostility During:	
	June 28-July 28	*July 29-August 4**
Austria-Hungary		
Franz Joseph (monarch)	4.55	5.95
Berchtold (foreign minister)	4.28	5.20
Forgach (div. chief, foreign office)	3.77	5.90
Szögyény (ambassador to Germany)	4.11	4.47
Germany		
Government**	5.53	5.87
Wilhelm II (monarch)	4.40	5.78
Bethmann-Hollweg (chancellor)	4.08	6.47
Jagow (sec. state, foreign affairs)	3.59	6.08
Great Britain		
Grey (foreign minister)	4.52	5.00
Nicolson (under-sec., foreign affairs)	5.25	5.43
Goschen (ambassador to Germany)	4.09	5.71
France		
Government**	4.34	6.63
Viviani (premier and foreign min.)	4.76	5.97
Bienvenu-Martin (dep. min., for. aff.)	4.51	5.85
Berthelot (act. dir., foreign office)	5.00	7.30
Russia		
Nicholas II (monarch)	7.00	5.86
Sazonov (foreign minister)	5.21	5.11
Serbia		
Paschich (prime and foreign minister)	3.97	5.66
Alexander (crown prince and regent)	4.23	7.67

*Austro-Hungarian documents available only through July 31, 1914.
**Documents issued by the government but author not identified.

This table from "Individual Differences in 'Definition of the Situation,' " by Ole R. Holsti is reprinted from *Journal of Conflict Resolution* Vol. 14, No. 3 (Sept. 1970), p. 306 by permission of the author and publisher, Sage Publications, Inc.

crisis or noncrisis accounted for differences in perception, Siverson, using level of violence in effect as a "situational" variable, did not find that it explained the variation in perceptions, but nonetheless did conclude that "the decision-makers at the United Nations evaluated the main parties to the conflict in a manner that was very similar to the perceptions of the decision-makers in their respective national foreign policy operations." [33] While there may have been a significant variation in each country among the four national leaders, his conclusions nonetheless tend to support Holsti's.

[33] Randolph Siverson, "Role and Perception in International Crisis: The Cases of Israeli and Egyptian Decision-Makers in National Capitals and the United Nations," *International Organization* 27 (Summer, 1973), p. 339.

Patrick McGowan and Howard Shapiro cite W. Eckhardt and R. K. White's study showing that President Kennedy and Premier Khrushchev were not significantly different from each other on several indexes of "conflict-mindedness." [34] Nazli Choucri analyzed the perceptions of Nehru, Sukarno, and Nasser towards the East, West, and the international system (on a good-bad dimension) and concluded that "the degree of variation among Indian, Egyptian, and Indonesian attitudes—as expressed before Afro-Asian audiences—are not significant." [35] Finally, a comparison of Presidents Kennedy, Johnson, and Nixon's utilization of rhetorical symbols (such as freedom, democracy, honor, will and commitment) in reference to Vietnam showed much less variation among them than we would expect if differing personalities affected that rhetorical output. By looking at the trend of such rhetorical symbols through time, it was not apparent when administrations changed; their overall level of rhetoric showed only that Johnson differed significantly from Nixon; and all three tended for the most part to favor the same symbols.[36]

It is unfortunate that few direct tests of personality exist, thus forcing a reliance on these indirect ones. Holsti cautions that his study does not give "license to disregard individual factors in the analysis of foreign policy and international politics," [37] and it should go without saying that in Siverson's Egyptian-Israeli study variation in perceptions may still be accounted for by differences among leaders in the "national" group.

Not one of these studies, therefore, can be read as disconfirming the link between personality and behavior, but they do raise questions about *what* behavior personality can account for. If the link between an individual's perceptions and his behavior—to be considered shortly—is an accurate one, then insofar as personality seems unrelated to perceptions, it may be unrelated to final decisions. This does not mean that personality is definitely not related to behavior, but rather raises the question of what *types* of behavior might be accounted for by personality.

In short, as with so much research on international behavior, the ques-

---

[34] W. Eckhardt and R. K. White, "A Test of the Mirror-Image Hypothesis: Kennedy and Khrushchev," *Journal of Conflict Resolution* 11 (September, 1967), pp. 325–32; cited in Patrick McGowan and Howard B. Shapiro, *The Comparative Study of Foreign Policy: A Survey of Scientific Findings* (Beverly Hills: Sage Publications, 1973), p. 184.

[35] Nazli Choucri, "The Perceptual Base of Nonalignment," *Journal of Conflict Resolution* 13 (March, 1969), p. 72.

[36] Michael P. Sullivan and Karen Peterson, "Presidential Rhetoric on Vietnam: Kennedy, Johnson, and Nixon," mimeographed, University of Arizona, Tucson: 1975; paper delivered at the 1975 International Studies Association/West meeting, San Francisco, April 4–5, 1975.

[37] Holsti, "Individual Differences," p. 309.

tion of the role of personality remains an unanswered one. Though we have numerous plausible linkages, many individual case studies illustrating what are apparent correlations between personality attributes and foreign policy behavior, as well as some systematically collected evidence on the role of personality, there is also evidence that in some areas personality appears to have little or no effect. As noted already, therefore, the debate should not be over whether—in some highly general sense—personality influences foreign behavior, but rather what the specific linkages are and the domains in which personality variables do, and do not, affect behavior.

Image Theories

Instinct and personality are relatively fixed aspects of the individual, although debate continues concerning that contention for personality. The "images" and perceptions that individuals possess are dynamic, however, for they often change. This section investigates how images affect behavior. As Kenneth Boulding has remarked, the naïve notion that we react to the world around us must be supplanted by the realization that we react to *our image* of the world—and the two may not be similar:

We must recognize that the people whose decisions determine the policies and actions of nations do not respond to the "objective" facts of the situation, whatever that may mean, but to their "image" of the situation. It is what we think the world is like, not what it is really like, that determines our behavior.[38]

Even if images are incorrect, in other words, they nonetheless play a role in a nation's behavior. Thomas Franck and Edward Weisband, stressing the importance of images, also argue that the "way two states 'see' each other will frequently affect the way they interact. A pattern of systematic cooperation is not likely to develop between states that perceive each other as evil, aggressive, and immoral."[39]

As Herbert Kelman points out, however, images can operate as independent as well as dependent variables, affecting and being affected. Our concern here is primarily with images as they affect international behavior; we thus forgo discussion of how images change and what causes

[38] Kenneth Boulding, "National Images and International Systems," in *International Politics and Foreign Policy: A Reader in Research and Theory,* ed. James N. Rosenau, rev. ed. (New York: The Free Press, 1969), p. 423.

[39] Thomas M. Franck and Edward Weisband, *Word Politics: Verbal Strategy Among the Superpowers* (New York: Oxford University Press, 1972), pp. 151–52.

those changes.[40] For the moment we shall also forgo a discussion of the manipulation of images, wherein the focus is not on an individual's images or perceptions in terms of how they explain his behavior, but rather on the manipulation by one actor of images held by other actors.[41] Because manipulation involves the attempt to influence others, it appropriately belongs in the discussions of bargaining in Chapter 7 where behavior is explained as a function of bargaining processes or attempts to wield influence.

A methodological note must be appended at this point before delving into the several different approaches to analyzing images or perceptions. There has always been much dispute concerning the "meaning" of people's statements, whether the analyst can find the "correct" meaning, and whether it is possible to actually get at people's perceptions. As with the disputes noted in Chapter 1, it is a very complex issue, and we cannot hope to deal with it completely at this point. But in order to put into perspective much of the research to follow, several basic assumptions must be laid out.

First, content analysis—whether in the form of traditional historical analysis of speeches and statements, or in the form of more contemporary systematic and empirical quantification of statements—makes the assumption that information of a verbal or written nature can have importance. Granted that statements may often be "political," or are meant to arouse ideological fervor, nonetheless if the research question is asked in the correct way, some of the political content may be gleaned out. Second, we will find that much research has relied on the fairly simple good-bad continuum, which uses as a starting point the research by Osgood and his colleagues on the "semantic differential." [42] They found that the three factors of "evaluation," "potency," and "activity" accounted for much of the variation in human judgement.[43] Put simply, when people think about or evaluate something, they tend to see it as good or bad, strong or weak, and active or passive.

Third, an essential ingredient of most content analyses—whether traditional or contemporary—is the assumption that *frequency* is equivalent

[40] Herbert C. Kelman, "Social-Psychological Approaches to the Study of International Relations: Definitions and Scope," in *International Behavior: A Social-Psychological Analysis,* ed. Herbert C. Kelman (New York: Holt, Rinehart, and Winston, 1965), p. 27.

[41] See Robert Jervis, *The Logic of Images in International Relations* (Princeton: Princeton University Press, 1970).

[42] Charles E. Osgood, George J. Suci, and Percy H. Tannenbaum, *The Measurement of Meaning* (Urbana: University of Illinois Press, 1957).

[43] Ibid., p. 325.

to *intensity*. Though some object to this assumption,[44] our common-sense appreciation of the world suggests that the equation is very often quite accurate. The term "evil Communist" is quite a bit different from "vicious, evil, and abominable Communist," and accordingly we assign them a different level of intensity.

Finally, we make the assumption that individuals' perceptions and images can in fact be gleaned from their statements or writings, and that this can be done in a quantitative fashion. Numerical summaries always tend to take the "flesh" out of someone's perceptions, but that drawback is enhanced by the manipulation that can then be done on the quantitative data.

IMAGES: GENERAL LINKAGES

The term "image," as we have already mentioned, covers a broad spectrum. The mere assertion that images must be important for understanding international behavior, however, does not provide theoretical links between what types of images are related to what types of behavior. De Rivera, for instance, points out in reference to the North Korean invasion of South Korea in 1950 that "the Assistant Secretary of State for Far Eastern Affairs did not expect an invasion, and hence, failed to detect it even when he was confronted with a rather strong signal." [45] The assistant secretary's image of the situation made him feel that invasion was an unlikely possibility, and, not surprisingly, he acted in consonance with that image.

David Lampton asserts that a decision-maker's image of an opponent "plays an important role in shaping his definition of the situation and his evaluation of alternatives." [46] Concerning the Korean situation in 1950, for example, an incorrect image of the Chinese "operational code" and a "deficient concept of what power means in Asia" meant that policymakers in the Truman administration did not accurately gauge Chinese intentions, motivations, and capabilities.[47] The same phenomenon occurred in the 1954 crisis over aid to Indochina during the Eisenhower

[44] Robert Jervis, "The Costs of the Quantitative Study of International Relations," in *Contending Approaches to International Politics,* ed. Klaus Knorr and James N. Rosenau (Princeton: Princeton University Press, 1969), p. 188.

[45] De Rivera, *Psychological Dimension of Foreign Policy,* p. 53.

[46] David M. Lampton, "The U.S. Image of Peking in Three International Crises," *Western Political Quarterly* 26 (March, 1973), p. 28.

[47] Ibid., p. 35.

administration. Contrary to what Washington thought, "the Chinese actually felt their limited aid to nationalist Ho Chi Minh was a low-risk policy option." [48]

In contrast, President Kennedy possessed a "relatively sophisticated analysis of Chinese goals and interests" in which Kennedy made sure that "none of China's minimum goals or interests were jeopardized." [49] Says Lampton of Kennedy's Indochina strategy, "The reason he was able to fully use his resources is that the analysis of most components of the ImOP [Image of the Opponent] was largely correct," [50] and thus "the three case studies demonstrate that perceptual accuracy does matter." [51] If decisionmakers' images of the world are incorrect, their policy will be different—perhaps "failure" rather than "success"—from what it would be if their images were correct.

As true as Lampton's findings are, they still lack generality to other cases. What images, in other words, are linked with what behavior? One attempt to assess that linkage is a study by Hermann and his associates, in which they found that when explaining the decision in a simulation to respond with nuclear attack rather than delay response, two perceptual variables of the decision-makers came into play. Leaders who perceived the situation as less ambiguous and who perceived more tension in the system in general were more likely to counterattack on warning rather than delay their response.[52] Contrary to this, the perception of the situation as accidental or nonaccidental was unrelated to the final decision.

Likewise Choucri compared the perceptions held of both east and west by Nehru, Sukarno, and Nasser to the actual behavior of those leaders' states toward the east and the west. While it was noted above that the perceptions of the three differed little, it was found that their actions did. Egypt showed significantly higher conflict toward the West than the East, whereas India and Indonesia reversed that pattern. Thus while differences existed in the behavior of Indonesia, these differences cannot be explained by differences in overall (positive or negative) perceptions by the leaders.[53]

[48] Ibid., p. 40.

[49] Ibid., p. 46.

[50] Ibid., p. 48.

[51] Ibid., p. 49.

[52] Hermann, et al, "Counterattack or Delay," pp. 98–99.

[53] Nazli Choucri, "The Nonalignment of Afro-Asian States: Policy, Perception, and Behavior," *Canadian Journal of Political Science* 2 (March, 1969), p. 13.

"MIRROR" IMAGES

A slightly more specific linkage between images and behavior is found in the "mirror" image study of Soviet-American relations by Uri Bronfenbrenner.[54] Although his observations are derived solely from a trip to the Soviet Union, he found that what he first thought to be merely Soviet distortion of American society and foreign policy was actually a dual misperception. Each side viewed the other as an aggressor, as exploiting its people, as having no popular support, as being untrustworthy, and as fostering a "mad" foreign policy. One clear inference seems to be that such images nurtured the Cold War; as Franck and Weisband noted, nations holding these images of one another are unlikely to partake in long-range and persistently cooperative behavior.

Ralph White isolated six mirror images that he claimed were present during World War I, World War II, and the Vietnam war.[55] Three reflect what we have seen already in terms of general dimensions, although the specifics are different: The enemy was viewed as diabolical (evil) while the self was viewed as both moral (good) and virile. Again the implication is that these mirror images are linked to the inception or continuation of war. White comments, for instance, that in 1914 Austria harped on the "criminal" character of Serbia, Hitler in 1939 pictured his enemies as having "hatred" for Germany, and Ho Chi Minh and the Vietcong consistently attacked the brutality and inhumanity of the United States during the Vietnam War. Conversely, the Austrians viewed themselves as peace-loving, civilized, orderly, and democratic; Hitler argued in 1939: "I have not conducted any war . . . I have expressed my abhorrence of war . . . I am not aware for what purpose I should wage a war at all";[56] the United States justified its activities in Vietnam in terms of morality and Western civilization; and the NLF and the Vietcong consistently referred to themselves as peaceful and as possessing respect for the independence of other nations.[57]

As logical as such mirror image hypotheses are, the images may not represent misperceptions at all, but be consciously utilized by decision-makers to rally their populations for war. Moreover, regardless of the voluminous historical illustrations that can be cited, no control exists showing that the images were not always present, or, if present, that they change in scope or intensity during wartime.

[54] Uri Bronfenbrenner, "The Mirror Image in Soviet-American Relations," *Journal of Social Issues* 17 (No. 3, 1961), pp. 45–56.

[55] Ralph K. White, "Misperception and the Vietnam War," *Journal of Social Issues* 22 (No. 3, 1966), pp. 1–164.

[56] Ibid., p. 12.

[57] Ralph K. White, *Nobody Wanted War* (Garden City, N.Y.: Doubleday, 1970).

BELIEF SYSTEMS

While the concept of mirror images is fairly simple and restricted, it and other image hypotheses can be cast in a broader framework by utilizing the notion of "belief systems." As normally conceived, belief systems operate as orientations or filtering elements for all individuals. Alexander George, for instance, has outlined basic elements of the belief system—or what he calls the "operational code"—of Bolshevik leaders. In terms of basic philosophical content, the Communist belief system viewed opponents as completely hostile and shrewd, and therefore saw the political universe as one of conflict. Even so, they possessed great optimism because the victory of communism would at some future time be insured. Further, the Communist belief system did not encompass chance events: Man can and does move history. Bolshevik leaders, therefore, tended to see very complicated planning behind events that in many cases may have been fortuitous.[58]

One can, it is hypothesized, understand Soviet behavior as a function of these basic parameters of their belief system. Soviet leaders would not be happy with merely "surviving"; rather they must maximize their gains. At the same time, despite their desire to push forward and engage in pursuit, their idea of the inevitability of their success leads them to "avoid adventures" and "know when to stop."[59]

American leaders, of course, have possessed their own belief systems. Henry Kissinger once labeled former Secretary of State John Foster Dulles's belief system about the Communists as an "inherent bad faith" model. Kissinger was implying that Dulles's view of Soviet hostility, filtered through his belief system, could not help but lead him to conclude that the behavior of the Soviets was not sincere but rather a function of their frustration or changing capabilities.[60] Because in Dulles's mind the Soviets were inherently evil, their behavior would not indicate to him what it might suggest to others. If this premise is true, then two hypotheses follow: Dulles's perception of the Soviet Union as hostile should decrease only as he saw its capabilities decreasing and its frustrations increasing. However, an actual decrease in Soviet hostility should be unrelated to his general evaluation of the Soviet Union.

Ole Holsti analyzed more than 400 documents authored by Dulles between 1953 and 1959 (including Congressional testimony, press con-

58 Alexander L. George, "The 'Operational Code': A Neglected Approach to the Study of Political Leaders and Decision-making," *International Studies Quarterly* 13 (June, 1969), pp. 204–5.

59 Ibid., p. 209.

60 Henry Kissinger, *The Necessity of Choice* (Garden City, N.Y.: Doubleday, 1962), p. 201.

ferences, and addresses), and discovered that the hypotheses were generally supported. Aggregating his data into twenty-five three-month periods, Holsti found that Dulles's perception of Soviet hostility correlated with his perception of their failure or frustration in foreign policy, and with their weakness.[61] However, his perceptions of decreased hostility notwithstanding, Dulles's evaluation of the Soviet Union generally (along the evaluative, good-bad continuum) remained unchanged. As Holsti concluded, these results "strongly suggest that [Dulles] attributed decreasing Soviet hostility to the necessity of adversity rather than to any genuine change of character." [62]

In Holsti's view, therefore, changes in Soviet hostility might not affect Dulles's evaluation of the Soviet Union. Specific Soviet cooperative moves—he mentions the treaty neutralizing Austria in 1955 and Soviet manpower reductions—would be reinterpreted by Dulles's belief system. The important question, however, is the effect this filtering had on United States foreign policy, and the answer is unclear. Using data on events between the United States and the Soviet Union along the positive-negative dimension,[63] we find only a very moderate correlation between U.S. actions and Dulles's evaluation.[64] Furthermore, given the fact that Dulles's evaluation of the Soviet Union changed very little between 1953 and 1959 (ranging from −2.69 to −3.00 on a 6-point scale), that small variation cannot account for the shifts that we do know occurred in Soviet-American relations (as we shall see in Chapter 7, and as reported in Gamson and Modigliani and in Goldmann's studies [65]).

Although removed somewhat from actual foreign behavior, Glen Stassen's study of belief systems not only confirms their importance, but also shows that they account for behavior that goes unaccounted for by the variable of "role." [66] Stassen takes off from an early study by James Rosenau who had found that party and committee roles determined what United States senators said about Secretaries of State Dean Acheson and

[61] Ole Holsti, "Belief System and National Images: A Case Study," in *International Politics and Foreign Policy: A Reader in Research and Theory*, ed. James N. Rosenau, rev. ed. (New York: The Free Press, 1969). The correlations were .58 and .55 (p = .01); see appendix, paragraph A.

[62] Ibid., p. 547.

[63] These event data were kindly provided by Professor Terrence Hopmann, University of Minnesota.

[64] The rank correlation is .42 (p = .16); see appendix, paragraph H. The correlation of the data on these events with Dulles's perception of hostility is .30 (p = .36).

[65] Gamson and Modigliani, *Untangling the Cold War*; Kjell Goldmann, "East-West Tension in Europe, 1946–1970: A Conceptual Analysis and a Quantitative Description," *World Politics* 26 (Octboer, 1973), pp. 106–25.

[66] Glen H. Stassen, "Individual Preference vs. Role Constraint in Policy-making: Senatorial Response to Secretaries Acheson and Dulles," *World Politics* 25 (October, 1972), pp. 96–119.

Dulles. Republicans were more likely to support a secretary under a Republican administration, and likewise for Democrats under a Democratic administration. Further, senators in the role of members of the Foreign Relations Committee were more supportive of secretaries—regardless of party—than were senators not in that role.[67]

No comparison was made with the potency of an individual variable, however, and Stassen classified senators according to the images of isolationism, alliance support, and cold warrior-moderate. He found that this individual "belief-set" model, as he calls it, more strongly related to senatorial comments about the secretary of state than the role variable, and, more important, it was capable of accounting for behavior left unexplained by the role model. For instance, nine Democrats supported Acheson, but these nine were also alliance-supporting moderates. The one Democrat opposing him, Patrick McCarran, was an isolationist moderate, and therefore "belief-set prevailed over his Democratic party role." [68] The same phenomenon occurred with the Republicans. Republican senators should oppose Acheson, and twenty did. Eighteen were cold warriors, however, and therefore their belief systems can also explain their opposition. There were four Republicans whose belief systems agreed with Acheson's, and for three of the four the belief-set prevailed over party role. Stassen concluded that "cognitive processing elements—perception patterns, expectations, evaluations, and belief-sets—deserve a much larger part of the credit or blame for foreign policy outcome than is often recognized." [69]

Robert Bernstein and William Anthony compared the potency of the belief system to other explanations of senators' votes on the antiballistic missile system in the late 1960s.[70] They found that variation on ideology (measured by variation on the senators' ACA-ADA ratings) took precedence over party commitment as well as over economic benefits in military hardware their states would derive from the new system. Moreover, the influence of ideology—at least on this issue—seems to have grown (Table 2-2); almost all changes in votes between 1968 and 1970 were undertaken by senators whose original votes were not in line with their ideology, and they moved to bring them into greater accord.

Joanne Loomba compared "the extent to which differing images of India and dissimilar political roles are associated with different foreign

---

[67] James N. Rosenau, "Private Preferences and Political Responsibilities: The Relative Potency of Individual and Role Variables in the Behavior of U.S. Senators," in *Quantitative International Politics: Insights and Evidence*, ed. J. David Singer (New York: The Free Press, 1968).

[68] Stassen, "Individual Preference vs. Role Constraint," p. 107.

[69] Ibid., p. 119.

[70] Robert A. Bernstein and William W. Anthony, "The ABM Issue in the Senate, 1968–1970: the Importance of Ideology," *American Political Science Review* 68 (September, 1974), pp. 1198–1206.

Table 2-2. Deviation from Expected Position, Based on Ideology and Relative Change in Position, 1968-1970

Relative Change in Position, 1968-1970	Deviation from Position, 1968		
	More Anti-ABM than Expected	As Expected	More Pro-ABM than Expected
Pro-ABM Move	5	0	0
None	10	55	5
Anti-ABM Move	0	1	10

Robert A. Bernstein and William W. Anthony, "The ABM Issue in the Senate, 1968-1970: The Importance of Ideology," *American Political Science Review,* 68 (September 1974), p. 1203.

aid orientations." [71] She hypothesized that attitudes regarding foreign aid for India would be related to differing images of India. These images pertained to evaluations of India's international behavior and domestic situation, its leaders and people, and its political, military, economic, and social transactions with the United States. Role variables included the dichotomies of executive-legislative, Senate-House, and Democratic-Republican, as well as geographic region and membership in specific groups such as the Senate Foreign Relations and House Foreign Affairs committees. She concluded that "a study of certain aspects of images of India is more likely to uncover significant differences in aid orientations across time than is an examination of the political affiliations of American foreign policy makers." [72] Regardless of the fact that three role variables—Senate or House membership, region, and service on the House Foreign Affairs, Appropriations, or Agricultural committees—do attain statistical significance in some cases, "region of the country represented and service on the various House committees are virtually worthless when directional expectations are included in the hypotheses." [73] That is, directional hypotheses would suggest not only differences between those who hold positive and negative images about India, but would also suggest those with more positive images would favor aid more. Likewise, directional hypotheses on the role variables would not only suggest differences for different roles, but also suggest that congressmen from the Northeast section of the country, as well as those on the Foreign Affairs and Foreign Relations committees would be more favorable to-

[71] Joanne Loomba, "The Relationship of Images and Political Affiliations to Orientations Toward Foreign Aid for India," *Internation Studies Quarterly* 16 (September, 1972), p. 352.

[72] Ibid., p. 363.

[73] Ibid., p. 369.

ward aid. In fact, when testing these directional differences, Loomba found the image hypotheses to be much more potent.

Although findings from these three different studies all show the effect of belief system, unfortunately the behavior in two is verbal behavior or attitudes, while Holsti's study of Dulles deals with perceptions that seem to be related only moderately to patterns of United States foreign policy during that period. In addition, as George points out, belief systems are not static entities; they do undergo change. In George's analysis, particularly, he noted how under Khrushchev the Soviets' belief in the possibility of annihilation seemed to subside, which in turn affected their urgency for immediate and total victory.[74]

Despite such limitations, these studies do suggest that the hypothesis that "images are important" should be refined to specify what *types* of images are important. For one thing, it appears that evaluative (good-bad) perceptions, as well as certain ideologically or politically oriented ones, are very basic and very important. Moreover, studies suggest, at least Stassen's and Loomba's, that the alternative explanation of *role* was found less capable of accounting for variation in behavior than image or belief system. The effect of belief-system and images remains to be applied systematically to variation in actual state behavior, but these studies constitute clear evidence that, at a minimum, verbal behavior is dependent on the construct and content of belief systems.

IMAGE: DEFINITION OF THE SITUATION

Image theory in a general sense, then, does not carry the potency that more particular *types* of images do. "National interest" and "definition of the situation"—both traditional concepts in the study of international politics—can be considered very general images or perceptions, and as such carry little explanatory power. To contend that an individual acted because of the way in which he defined the situation may be valid, but not very specific. Similarly, to argue that states act because "their national interest is at stake" may be valid, but almost solely by definition. In neither case can it account for variation other than post facto. If a state acts in a given situation, then logically *some* interest is at stake, and one need only search through the situation to come up with one—status, image, economic considerations; there is always something to fall back on. Note, however, that the presence or absence of the independent variable—national interest—is measured by the presence or absence of the state's action, a clearly invalid method of research.

74 George, "The 'Operational Code,' " pp. 216f.

The definition of "national interest," furthermore, is all-encompassing. As illustrated by Quincy Wright, it includes the

spread of . . . ideologies, observance of commitments; realization of . . . policies, preservation of national character, gaining of prestige, satisfaction of pride, augmentation of power, security of independence, territorial integrity, and continued existence.[75]

Hans Morgenthau divided the concept of "national interest" into two parts, the first being the residual meaning inherent in the concept itself, and the second constituting all the logical possibilities compatible with it determined by a given context.[76] Nonetheless, such concepts are very difficult to operationalize and often require a post-hoc assessment. Quincy Wright's attempt at such analysis is interesting, although subjective. In separating numerous conflicts into four categories—no military hostilities, hostilities with no escalation, hostilities with escalation, and World Wars" —his post-hoc assessment of the respective national interests involved in each conflict produces the following average scores per category (range 1 to 100): 17.2, 22.7, 36.4, and 57.5.[77] Clearly the greater the felt national interest, the greater the violence, but such subjective and post-hoc asssesments are questionable, to say the least. To employ the term "national interest," however, is really one way of defining a situation, or type of "issue." If the types of issues with which countries become concerned change, and if their behavior is dependent on the type of issue, then different and changing issues—one being the "national interest"—may relate to specific state behavior.

A wide variety of literature contends that the more general, broader, symbolic, or intangible an issue, the more likely it is that parties to a conflict will act in an aggressive or hostile way.[78] Druckman, putting it another way, offers two specific hypotheses: "The more limited the scope of the issues to be discussed in negotiations, the more likely that a resolution will be attained," and, "The more resolutions attained on 'smaller'

[75] Quincy Wright, "The Escalation of International Conflicts," *Journal of Conflict Resolution* 9 (March, 1965), p. 445.

[76] Hans Morgenthau, *Politics Among Nations: The Struggle for Power and Peace,* 3d ed. (New York: Knopf, 1965), p. 9.

[77] Quincy Wright, "The Escalation of International Conflicts," pp. 443–45.

[78] James N. Rosenau, "Pre-Theories and Theories of Foreign Policy," in *Approaches to Comparative and International Politics,* ed. R. Barry Farrel (Evanston: Northwestern University Press, 1966); Kal Holsti, "Resolving International Conflicts: A Taxonomy of Behavior and Some Figures on Procedure," *Journal of Conflict Resolution* 10 (September, 1966), pp. 272–96; Daniel Katz, "Group Process and Social Interaction: A System Analysis of Two Movements of Social Protest," *Journal of Social Issues* 23 (No. 1, 1967), pp. 3–22.

issues, the more likely will parties be able to negotiate their differences on the broader issues." [79] One study compared the six-week crisis leading up to the outbreak of World War I, the ten days of the Cuban Missile Crisis, and the six years of the Vietnam War.[80] It found that in the first and third cases the issues as perceived by the decision-makers (and elite newspapers in the last case) changed from more specific and tangible to more symbolic and intangible as the crisis in 1914 and the war in Vietnam progressed in intensity. For the Cuban Missile Crisis the change did not occur. Of note here is that the 1914 case and the Vietnam War were both violent conflicts whereas the 1962 Cuban Missile Crisis became extremely, but only temporarily, intense.

A later study delved even more particularly into the entire Vietnam War, with a content analysis of every presidential document by Kennedy, Johnson, and Nixon in which Vietnam was mentioned from 1961 to 1973. The content analysis was a relatively simple one; it consisted of a frequency count of the appearance of thirty-two different "symbols" such as "freedom," "democracy," and "honor." Without going into specifics, the results showed that, taking the three administrations together, the definition of the situation along a symbolic dimension was related roughly to the progress of the war. During the early years the symbolic issues were less prominent than during the 1965-1968 period when American intervention escalated and casualties rose, whereas between 1969 and 1973 the symbolic issues declined as the war decreased in intensity. The relation becomes stronger when using documents that pertain largely to Vietnam and that are moderately lengthy (Figure 2-4); even analyzing Johnson and Nixon separately, the same general relationship emerged, despite the fact that Johnson used a higher overall amount of symbols.[81] Causal relationships were difficult to tease out of these data (partly due to the presence of methodological problems—see appendix, paragraph D), but those that did emerge seemed to indicate that the symbolic rhetoric of Johnson tended to precede the trend of the war, while for Nixon it appeared to follow the progress of the war. (No patterns were discernible during the Kennedy years.)

Earlier evidence collected for different reasons by Ithiel deSola Pool and his associates is in general agreement with these findings. "Ideological" symbols increased in newspaper editorials in the *London Times*

[79] Druckman, *Human Factors in International Negotiations*, p. 18.

[80] Michael P. Sullivan, "Commitment and the Escalation of Conflict," *Western Political Quarterly* 25 (March, 1972), pp. 28–38.

[81] Michael P. Sullivan, "Symbolic Commitment and the Escalation of the Vietnam War: Kennedy, Johnson, and Nixon," mimeographed (Institute of Government Research, University of Arizona, 1975).

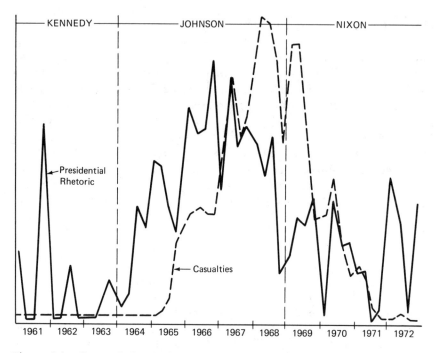

Figure 2-4. Quarterly level of United States casualties in Vietnam, and presidential symbolic rhetoric in major documents.

and *New York Times* during the two world war periods and decreased during peacetime.[82] During World War I, Pool reports that the symbol "democracy" increased from appearing in 2 percent of all editorials in 1914 to 12 percent in 1918. Pool notes, with no data presented, that the next significant increase in the frequency of occurrence of the symbol "democracy," especially in Great Britain and the United States, was near the end of the 1930s, prior to the outbreak of World War II. (The symbol was used less in France, and not at all in Russia and Germany.[83]) Pool found that the effect of fighting on the use of symbols varied, "but again one may generalize that when the physical danger became sufficiently acute ideological arguments were used less." [84] A somewhat similar pattern occurred in Lyndon Johnson's references to symbolic issues in the Vietnam War: after the war escalated in 1965, one measure of his rhetoric dropped sharply in 1966.

The theoretical implications of these studies are that national interest

---

[82] Ithiel deSola Pool, *The Prestige Papers: A Comparative Study of Political Symbols* (Cambridge: MIT Press, 1970), p. 74.

[83] Ibid., p. 158.

[84] Ibid., p. 216.

is only one issue, that it is of a type called "symbolic," and that it—along with other issues of the same type—reflect how decision-makers define a situation. More important, the entire constellation of "symbolic" images appears to relate to actual state behavior, although as noted we must be cautious as to whether it is affecting or being affected by actual state behavior.

IMAGE: INTERVENING VARIABLE

Belief systems contain images that are on the whole unchanging, mirror images take long periods of time to change, and images as definitions of a situation are also usually conceived as fairly stable. Moreover, these several perspectives usually view the image as the independent agent, unaffected—for the most part—by external elements. The image, however, can also be an intervening variable that undergoes change, a variable that exists between the external elements that are perceived (and which themselves might account for behavior) and the behavior. For example, North Vietnamese behavior in South Vietnam during the Vietnam War (an external element) might in actuality have been very non-provocative, but American decision-makers might have perceived it in a much more provocative sense. Their resultant behavior may be affected by their perception, which serves as the intervening variable between North Vietnamese behavior and subsequent American behavior.

Image in this perspective is best considered in terms of stimulus and response. An organism responds to stimuli it receives from the world; given certain stimuli, it will respond in certain ways. The classic reference, of course, is to the Russian scientist Pavlov's discovery that he could train a dog to salivate at the sound of a bell simply by ringing it every time he fed the dog. While at first the dog salivated only at the presence of food, the association of the bell with the food soon transferred that response from the food to the bell.

Needless to say, human beings are quite a bit more complex, and therefore the transference of the simple stimulus-response model to human beings is questionable. Yet national leaders often seem to operate within a strict stimulus-response framework. Many U.S. officials during the 1950s, very clearly felt that all Communist countries would back down if *only* the United States showed the "will" and the "strength" to oppose them. In other words, if America presented a specified stimulus (S) in each situation—strength, an image of a strong will, and perhaps a strongly worded threat—it could expect a specific response (R), namely, that the opposition accede to its wishes. One crucially important intervening variable between S and R may be the perception or image that the individual has of the specific external stimulus. In a sense, Holsti's study of Dulles investigated the intervening variable of perception, but not in terms of what has been called specific "congruence" across the stimulus-response model. To illustrate, assume a Soviet premier accuses the United States of aggression; this accusation represents a stimulus (S) for the United States, which then *perceives* it in some way, and, normally, responds to it (R). The United States may perceive the stimulus as very hostile, and decide to respond with a threat. This response (R) by the United States then becomes a stimulus (S) for the Soviets, who in turn will perceive it in some way and—once again, normally—respond. This perspective has been generalized into a "mediated" stimulus-response model in the following way:

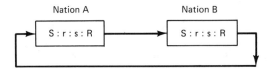

The response (R) on the far right-hand side serves, of course, as the stimulus (S) on the far left-hand side; likewise, the R and S in the middle of the diagram are similar. The lower-case "r" and "s" within each nation represent, respectively, the nation's perception of the external stimulus and its perception of its own response. In the above example, the United States might perceive the Soviet action as very hostile and respond with a hostile action, but yet have a perception ("s") of its own response as being only mildly hostile.

To reiterate, the *mediated* stimulus-response model assumes that with nation-states a simple S-R model would leave too much of the variation in state behavior (R) unexplained. As Holsti, Brody, and North see it:

> The basic problem is this: given some action by Nation B, what additional information is needed to account for Nation A's foreign policy response? . . . If the real world for a President, Prime Minister or Foreign Secretary—and for their counterparts in friendly and hostile nations—is the world as they perceive it, perceptual [or intervening] variables are crucial in a conflict situation.[85]

Unfortunately, results from numerous studies are mixed. In one analysis, Holsti and his colleagues suggest that less involved nations—those with less intense behavior in the crisis—are likely to have a higher congruence across the model than nations that are more highly "involved,"

[85] Ole R. Holsti, Richard A. Brody, and Robert C. North, "Measuring Affect and Action in International Reaction Models: Empirical Materials from the 1962 Cuban Crisis," in *International Politics and Foreign Policy: A Reader in Research and Theory,* ed. James N. Rosenau, rev. ed. (New York: The Free Press, 1969), pp. 683–684.

the assumption being that involved individuals (or, in this case, groups of individuals) are less likely to perceive objective reality as it really is, and are more likely to let their own perceptions enter in. They tested this theory on the crisis in 1914 using the Dual Alliance and Triple Entente as the two units. Data on state actions (S and R) were collected from contemporary accounts and histories of the period; perceptions (r and s) for all decision-makers were derived from official documents—almost all of which have been released. The perceptions were categorized into these variables: hostility, friendship, frustration, satisfaction, and change in the status quo, while the behavioral variable was that of violence.

They are quite right when they conclude that the differences between S and R for both alliances showed that the Dual Alliance more consistently overreacted to the input stimulus, whereas the Triple Entente underreacted; that the Dual Alliance consistently overperceived the actions of the Triple Entente; and that R cannot be predicted solely from S.[86] Their report of the findings are somewhat contradictory, however, and in spite of the fact that differences in perception were present, when the stimulus and the perception are correlated with the response (R), only for the Dual Alliance is the relation between perception (r) and response (R) stronger than between the stimulus (S) and response (R). For the Triple Entente, stimulus is slightly better related to response than perception (Table 2-3).[87]

The central conclusion, therefore, is that although in neither case is the response (R) highly determined by either the stimulus, the perception of that stimulus, or a combination of the two, in only one case does the perception take precedence over the stimulus and even in that one case the stimulus still accounts for a moderate amount of the variation in response.

Similar data for the 1962 Cuban Missile Crisis suggests that congruence across the stimulus-response model was much greater in that case, meaning that both the United States and the Soviet Union perceived stimuli more accurately, at least in terms of a gross level of hostility.[88] Table 2-3 also shows, however, that while for the U.S. perceptions correlated slightly higher with its action than stimuli did, the difference was

[86] Ole R. Holsti, Robert C. North, and Richard A. Brody, "Perception and Action in the 1914 Crisis," in *Quantitative International Politics; Insights and Evidence*, ed. J. David Singer (New York: The Free Press, 1968), pp. 152–53.

[87] The correlations presented in Table 2-3 are rather different from those presented in the original article. Moreover, even using percentage change from time period to time period for the Dual Alliance (this analysis cannot be done for the Triple Entente because of the presence of so many ties), the correlations between perception (r) and response (R) are —.24, and .06 with the response (R) variable lagged one time period behind the perception (r) variable.

[88] Holsti, et al., "Measuring Affect and Action."

Table 2-3.   Correlations of Stimulus, Perception, and Response, in Three Historical Situations

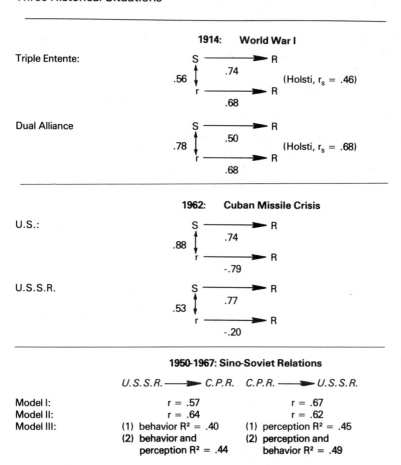

1914:   World War I

Triple Entente: S ————————▶ R

.56 │   .74   (Holsti, r_s = .46)

r ————————▶ R

.68

Dual Alliance   S ————————▶ R

.78 │   .50   (Holsti, r_s = .68)

r ————————▶ R

.68

1962:   Cuban Missile Crisis

U.S.:   S ————————▶ R

.88 │   .74

r ————————▶ R

-.79

U.S.S.R.   S ————————▶ R

.53 │   .77

r ————————▶ R

-.20

1950-1967: Sino-Soviet Relations

	U.S.S.R. ——▶ *C.P.R.*	*C.P.R.* ——▶ *U.S.S.R.*
Model I:	r = .57	r = .67
Model II:	r = .64	r = .62
Model III:	(1) behavior R^2 = .40 (2) behavior and perception R^2 = .44	(1) perception R^2 = .45 (2) perception and behavior R^2 = .49

not great; more importantly, however, the relationship between the Soviet's perception of action by the United States and its own response to that action was not very close.[89]

Dina Zinnes utilized basically the same question in analyzing similar data again from the 1914 crisis, but her concern was solely on the link between perception and behavior. She tested four different hypotheses and found that when states perceive hostility they will express hostility, and tend to express it toward the offending state. Moreover, she found that an *imperfect memory* model, in which current perceptions and those

[89] Perceptions had been measured along the positive-negative dimension, and for this case the percentage of all perceptions that were negative was used as the perceptual variable. For the behavioral—or "action"—data, each day of the crisis was ranked in terms of level of hostility on a 1–10 scale.

formed over the previous three days worked better than a *no memory* or *perfect memory* model. Hypotheses concerning A's expression of hostility toward B and his subsequent perception of it and expression of hostility back to A, however, were not confirmed, but as Zinnes notes these findings (which turned out in fact to be negative, the opposite of the expected relation) were very likely the result of incorrect time models.[90]

A later study by Zinnes, however, which treated the perception or expression of hostility in a much more gross sense (merely dichotomizing into perception versus no perception and expression versus no expression), found that "when there is no perception of hostility there is no expression of hostility, but when hostility is perceived it is replied to with hostility." [91]

Gordon Hilton, analyzing the change in perception or expression of hostility in World War I, found no relation between the two variables during the same time periods. It was only when the expression of hostility was delayed two and three days after the perception of it that significant results turned up between the two variables, but only for the Triple Entente and not for the Dual Alliance. Hence, the role of perception of hostility in its effect on the expression of hostility is not a simple one, and does not fit all cases.[92]

Franz Mogdis' study of Sino-Soviet relations also investigated the importance of perceptions.[93] He found that perceptions of each side were important in accounting for subsequent behavior. Behavior was a *combined* dimension of Sino-Soviet relations, that is, the behavior in question was a conflict-cooperation dimension, including the exchange of technicians, military aid to China, trade, the number of Communist Chinese forces at the Sino-Soviet border, and the number of border incidents. The perceptions were derived from official sources such as the *People's Daily* (China), and *Pravda* (U.S.S.R.), and were scaled along a positive-negative dimension. Table 2-3 shows the results when comparing Mogdis' perceptual data with Sino-Soviet actions collected in an independent study.[94]

[90] Dina Zinnes, "The Expression and Perception of Hostility in Prewar Crisis: 1914," in *Quantitative International Politics: Insights and Evidence,* ed. J. David Singer (New York: The Free Press, 1968), p. 117.

[91] Dina A. Zinnes, Joseph L. Zinnes, and Robert D. McClure, "Hostility in Diplomatic Communication: A Study of the 1914 Crisis," in *International Crises: Insights from Behavioral Research,* ed. Charles F. Hermann (New York: The Free Press, 1972), p. 160.

[92] Gordon Hilton, "A Closed and Open Model Analysis of Expressions of Hostility in Crisis," *Journal of Peace Research* 8 (Nos. 3–4, 1971), pp. 258–59.

[93] Franz Mogdis, "The Verbal Dimension in Sino-Soviet Relations: A Time Series Analysis," mimeographed, presented at the Annual Meeting, American Political Science Association, Los Angeles, California, September, 1970.

[94] See footnote 63.

Model I uses perception as the independent variable predicting to subsequent behavior; Model II uses the other side's actions as the independent variable predicting to subsequent behavior; and Model III combines both perception and behaviors as independent variables. For the Chinese People's Republic, perception is more important in accounting for its action, whereas for the U.S.S.R. the relationship is reversed. However, both perception as well as action by the other side are highly related to the subsequent actions of each side; model III shows that the combination of both independent variables does not appreciably add to the predictive power.

This section has ranged over considerable territory, and conclusions should remain for the following section. Be it noted here, however, that what has been termed "image theory" really covers a conglomerate of theories and hypotheses that generally focus on the potential role of the individual's image of the world and how it might explain that individual's behavior. In that sense, it is not a neatly contained theory. It is hoped, nonetheless, that the above subsections have illustrated the different ways in which to "cut into" the general image theory.

Conclusions and Implications

This chapter posits the individual—his instinct, personality, and images or perceptions—as a crucial independent agent accounting for international behavior. The assumption is that man controls his environment, that somehow man makes a difference, and that therefore *he* must be considered in trying to explain international phenomena. The conclusions to be drawn from this assumption, and its implications, can be separated into the theoretical and the policy categories.

THEORETICAL IMPLICATIONS

No single chapter could possibly do justice to this broad subject. What we have attempted here is the establishment of parameters. Man has long felt that he can influence his environment, and that his behavior in international affairs is due, at least partly, to factors internal to himself. Unfortunately, though there exists much ad hoc theorizing and volumes of individual case studies that can be read as illustrating an individual's effect on foreign policy,[95] we still lack much systematic evidence confirming this hypothesis or illustrating its domain.

---

[95] Such as Rogow, *James Forrestal;* Garry Wills, *Nixon Agonistes: The Crisis of the Self-Made Man* (Boston: Houghton Mifflin, 1969); Tom Wicker, *JFK and LBJ: The Influence of Personality Upon Politics* (New York: Morrow, 1968); David Halberstam, *The Best and the Brightest* (New York: Random House, 1969).

In terms of the role of personality, two basic problems stand out. First is the difficulty of theorizing in a specific sense about exactly what personality variables or attributes have exactly what type of effect in exactly what kind of situation. With the exception of a few personality studies, the theorizing remains ad hoc. A recent review of international relations literature puts it well:

The mechanism by which individual psychic attitudes and complexes of a quasi-pathological character are translated into the concrete political decisions of leaders building up toward the actual outbreak of organized conflict has not yet been adequately defined and described. . . . Undoubtedly the frustrations of human beings form an important part of the total matrix out of which social conflict arises. . . . To admit this is not to deny that the hypothesis contains serious difficulties. We still do not know, for example, what exactly is the relationship between childhood frustration experiences (with their accompanying effects upon personality) and adult socio-political attitudes. Nor is there any way to determine whether childhood experiences or contemporary adult frustrations are more important as influences on behavior.[96]

In other words, the relationships simply have not been spelled out even on the theoretical level.

The second problem is that adequate measurement of personality determinants or characteristics is difficult in international affairs. Unconscious determinants are extremely difficult to "get at," and variation in personality attributes has not been well measured for national decision-makers and then applied to their variation in decision-making. This difficulty in acquiring or creating data means that only a small number of cases, usually of aberrant personalities like Stalin and Hitler, are used as evidence about the influence of the individual. Systematic evidence linking personality characteristics to decisions or trends in decisions is sorely lacking. Furthermore, the indirect tests utilized here showed that in instances where changes could be expected in behavior if personality were a potent variable failed to produce such changes. Specific decisions such as MacArthur's landing at Inchon during the Korean War might be accounted for by personality, but almost without exception such explanations are post facto, and in that sense it is not too difficult to find some personality characteristic that seems to be present and that plausibly explains a given decision.

Specific decisions, however, are only one kind of behavior in international politics, and they are no more nor less important than other types of behavior. Quite clearly, then, the problem is not solely one of measurement nor—given the extensive work by personality theorists and the small number of excellent personality studies referred to already—one

---

[96] James E. Dougherty and Robert L. Pfaltzgraff, Jr., *Contending Theories of International Relations* (Philadelphia: Lippincott, 1971), pp. 220–21.

of a lack of theory. Rather, the difficulty in assessing the importance and domain of personality derives from a rather fuzzy picture of the behavior that personality is thought to explain. Our first inclination is to hypothesize that personality will have its greatest effect on individual decisions, but Margaret Hermann's results, for example, suggest that composite personality types will also be related to a nation's overall outlook on foreign affairs as well as its level of cooperative behavior.[97] Personality variables also seem to be highly related to specific attitudes about foreign affairs.[98] Quite clearly personality does not apply equally strongly to all aspects of international behavior; but until some of those specifications begin to be developed, we must be content with only scattered findings on the actual effect of personality variables.

Image theories appear to cover a larger empirical domain, but that is very likely a function of easier access to data on images and perceptions. "General" images (such as Lambton's "image of the opponent" or Wright's broad conception of "national interest") are very plausibly linked to large sweeps of behavior, but because they are so general we run the risk of being tautological when we use them. The theory of an internal belief system contains impressive backing, but unfortunately the behavior analyzed in connection with such a system has almost without exception been verbal, attitudinal, or voting, none of which is truly descriptive of international behavior. Even Holsti's study of Dulles did not ultimately relate Dulles's filtering element to United States behavior, and when that was done later, the correlation was only moderate. Systematic studies concerned with "definition of the situation," such as "the national interest," are very few, and the two cited here (Sullivan's and Pool's) lend only very moderate support to the relation between a certain mode of definition and the pattern both of war as opposed to non war as well as the escalation of an on-going war.

None of this is to say that belief systems do not relate to actual international behavior, but only that the empirical link has not been forged. It might be argued on the one hand that the link to actual international behavior would appear very strong because of the potency of the belief system variable across several studies. On the other hand, it might also be argued that actual international behavior is so large-scale that it is not susceptible to the effect of individual belief systems. Implicit in Holsti's study of Dulles, however, was the additional variable of personality; Dulles, categorized as having a "high self-esteem" personality, would more likely possess a rigid belief system, whereas individuals on the opposite end of the "esteem" continuum would be less rigid. Interaction between personality and belief system provides a more plausible

[97] M. Hermann, "Leader Personality and Foreign Policy Behavior," p. 225.
[98] Scott, "Psychological and Social Correlates of International Images."

combination of independent variables potentially affecting a broader range of international behavior. But the measurement problems that have been noted throughout are no doubt the reason why such interaction has not been tested. As we will find in Chapter 3, the situational variable of "crisis" also affects decision-makers, and the addition of this third variable would result in a more complex and possibly more accurate model. We might expect a rigid personality with a strong belief system to react to a crisis much differently from a nonrigid individual with a weak belief system; we might also expect the same outcome in a noncrisis situation, but the impact might not be as great. These assertions, however, remain little more than hypotheses. As mentioned already, the impact of variables, individually or collectively, can best be assessed when we have made clear what the behavior is that they should affect.

Perhaps the most interesting set of findings discussed in this chapter were those pertaining to perceptions as intervening variables. Almost without exception, trends, levels, and changes in levels of hostility were not dependent on the perception of the level of hostility of incoming stimuli. In fact, in several cases the perceptions of the stimuli were shown to be quite inadequate in accounting for the resultant action by the state. The sole exception was Zinnes's analysis of data from the 1914 crisis, and as noted some of her findings were qualified in a later analysis by Hilton, and her earlier finding may have been a result of inadequate models relating incoming stimuli to response. As a general statement, therefore, the mere assertion of the "importance" of such perceptions is not upheld.

These conclusions apply for the most part to behavior viewed as trends, levels, or changes in levels of certain phenomena, usually hostility or conflict, and to the indirect tests of personality. As such, they may rule out the importance of perceptions and personality for understanding trends, but may not rule them out for understanding more specific decisions. To make that statement, however, is not to say that perceptions *will* be important nor does it provide a hint as to *what* perceptions and *what* decisions will be linked. The greatest amount of research on perceptions has gone into the analysis of their evaluative—or positive-negative—dimension. While such a concentration of effort is to be lamented because it represents only one dimension, nonetheless it is a very important dimension, as the research by Osgood and his associates discovered. The studies on the 1914 crisis found that of the many perceptual variables utilized, such as friendship, satisfaction, and frustration, the hostility variable was the most highly correlated to foreign behavior.[99] All these studies seem to suggest that in talking about the

[99] Robert North, "Perception and Action in the 1914 Crisis," *Journal of International Affairs* 21 (No. 2, 1967), pp. 103–122.

importance of perceptions, the *evaluative* (good-bad, positive-negative, hostile-cooperative) perception may be a dominant one. This is further supported by the potency of the evaluative image in the belief system study of Loomba. Theories of images or perceptions therefore, may be theories that focus on one key dimension rather than rely on a wide range of vaguely defined perceptions.

These research findings—and especially the judgments about domain and validity—are not cast in bronze. On a theoretical level, the approach embracing "man" and his "images" covers a broad area of investigation, and the empirical links between these generally defined concepts and international behavior are not well spelled out. Some patterns do appear to emerge from the research, and several studies do demonstrate the importance of the individual-level variables, but the indirect tests have shown that numerous types of behavior are relatively unaffected by individual differences. Furthermore, while perceptual variables often do explain variation in subsequent behavior, it has been demonstrated that other variables could just as easily explain the same behavior— and in fact precede the perceptual data in time, potentially making it more causally important. What has become clear is that once we go beyond the ad hoc general statements of everyday common sense, solving the puzzles of international behavior in an empirically satisfactory way is more difficult than it first appears, and on the whole, attitudes and verbal behavior appear to be much more susceptible to individual-level variables than are large-scale decisions or long-range trends.

POLICY IMPLICATIONS

As we mentioned in the introductory chapter, the recent concern with "policy" analysis and "policy relevant" studies is understandable and welcome, but much confusion remains about what these terms mean. There is no intention here or in the following chapters to provide a handy "guide" for the State Department official involved in formulating day-to-day foreign policy. At the present stage of research such a goal would be impossible, not only because of a lack of empirically verified findings, but also because the everyday "operative" is faced with such a multitude of problems that it would be impossible to second-guess each specific issue that he is likely to face. Rather, the intention here is to suggest general guidelines wherein research might be conducted—and how it might be conducted—and to point out areas where research would be useless for the policy-maker because his problems are quite different. It should be recognized that it is only insofar as the policy-maker's current, specific problem can be generalized that *any* research will be helpful to him.

On the most general level, it is relatively unsophisticated to suggest that psychological deviants should not be allowed into high office, not only because of the difficulties involved in trying to implement that dictum, but because we have no really accurate way of assessing such characteristics. Furthermore, even the popular linkage drawn by de Rivera between aberrant personalities and their behavior in office—"one does not feel confident that either Stalin or Hitler would have hesitated to begin a nuclear war if it were the only way to save their power" [100]—is empirically questionable, for the same argument could easily be made about almost all national leaders. One could argue that the process of "natural" political selection at work, particularly in democratic systems, tends to weed out blatantly irresponsible individuals. Because the criteria for psychological fitness to hold high office are unclear, few people would be willing to have all candidates screened by psychologists.

Obviously more important, however, is the question of how one should take into account the personalities of other leaders in one's own calculations. It seems safe to say, in light of the indirect tests here, that policy-makers need not be overly concerned about sudden changes in the leadership of other countries, at least in terms of short-range trends in their foreign behavior; nations appear to behave very similarly when heads of state change, and shifts that do occur happen some time after new leaders take over. Thus, even if personality variables such as nationalism and cognitive complexity do appear to relate to levels of conflict and cooperative behavior,[101] personality shifts may take some time to bring about changes in those behaviors.

As for short-term—perhaps crisis—decisions, endless speculations could be made about the potential effects of personality variables, but systematic linkages between personality and crisis behavior have not been established, even across a moderately broad range of cases. We have no doubt that *some* personality attributes are going to effect *some* specific decisions, but that constitutes only the most general of hypotheses, of little use to a policy-maker. Furthermore, the following chapter will suggest that organizational constraints and procedures may have a great influence even in such immediate decision situations.

Implications flowing from theories concerning images and perceptions are difficult to summarize and extend because many analyses have dealt with behavior that cannot strictly be termed "international." While images are potent for explaining some non-international behavior (attitudes, voting), it is unclear whether and how they can be extended to international behavior. It seems very likely, however, that other states react in kind to our own actions (a subject taken up again in Chapter 7),

100 De Rivera, *Psychological Dimension of Foreign Policy*, p. 195.
101 M. Hermann, "Leader Personality and Foreign Policy Behavior," pp. 220, 222.

and this likelihood should be kept in mind when thought is given to attempting to change the perceptions of other leaders. Furthermore, though no one would argue against the proposition that national leaders should have a correct image of the opponent and his goals and interests,[102] such advice is of little use if there is no criterion by which the policy-maker can distinguish correct from incorrect images.

In a sense, the same implications are generated by the studies investigating belief systems. To prevent the misinterpretation of external stimuli, constant "reality-testing" of one's own belief system must be undertaken to point out when discrepancies exist between external behavior and our perception of it. Further, policy implications from the study of definition of the situation as "national interest" suggest that in escalating conflicts the emergence of symbolic issues may signal further escalation. As such, slowly escalating conflict may feed back onto the perceptions of the decision-makers, increasing perception of symbolic issues, fostering the necessity for further escalatory behavior. Decision-makers locking themselves into such expressions of symbolic concern might be unwittingly feeding the escalatory fires. An honest concern for defusing an international conflict could well be an awareness of the possible self-perpetuating escalatory nature of such definitions of the situation. Of course, turning this advice on its head, decision-makers might read an opponent's concern for symbolic involvement, in which less use of symbols would equate with an interest in negotiation. Although not tested, these implications could also apply across the bargaining table.

Perception as an intervening variable in the limited dimensions in which it has been tested does not appear that important. The numerous studies using the mediated stimulus response model showed that perception of a stimulus along a given dimension (usually hostility) was not markedly superior to the stimulus in predicting the other state's level of response. Hence, images either reflect the stimulus fairly well or are not that important in terms of the final reaction. At the same time, very strong and very important policy implications might be derived if there were patterns distinguishing cases in which perceptions clearly predominated and those in which they did not. In the comparison of the 1914 case to the 1962 case, however, no such pattern seemed to emerge, unless we assume the Soviet Union was less involved in the Cuban Missile Crisis than the United States, in which case involvement is one crucial distinguishing factor. That assumption for the 1962 case is not particularly tenable, however. Even so, the implication from these studies is that one nation's actions aimed at other states are extremely important

---

[102] Lampton, "U.S. Image of Peking," pp. 48–49.

in terms of their subsequent responses. Although no tests have been conducted on this hypothesis, it might be suggested that even efforts to modify an opponent's image or perception will not prove too availing, and that the best way to affect an opponent's response is to act differently.

It is understandable that man views himself as the center of the universe and as affecting that universe. Explanations of international behavior on the individual level have been widespread and popular. But if one conclusion is valid from the brief examination of the material referred to in this chapter it is that such explanations have not yet systematically showed what this approach *can* explain and what it *fails* to explain. It is extremely easy to utilize image or perceptual explanations that are in essence tautologies, such as "incorrect images of the opponent will lead to incorrect or 'failing' foreign policies." Yet it is obvious from several analyses in several domains that some international behavior is *not* dependent on the individual's images or perceptions. These individual-level approaches will become much more firm once their range and domain have been established.

chapter 3 Decision-Making

The decision-making approach to the study of international relations broadens the scope of foreign policy analysis. It places individuals within different social contexts, and it views their decisions—or outcomes—as a function of those contexts. As James Robinson and Richard Snyder put it, "the main purpose of inquiries about decision-making processes is to determine whether and how decision process affects the content of decision outcome." [1] To put it another way, the decision-making approach is concerned with different external stimuli that influence the decision-making *process*—and the decision itself. It seeks to determine whether different decision-making processes have different outcomes, and whether, again to quote Robinson and Snyder, "different combinations of situation, individuals, and organizations produce different policies." [2]

There are numerous decision-making approaches. One, which should be familiar because it contains the same basic parameters and assumptions that are the central theme of this book, tries to build theories concerning the interaction of variables in a decision situation. These decision *theories* attempt to define the variables not only carefully but operationally. It is an approach that collects information on independent

---

[1] James A. Robinson and Richard C. Snyder, "Decision-Making in International Politics," in *International Behavior: A Social Psychological Analysis,* ed. Herbert C. Kelman (New York: Holt, Rinehart, and Winston, 1965), p. 456.

[2] Ibid.

variables thought to affect the final decision or the decision process or trend.

In recent years, however, increasing interest has turned to the analysis of decision-making models, which, although often related to the theories, are for the most part much "looser" and less rigorous. In spite of this drawback, they help to establish the parameters of decision-making, and bring into the open contrasting assumptions about how decisions are made. Consequently, they present different broad-scale explanations for decisions.

For our purposes a model will be a very general picture of how decisions are made; it will be concerned with overall processes of decision-making. Each model possesses quite different assumptions about those processes, and therefore each paints a different picture of how individuals make decisions resulting in foreign policy. Decision-making theory, however, is more concerned with specific hypotheses predicting the outcome of decision processes. The distinction is not a perfect one, for hypotheses are involved in decision-making models, and decision-making theories rely on different models. Nonetheless, it will be important to understand the difference between theories and models in terms of *how* and *what* they explain.

Before turning to the decision-making models, a word is necessary on the "rationality" of decisions. Whenever we attempt to analyze decisions made by national leaders, this question arises: If decisions are in part irrational, how can anyone hope to analyze them systematically as if they were rational? Sidney Verba has dealt with the question and convincingly suggests that the "nonlogical" model—that decisions are a function of nonlogical as opposed to logical reasons—probably does not suffice as *the* model of foreign policy decision-making, and that, therefore, it most likely does not account for a large number of decisions in international politics.[3] Because of that he suggests the use of what he terms the "logical" model, which in turn resembles one of the models to be considered in the next section. The point here is that the time-worn attack on those trying to analyze foreign policy decisions—that such tasks are impossible because such decisions are likely a function of irrational decision-makers —does not apply to most decisions or decision-makers.

Decision-Making Models

Decision-making as a distinct type of analysis came into its own during the 1950s. It is not a new form of analysis, of course, for scholars have

[3] Sidney Verba, "Assumptions of Rationality and Non-Rationality in Models of the International System," in *International Politics and Foreign Policy: A Reader in Research and Theory*, ed. James N. Rosenau, rev. ed. (New York: Free Press, 1969).

always analyzed decisions. They have always relied on—usually implicit— models, although they may not have graced their analyses with that term. Perhaps the oldest type of decision model is the strictly historical de- scription of a decision, in which decision-makers are portrayed as acting within loosely defined environments that impinge on them, forcing them to establish their goals and act on them. The primary emphasis has been on description, and—as noted in Chapter 1—the explanation seems to flow from the description itself. As a result, multitudes of historical case studies of decisions have been produced. Thus, one type of model con- sists primarily of a description of events. It often includes hypotheses and linkages, though not necessarily explicitly.

SNYDER

In 1954 Snyder and his colleagues proposed what at the time was viewed by many as a revolutionary idea in the study of foreign policy decisions. They suggested that political scientists learn from their fellow social scientists in economics and public administration and recognize that decisions are a *type* of behavior or process, that while decisions do exhibit some differences, there are substantial, comparable similarities.[4]

Snyder had to make some simplifying assumptions, namely, that the *de jure* decision-makers were in fact the ones making the decisions, and that those decisions were the important and authoritative ones. If other individuals were making the decisions, but did not possess the authority to do so, they were excluded from the analysis. Snyder and his associates focused on the decisions made by the *de jure* decision-making groups, and they described the decision as the group members saw it. In short, they wanted to analyze the decision, not evaluate it.

The Snyder model represented nothing substantively new; the differ- ence rested in viewing it as an approach to compare decisions, and in establishing quite specifically the dimensions along which decisions were to be compared and explained. These dimensions consisted of three variable "clusters" that were considered to be the determinants of deci- sion-making behavior. The first, called "spheres of competence," consti- tuted the *characteristics* of a decision-making organization or unit— whether it was tight or loose, formal or informal; whether it had the ability to change; what its level of bureaucratization might be. The "communication and information" cluster pertained to the *communica- tion networks* within an organization—who communicates with whom;

[4] Richard C. Snyder, "A Decision-Making Approach to the Study of Political Phenomena," in *Approaches to the Study of Politics,* ed. Roland Young (Evanston: Northwestern University Press, 1958), pp. 3–37.

how they do it; what blocs exist in communication; how much information comes from outside the unit; how flexible the unit is in accepting it. Finally, the cluster called "motivation," which to Snyder was admittedly a "ball of snakes," related to the objectives of the entire decision-making unit, the norms and values of those within the unit, and any values of the community.

Needless to say, the Snyder scheme was almost all-inclusive. In fact, one of the continuing criticisms leveled at the design has been its unworkability. Rather than providing a useful tool for reducing the complexity of decision-making processes in order to compare them, the Snyder model requires the retention of almost all of the original historical data. Only one major study—of the U.S. decision to respond to the North Korean invasion of South Korea in 1950—has been carried out using it, and was conducted by Glenn Paige.[5] On analysis, Paige's study turns out to be quite revealing, for more than 250 pages of the 366-page manuscript are devoted to recapturing the historical conditions of the era as well as a day-by-day account of the actual decision. Though Snyder considered the three variable clusters as "factors which determine the choices of . . . decision-makers,"[6] Paige presents a series of *five* hypothesis clusters all revolving around the effect of "crisis" on the three variables suggested by Snyder.[7] These clusters, then, become dependent on the level of crisis and are not thought of as the determinants of decision-making.

In spite of these problems, Snyder's scheme was a rather sharp break from the then-prevalent historical model because it suggested abstracting the common elements of decisions. Decision-making studies in foreign policy before that time had never *explicitly* done that. The Snyder model proposed that decisions could be analyzed as a *type* of behavior, that similar determinants might be responsible for a wide array of decisions, and that those determinants could be studied in a systematic way. It also focused to some degree on decisions as the result of a *rationalized process.*

SIMON AND LINDBLOM

Basic to conceiving of decisions as a rational process (*not,* it should be noted, necessarily producing *rational* decisions, whatever they may be) is the psychological model of "rational man," in which goals are established and then means found to maximize them. Herbert Simon, however, suggested that men do not go about maximizing their goals,

---

[5] Glenn Paige, *The Korean Decision: June 24–30, 1950* (New York: Free Press, 1968).

[6] Snyder, "A Decision-Making Approach," p. 24.

[7] Paige, *The Korean Decision,* p. 315.

but—given the great difficulty of making decisions—merely "satisficing" them, a term he uses to describe the process of considering alternatives sequentially, or incrementally, until one comes along that seems to meet certain requirements.[8] The ideal of rationally processing alternatives according to some criteria until the best one is found seems to be contradicted by much of what we see every day, even in our own lives.

Charles Lindblom likewise questioned what he called the "rational-comprehensive" model, arguing that not only do individuals *not* follow that process very closely, but at times they violate the basic assumptions of the model.[9] Table 3-1 lists the assumptions underlying the rationalized process along with the alternative model that Lindblom suggested, called the "successive limited comparison" model.

A rationalized process implies that decision-makers establish their goals first, and then consider all the alternatives open to them. The "best" policy or decision, then, emerges from the many alternatives as

Table 3-1.

Rational-Comprehensive Model	Successive Limited Comparison Model
1. Clarification of values or objectives distinct from and usually prerequisite to empirical analysis of alternative policies.	1. Selection of value goals and empirical analysis of the needed action are not distinct from one another but are closely intertwined.
2. Policy-formulation is therefore approached through means-end analysis: First the ends are isolated, then the means to achieve them are sought.	2. Since means and ends are not distinct, means-end analysis is often inappropriate or limited.
3. The test of a "good" policy is that it can be shown to be the most appropriate means to desired ends.	3. The test of a "good" policy is typically that various analysts find themselves directly agreeing on a policy (without their agreeing that it is the most appropriate means to an agreed objective).
4. Analysis is comprehensive; every important relevant factor is taken into account.	4. Analysis is drastically limited: (a) Important possible outcomes are neglected. (b) Important alternative potential policies are neglected. (c) Important affected values are neglected.
5. Theory is often heavily relied upon.	5. A succession of comparisons greatly reduces or eliminates reliance on theory.

Charles E. Lindblom, "The Science of Muddling Through," *Public Administration Review,* 19 (Spring, 1959), p. 81.

[8] Herbert A. Simon, *Models of Man: Social and Rational* (New York: Wiley, 1957).

[9] Charles E. Lindblom, "The Science of Muddling Through," *Public Administration Review* 19 (Spring, 1959), pp. 79–88.

the one most ideally suited to reach the desired end. In other words, the analysis is comprehensive because all factors are taken into account. Just as image theory was called the "normal" individual model of international relations in the last chapter, the rational-comprehensive model can be called the "normal" decision-making model because most people like to think they make decisions in just this "rational" way. But Lindblom made the rather startling—although in retrospect quite perceptive and probably accurate—suggestion that we rarely make decisions according to the rational-comprehensive model. Rather, humans more often rely on a "successive limited comparison" model in which means and goals are intertwined, and in which the goals are often affected by the desirability of specific means. The "best" policy, moreover, is now not necessarily the one most able to realize the goal, but rather the one the decision-makers feel they can finally agree on. Most importantly, of course, is the assertion, following Simon, that human beings are not capable of analyzing vast amounts of information and therefore many possible outcomes as well as possible alternatives are often simply not considered.

The successive limited comparison model suggests that making decisions is often a very costly process, one, therefore, that may be put off— *even if* information is high and many alternatives are possible. Indeed, it is just when information is extremely high and alternatives are numerous that the human decision-making system begins to break down from "overload." Humans tend to eliminate alternatives, not because some are bad but because they simply cannot handle more than a small number of them at once. They deal with decisions, that is, one at a time, incrementally, successively. They often cannot see the long-range implications of making the small, incremental decisions they face every day. This way of going about making a decision may not appear to be the most "rational"; nonetheless, most people will recognize here their own behavior pattern. Moreover, one scholar has even advocated that complex decisions *should* be broken up and made incrementally.[10]

ALLISON

More recently Graham Allison has suggested that the foreign policy literature on decision-making actually contains three quite distinct models. In most instances, however, he points out that they are not recognized as distinct nor are their parameters and assumptions made

---

[10] Alexander George, "Policy-Oriented Forecasting," *International Studies Notes* 1 (Spring, 1974), p. 2.

explicit.[11] Allison's first model, the "rational policy" model, resembles Lindblom's rational-comprehensive model, and is the "normal" model of foreign policy decisions. It asserts that important events have important causes; that monolithic units perform large actions for big, important reasons; and that in any foreign policy decision situation a *purpose or intention* exists that must be explained, that is, actions that a state chooses are calculated ones directly responsive to the large strategic problem the state faces. Ultimately, the model asserts that a sufficient explanation of the state's decision consists in showing what goal the state was pursuing through its action. Thus state action is understood in terms of decision-makers' rationally planning and executing a policy for large-scale reasons. These important actions do not merely "happen." Decision-makers must have had overwhelming reasons for executing them.

Allison's second model is the "organizational process" model, and it bears some resemblance to Lindblom's limited successive comparison model. Governments are large organizations, with fixed sets of procedures, and their behavior is dependent on these procedures. Organizations do change, but their greater propensity is to retain certain tendencies and routines, which permit them to reduce the uncertainty in their environment. All large organizations must have rules so they are not caught off-guard. Anyone who has dealt with these organizations—the army, General Motors, universities, passport offices, the telephone company, Internal Revenue Service—has stories to tell of their intransigence, the very characteristic that forces an organization to act today as much as possible like the way in which it was acting yesterday. The significance of the organizational model is that even in the area of foreign affairs, where we often assume presidents and prime ministers have complete control, the organizations narrow their alternatives for them.

The third model offered by Allison is the "bureaucratic politics" model, which also resembles a nonrationalized perspective. Decisions under this model result from bargaining and compromise within the decisional unit. Each bureaucratic "player" has different perceptions and priorities, and each vies for power, promotion, and retention of his own position even after the crisis has passed. The policy problems that the historian isolates with hindsight, then, are different from those facing the members of the political unit making the decision.

As noted earlier, models represent generalized views of how decisions are made. Each constitutes a different way of explaining decisions. The overlap between the different authors is high; Lindblom's rational-comprehensive model resembles Allison's rational process model; his suc-

[11] Graham Allison, *Essence of Decision: Explaining the Cuban Missile Crisis* (Boston: Little, Brown, 1971).

cessive limited comparison model more closely fits Allison's second and third models; and all three are at least indirect offshoots from Simon's earlier work on organizational processes. Before elucidating the models through two case studies, some mention must be made of the problems of evidence in utilizing decision-making models.

MEASUREMENT

Decision-making models do not focus on testing specific hypotheses, and the "variables" they employ are much looser than we would prefer. The "measurement" of these models, therefore, is problematic, and an evaluation of competing models presents severe problems.

The greatest drawback in any decision-making study is access to material. The amount of legwork done by Allison in his study of the Cuban Missile Crisis, which we turn to in the next section, is an illustration of this handicap. Because few criteria exist for what is necessary information in these studies, the tendency is to gather as much minutia as possible, and string it all together in chronological sequence with the hope that out of the plethora of data an explanation will somehow emerge.

The very looseness of the concepts ("organizational process," "bureaucratic politics"), moreover, creates further problems of data gathering. Generalized concepts abound, but few specific concepts have been proposed. Consequently, everything plausible is thrown under a kind of conceptual tent. Needless to say, this creates a certain laxity about what exactly is being demonstrated with what evidence.

Even so, despite these very real and limiting problems, some attempt must be made to go beyond the mere presentation of plausible explanations or models. One method, to be proposed in the concluding section of this chapter, is to think about models in competitive terms, and to evaluate one against the other. In this connection, three questions might be kept in mind as we proceed to discuss the case studies that follow. First, what are the assumptions of each of the models, and how realistic are they? The more realistic assumptions, namely, those that are more likely to be true in a given situation, are preferable. Second, does the evidence that supports one model also tend to support another? The evidence, as noted, is not always as clearly spelled out as we would like, and sometimes can be interpreted to support more than one model. Finally, what types of behavior do the models purport to explain? We will find, particularly in Allison's study of the Cuban Missile Crisis, that the different models are actually applied to different decisions and therefore are not strictly competitors. As has been noted already, it will often help to set out what exactly the models are capable of explaining. Because the assessment of decision models is virtually virgin territory, these questions can be in no way definitive. They are suggested here merely as illustrative methods one might use in attempting to assess the potency of different models.

VIETNAM AND CUBA: RATIONAL PROCESS

If the rational process model explains why decision-makers do what they do, then there should be evidence of a big problem analyzed in a sequential way, resulting in the decision to act. One can point to evidence that there was a big problem called "Vietnam" which decision-makers reacted to in a "big" way.[12] Analysts in *The Pentagon Papers*, for instance, cite the Truman administration's aid to France as "directly involving" the United States in Vietnam and "setting" the course of American policy in Southeast Asia.[13] When a 1954 National Security Council paper outlined American policy in Vietnam, " 'American policy toward post-Geneva Vietnam was drawn.' The commitment for the United States to assume the burden of defending South Vietnam had been made." [14]

Later, although President Kennedy grumbled about being "over-committed" in Southeast Asia, he too felt he must continue U.S. efforts there lest he disrupt, as Roger Hilsman put it, "the whole balance of power and fabric of the security structure of the region, where so many countries had based their policy on continued American involvement." [15] After Kennedy's assassination, President Johnson was under emotional stress and did not want Vietnam to go the way China had. Says Tom Wicker: "The tragedy of Lyndon Johnson . . . was set in motion barely 48 hours after he had taken the oath [of office]." [16] Further, many assert that the Tonkin Gulf resolution of 1964—which later served as the quasi-legal justification for prosecuting the war—had been prepared long

---

[12] Data on the Vietnam case in this and the following sections comes from Michael P. Sullivan, "Vietnam: Calculation or Quicksand? An Analysis of Competing Decision-Making Models," Research Series 13, mimeo, Institute of Government Research, University of Arizona, Tucson, October, 1972, portions of which were reprinted in *The Theory and Practice of International Relations*, 4th ed., ed., Fred A. Sondermann, William C. Olson, and David S. McClellan (Englewood Cliffs, N.J.: Prentice-Hall, 1974).

[13] *The Pentagon Papers*, as published by the *New York Times* (New York: Bantam Books, 1971), p. xi.

[14] Ibid., p. 15.

[15] Roger Hilsman, *To Move a Nation* (New York: Delta, 1968), p. 420.

[16] Tom Wicker, *JFK and LBJ: The Influence of Personality upon Politics* (New York: Morrow, 1968), p. 205.

before the alleged "attack" on American ships had occurred,[17] and that bombing targets were placed on Johnson's desk the day after his election victory in 1964.[18]

All of this information suggests that American decisions on Vietnam were carefully planned. Leslie Gelb cites "high objectives" as the driving force behind years of United States planning and action. Says Gelb: "Statements about the vital importance of Vietnam to United States national security are a matter of the yearly public record." [19] In 1948, for example, the State Department asserted that the objective in Southeast Asia was "to eliminate so far as possible Communist influence in Indochina." Sixteen years later President Johnson said: "We seek an independent, non-Communist South Vietnam."

Furthermore, at every step, the rational process model would argue, the decision-makers knew what they were in for. After the important mission to Saigon by General Maxwell Taylor and White House adviser Walt Rostow in late 1961, their recommendation was to provide minimal assistance to Vietnam "but with the significant warning that much greater troop commitments were likely in the future." [20] With less than 1,000 Americans in Vietnam in 1961, Secretary of Defense Robert McNamara said, "I believe we can assume that the maximum United States forces required on the ground in Southeast Asia will not exceed . . . 205,000 men." [21]

As *The Pentagon Papers* disclosed, analysts noted that in the summer of 1965, with the commitment of forty-four battalions:

> The choice . . . was not whether or not to negotiate, it was not whether to hold on for a while or let go—the choice was viewed as winning or losing South Vietnam. . . . Final acceptance of the desirability of inflicting defeat on the enemy rather than merely denying him victory opened the door to an indeterminate amount of additional force.[22]

In November, 1965, as the American troop buildup ballooned, Mc-Namara, although agreeing with the recommendation that 400,000 troops be sent to Vietnam by the end of 1966, expressed reservations about how successful the new deployments would be. "The odds are even," he said,

17 Ibid., p. 225.

18 David Halberstam, *The Unfinished Odyssey of Robert Kennedy* (New York: Random House, 1968), pp. 20–21.

19 Leslie Gelb, "Vietnam: Some Hypotheses about How and Why" (Paper delivered at the Sixty-sixth American Political Science Association, Los Angeles, September 8–12, 1970), p. 11.

20 *Pentagon Papers*, p. 85.

21 Ibid., p. 149.

22 Ibid., pp. 416–17.

"that we will be faced in early 1967 with a 'no decision' at an even higher level." [23] In October, 1966, McNamara noted in a memo to the President:

The prognosis is bad that the war can be brought to a satisfactory conclusion within the next two years. The large-unit operations probably will not do it; negotiations probably will not do it. *While we should continue to pursue both of these routes in trying for a solution in the short run, we should recognize that success from them is a mere possibility, not a probability.*[24]

This evidence, selective as it is, nonetheless suggests three main conclusions: that Vietnam occurred (1) because there was a large-scale goal (to prevent South Vietnam from becoming Communist), even as far back as the Truman and early Eisenhower years, (2) that decision-makers involved throughout the war knew what they were getting into, and, (3) by implication, their decisions resulted from a rational process in attempting to achieve their goals.

Allison applies his version of the rational process model to the Cuban Missile Crisis. Why did the Soviets decide to place missiles in Cuba, and why did the United States respond with the blockade of Cuba? Numerous explanations can be offered using the rational model: the Soviets may have viewed the missiles as a bargaining ploy; the missiles may have represented a diversionary tactic; they could honestly have been put there for Cuban defense; Soviet prestige would increase; or Soviet military capabilities—power—might be enhanced. Although all are plausible, Allison notes drawbacks for each. The Soviets were placing sixty-six missiles in Cuba, whereas the United States had only fifteen in Turkey. Using Cuba as a diversion did not make sense because they placed numerous Soviet citizens in Cuba in a perfect position to be attacked. Conventional ground forces would have been more advantageous for the actual defense of Cuba than intercontinental ballistic missiles. Allison sees the power explanation as the most plausible, that the missiles in Cuba would immediately enhance Soviet worldwide military power.

The same analysis can be applied to the United States decision to respond with a blockade. According to the rational policy model, of the many alternatives proposed during the week of decision, the blockade was the best alternative for steering a middle course between doing nothing and taking outright, aggressive action. It left the next move up to the Soviets and militarily placed them in a disadvantageous position because the confrontation would come in the Caribbean, far from their home base. To explain the Soviet withdrawal of missiles, the rational

---

[23] Ibid., p. 466.
[24] Ibid., p. 549, emphasis in original.

process model might view Kennedy's action as a clear threat, in the face of which the Soviet leaders decided to back down.

The point here is not which of the explanations is *the* correct one but rather that they all had a common denominator. For each explanation, action is explained by assuming that the decision-makers faced a large-scale problem, that they therefore possessed a large-scale or long-range goal, and that their final decision was viewed as the path toward achieving that goal. To arrive at that decision, however, they followed a rational process of considering all alternatives and all information until the right alternative presented itself.

VIETNAM AND CUBA: ORGANIZATION, BUREAUCRATIC, AND INCREMENTAL PROCESSES

As compelling and as popular as the above explanations for behavior in Vietnam and Cuba are, they nonetheless constitute only *one* model for explaining those decisions. Here a second model is offered, combining Allison's organizational process and bureaucratic politics models (because of their similarity) with Simon's incremental and Lindblom's successive limited comparison models. The evidence again is fragmentary, open to subjective interpretation, and therefore very difficult to work with. Yet these models do paint a drastically different picture of both historical cases.

Was Vietnam a vital, important issue? In November, 1961, President Kennedy reportedly asked whether it was really important to save South Vietnam and Laos.[25] In June, 1964, President Johnson asked the CIA to assess whether the rest of Southeast Asia would fall if South Vietnam came under Hanoi's control (its answer was basically "no"). Tom Wicker argues that "all the evidence visible at the time, and much testimony gathered since, suggests that, in 1964, Johnson was not deeply concerned about Vietnam."[26] Some $3.5 billion in military aid went to France before 1954, much of it no doubt ending up in Indochina, but Agency for International Development figures show a similar amount—$3.3 billion—going to France between 1953 and 1961, a period when France's operations there were greatly reduced. Vietnam ranked eleventh during the 1953-1961 period in total military aid received (behind the Netherlands, Korea, Italy, and others).[27]

[25] Ibid., p. 108.

[26] Wicker, *JFK and LBJ*, p. 229.

[27] AID, *U.S. Overseas Loans and Grants, and Assistance from International Organizations,* Special Report Prepared for the U.S. House Foreign Affairs Committee, May 14, 1971 (Washington, D.C.: GPO, 1971).

Did Vietnam result from long-range, well-thought-out and widely agreed-to plans? In mid-1965 Ambassador Taylor cabled Washington: "I badly need a clarification of our purposes and objectives." [28] In the same year, when bombing was proposed as an alternative to sending in more troops, the decision-makers agreed to it

not because they really believed in bombing for there was a good deal of private hedging on what the bombing might accomplish ("This bombing bullshit," Lyndon Johnson called it), but because there was nowhere else to go and they did not want to send troops.[29]

As Pentagon Papers point out regarding the massive bombing campaign in 1965, called Rolling Thunder, "the decision to go ahead with [it] seems to have resulted as much from the lack of alternative proposals as from any compelling logic in their favor." [30]

In actuality, of course, the alleged large-scale goals supposedly driving the Americans on in Vietnam did undergo constant scrutiny, and did change. In May, 1967, McNamara asked Johnson to eliminate the ambiguities from the objectives in Vietnam, and suggested the U.S. commitment (1) be defined in terms of the ability of the South Vietnamese people to determine their own future, and (2) cease if South Vietnam ceased to help itself. Further, he said, the commitment should *not* be to insure one group's continuation in power in South Vietnam, nor that the government remain non-Communist, nor that South Vietnam remain separate from North Vietnam.[31] McNamara's request represented a serious break from National Security Action Memorandum 288 which had seen America's goal as "an independent non-Communist South Vietnam." [32] The Joint Chiefs of Staffs replied on May 31 that McNamara's changes "would undermine and no longer provide a complete rationale for our presence in South Vietnam or much of our efforts over the past two years." [33]

Finally, many decisions in Vietnam were incremental. Although Daniel Ellsberg, a member of McNamara's staff who worked on the Pentagon Papers project, argues that all of Kennedy's advisers saw the program Kennedy ultimately chose as "inadequate not only to achieve long-run success but to avoid further deterioration in the mid-term," [34] he fails

---

[28] *Pentagon Papers,* p. 445.

[29] David Halberstam, "The Programming of Robert McNamara," *Harpers* (February, 1971), p. 64.

[30] *Pentagon Papers,* p. 344.

[31] Ibid., p. 514.

[32] Ibid., p. 536.

[33] Ibid., p. 538.

[34] Daniel Ellsberg, *Papers on the War* (New York: Simon and Schuster, 1972), p. 64.

to demonstrate that Kennedy's decision to go against his advisers meant he *knew* and *believed* the move would be unsuccessful, and that further commitments would be needed. To the contrary, his decision to slowly increase the number of American advisors in Vietnam can very easily be interpreted as one simply to "buy time." When George Ball warned that an 8,000-man force would blossom into hundreds of thousands in a few years, Kennedy reportedly replied: "George, you're crazy as hell!" Ellsberg describes the incremental pattern well in saying that the solutions taken during the war by American decision-makers were to ignore long-term objectives and to concentrate "almost exclusively upon the aim of minimizing the short-run risk of anti-Communist collapse or Communist takeovers." [35]

The incremental model fits even the last decisions before the dramatic turnaround in March, 1968. When another request for troops arrived in early 1968, "several insiders later suggested that a smaller request, for 30,000 to 50,000 men, would probably have been granted and the Administration's crisis would have been avoided or at least delayed." [36]

These data support quite a different explanation for Vietnam than the rational policy model. Specific decisions were not necessarily tied into long-range goals, alternatives were frequently followed not because they would reach a final goal but because there were no other perceived options and it was better to do something rather than nothing.

Consideration of this model also sheds quite a different light on the decisions in the Cuban Missile Crisis. If the missiles represented long-range planning by the Soviets—perhaps a fait accompli in time for the Soviet Central Committee Plenary Session or Khrushchev's proposed United Nations visit, both in late November, 1962—it was necessary that they be firmly established. Allison shows that even round-the-clock work could not have achieved that goal. Moreover, there was no camouflage at the missile sites, providing a dead giveaway of the presence of missiles. The Soviets knew about the U.S. U-2 flights over Cuba. Why then, did they not take the precaution of camouflaging the missiles?

These events can be explained by investigating organizational procedures within the Soviet Union. Although constructing SAM missile sites in a trapezoidal pattern reduced the desired secrecy of the missiles, Allison suggests it was done that way because that was the way the Soviets always did it. Camouflage of the sites was not considered, very simply, because the organization had understandably never been concerned with that problem in the Soviet Union. Why the establishment of large intermediate range ballistic missiles rather than mere medium

[35] Ibid., p. 105.
[36] *New York Times*, March 5, 1969, p. 14.

range ballistic missiles? Perhaps, very plausibly, because the Soviet military, unlike Khrushchev, may have been more concerned with the strategic military balance, and the IRBMs would achieve that goal but the MRBMs would not.

Understandably, more information is available concerning American behavior in the crisis, and therefore an illustration of the organizational and bureaucratic politics model for the American decisions is more complete. Allison shows that "organizational procedures" clearly affected intelligence gathering, the options considered, and the final implementation of the blockade. A ten-day delay in intelligence-gathering photographic flights over Cuba, for instance, was caused largely by interorganizational bickering between the CIA and the Air Force over which group would carry out the mission. *Their* immediate goals obviously were different from finding out whether there were Russian missiles in Cuba.

The option of an air strike against Cuba was never as carefully considered as the rational policy model would suggest, for the Air Force simply dipped into its organizational bag of alternatives, and came up with an already prepared contingency calling for "extensive bombardment of all storage depots, airports, and (in deference to the Navy) the artillery batteries opposite the naval base at Guantanamo, as well as all missile sites." [37] The political leaders were amazed at the extent of the Air Force's proposed "surgical" strike—and not surprisingly, because they were talking about something quite different from what the military leaders proposed.

In terms of finally implementing the blockade, Allison concludes that despite Kennedy's desire to move the blockade closer to Cuba to allow Khrushchev more time to deliberate, the Navy opposed the plan because of danger from the proximity of Cuban MIGs. And the Navy had its way. The blockade was not moved, despite Kennedy's order.

Allison's third model suggests that bureaucratic and political elements also have an influence on the final decisional outcome. In 1962 Kennedy had been campaigning in the midterm election on a pledge that no Soviet missiles would be put on Cuba. When information surfaced suggesting missiles were being placed there, Kennedy saw the information as politically tinged—CIA head John McCone had traditionally been a hard-line anti-Communist, and Kennedy was suspicious of information of that nature given its source. In addition, however, the CIA was reluctant at that juncture to incur further adverse publicity for itself; in September, an American U-2 had strayed over Siberia for nine minutes, and another flown by Nationalist Chinese had been downed over Mainland China. Both episodes had prompted the CIA to restrict further U-2 flights over

[37] Allison, *Essence of Decision*, p. 125.

the western tip of Cuba, where they knew missiles were becoming operational, to prevent another downing.

Furthermore, the issue in the missile crisis was quite different for all involved. For Kennedy it was a political issue ("He [Khrushchev] can't do this to me!"). For Secretary of Defense McNamara it was a question of "hardware": a missile was a missile regardless of where it was. For some it was a major Cold War ploy on the part of the Russians; for others it was a minor irritant. Finally, in terms of the actual choice, Allison shows that it was not the result of a sequential, rationalized decision-making process, but the result of immense hauling and tugging between all the political participants, each with his own separate goals.

Whether they are called incremental, organizational, or bureaucratic, the models outlined here all point to the fact that decision-makers' actions cannot always be attributed to rationally thought-out goals and means. Humans simply do not behave in the way the rational process model would have us believe. They often don't want to make decisions—and therefore don't, which in itself is a type of decision—and their alternatives can be very severely restricted by large-scale organizational contexts or processes. Explaining that final decision (or decisions), then, takes on quite a different cast.

Decision-making models, then, focus on *how* decisions are made in a very general way. The models that have normally been used, as illustrated here, usually pit a rational process approach against an incremental model. Two questions remain to be answered, which will be postponed until the conclusion of the chapter. First, are there any evaluative procedures one can utilize to assess the accuracy of one model over another? Second, are there any policy or theoretical implications that can be derived from these models?

Theories of Decision Processes

Decision-making models are helpful because they compel anyone investigating foreign policy decisions to put on different "thinking caps," thereby gaining different viewpoints and explanations. Their obvious drawback, of course, is that decision-making models fail to show clear relationships between specified variables in the decision process. Snyder, for example, in commenting recently about his own work, noted that he had failed to spell out the basic factors postulated to have an influence on the decision outcome. In his words:

No hypotheses linking the variables were stated, and therefore no bases for prediction existed and no explanation—even *post hoc*—was possible without further operations implied by the scheme but certainly not explicitly set forth in the initial version.[38]

Decision-making theories, however, should go beyond the looseness of the models, for they not only set out the independent variables affecting the decisional outcome—including specific decisions as well as trends in decisions—but also *what* those effects are. Organizing the vast amount of literature on decision-making is formidable. Robinson and Snyder have presented perhaps the best outline, using three general categories: the occasion for decision, the individual decision-makers, and the organizational context.[39] Some authors also focus on the decisional result as a separate category, but that obviously becomes the dependent variable in our context, and our interest is in isolating the important independent variables that have a bearing on the outcome.

The occasion for decision—or what some call the "decision situation" —refers to elements that are for the most part external to the decision-making unit. These elements are usually considered to have an effect on the unit, and therefore ultimately on the decision itself. The variable of the individual decision-maker has been referred to already in Chapter 2, but is here considered as part of a unit, one that interacts within that unit. Finally, the organizational context refers to what goes on within the decision-making unit, group dynamics, communication patterns, and characteristics of the unit. Each of these is viewed in terms of its influence on the ultimate decision.

OCCASION FOR DECISION:
SITUATIONAL RESTRAINTS—"CRISIS"

The occasion for the decision itself is, in most instances, nothing the decision-maker has much control over—other than his perception, of course, that a decision is needed at a given point. The occasion amounts to an external, situational restraint on the decision-maker. The most widely researched situational variable—and the only situational restraint Robinson and Snyder considered—is "crisis." This concentration on crisis no doubt stems from the understandable interest in severe international confrontations during the nuclear era. Most researchers of crises have settled on three components as defining this emergency situation: whether the situation itself has been anticipated or not; whether the time to make a decision is long or short; and whether important or unimportant values are involved. For all the research that has gone into

[38] Richard C. Snyder, "Introduction," in Paige, *Korean Decision*, p. xiii.
[39] Robinson and Snyder, "Decision-Making in International Politics."

the concept of crisis, most attention has been given to its effect on the decisional process, which, to be sure, is assumed to relate to the decisional outcome. Little attention has been given to the final decision, however.

The very components of the definition of crisis suggest what impact it has on the decisional process. An unanticipated decision situation is more likely to result in a hasty, quick, perhaps temperamental decision, whereas an anticipated situation, where decision-makers can think, process information, and calculate their response much more carefully, is more likely to result in a decision more closely attuned to external realities, or, in a word, more "rational." Robinson and Snyder suggest that *time* may be related to individual psychological variables such as intelligence, mental agility, and creativity, which in turn may be related to the decision outcome.[40] The link between "values" and decision is more tautological: If the decision-makers perceive greater values are involved, their decisions will usually be different than if they feel less important values are involved.

Little or no evidence exists on the effect of these separate indicators, but research has been done on what happens on various dimensions in the decisional process as a function of change from noncrisis to crisis or from low crisis to high crisis situations. Robinson, Charles Hermann, and Margaret Hermann reviewed several studies and found that in simulations of foreign policy decision-making, less search for alternatives occurred in the crisis-induced situation than in the noncrisis situation.[41] However, the hypothesis that fewer alternatives would be *identified* in crisis situations was not supported. They concluded that crisis may induce "poor" decision-making in that decision-makers search less for sufficient alternatives. Contradicting that view were their findings that decision-makers in crisis situations actually identify more alternatives than in noncrisis.

Holsti tested similar propositions with regard to the perceptions of decision-makers during the 1914 crisis leading to World War I. He investigated the influence of crisis on perceptions of alternatives, perceptions of "time," and changes in communication patterns. He found the "high stress" period near the end of July, 1914, induced more concern or perceptions about "time" by the decision-makers than the earlier, low-stress period, and that they were more concerned with "current" time than future time. Table 3-2 shows the number of perceptions of "choice," "necessity," and "closed" alternatives open to one's self, one's

[40] Ibid., p. 441.

[41] James A. Robinson, Charles Hermann, and Margaret Hermann, "Search under Crisis in Political Gaming and Simulation," in *Theory and Research on the Causes of War*, ed. Dean Pruitt and Richard C. Snyder (Englewood Cliffs, N.J.: Prentice-Hall, 1969).

Table 3-2. Perceptions of Three Different Alternatives in 1914 Crisis: Britain, France, Germany, Russia, and Austria-Hungary

	Choice	Necessity	Choice	Closed
Self	38	242	38	62
Enemies	60	12	60	3
	(Q = .94)		(Q = .95)	
Allies	43	37	43	10
Enemies	60	12	60	3
	(Q = .63)		(Q = .64)	

Based on data presented in Ole R. Holsti, "The 1914 Case," *American Political Science Review* 58 (June, 1965), pp. 371 and 374.

enemies, and one's allies.[42] The data here have been aggregated from the five separate countries Holsti presents, and it should be noted that when considered separately, the relationships in Austria-Hungary are not in line with the hypothesis. The table shows, nevertheless, that the decision-makers tended to see themselves as faced with either "closed" or "necessity" alternatives and that they were more likely to view their opponents as having some "choice" in their alternatives.

Holsti also found that perceptions of alternatives were different in periods of low and high stress. In high stress situations, there were a proportionately greater number of perceptions wherein the decision-makers viewed an alternative as necessary or that other alternatives had been closed off to them, than there were cases in which they felt they had a "choice." This pattern also applied to one's allies but not to one's enemies; the relationships were stronger in the Dual Alliance than in the Triple Entente. Finally, as expected, the crisis produced an increase in the volume of messages; moreover, a process of polarization developed whereby more communications were transmitted within alliances than between alliances.[43]

With few exceptions, therefore, the situational constraint of *stress* (crisis) affected several decision or decision-related processes in the 1914 crisis thought to have an ultimate impact on the decision made. Holsti also contends that the same processes worked in 1962, but on Cuba his evidence is almost completely anecdotal.[44] What systematic evidence he does present—concerning perceptions of time and its relation to crisis— partially contradicts the findings for the 1914 crisis, depending on how

[42] Ole R. Holsti, "The 1914 Crisis," *American Political Science Review* 59 (June, 1965), p. 371.

[43] See appendix, paragraph A.3., for a further analysis of Holsti's data.

[44] Ole R. Holsti, *Crisis, Escalation, War* (Montreal: McGill-Queens University Press, 1972), pp. 180–92.

one analyzes the evidence.[45] In one method, we can assume that the middle days of the crisis are the most stressful, as measured not necessarily in terms of overall levels of violence or hostility but in terms of their having constituted the period when face-to-face confrontation occurred. That is, from October 24 through October 27, the quarantine went into effect, the Soviet ships turned back, the Soviets acknowledged the existence of missiles in Cuba, and an American U-2 was shot down. These were also generally the days of highest perception of time (combining both U.S. and U.S.S.R. perceptions).[46] A second method, however, is to treat the degree of violence on any given day as stress, and correlate it with the actual perception of time.[47] The correlations in every instance are very small, and therefore the evidence in the 1962 case cannot be used as confirmation of the effect of crisis on decisions.

From his extensive study of the United States's decision to respond in Korea, Paige likewise establishes stress or crisis as crucial in its effect on the decision process.[48] He concludes that the greater the crisis, the more frequent and more direct will be interactions with friendly leaders in the external setting, not unlike Holsti's finding of polarization in communication patterns. Partially contradicting and partially supporting Holsti's hypotheses about 1914, Paige concludes that the greater the crisis, the greater the felt need for information; and the more prolonged the crisis, the greater the sense of adequacy about information. In other words, crisis produces a search for information, but as the crisis continues, the leaders, at least in the 1950 decision over Korea, became more satisfied with the information they found.

Linda Brady investigated the three situational conditions of threat, short time, and surprise in a large number of situations. She discovered that all three conditions tended to produce hostile as opposed to cooperative behavior, but that the amount of variation in both behaviors that was accounted for by the three situational conditions was extremely small.[49]

The evidence on the effect of situational variables, to say the least,

[45] These conclusions are drawn from data presented in two different sources: Holsti, *Crisis, Escalation, and War*, pp. 190–91; and Ole R. Holsti, Richard A. Brody, and Robert C. North, "Measuring Affect and Action in International Reaction Models: Empirical Materials from the 1962 Cuban Crisis," in *International Politics and Foreign Policy: A Reader in Research and Theory*, ed. James N. Rosenau, rev. ed. (New York: The Free Press, 1969), pp. 686–87.

[46] Holsti, *Crisis, Escalation, and War*, p. 183.

[47] Ibid.

[48] Paige, *Korean Decision*.

[49] Linda P. Brady, "Threat, Decision Time, and Awareness: The Impact of Situational Variables on Foreign Policy Behavior," CREON Publication No. 31, Unpublished Ph.D. Dissertation, Ohio State University, March, 1974.

is scanty. Holsti's study encompasses only 1914 and Cuba and the evidence clearly supports only the former. Paige studied only Korea. In sum, we have some evidence of the situational constraint of crisis on decision-making processes, but to date the further linkage between situation and final decision has not been made. As de Rivera notes, studies are still lacking "on the effects of natural stress on top American decision-makers although there is anecdotal evidence of the impact." [50]

INDIVIDUAL DECISION-MAKERS

Robinson and Snyder's second general category is the individual decision-maker. It is broken down into three subcategories: the personality of the decision-maker, his background, and his values. Obviously this is one of those crucial junctures where levels and approaches begin to mesh into each other.

Personality has been considered in the previous chapter as an isolated variable, with the conclusion suggested there that while reams of plausible connections exist between personality variables and foreign policy, the exact specification of the range and domain of personality's effect has not been made. Further, it was concluded that some aspects of international behavior are relatively unaffected by personality. Robinson and Snyder also note that although the field of psychology is one of the more advanced of the social sciences, and although common sense dictates "the importance of personality in politics, applications of psychology to political and especially to international decision-making are relatively few." [51] For this reason, and because personality was treated in the preceding chapter, and, further, because no studies in foreign policy decision-making have specifically spelled out the effect of personality on group decision-making, we shall move on to consider Robinson and Snyder's subcategory of background.

Social background also offers a plausible explanation for foreign policy, but the evidence again is anecdotal and often does not confirm the hypothesis. Snyder and Robinson, for instance, found that one study has shown that foreign travel may alter the *bases* and *rationale* of businessmen's views of foreign trade policy, but it may *not* alter the direction of their attitudes. They note further that although much research has been done on the social backgrounds of decision-makers for theoretical reasons other than decision-making, "it is often difficult to relate differ-

[50] Joseph H. de Rivera, *The Psychological Dimension of Foreign Policy* (Columbus, Ohio: Charles E. Merrill, 1968), p. 152.

[51] Robinson and Snyder, "Decision-Making in International Politics," p. 443.

ences in background and experience to variations in decisional per-formance." [52]

The same conclusion holds true, unfortunately, for the variable of a decision-maker's "values." Snyder and Robinson do cite evidence, but the linkages they draw are tenuous. For one, they note that public op-position in the United States to Bolshevism in the 1930s contributed to the delay in the decision to recognize the Soviet Union.[53] They also cite several instances where espoused values seemed *not* to be able to predict to subsequent behavior: the shifting attitudes toward the Soviet Union; the small number of draft resisters among American youth in 1943 even though half a million had declared in 1937 they would not fight; de Gaulle's shift in French policy toward Algeria despite his earlier values about overseas territories. Certainly one of the most pronounced and perhaps far-reaching changes in values in recent times was Richard Nixon's shift from being an intense Cold Warrior and anti-Communist as legislator and vice president to being the first American president to visit Mainland China. Further, although Robinson as well as Warren Miller and Donald Stokes found correlations between foreign policy attitudes and foreign policy behavior among congressmen, Snyder and Robinson conclude that "the relationship of values and attitudes to behavior is not perfect." [54]

These conclusions do not imply that values play no role in foreign policy decision-making, but only that they may do so in certain very large-scale domains, relevant to long-term trends in behavior. Moreover, values are changeable, and therefore behavior seen as a function of values is ultimately dependent on what changes the values. As with images, it is a big step to move from the general assertion that values are im-portant to the specification of exactly what their linkage is with decisions.

ORGANIZATION CONTEXT:
INTERNAL PROCESSES

Once we move inside the organization itself, the linkages between variables and decisions become a bit clearer. The evidence is also a bit

[52] Ibid., p. 446. Illustrations of such work would include D. R. Matthews, *The Social Background of Political Decision-Makers* (Chapel Hill: University of North Carolina Press, 1954); James A. Robinson, *Congress and Foreign Policy-Making: A Study in Legislative Influence and Initiative* (Homewood, Ill.: Dorsey Press, 1962); L. A. Froman, Jr., *Congressmen and Their Constituencies* (Chicago: Rand McNally, 1963).

[53] Robinson and Snyder, "Decision-Making in International Politics," p. 447.

[54] Ibid. See also Robinson, *Congress and Foreign Policy-Making;* Warren E. Miller and Donald Stokes, "Constituency Influence in Congress," *American Political Science Review* 57 (March, 1963), pp. 45–56.

stronger, though much of it still remains anecdotal. Allison's organizational and bureaucratic politics models must be examined here for what they imply about what goes on inside a decision-making unit. Implicit in Allison's models, as noted already, is that only by considering all the minute events occurring within the unit can one understand the final decision. Because no specific variables are isolated, however, decision theory suffers.

Raymond Tanter has suggested an intriguing test of a rather simplified notion of Allison's organization model on real-world data. Tanter's test can be done in such a way that it can falsify the main proposition of the organization model. His proposition was that today's behavior will be similar to yesterday's behavior. Utilizing events data collected for the Berlin crisis, Tanter tested Allison's organization model against a competing one—an "interaction model" that says an organization's behavior results from an opponent's behavior toward it. Because the events Tanter used were scaled along a conflict-cooperation continuum, he could test the hypothesis that the North Atlantic Treaty Organization (NATO) and the Warsaw Treaty Organization (WTO) acted during a given time period the same way it had acted during the previous time period.[55] The results showed that neither model was able to predict behavior very well. (Several questions might be raised about Tanter's research design; see appendix, paragraph E.) Other evidence, however, supports a modified organizational model. Michael Dennis tested the model on the acquisition of weapons systems by four large naval powers, and found that the rate of acquisition of weapons systems was very constant over long periods of time, and that changes in that constant acquisition could be easily identified as caused by something outside the organization itself.[56]

Snyder and Robinson suggest that organizations be arranged into different typologies and that these be converted into dimensions of decision-making organization. One dimension would be bureaucratization. Others, introduced by Snyder in his early work, would be hierarchies and centralization. Unfortunately, again, despite the intuitive appeal of these variables little research specifically linking variation on them to variation in decisional outcome has been done. In fact, Brady's study found that though the situational conditions of threat, short time, and surprise were very moderately related to behavior—especially conflict—elements of the bureaucratic process such as centralization of authority and level of bu-

[55] Raymond Tanter, "International System and Foreign Policy Approaches: Implications for Conflict Modelling and Management," *World Politics* 24 (Spring Supplement, 1972), pp. 7–39.

[56] Michael F. H. Dennis, "The Policy Basis of General Purpose Forces: A Model for Quantitative Analysis, *Journal of Conflict Resolution* 18 (March, 1974), p. 29.

reaucratic opposition were not directly linked to foreign policy.[57] To that extent, we are unclear as to the effect of organizational structure on decisions, at least in the foreign policy area.

Again, what information does exist on the organization model is primarily anecdotal. It is interesting information, but it should be evaluated carefully. Townsend Hoopes, for instance, focuses on communication patterns in his discussion of the central position Walt Rostow occupied in the White House under Johnson. It was a position that enabled Rostow to filter out information going to the president that would have contradicted Rostow's own hawkish views on the Vietnam War[58] Hoopes implies that Rostow was a crucial factor in the continual decisions to escalate the war, for he eliminated information that would have cast doubt on escalation as an option.

De Rivera, however, using another proposition concerning the organizational process, suggests by inference that Hoopes's assessment of Rostow's importance during the Vietnam War may be an inaccurate reason for Johnson's decisions. Because, says de Rivera, "communication of information is affected by rewards and costs," the "entire communication system is biased by the ideas and plans of the top decision makers. . . . Hence, subordinates soon learn their superior's ideas, plans, and way of thinking." [59] If de Rivera's proposition is correct, then pointing to Rostow as the prime influencer on the Vietnam decisions would be inaccurate for two reasons. First, Rostow's hawkishness may have derived as much from Johnson's predilections as from his own orientation: Johnson would only appoint someone who agreed with him. Second, Rostow need not have done the filtering at all because subordinates under him would already have done it: the process works on down through the communications structure. In this case too, therefore, equally plausible, but almost totally contradictory, explanations arrive at the same conclusion.

Such contradictions regarding the organizational context can be exhibited in yet another proposition by de Rivera. Analyzing the Korean decision, he notes that Truman's inclinations on Korea hardened "with the press of events *and the support of his advisors, the Congress, the public, the press, and his allies.* Had these elements not supported his earlier tentative moves," de Rivera says, "the later moves might not have been made." [60] Although his proposition is not systematically formulated, the inference is clear that these elements played a key role in Truman's decisions on Korea. "The opinions of his advisors and the reaction of the

[57] Brady, "Threat, Decision Time, and Awareness."

[58] Townsend Hoopes, *The Limits of Intervention* (New York: David McKay, 1967), especially pp. 59–61.

[59] De Rivera, *Psychological Dimension of Foreign Policy,* p. 57.

[60] Ibid., p. 138. Emphasis in original.

Congress were wind, sun, and rain that affected the final product." [61] To apply de Rivera's proposition to Johnson and Vietnam, however, produces evidence inconsistent with the proposition. Why did such elements as growing opposition toward Johnson's actions during the Vietnam war fail to force a reversal, and why, in spite of this opposition, did Johnson's inclinations "harden?" Although early in the war public support for the war was high, Johnson was consistently concerned about it, and in 1966 that support began to wane. Yet none of this appeared to affect his decisions; to the contrary, some feel it made him even more convinced that he should continue his escalating actions. To be sure, March, 1968, did produce a turnaround and a basic de-escalating pattern was begun—at a time when public opposition to the war was very high. But this turn of affairs still fails to resolve the contradiction between Truman's early resolve being strengthened by the support he received in 1950, and Johnson's early resolve being strengthened by increasing opposition, at least through 1966.

Most likely the situational constraint of crisis played the important intervening role, although de Rivera does not make that point. We know now that crises, especially those in foreign affairs, are almost certain to boost a president's popularity; witness Kennedy's increase in popularity after the Bay of Pigs fiasco. They force a "rallying-around" process absent in noncrisis situations. For this reason, the crisis atmosphere of June, 1950, over Korea produced the outpouring of support that Truman then relied upon, whereas Johnson's escalating decisions from 1964 to 1967 were not triggered by crisis, with one exception. That exception—the Gulf of Tonkin incident of August, 1964—rather ironically produced a great deal of public support. In building a model of decision processes, therefore, the situational constraint of crisis or noncrisis would appear—if the evidence is valid—to play the dominating role over other effects on the organizational process.

Charles Hermann and two of his colleagues found that the variables of "collective" decision-making and the number of alternatives isolated were related to whether a decision unit in a simulation decided to counterattack immediately upon warning of a nuclear attack, as opposed to delaying their response. The greater the process of collective—as opposed to single individual—decision-making in their simulation runs, the greater the probability to delay response, and the greater the number of alternatives, the less the chance of immediate counterattack. However, when assessing the effect of each variable while controlling for the effect of all others—such as the individual-level variable of self-esteem and the national attribute variable of capabilities—the number of alternatives then appeared to have little influence, whereas collective decision-making style did.[62]

Another organizational process variable is the composition of the decision unit. As Paige observes, "the fundamental assumption of decision-making analysis [is] that decisions tend to vary with the composition of the decisional unit."[63] In terms of the Korean decision, for example, he says that the initial decision to follow a diplomatic path in the crisis—with an emphasis on international law and organization—was a function of the presence of individuals in the decision-making unit who had been involved with the United Nations, and were then with the State Department. Paige presents data showing that 80 percent of those involved in the first decision on June 24—to call for a U.N. Security Council meeting—were State Departmental personnel. For the remaining five primary decisions (see Table 3-3), the percentage of military personnel ranged from 57 to 100, and each one of those decisions would have to be classified as a military decision. The two most serious military decisions (numbers

Table 3-3. Relative Representation of State Department and Defense Department Personnel in Six Decisions during Korean Crisis, June 24–June 30, 1950

Decision	Percent State	Percent Defense
1. Call for a U.N. Security Council meeting	80	20
2. To adopt a strong posture of resistance	38	62
3. To commit sea-air forces; to keep conflict limited	36	64
4. To extend operations into North Korea and to employ combat troops as evacuation cover	29	57
5. To commit one regimental combat team to combat	0	100
6. To commit necessary ground forces	18	82

Reprinted with permission of Macmillan Publishing Co., Inc. from *The Korean Decision* by Glenn D. Paige. Copyright © by The Free Press, a division of The Macmillan Company.

[62] Charles F. Hermann, Margaret G. Hermann, and Robert A. Cantor, "Counterattack or Delay: Characteristics Influencing Decision-Makers' Responses to the Simulation of an Unidentified Attack," *Journal of Conflict Resolution* 18 (March, 1974), pp. 98–99.

[63] Paige, *Korean Decision*, p. 284.

five and six) had 82 percent and 100 percent military personnel in attendance.

Roger Benjamin and Lewis Edinger also found several variables concerning organizational process that were related to military control over the final decision of a unit.[64] Using sixty-two historical cases, they found that a military as opposed to civilian outcome was more likely when the military leaders served a representational rather than a purely informational role, that is, when they provided means or end values, or both, instead of information alone. Second, not surprisingly, when the perception of both the military and the civilian leaders was that military leaders should be dominant in foreign policy-making, the military outcome was the more likely.[65] The first finding is of more theoretical importance in the present context, for it suggests the outcome is dependent upon how the military leaders present themselves within a decision-making unit.

Theories of foreign policy decision-making have filled volumes of literature on what *should*—intuitively and plausibly—explain an outcome. And they have included a vast array of illustrative, anecdotal material, and the results of substantial research in *non*-foreign policy areas. But systematic evidence confirming the operation of decision variables in foreign policy is small.

Similarly, descriptions of certain characteristics of foreign policy decision-making organizations do not constitute theories. To note that "conflict is pervasive" in such organizations because of the different viewpoints of different agencies, and therefore that conflict-resolution processes must go on inside the unit for a decision to occur, still does not link that phenomenon to differences in the actual outputs. Though it is true that foreign policy decisions are made in a context that has its own political forces and "rules of the game," and that the processes of conflict resolution and consensus building "will affect what can be done and how long it will take," [66] it is difficult to ferret out exactly *how* that effect will take place or *what* it will be. The central questions that make up the distinctive character of the decision-making approach seem all too often to be skirted. Descriptions of the process of decision-making as reconstructed by an outsider, of the actors and their interactions with one another, of their goals and personalities, are all interesting, but they do not constitute theories of decision-making.

[64] Roger W. Benjamin and Lewis J. Edinger, "Conditions for Military Control over Foreign Policy Decisions in Major States: A Historical Exploration," *Journal of Conflict Resolution* 15 (March, 1971), pp. 5–32.

[65] Benjamin and Edinger present two different correlations (Cramer's V of .34 and .08) for the variable of military communication through informal, nonstructured channels to the civilian leader, and therefore it is impossible to tell whether this variable is in fact significant or not.

[66] Robinson and Snyder, "Decision-Making in International Politics," p. 451.

Conclusion

THEORETICAL EVALUATION

The decision-making approach to an analysis of foreign policy has in some ways come full circle. Considering the movement from strict historical descriptions to the analytical categories suggested by Snyder and the numerous propositions presented by Paige in his Korean decision, the conclusion seems clear that the study of decision-making has progressed. Further, the analyses by de Rivera, using numerous psychological, sociological, and social-psychological propositions, as well as the tests made by Hermann, Robinson, Holsti, and others, all point to some accumulation of knowledge about decision-makers and decisions.

At the same time, the construction of theories in the field of foreign policy decision-making—implying the isolation of key variables and generalizations about their effect on decisions—has not fared particularly well. In fact, with the failure of theories, the circle has been fully completed by emergence of decision-making models. These models, popular in recent years, require that equal attention be given to the many "bits" of historical information that develop in every decision process—with the implication that each bit adds up to the explanation of the decision.

Perhaps the most serious drawback still involves the extent of the information seemingly required in so many decision studies. The "entire picture" of a decision can never be made; any description must exclude some information. But no criteria have as yet been spelled out concerning what information is to be left out and what is to be included. It is quite possible that many of the details in decision studies may constitute "noise," to use a technical term from communications research. Interesting though noise may be, it is not clear what effect each piece of information has on the final decisions. *If* the surgical air strike in Cuba had been considered differently during the missile crisis, for instance, the final decision might have been the same. There is no way of knowing for sure what effect that organizational quirk had. The usual objection to this line of argument is that because we don't really know what elements were noise and what were not, we must include everything. But to do that is to forsake the role of theorizing, or the search for the important variables.

Evaluating theories of decision-making in foreign policy is fairly straightforward. Evaluating historical case studies, or decision-making models, is quite different, and in numerous ways much more difficult. However, given the emphasis in recent years on models, and the fact that almost without exception the case studies on foreign policy decisions rely implicitly or explicitly on one or more of the models, some attempt must be made to at least suggest evaluative criteria.

ASSUMPTIONS

One technique in arriving at evaluative criteria is to examine the assumptions on which the model rests. The rationalized model *assumes* that large-scale events do not just "happen." Smaller decisions may come about simply out of neglect, but nothing as momentous as the Vietnam War, for example, could just "happen." Ellsberg illustrates this "assumption" when he asks four American presidents involved in Vietnam how they could have, "in the face of intelligence estimates and program analyses and recommendations," so persistently chosen programs that were "almost surely inadequate in the long run, while potentially costly and risky, instead of measures purported to be either more effective or else requiring *lesser* involvement?" [67] The assumption here, of course, is that the decision-makers—the presidents—must have had reasons for their actions, for making the choices they did, and the very actions themselves imply reasons. This assumption does not allow for the possibility that they had equally plausible reasons for not doing what in fact they did not do.

A second assumption underlying the rationalized model concerns evidence. Evidence, for one thing, means that authentic reasons for, say, presidential actions can be found in presidential statements. In the Vietnam case, reference by decision-makers to how vital Vietnam was to American interests supposedly reflected their real attitudes. On Vietnam it is possible to find statements asserting how important it was to the United States, but the question is whether those statements reflected real perceptions, and exactly how persistent they were. A simple page count, by year, from 1946 to 1969 of documents reproduced in the *New York Times* and the Senator Mike Gravel editions of *The Pentagon Papers* indicate (Figure 3-1) that the two periods from 1946 to 1951 and 1956 to 1959 were ones in which U.S. decision-makers paid comparatively little attention to Vietnam. Not surprisingly, in 1954 and 1955, the years of the fall of Dien Bien Phu and the Geneva conference on the future of Vietnam, much more attention was given to Vietnam. But aside from 1954, this documentary measure does not show any high and constant attention being paid Vietnam by American decision-makers before the early 1960s—with the peak years being 1963 to 1965. This evidence is far from the best, but it would certainly confirm a model that viewed "attention to Vietnam" not as a function of some prior, well-thought-out

[67] Ellsberg, *Papers on the War*, p. 74. Emphasis in original.

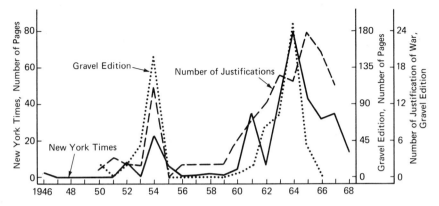

Figure 3-1. How vital was Vietnam? Number of pages of official documents reprinted in *New York Times* and Gravel Editions of the *Pentagon Papers;* and number of justifications of war cited in Gravel Edition, by year.

plan, but as a function merely of increasing or decreasing activity in Vietnam. The logical rejoinder to this argument would be that increased attention does not prove the situation was unimportant before the increase took place. Although this premise certainly has validity, the burden of its proof remains on those arguing that Vietnam was of relatively constant importance.

There is, of course, another factor involved here. The fact that the presidents referred to Vietnam as "vital" does not necessarily testify to their high and constant concern. In this regard, it is reported that Senator Mike Mansfield met with President Kennedy in the spring of 1963, after the senator had been arguing that increased American involvement was a mistake, and that Kennedy told Mansfield he agreed with him. He contended, however, that he could do nothing until after the 1964 election. According to Presidential Assistant Kenneth O'Donnell, Kennedy told Mansfield that "if I tried to pull out completely now, we would have another Joe McCarthy red scare on our hands, but I can do it after I'm reelected. So we had better make damned sure that I *am* reelected." [68] This account hardly squares with the picture of Kennedy—as one involved in Vietnam decision-making—viewing Vietnam as vital to American interests, and it raises serious doubt as to the forthrightness of Kennedy's public posture concerning Vietnam.

Assumptions underlie not only the rationalized model so far as Vietnam is concerned, but also what might be called the "quagmire model." This model assumes that (1) decision-makers are optimistic at important decision points, and that (2) each new small commitment is perceived

[68] Ibid., p. 97.

as promising to do the job "for good." Ellsberg raises serious questions about these assumptions in connection with Vietnam, for there is evidence that in 1961 the decisions to aid Vietnam *short* of a large-scale military Task Force were not the result of optimism that these decisions would "do it." [69] Both Taylor and McNamara pointed out that the proposed solutions would not necessarily take care of the problem. However, Taylor added that real disadvantages were present even with a Task Force proposal: it would weaken the strategic U.S. reserve force, American prestige would then become involved, and if the first contingent failed, pressures would rise for further commitments.[70] Hence, instead of optimism, pessimism surrounded Kennedy's early and important decisions. Both the rationalized model, as well as the strictly defined quagmire model, then, require either assumptions that are questionable, or evidence that we know not to be true regarding Vietnam. This discussion illustrates the difficulty of evaluating competing models, for one can argue persuasively for both perspectives.

EVIDENCE: WHAT IS NEEDED?

Another procedure for evaluating models, one not often used in the social sciences and one that tangentially involves assumptions, is to speculate about what evidence would have to exist in order to confirm a model. In other words, rather than make an *a priori* assertion that one of the models explains the behavior in question, and then institute a search for evidence to support it, this method stipulates beforehand what evidence must exist to validate each of the models. Three sets of evidence would rather clearly support the rational policy model: first, if there had been one big decision to stay in Vietnam; second, if it could be shown that Vietnam was absolutely vital to the United States; and third, if decisions to escalate were made not only long before they were announced, but also long before they were patently *needed* to react to the enemy.

Although there are several incidents that might constitute that "big" decision—Kennedy's increase in advisors, Johnson's bombing decision, as well as higher troop commitment—serious doubt can be raised as to whether (1) they sufficiently satisfy the criteria for a "big" decision, and (2) how solid and irrevocable they were in light of the serious doubts raised about Vietnam at several junctures. Second, evidence on the vitalness of Vietnam, as already noted, is questionable. Finally, there is only scant evidence that long-range escalatory decisions were made prior to any observed *need* for escalation. There are certainly hints of this

[69] Ibid., chap. 1.
[70] *Pentagon Papers*, p. 141.

throughout the early 1960s, but there are equally solid bits of evidence showing that many of the escalatory moves were made because no other options existed and merely because "something" had to be done.

For the quagmire model, decision-makers must be optimistic about their decisions and perceive them as permanent solutions. Ellsberg has presented strong evidence that optimism was not present during the making of the so-called crucial decisions throughout the Vietnam War. This evidence does not mean that pessimism was paramount, though evidence presented here does indicate that pessimism was attached to almost all options considered at several points. Leaders are, of course, constantly torn between optimism and pessimism on any decision. To focus only on certain pronounced pessimistic comments is misleading, for it ignores the fact of the decision itself. Therefore, evidence supposedly against this model does not appear as strong when these factors are taken into consideration.

For a strictly incremental model, decision-makers need only view their decisions as possible solutions *for the time being,* and we have already reviewed evidence that would tend to support that model for Vietnam. Kennedy's early decision to send Taylor and Rostow to Vietnam and later to increase the number of advisors; Johnson's immediate response to the Tonkin Gulf incident and his later bombing decisions: these and many others could be cited as evidence of incremental decisions, made for the moment. Presidents soon learn to question arguments that they *must* act immediately or face dire consequences; they often convert decisions into small, sequential ones rather than large-scale ones; and they develop—as politicians—short-run perspectives with the belief that, usually, things work themselves out "in the long run." [71]

Two problems regarding these evaluative procedures remain. First, have the requirements for evidence on the models been too harsh? Second, isn't it possible that all of the models apply, but that their application is limited only to certain decisions?

In terms of the first problem, the rationalized model does require somewhat stricter assumptions in terms of the evidence needed to support it. Of course, making those large assumptions means that one can explain large sweeps of history with that model. The incremental or quagmire models require more realistic assumptions and are in accord with numerous everyday decisions made in many areas of life. The requirements, although harsh and—unfortunately—subjective in their interpretation, force the analyst to spell out clearly what each model does imply. The harsher the requirements, the greater the reliability in the findings.

[71] Ellsberg, *Papers on the War,* p. 78.

The second problem is more formidable. For instance, many might argue that large-scale goals—the basic element in the rational policy model—such as "containing Communism" provided the rationale and therefore explains the "occurrence" of the entire Vietnam War. At the same time, more tactical, immediate, day-to-day decisions may not have been tied into that large-scale goal, but resulted more from the incremental process of decision-making. This argument, however, assumes a neat separation between "large" and "small" decisions. Ellsberg, for instance, isolates four "large" decisions in Vietnam: the 1950 aid to the French, increased support for Ngo Dinh Diem in 1954, Eisenhower's increase of advisers in 1960, and the inauguration of bombing in 1964. Other decisions, such as Kennedy's increasing the number of advisers, or Johnson's increase in the troop commitment after 1965, are "merely quantitative" for Ellsberg. This procedure, however, imposes on the data the very model that is being tested; to assert that there *are* "large" decisions and that others are "merely quantitative" stacks the cards in favor of a model that assumes such large or important decisions exist. None of these large decisions occurred in a vacuum, however. Kennedy's decision to send General Taylor to Vietnam in 1961 may have been prompted by reasons unrelated to "saving" Vietnam. Once the mission occurred, however, and recommendations made, the situation was transformed: a further decision had to be made on the recommendations. Similarly, indications are that some of Johnson's early bombing decisions were little more than "feelers," to see "what would happen." Although certainly cloaked in broader concerns, much evidence suggests that they were partially seen as promising responses "for the moment." The difficulty, of course, is that each "promising response," each "feeler," each small decision thereby *changed* the existing situation. Isolating supposed "large-scale decisions" may fail to show the effect that earlier decisions had on them.

In sum, combining the models by applying them to different levels requires criteria for importance of decisions and imposes an artificiality on the distinctions between different types of decisions that may not exist. To act as if "large" decisions occur unrelated to what went before them is empirically incorrect. The incremental model requires no such "large" decisions.

The goal here has not been to show the accuracy of one model over another, but to suggest that using the models in more than just a plausible fashion requires some assessment by the analyst as to each model's accuracy. The thrust of Allison's report on the Cuban Missile Crisis was that narrow and perhaps faulty explanations arise from utilizing only one model. But merely to propose other models does not entirely solve the problem, for in most cases the other models are equally plausible.

The methods sketched out here are meant to set out at least some rough categories of comparative evaluation for decision-making models.

To summarize on the theoretical level, this chapter has suggested that there are two perspectives to take on decision-making, one being the use of broadly defined models and the other being the testing of specific hypotheses in a strictly defined situation. Emphasis in more recent years has seemed to move more toward the broadly defined "models," [72] and away from testing specific hypotheses. This trend no doubt results primarily from the difficulty of collecting the necessary data concerning decision-making units and interactions within those units. It also no doubt results from the difficulty of conceptualizing the important internal decision-making variables in conjunction with the important differential situations that have been linked to decisional outcomes.

POLICY IMPLICATIONS

Not surprisingly, the variable of "stress" or "crisis" offers the most empirically grounded policy implications because it has been the most researched variable in the area of decision-making. The evidence does not speak with one voice on this matter, but the results of most of the research indicates that stress affects the search for alternatives and that as stress increases beyond a certain optimum level, alternatives become limited, and decision-makers become more inward-looking and less empathetic.

The proper advice, of course, would be to change one's decision-making style during crisis or stressful situations to accommodate these changes and possibly allay any adverse effects. Unfortunately, decision-makers in real-life decision situations are unlikely to heed such advice because they will be operating under the very forces and being influenced by the very variables that the findings suggest will have a great impact on them.

The decision-making models can be helpful if they force leaders to use different perspectives in inferring motives to *other* decision-makers. The rationalized model of decision-making elicits drastically different inferences about Soviet motives and intentions from the internal organizational, bureaucratic, or incremental models. Specific recommendations from the models are scarce, however, as befits an analytical method

---

[72] Allison, *Essence of Decision;* Graham Allison and Morton Halperin, "Bureaucratic Politics: A Paradigm and Some Policy Implications," *World Politics* 24 (Spring supplement, 1972), pp. 40–79; Morton H. Halperin, with the assistance of Priscilla Clapp and Arnold Kanter, *Bureaucratic Politics and Foreign Policy* (Washington, D.C.: The Brookings Institution, 1974); Leon V. Sigal, "The 'Rational Policy' Model and the Formosa Straits Crises," *International Studies Quarterly* 14 (June, 1970), pp. 121–56.

that is itself nonspecific. Allison and Halperin claim to derive policy implications from the organizational model concerning an opponent's behavior, but for the most part these implications are little more than further explications of the model. Their implications take the form of "warnings" to the policy-maker:

Be suspicious of explanations that depend on the assumption that one can reason back from detailed characteristics of specific behavior to central government intentions. . . . Recognize that in most cases the full range of behavior exhibited by a government was not intended by a single participant.[73]

Both "policy implications" merely reiterate the fallacy of relying solely on the postulates of the rational policy model.[74]

The inability to move beyond the parameters and outlines of the models themselves, of course, results in the paucity of policy implications. To go beyond repeating the axioms of the models as if they were policy implications would involve operationalizing the components of the models, such as "organizational process" or "bureaucratic politics." The models might be used as sensitizing aids for the policy-maker, forcing him perhaps to make explicit exactly what model he is employing, and in turn forcing him to investigate whether the assumptions and the parameters of that model are correct. But the models are unable, at least as they have been developed to date, to surpass that sensitizing role and provide actual recommendations. On the other hand, the decision theories also fall down in this respect, primarily from the lack of evidence. The studies on crisis and on the effect of unit makeup, as well as on the type of interaction within the unit [75] are very few in number. But the studies carried out in this fashion—testing decision-making propositions, some of which come from the decision models—hold probably the greatest hope for aid to policy-makers because they focus more closely on clearly specified variables describing the unit and the process.

Decision-making studies are a very difficult enterprise. Because of the understandable hold that traditional, historical descriptions have on the study of decisions, progress toward theory-building has not been spectacular. However, if nothing else, the recognition of the difficulty of analyzing decisions, regardless of the perspective, is itself helpful. Historical case studies tend to carry high plausibility but low reliability.

[73] Allison and Halperin, "Bureaucratic Politics," p. 70.

[74] The same critique applies to further alleged policy implications by Allison and Halperin, as well as to certain of their predictions; see ibid., pp. 71–72.

[75] The reference is primarily to Benjamin and Edinger, "Conditions for Military Control."

Useful insights into the decision process are certainly abundant in historical descriptions, but their drawbacks for theory are momentous. To go beyond plausibility, we must have evidence of the comparative utility of differing theories and models, a strict criterion, to be sure, but certainly one to work toward.

chapter 4 National Attribute Theory:

Domestic Sources

of Foreign Policy

The basic premise of the national attribute theory is manifested not only in foreign policy literature but in a great deal of traditional and contemporary international politics. It assumes that a state's characteristics are a primary cause of its foreign policy behavior. Just as analysis of an individual asserts that his personality characteristics shape his behavior, so national attribute theory suggests that a state's attributes affect its behavior.

Some might argue that the national attribute theory unrealistically bypasses decision-makers and that national attributes can work only as *constraints* on the decision-makers and not necessarily as direct forces on foreign policy. Although true in the ultimate sense that decision-makers make the decisions, national attribute theory asserts only that states should *tend to be constrained in similar ways* if possessing similar attributes. Rosenau says, for instance, that those utilizing this general approach of national attributes would "assume that a society's economic institutions, social structure, educational system, major value orientations, even its family life . . . underlie the actions of its decision-makers." [1] Although he implies that decision-makers' actions result from concern or response to internal elements, national attribute theory need not utilize that assumption. Just as a schizoid personality, for instance,

[1] James N. Rosenau, "Actions of States: Theories and Approaches, Introductory Note," in *International Politics and Foreign Policy: A Reader in Research and Theory,* ed. James N. Rosenau, rev. ed. (New York: The Free Press, 1969), p. 172.

acts not from conscious response to his schizoid character, but simply because that attribute constrains him to act in certain ways, attributes of nations in a sense "force" them to behave in certain ways. National attributes, then, are causal factors even though the process must certainly be filtered through the decision-making unit.

For present purposes, we will define a national attribute as anything that describes the makeup of a nation, differentiating one state from another in terms of political, social, economic, or, as some might argue, psychological characteristics. National attributes also cover what are referred to as "domestic sources" of foreign policy, although some will dispute this point. Common examples of national attributes are size and economic or political development. Examples of domestic sources of foreign policy would include the level of internal conflict or the type of leadership structure. While it is true that the leadership structure is not strictly an attribute of a nation, it is nevertheless considered one by national attribute theorists because they view foreign policy as a function of state-level variables. The following section reviews national attribute formulations found in traditional international relations literature and then relates these formulations to more recent empirical analyses.

NATIONAL ATTRIBUTE THEORY
IN HISTORY

Perhaps the earliest national attribute conception was that of geopolitics. Holders of this concept thought that the geographic location, climatic conditions, and the availability of natural resources were all crucial variables for understanding the behavior of nations. Alfred Thayer Mahan, for instance, contended that the rise of British power paralleled its increased strength on the high seas, that naval power made a nation different, and that in Britain's case it made it more powerful.[2] British geographer Sir Halford (John) Mackinder argued in his famous "heartland" thesis that whoever ruled the "heartland," namely, central Europe, would rule the world because railroads would provide mobility, the area was inaccessible to naval attack, and it possessed abundant natural resources. Likewise, Robert Holt and John Turner have maintained that insular polities will have different kinds of foreign policies than noninsular polities. Island nations will try to align with states outside of their region, and will likely try to dominate the large land masses proximate to them in order to prevent invasions.[3]

[2] James E. Dougherty and Robert L. Pfaltzgraff, Jr., *Contending Theories of International Relations* (Philadelphia: Lippincott, 1971), p. 52.

[3] Robert T. Holt and John E. Turner, "Insular Polities," in *Linkage Politics*, ed. James N. Rosenau (New York: The Free Press, 1969).

Second to the geopolitical formulation of national attribute theory, Lenin's ideas on imperialism are probably the most well-known. Capitalist economic systems ultimately deplete their own natural resources and use up the finite amount of investment possibilities, resulting in a falling rate of profit. At that point, capitalist countries, says Lenin, must go beyond themselves, not only looking for markets where they can peddle their goods, but also searching for raw materials that have become scarce at home. This activity produces conflicts of interest between countries, and hastens international wars. Capitalist nations become involved in conflicts with other capitalist countries searching for goods, and all of them try to dominate the less powerful states. Thus, argues Lenin, capitalist countries possess the attribute of imperialism, which forces them into wars more often than noncapitalist countries.

Kenneth Waltz relates the traditional liberal-democratic notion that sees nondemocratic states as the cause of wars. The liberal, democratic polities, which are "good" because they supposedly provide decentralization, economic well-being, and participation, are the peaceful states. Waltz equates rationality and harmony with democratic states. War, therefore, would become an anachronism as more states achieved democratic status, because they would live more peacefully and contentedly with one another, settling their differences in a logical way.[4]

Henry Kissinger's classic study in national attributes focuses not on the economic or political system but on "leadership types." He distinguishes three types of domestic structures: a bureaucratic leadership structure, such as the United States; a revolutionary leadership, such as the People's Republic of China; and a charismatic leadership, such as Cuba in the 1960s.[5] Two general types of propositions flow from this categorization, one on the national level and the second on the systemic level. The national attribute hypothesis would contend that each leadership structure, with contrasting perceptions, priorities, and internal procedures, holds diverse ideas of what constitutes legitimate foreign policy acts or legitimate responses to actions by other countries. Therefore each leadership structure's behavior will differ based on those internal characteristics. Note that while individual-level data might be utilized in these analyses, such as perceptions and values, the analysis does not take place on that level because persons within the same system should possess relatively similar values and perceptions. Variation, therefore, occurs not on the individual level but across states. The systemic hypothesis, which

---

[4] Kenneth Waltz, *Man, the State, and War* (New York: Columbia University Press, 1959), p. 101.

[5] Henry Kissinger, "Domestic Structure and Foreign Policy," in *International Politics and Foreign Policy: A Reader in Research and Theory,* ed. James N. Rosenau, rev. ed. (New York: The Free Press, 1969), p. 267ff.

will be considered in a later chapter, pertains to the *interaction* of different kinds of structures in the international system as the causal variable leading to instabilities. For purposes of this chapter the national attribute hypothesis can be clearly grounded in Kissinger's categories of leadership structures. (An investigation of the problems involved in Kissinger's categories is contained in the appendix, paragraph B.)

Rosenau's "pre-theory" of foreign policy contains two variables located at the national attribute level: the "governmental" variable and the "societal" variable. The governmental variable refers to "those aspects of a government's structure that limit or enhance the foreign policy choices made by decision-makers. The impact of executive-legislative relations on American foreign policy exemplifies the operation of governmental variables." [6] The governmental variable also distinguishes between open and closed political systems. A democratic, open system, for example, may be less free to act in foreign policy and therefore its policy should be more stable. It may be less capable of using internal disruptions as an excuse for fomenting external conflict, and therefore may simply have less external conflict. Or, as Waltz might argue, democratic leaders might be much more interested in rationally solving conflicts of interest and less likely to resort as quickly to war or violence. Totalitarian or single-leader regimes possess much more flexibility, and thus are much more capable of rapid changes of policy. They are able to foment foreign conflict with less worry about having to account domestically for their decisions. And, contrary to democratic countries, they may just see conflict as a much more usable and preferable alternative to solving a problem.

The societal variable, according to Rosenau, refers to "those non-governmental aspects of a society which influence its external behavior." [7] Rosenau has in mind here such attributes of a nation as its value orientations, unity, and degrees of industrialization, all of which can, as he puts it, "contribute to the contents of a nation's external aspirations and policies." [8]

Societal variables would also include country size and level of economic and social development. Large, developed systems are likely to be more active in foreign affairs, and because they have more actions and more international interests, they may be involved in more conflicts as well as more alliances. They are also—because of their military capabilities—likely to be more militaristic in their foreign policy. Small coun-

6 James N. Rosenau, "Pre-Theories and Theories of Foreign Policy," in *Approaches to Comparative and International Politics,* ed. R. Barry Farrel (Evanston: Northwestern University Press, 1966), p. 43.

7 Ibid.

8 Ibid.

tries, when they engage in conflict, are apt to rely more on verbal abuse and sorties across borders rather than invasions.

The differing hypotheses offered above have been culled from traditional and contemporary writings positing national attributes as an explanation of foreign behavior. While an investigator can usually find numerous domestic sources in any one situation to explain a particular foreign policy, action, or trend, the next section suggests several general categories of national attributes.

Contemporary Empirical Analysis

Organizing the many potential national attribute variables into a coherent framework is not as difficult as it might first appear. The traditional and contemporary historical literature, as well as our common sense, dovetails remarkably with recent empirical studies outlining the general categories of nation-state attributes. Of the five general variables set forth in his pre-theory, for instance, Rosenau suggests that the large-small, open-closed, and developed-undeveloped variables have considerable value in explaining international behavior. In reports by Jack Sawyer, Bruce Russett, and, especially, Rudolph Rummel,[9] similar dimensions appear that are basically uncorrelated with one another. Sawyer uncovered the characteristics or attributes of size, wealth, and politics; Russett found economic development, communism, intensive agriculture, size, and "Catholic culture"; and Rummel isolated seven different attributes: economic development, size, politics, Catholic culture, density, foreign conflict, and domestic conflict.

This chapter focuses on three broadly defined national attributes or domestic sources of foreign policy, a categorization derived from intuition, from the historical works reviewed above, and from an analysis of the work by Russett, Sawyer, and Rummel. The three categories are size and economic wealth, type of governmental system, and political or social unrest or strain. Some justification is needed for the choice of these specific categories because they do not agree entirely with those of Rummel, Russett, and Sawyer—nor do those authors entirely agree among themselves on the important and distinctive attributes of nations.

Factor analysis was used as the primary method to separate out the important variables. We can therefore make some assessment concerning

[9] Jack Sawyer, "Dimensions of Nations: Size, Wealth, and Politics," *American Journal of Sociology* 73 (September, 1967), pp. 145–72; Bruce M. Russett, *International Regions and the International System: A Study in Political Ecology* (Chicago: Rand McNally, 1967); R. J. Rummel, "Indicators of Cross-National and International Patterns," *American Political Science Review* 63 (March, 1969), pp. 127–47.

their generality and importance by referring to those results. First, in every study economic development or wealth emerges as the factor accounting for the greatest amount of variation among nations, which means that nations can be discriminated most effectively by the variables underlying that dimension (see appendix, paragraph C); consequently, it must play a prominent role in any attempt to differentiate nations empirically. Second, size follows economic wealth in importance in Rummel's study, ties with politics for second place in Sawyer's study, and is fifth in Russett's. We have combined economic development (or wealth) and size not only because several indicators correlate highly with both of these dimensions,[10] but also because they intuitively tend to be combined. Furthermore, the entire concept of power is intimately tied up with these two variables. The two variables, then, although treated separately at times, are considered here as a group distinct from the other two general attributes.

The second category or general attribute, the type of governmental system, or "politics," consists primarily of variables that measure accountability or type of political system along the open-closed dichotomy (freedom of opposition, freedom of the press, voter choice, Communist party memberships).

The third category of national attributes is domestic conflict, and here we are referring to political or social unrest or instability. This category is included primarily because of the numerous hypotheses generated in the literature and because of the large amount of research testing these hypotheses in recent years. Moreover, Rummel isolated domestic conflict as a separate dimension in his study, although a minor one compared with the others.

The other dimensions from the numerous factor analyses are not used either because they do not make as much clear theoretical sense (i.e., Catholic culture), or because the variables indexing those dimensions load on other dimensions also. For example, two variables in Russett's Catholic culture dimension load moderately high on development and the three variables in Rummel's study delineating Catholic culture load in Sawyer's study on one of his three dimensions. Another reason remaining dimensions mentioned above are not used is because they represent one of the behaviors we are trying to explain, namely foreign conflict.

MEASUREMENT

National attributes encompass the multitude of elements that make up a nation-state. They range from size and development to character and

___

10 Sawyer, "Dimensions of Nations," p. 165.

morale. Most of the research in recent years in attribute theory has been done on attributes that can be easily measured with available aggregate data. This measurement of only a certain kind of attribute serves as a drawback on the development of theory because it may be that the less easily measured attributes have a greater impact on behavior. However, given the overwhelming attention to variables in traditional literature than *can* be measured with available aggregate data, research in these areas has clearly not been totally a function of data availability.

The three attribute clusters of size and wealth, type of government system, and internal unrest or dissatisfaction are all amenable to measurement, although to differing degrees of accuracy. Size and wealth will in most cases be measured by population and gross national product per capita, indicators that correlate highly with scores of other indicators all clearly measuring the same basic concept. Type of political system has been measured in several ways. Some have used a measure of freedom of the press,[11] which is admittedly subjective, but investigation of the scores given to countries shows that it agrees with our intuitive judgment and therefore has validity. Others have factor analyzed numerous political components of countries from data in the survey by Arthur Banks and Robert Textor,[12] finding that countries tend to fall into fairly clear political groups.[13] Still others have used ordinal or interval groupings of countries on such variables as "freedom of opposition." [14] Finally, internal unrest, conflict, or strain has been measured in one of two ways: either by general societal stress *thought to be* a concomitant of rapid industrialization (level of suicide or homicide rates, for example) or by specific social acts (rioting, rebelling, demonstrating, committing physical violence).

In sum, most measures used to describe national attributes relate to social, political, economic, or physical elements of the state. As we will note in Chapter 5 concerning the measurement of power, however, such indexes can very plausibly be related to—and perhaps substitute for—more nebulous psychological or morale characteristics.

[11] Charles Lewis Taylor and Michael C. Hudson, *World Handbook of Political and Social Indicators,* 2d ed. (New Haven: Yale University Press, 1972), p. 51.

[12] Arthur S. Banks and Robert B. Textor, *A Cross-Polity Survey* (Cambridge: MIT Press, 1963).

[13] Arthur S. Banks and Phillip M. Gregg, "Grouping Political Systems: Q-Factor Analysis of *A Cross-Polity Survey,*" *American Behavioral Scientist* 9 (November, 1965), pp. 3–6.

[14] See Jack Sawyer, "Dimensions of Nations," pp. 145–72.

Size and Development

The national attributes of size and economic development have always been important in the study of international politics and foreign policy as well as in comparative politics. Their importance stems from Marxist notions about the primary significance of economics and from the literature on international relations that is concerned with the power of nation-states. Size is a crucial factor, therefore, because it is usually associated with the great powers, and these powers tend to be the countries that are also economically developed. The question of power is treated more extensively in the following chapter, but let it be noted here concerning attributes that large, developed states are usually thought to be the most powerful because they have greater capacities than smaller states for carrying out policies. They normally possess trained, highly educated elites, vast armies, and immense bureaucratic structures.

In view of these attributes, it has long been felt that the powerful should act differently than the non-powerful. Maurice East and Charles Hermann use such reasoning to propose numerous hypotheses concerning the effect of size and development. For size, they hypothesize that large states are more active, that their heads of state and bureaucratic organizations are more involved in these actions, that they are engaged in more conflict, and so forth.[15] While economically developed states should exhibit some of these same patterns, they also suggest that developed states will differ from large states in having a lower percentage of acts involving heads of state and verbal events, while using a higher percentage of events involving military skills and resources.[16]

PARTICIPATION, CONFLICT, AND COOPERATION

Numerous factor analyses differentiate between size and development, but the effect of both variables on foreign policy is not so easily determined. It is not particularly surprising that the larger and more economically developed states are the more active participants in the international system; they have more at stake in the world. Later research

---

[15] Maurice A. East and Charles F. Hermann, "Do Nation-Types Account for Foreign Policy Behavior?" in *Comparing Foreign Policies: Theories, Findings, and Methods*, ed. James N. Rosenau (New York: Wiley, 1974), p. 274.

[16] Ibid., p. 276.

will suggest that the intervening variables of *needs* and *resources* are the crucial ones that influence their level of participation.[17] For the moment it can be said that numerous studies have found some correlation between size, modernization, and activity. However, going beyond the level of participation to the level of different types and degrees of conflict and cooperation presents a more interesting approach to analysis.

According to Rummel, studies by Raymond Cattell show little or no relation between war deaths, number of wars, and foreign clashes, on the one hand, and national income per capita, telephones per capita, and railway length per capita, on the other. Rummel also found few strong relationships between foreign conflict behavior—as measured by thirteen variables of foreign conflict—and economic development.[18] Because Rummel's findings have been repeatedly cited as denying the role of development in international behavior, Table 4-1 presents nine of his thirteen foreign conflict variables and several measures of size and wealth. While it is true that in Rummel's entire data set roughly 10 percent of all his correlations between foreign conflict and national attributes were above .30, and only 12 percent of those between size and wealth are above .30, the table suggests a slight reworking of that conclusion. First, four of the indicators—protests, expulsion of low-level diplomats, troop movements, and accusations—all correlate much more highly than the other nine indicators. Second, numerous factor analyses [19] indicate that states' behavior is patterned. Severance of relations and foreign demonstrations seem to form one pattern, protests and accusations another, expulsions of diplomats and troop movements a third, and war and the number of individuals killed in foreign wars a fourth (along with mobilization and military acts; see appendix, paragraph C).

Third and most important, perhaps, there seems to be a clear pattern for larger states to make more protests and accusations (verbal acts), to expel lesser officials and engage in troop movements (diplomatic acts), and take up arms (war acts). Wealthy or developed states, however, do not protest, accuse, or partake in troop movements—there is no relation with these variables at all—but they do tend to expel lower officials. Moreover, while the smaller and less-developed states participate less in

[17] James G. Kean and Patrick J. McGowan, "National Attributes and Foreign Policy Participation: A Path Analysis," in *Sage International Yearbook of Foreign Policy Studies*, ed. Patrick J. McGowan, Vol. 1 (Beverly Hills: Sage Publications, 1973).

[18] Rudolph J. Rummel, "The Relationship between National Attributes and Foreign Conflict Behavior," in *Quantitative International Politics: Insights and Evidence*, ed. J. David Singer (New York: Free Press, 1968), p. 205.

[19] See Dina A. Zinnes and Jonathan Wilkenfeld, "An Analysis of Foreign Conflict Behavior of Nations," in *Comparative Foreign Policy: Theoretical Essays*, ed. Wolfram F. Hanrieder (New York: David McKay, 1971), p. 173.

Table 4-1. Correlations of Selected Size and Development Indicators with Selected Foreign Conflict Behaviors, 1955-1957

Size	Protests	Accusations	Severance of Relations	Foreign Demon-strations	Expel Ambass.	Expel Others	Troop Move-ments	War	Foreign Killed
Population (1.00)[a]	.38	.36					.49		
GNP (.82)[b]	.42						.43		
National income (.80)[b]	.40	.45				.37	.45		
Defense exp. (.74)[b]	.48	.55		.32		.32	.51		
No. in mil. (.79)	.45			.32		.45		.31	.35
Resources available (.70)	.32	.32				.35	.43		
Pop. x energy prod. (.80)[b]	.35					.34	.32		
Total energy consumption (.68)[b]	.35					.39	.33		
RR freight per RR length (.58)[b]	.53	.40				.38	.50	.36	.33
Development									
GNP per capita (1.00)			−.35			.31			
Calories consumed—Req./Required (.80)			−.46						
Life expectancy (.81)			−.31			.40			
Trade (.68)[b]	.37					.42			
Newsprint consumption per capita			−.35			.35			
Illiterate (.83)			.33						

[a] Correlations in parentheses after each indicator are the correlation with the dimension.

[b] Indicates that the variable correlated with both size and development, but higher with the category under which it is listed; see Jack Sawyer, "Dimensions of Nations: Size, Wealth, and Politics," *American Journal of Sociology* 73 (September, 1967), pp. 145-172.

Based on Table 1 in R.J. Rummel, "The Relationship Between National Attributes and Foreign Conflict Behavior," in *Quantitative International Politics: Insights and Evidence,* ed., J. David Singer.(New York: The Free Press, 1968), pp. 188-199.

the actions described above, they tend to sever relations more often than the more wealthy states.

Rummel is certainly correct in noting that the correlations are low. Table 4-1 nonetheless suggests at least a pattern that might be investigated. Furthermore, in a later analysis, Erich Weede reanalyzed Rummel's data and found high correlations between verbal and violent foreign conflict and certain measures of size.[20] Jack Vincent and his associates also found that measures of high power were generally associated with high conflict, that high economic development was associated with high cooperative behavior (trade, common International Organization (IO) membership, and diplomatic exchanges);however, the measures of power and economic development tended to resemble each other.[21] Perhaps Rummel's conclusion that national attributes are unrelated to foreign behavior is true in a broad sense concerning all national attributes and all foreign conflict behavior. It may also be correct insofar as attributes could not account for the bulk of variation in behavior. But these conclusions do not equate with saying attributes have *no* effect on international relations.

Michael Skrein's study of the impact of attributes on foreign policy used quite different data—especially for foreign behavior—and his conclusions differ somewhat from those of Rummel.[22] He found that in nineteen British Commonwealth countries, those that were developed had a high ratio of cooperative to noncooperative behavior toward other nations, whereas the acts of smaller, newer countries in the Commonwealth were more noncooperative.[23] Skrein confirmed in a larger study of sixty-nine countries the finding that size and development also relate to total output (larger countries use more actions than smaller countries), but that the relationships drop when the *ratio* of cooperative to uncooperative acts is considered. Though small, however, the correlations showed that developed countries used a moderately smaller proportion

[20] Erich Weede, "Conflict Behavior of Nation-States," *Journal of Peace Research* 7 (No. 3, 1970), pp. 229–35. Weede's analysis was different from Rummel's, which might account for his different results.

[21] Jack Vincent, Roger Baker, Susan Gagnon, Keith Hamm, and Scott Reilly, "Empirical Tests of Attribute, Social Field, and Status Field Theories on International Relations Data," *International Studies Quarterly* 17 (December, 1973), pp. 405–44.

[22] Michael Skrein's nation-state behavior comes from the twenty-two category coding scheme of the World Event/Interaction Survey (WEIS), which includes cooperation as well as conflict actions. See Barbara Fitzsimmons, Gary Hoggard, Charles McClelland, Wayne Martin, and Robert Young, "World Event/Interaction Survey Handbook and Codebook," Technical Report 1, mimeographed (Los Angeles: University of Southern California, 1969).

[23] Michael Skrein, "The Commonwealth: An Application of Event/Interaction Data," Support Study 2, mimeographed (Los Angeles: University of Southern California, 1969).

of conflict acts than smaller, undeveloped nations. When broken down into verbal and physical conflict, Skrein's findings were mixed for verbal but showed rather clearly that the developed states had a smaller ratio of physical violence to their total behavioral output. Thus, while the danger of conflict emanating from the developed nations remains high, as a proportion of their total action their physical conflict action is less. Steven Salmore and Charles Hermann likewise showed that size and development are related to behavior. Using categories derived from the World Event/Interaction Survey (WEIS),[24] they determined, however, that these attributes relate significantly only to "defensive verbal conflict" (rejections, protests, and denials) and that the larger and developed states use these behaviors a good deal more than do the smaller, less developed states. In spite of the fact that the other relations are not statistically significant, the pattern is for the smaller and less developed states to use more offensive verbal conflict—accuse, demand, warn, and threaten—and to engage in acts of conflict more than do the larger, developed states.[25]

Other studies, using the same data, raise some doubts about these findings, but the discrepancies are not momentous. For instance, Richard Chadwick found the highest attribute correlations with threats, accusations and protests to be energy production and military personnel,[26] but Maurice East and Phillip Gregg, using Rummel's data, report that one measure of development (telephones per capita) was basically unrelated to the number of threats that a country used.[27] Even so, this discrepancy occurred on only one measure; in Rummel's study, threats were related to railway freight in proportion to railroad length, defense expenditures, number of military, national income, and population.

Moreover, Michael Haas reported that urbanized and wealthy countries (as measured by U.N. assessments) showed slightly higher conflict, and that the most and least developed countries had more foreign conflict. Although Haas treated his data differently,[28] the findings in a very

[24] Fitzsimmons, et al., "World Event/Interaction Survey Handbook and Codebook."

[25] Steven A. Salmore and Charles F. Hermann, "The Effect of Size, Development and Accountability on Foreign Policy," *Peace Research Society Papers* 14 (1970), pp. 27–28.

[26] Richard W. Chadwick, "An Inductive Empirical Analysis of Intra- and International Behavior Aimed at a Partial Extension of Inter-Nation Simulation Theory," *Journal of Peace Research* 6 (No. 3, 1969), pp. 193–214.

[27] Maurice A. East and Phillip M. Gregg, "Factors Influencing Cooperation and Conflict in the International System," *International Studies Quarterly* 11 (September, 1967), pp. 244–69.

[28] Michael Haas, "Societal Approaches to the Study of War," *Journal of Peace Research* 2 (No. 4, 1965), pp. 307–23; rather than utilizing the original interval data on his measurements, Haas categorized his variables into nominal or ordinal levels (such as high, medium, and low development) and placed countries into the categories. His findings, therefore, are less reliable and accurate since he loses information in that process.

general way support those reported earlier. Skrein, also using the WEIS data but in another form, showed that politically developed systems (using Cutright's measure)[29] have a higher cooperative to uncooperative ratio in their foreign affairs, a higher percentage of noncoercive acts, and a lower percentage of coercive acts.[30] Likewise, in Hermann's simulation investigating variables related to the decision to counterattack upon warning as opposed to delaying a response, wealthy, developed countries were more likely to counterattack than undeveloped countries.[31]

Rummel's general finding can be reiterated—size and development are not highly related to level of conflict—but the evidence does support a much more moderate relation, and one that differs depending on what measure of conflict is used. Overall conflict, different types of conflict, and conflict as a proportion of total behavior are quite different phenomena. On the whole, developed states have more conflict because they take more actions. However, when total number of actions are controlled for, large, developed states have a higher percentage of cooperative actions than smaller, undeveloped states. Also, there is a slight tendency for large developed states to use protests more than other states, while the latter engage in more conflict acts, especially in the severing of relations.

INTERNATIONAL ORGANIZATION
BEHAVIOR

Though conflict and cooperation are of central concern in international relations, Vincent has found that United Nations voting behavior and the attitudes of U. N. delgates toward the United Nations are strongly related to the level of their country's economic development. Delegates from larger, more developed states for example, tend to be more negative in their evaluation of the United Nations; those from smaller, developing states more positive. Similarly, larger states are inclined to vote *against* more measures more often than the smaller, developing states. Highly developed states would thus be characterized

[29] Phillips Cutright, "National Political Development," *American Sociological Review* 28 (April, 1963), pp. 253–64.

[30] Michael Skrein, "National Attributes and Foreign Policy Output: Tests for a Relationship," Support Study 4, mimeographed (Los Angeles: University of Southern California, 1970), pp. 45–47.

[31] Charles F. Hermann, Margaret G. Hermann, and Robert A. Cantor, "Counterattack or Delay: Characteristics Influencing Decision-Makers' Responses to the Simulation of an Unidentified Attack," *Journal of Conflict Resolution* 18 (March, 1974), p. 99.

as "negative," "oppositional," "nonprogressive," or status-quo oriented.[32] Vincent's findings were applicable to the 1961, 1963, 1968, and 1969 General Assemblies. Developed states were also found to be against a general "change orientation," defined as changes in the law of the sea, in the definition of aggression, and in the willingness to accept Mainland China's participation in the U. N.[33]

Studies also show that developed countries have relied more heavily on the Permanent Court of International Justice and on the International Court of Justice than on the League of Nations or the U. N. More than 60 percent of the cases in the first two organizations related to developed states, whereas less than 40 percent in either the League or the U. N. involved developed states.[34] Furthermore, the developed states were more active in initiating cases in the two court institutions, and the less developed were much more active in initiating them in the League and United Nations. Not unexpectedly, nondeveloped states were much more likely to use nonjudicial institutions after World War II —during the heyday of newly independent countries.[35]

A series of other studies has also indicated that economic development or power, that is, size, was related to office-holding in the United Nations. According to M. R. Singer and B. Sensenig, the more powerful countries were more successful in U. N. elections,[36] though this relationship has decreased over time. R. W. Gregg, measuring power by the country's U. N. assessment, also found a very high relation between power and election to offices in both the United Nations Security Council and the General Assembly.[37] K. M. Weigert and R. E. Riggs showed that developed and large countries were more successful at U. N. office-holding, had a larger permanent mission at the U. N., and sponsored

---

[32] Jack Vincent, "Predicting Voting Patterns in the General Assembly," *American Political Science Review* 65 (June, 1971), pp. 471–98; Jack E. Vincent, "National Attributes as Predictors of Delegate Attitudes at the United Nations," *American Political Science Review* 62 (September, 1968), pp. 916–31.

[33] James E. Todd, "The 'Law-Making' Behavior of States in the United Nations as a Function of Their Location within Formal World Regions," *International Studies Quarterly* 15 (September, 1971), pp. 297–316.

[34] William D. Coplin and J. Martin Rochester, "The Permanent Court of International Justice, the International Court of Justice, the League of Nations, and the United Nations: A Comparative Empirical Survey," *American Political Science Review* 66 (June, 1972), pp. 529–50.

[35] Ibid., pp. 534–35.

[36] M. R. Singer and B. Sensenig, III, "Elections within the United Nations: An Experimental Study Utilizing Statistical Analysis," *International Organization* 17 (Autumn, 1963), pp. 901–25.

[37] R. W. Gregg, "The Latin American Bloc in United Nations Elections," *Southwestern Social Science Quarterly* 46 (September, 1965), pp. 146–54.

more resolutions and amendments.[38] Hayward Alker's study on supranationalism reiterates Vincent's findings: more developed countries were
less likely to vote for issues of a supranational nature, which he defined
as "a commitment to use and to be bound by political institutions
transcending the nation-state." [39] J. F. Clark, M. K. O'Leary, and E. R.
Wittkopf determined that size, gross domestic product, and per capita
GDP correlated with measures of U. N. support, supranationalism, and
a willingness to pay for U. N. operations, the larger countries conform-
ing to U. N. behavior in terms of support through number of diplomats,
the wealthy and more developed countries being less supranational and
paying more for the U. N.'s upkeep.[40] Thomas Volgy and Jon Quistgard,
while confirming that basic relationship, discovered that other variables
—such as the size of a nation's mission at the U. N. and its total "involvement" in the international system—were somewhat more potent predictors.[41]

Attribute theory does not play a pivotal role in explaining certain
behavior within alliances, however. John D. Sullivan has summarized
the research investigating the hypothesis that the more highly valued a
country views an alliance, the more it will contribute to maintaining it.
National attributes come into play here because the value of an alliance
is usually measured by size of country—its GNP. Although cast in terms
of the theory of collective goods,[42] GNP is a national attribute. Sullivan
reports research on the U.N. and NATO supporting the hypothesis.[43] For
other alliances, however—the Rio Pact, the Warsaw Pact, the Arab
League—the relationship did not emerge as expected. In some cases
members did not join voluntarily and may have been coerced into supporting the alliance. In short, the hypothesis was not well supported,
and, therefore, national attributes of size or development do not explain
how the burdens within alliances are shared. Sullivan does admit that

[38] K. M. Weigert and R. E. Riggs, "Africa and United Nations Elections: An
Aggregate Data Analysis," *International Organization* 23 (Winter, 1969), pp. 1–19.

[39] Hayward R. Alker, Jr., "Supranationalism in the United Nations," *Peace Research Society Papers* 3 (1965), p. 200.

[40] J. F. Clark, M. K. O'Leary, and E. R. Wittkopf, "National Attributes Associated
with Dimensions of Support for the United Nations," *International Organization* 25
(Winter, 1971), pp. 1–25.

[41] Thomas Volgy and Jon Quistgard, "Correlates of Organizational Rewards in the
United Nations: An Analysis of Environmental and Legislative Variables," *International Organization* 28 (Spring, 1974), pp. 179–206.

[42] Bruce Russett and John D. Sullivan, "Collective Goods and International Organization," *International Organization* 25 (Autumn, 1971), pp. 845–67.

[43] John D. Sullivan, "International Alliances," in *International Systems: A Behavioral Approach,* ed. Michael Haas (New York: Chandler Publishing, 1974), pp. 99–
122.

the measure of country size may not accurately reflect the value of an alliance to the country.

SUMMARY

Size and development, then, relate in numerous domains to several different types of foreign policy behavior, but the relationships are not simple. Large and developed states use a greater proportion of cooperative as opposed to conflict behavior than do smaller and less-developed states. When they do resort to conflict, however, they rely more on its verbal aspects, especially protests. Underdeveloped states are more conflictual, and tend toward more coercive types of conflict. As noted, this is not to say that the damage wrought by the type of conflict practiced by the developed countries is any less—on the contrary, it is probably greater because of the greater extent of their actions—but merely that their attributes demand that they cooperate more than they fight. Developed states also take a different view of the United Nations, act differently within it, and use other international organs differently from the way in which smaller and less developed states use them.

Type of Government

Because political scientists have focused so much on governmental structures, it is not at all surprising that scholars of international politics have viewed the type of government as a key factor in a country's foreign policy. Earlier in the chapter we outlined the most consistent hypotheses on type of government as a national attribute. Democratic systems, it is argued, permit a certain type of freedom within government that tends to inhibit leaders of these systems from using their position to trample over other countries in foreign affairs. If we assume people do not like war, then systems where the leaders are accountable to the people are much less likely to become involved in wars.

CONFLICT, COOPERATION,

AND CONFORMANCE

Jonathan Wilkenfeld and Dina Zinnes divided countries into three different types—personalist, centrist, polyarchic—and related those types to Rummel's foreign conflict behavior for the years 1955 to 1957. The personalist group of countries were primarily one-man governments or dictatorships (Guatemala, El Salvador, Panama, and Honduras are examples). Centrist countries tended to be socialist or Communist (Bulgaria, Albania, East Germany, Hungary, and North Korea). Polyarchic countries were primarily "democratic" governments (United States, Norway, Ireland, West Germany, Sweden, Australia).

There is a slight tendency for centrist countries to exhibit more foreign conflict than would be expected by chance, whereas the polyarchic group exhibits less. The Personalist group, accounting for 20 percent of all countries, also accounts for 20 percent of all foreign conflict. Larger differences occurred, however, when various types of conflict were investigated. Centrist countries clearly exhibited more warlike behavior than expected.[44]

Haas also reports that democratic countries appear to have slightly less conflict.[45] Salmore and Hermann found that type of government was more important than size and development, with open systems using significantly less offensive verbal conflict than closed systems. On the whole, open systems are more cooperative, especially in terms of verbal behavior; they participate more, and use less offensive verbal conflict and fewer conflict acts.[46]

Contrary to what Marxist-Leninist theory would have us believe, Quincy Wright has shown that capitalist countries tend to be more peaceful than socialist countries.[47] Dougherty and Pfaltzgraff also argue that history simply does not support the contention that the capitalist countries have always been entering into foreign conflicts as a function of their imperialistic drives.[48] In other words, the general evidence seems to support the traditional thesis that open systems are less likely to use conflict than closed systems, although they do seem to use at least one type of verbal conflict more often.

Ole Holsti and John Sullivan's investigation of "non-conforming alliance behavior," while focused on a rather distinct type of behavior, does relate—albeit obliquely—to the behavior of open and closed systems. They were concerned with the behavior by France and China toward their respective alliances during the Cold War era, when both countries were felt to be mavericks. De Gaulle's behavior toward NATO and the West, on the one hand, and Mao's behavior toward the Soviet bloc were constant irritants to other leaders in both blocs. Although the individual

---

44 Dina A. Zinnes and Jonathan Wilkenfeld, "An Analysis of Foreign Conflict Behavior of Nations," in *Comparative Foreign Policy,* ed., Wolfram F. Hanrieder (New York: David McKay, 1971), p. 208.

45 Haas, "Societal Approaches to Study of War."

46 Salmore and Hermann, "Effect of Size," p. 28.

47 Quincy Wright, *A Study of War* (Chicago: University of Chicago Press, 1964), pp. 302 and 305.

48 Dougherty and Pfaltzgraff, *Contending Theories,* p. 182.

personalities and goals of de Gaulle and Mao might explain their behavior, Holsti and Sullivan contend that such anecdotal and unsystematic evidence limits generalizations to other nonconforming polities. They hypothesized that France's nonconforming behavior would be confined to a limited number of "issue areas," with little tendency to spill over, whereas China's deviations would tend to spill over into many issue areas, based on the fact that France was an open system while China was a closed one. In open, pluralistic systems, elites are under constraints against sudden changes in policy, and have a limited capability to mobilize *all* groups within the system behind their policies. Systems in which single decision-makers make more of the decisions, however, are likely to have the same trends in their foreign policy in more areas simply because of the mental consistency for the decision-makers. Chinese alienation from the Eastern bloc should then spread to more issue-areas than France's alienation from the West.[49]

By and large, the hypothesis was strongly supported with multiple indicators. Chinese actions toward the Eastern bloc showed that the split between China and the Soviet bloc not only became more serious over time, but occurred in the five issue areas of human resources, nonhuman resources, status, territory, and security. For French actions toward the West, on the other hand, there was little spillover; negative relations were predominant only in the area of security (see Figure 4-1).

Elite attitudes confirmed the pattern. Chinese leaders were consistently critical of the Soviet Union in all five issue areas, while praising them in none; the French were critical toward the West only on the security and status issues. Trade and treaty-making patterns also confirmed the hypothesis, with Chinese intra-bloc trade decreasing and *non*-bloc trade increasing, whereas French trade with the United States underwent very little change. Chinese treaty-making with the Communist bloc declined in all issue areas, but French treaties with the United States actually increased. Thus, France's open system restricted its deviations from the Western bloc, while China's closed system permitted it to exhibit negative behavior toward the members of its bloc in all areas.

UNITED NATIONS, INTERNATIONAL
ORGANIZATION BEHAVIOR

Type of political system also affects international organizational behavior. William Coplin and J. Martin Rochester present data showing that the openness of a political system affects its propensity to use inter-

---

[49] Ole Holsti and John D. Sullivan, "National-International Linkages: France and China as Non-Conforming Alliance Members," in *Linkage Politics,* ed. James N. Rosenau (New York: Free Press, 1969).

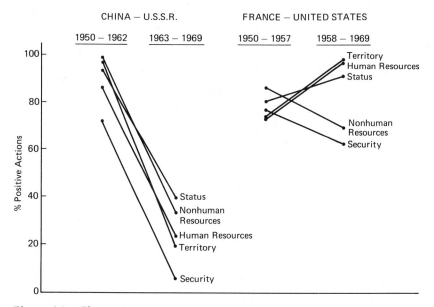

Figure 4-1. Change in positive actions, China-U.S.S.R. and France-U.S.

national courts or general international organizations. The Permanent Court of International Justice and the International Court of Justice are more likely to be used over the League or the United Nations by open political systems, and the tendency was more pronounced in the interwar period (League and PCIJ) than in the postwar period (U.N. and ICJ). Not only do open systems tend to use these organizations more, but they initiate more actions: open systems are more likely to bring cases before these four institutions than are closed systems.[50]

CONCLUSION

The type of a nation's government, therefore, does relate to its foreign policy. That it does, supports much traditional liberal thought about democracy as well as more recent formulations like Rosenau's "pre-theory." In terms of Rosenau's hypothesis, McGowan's study on Africa is to be noted for what it says about the difference between attribute theory and other theories such as "distance" theory (Chapter 5, 6, and 8). McGowan's study of the behavior of African states toward the two major blocs in the Cold War was, on the surface, a test of several pre-theory

[50] Coplin and Rochester, "Permanent Court of International Justice," p. 534.

variables, including open-closed. The interpretation of his findings, however, is subject to serious question.[51]

A behavioral variable McGowan called "interaction with the Communist bloc" was indexed by several measures: economic technicians in the Soviet Union, credits and grants from the Soviet Union, students trained in the East, trade.[52] The open-closed variable did correlate on two measures (government control of trade unions and freedom of the press) with the bloc interaction index: closed systems interacted more with the Soviet Union. Though superficially this conclusion seems to support attribute theory, the real reason these countries had greater interaction with the Soviet Union was not necessarily because they are closed systems but because the Soviet system is also closed. In other words, their interaction is high because both countries are similar, possessing closed systems, and not because Country X has a specific attribute. The distinction is crucial. If national attribute theory were the operative reason, then closed systems would act in similar ways; the data in McGowan's study show that closed systems interacted in certain patterned ways with another closed system, whereas the open systems acted differently toward that closed system (the Communist bloc). The explanation for the behavior therefore may be *distance* on ideology between the systems, not merely the country's attribute.

Type of government, even so, does make a difference in a country's foreign policy, although that variable alone—like size and wealth—does not have a drastic influence. Open systems are more cooperative, partake in slightly fewer wars on the average, and have foreign policies that are more compartmentalized, with less spillover—at least in the area of behavior within an alliance. They are also more frequent users, and supporters, of international organs for adjudication, and rely on the court systems more than on international membership bodies such as the United Nations. Open and closed systems, therefore, possess quite distinct foreign policy patterns, though these patterns cannot be *accurately* predicted from the governmental system variable alone.

Social and Political Stability

Perhaps more than any other attribute, the stability of a nation's social and political system has been viewed as a crucial variable affecting

[51] Patrick McGowan, "Africa and Non-Alignment: A Comparative Study of Foreign Policy," *International Studies Quarterly* 12 (September, 1968), pp. 262–95.

[52] See appendix, paragraph B, for discussion of the validity of McGowan's index and validity in general.

its foreign affairs. The common hypothesis is that the greater the domestic unrest, the greater the external conflict, for leaders in trouble internally try to take care of their problems by focusing public attention on an external enemy. National leaders, that is, "use" their international involvement to foster internal unity, a rallying-around-the-flag tactic.

Although certainly a time-worn hypothesis, it became more popular in the middle of the twentieth century, when sociologists began concentrating on the sociology of conflict, arguing that conflict is not entirely bad and that it does serve certain functions. Conflict with an "out-group" *defines* the "in-group," preserves the group as a group—which might have fallen apart had conflict with the out-group not existed. Hypothetically, outside conflict brings about internal cohesion.[53] The question, of course, is which way the causal arrow moves: conflict with another group may lessen within-group conflict, but that is not necessarily equivalent to saying that internal conflict will always force leaders toward foreign conflict in order to reduce domestic unrest. Nonetheless, the studies by Waltz and Wright, cited earlier, and by Alan Whiting and Ernest Haas [54] certainly do rely on the latter hypothesis. Furthermore, as normally posited, the hypothesis views conflict internally in terms of specific acts of civil war, coup d'états, revolutions, or other phenomena directly injurious to the ruling elite or government.

A much broader hypothesis can be formulated, however, that views not only specific acts of political or social unrest, but also general societal stresses or strains as potential causes of external adventures or conflict. Societies in times of internal strain may simply react to external situations in one way and in another when domestic harmony prevails. The first hypothesis—involving the factor of domestic unrest—views leaders reacting rationally to their internal problems; the second formulation—involving the factor of domestic stress—implies an organizational framework. The conclusions to be drawn from both hypotheses are—theoretically—the same. Although both formulations are equally logical, the greatest interest has focused on the first: physical unrest within societies.

INTERNAL CONFLICT: GENERAL

Pitirim Sorokin investigated the relation between internal disturbances and international war for several countries and empires from the twelfth to the twentieth centuries.[55] Sorokin claims that no correlation exists, but in analyzing his data there does appear to be some connection

---

53 Lewis Coser, *The Functions of Social Conflict* (New York: The Free Press, 1956).

54 Allen S. Whiting and Ernest B. Haas, *Dynamics of International Relations* (New York: McGraw-Hill, 1956).

55 Pitirim Sorokin, *Society, Culture, and Personality: Their Structures and Dynamics* (New York: Harper & Row, 1947), p. 484.

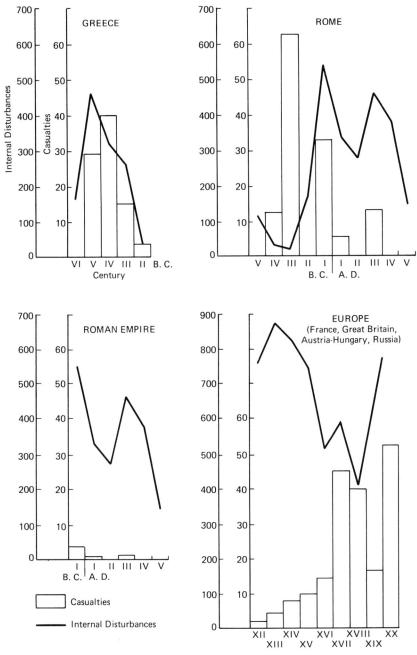

Source: Pitirim Sorokin, *Society, Culture, and Personality: Their Structures and Dynamics* (New York: Harper & Row, 1947), p. 484.

Figure 4-2. Relative war magnitude by casualties and internal disturbances.

between the two phenomena (Figure 4-2). With the exception of the seventeenth century, internal disturbances were declining in the European countries he investigated from the thirteenth to the eighteenth century; at the same time casualities and army strength were both increasing. Likewise his data show war decreasing in the nineteenth century, when disturbances increase. Yet the data he presents concerning Greece and the Roman empire show generally a positive relationship, especially for Rome. Interpretation of these data is very difficult because all cases can be viewed as support for the hypothesis. For the European countries, one could argue that the increased army strength and concomitant casualties were in fact effective in reducing internal disturbances. For the Greek and Roman empires, however, one could also argue that increased casualties were brought about by increased internal disturbances and that when those dropped off, casualties likewise dropped off. In other words, interpreting data of this nature, aggregated into such long time periods, is extremely difficult. Nonetheless, if nothing else, the two variables do appear to be related to one another, even if we cannot tease out the direction of causality.

GENERAL: CROSS-SECTIONAL

Sorokin's study is handicapped because, in dealing with vast periods of history, he was forced to use very approximate data. There is also the question about the advisability of aggregating the data by century (in which it is impossible to see what is happening *within* each of the centuries).[56] More recently, Rummel reopened the investigation of the hypothesis with a study of seventy-seven nations for the years 1955 to 1957. Though primarily concerned with delineating the dimensions of foreign and domestic conflict behavior, Rummel also investigated whether countries with high domestic conflict also exhibited high foreign conflict. He measured internal conflict by such indicators as assassinations, strikes, purges, and riots, and external conflict by such indicators as negative sanctions, protests, expulsions, threats, and troop movements, all data coming from public sources (*New York Times, Deadline Data, Facts on File*).

Rummel found three different dimensions of both foreign and domestic conflict. The domestic dimensions were turmoil, revolution, and subversion; the foreign were war, diplomacy, and belligerency.[57] He

---

56 See appendix, paragraph A.2.

57 The dimensions from the factor analysis (see appendix, paragraph C) mean, for instance, that countries scoring high on military acts and mobilizations—the war dimension—were very likely to be low on other foreign conflict behavior, such as severing relations and negative sanctions, labeled the "belligerency" dimension by Rummel.

determined that the foreign dimensions were almost completely independent of the domestic dimensions, that is, nations with high scores on any of the three internal dimensions of conflict did not necessarily have high scores on the foreign conflict dimensions. Of the forty countries scoring high on any of the three domestic or three foreign dimensions, only ten had high scores on *both* domestic and foreign measures; the remaining thirty did not cross this "boundary" at all (Table 4-2). The traditional hypothesis would suggest that countries *very* high on internal conflict should be high on external conflict. Of the seven states scoring high on *two or more* dimensions of domestic unrest, only two—India and

Table 4-2. Countries with High Scores on Domestic and Foreign Dimensions of Conflict, 1955-1957

Domestic Dimensions			Foreign Dimensions		
Turmoil	*Revolution*	*Subversion*	*War*	*Diplomacy*	*Belligerency*
France (3.16)	Argentina (4.07)	Cuba (4.08)	Israel (3.20)	U.S.S.R. (3.85)	Egypt (3.80)
Argentina (3.00)	China (2.69)	Burma (4.08)	Egypt (3.19)	U.S. (2.73)	Jordan (3.80)
India (2.25)	India (2.69)	Philippines (4.08)	France (3.18)	Dom. Rep. (2.65)	Pakistan (3.80)
Pakistan (1.72)	Guatemala (2.16)	Argentina (2.61)	U.K. (3.18)	Argentina (2.31)	Afghanistan (1.71)
Guatemala (1.71)	Brazil (1.85)	Indonesia (2.61)	Hungary (2.27)	Venezuela (2.31)	Chile (1.71)
Haiti (1.71)	Paraguay (1.85)	Columbia (1.14)	U.S.S.R. (2.27)	Hungary (1.61)	Rep. of China (1.71)
South Africa (1.68)	Hungary (1.62)	Costa Rica (1.14)	Syria (2.24)	Sweden (1.61)	W. Germany (1.71)
Iraq (1.54)	Syria (1.62)	India (1.14)	Yemen (1.31)	Iraq (1.19)	India (1.71)
Italy (1.44)	Haiti (1.54)	Lebanon (1.14)	Nicaragua (1.09)	Yugoslavia (1.19)	Iraq (1.71)
Jordan (1.44)	Egypt (1.09)				Peru (1.71)
cuba (1.41)	Burma (1.00)				Syria (1.71)
Indonesia (1.30)	Honduras (1.00)				
Poland (1.14)	Indonesia (1.00)				
Chile (1.11)					

From Rudolph J. Rummel, "Dimensions of Conflict Behavior Within and Between Nations," in *Conflict Behavior and Linkage Politics,* ed. Jonathan Wilkenfeld (David McKay Company, Inc., 1973), p. 85.

Argentina—scored among the higher countries on any of the three foreign conflict dimensions. In other words, only two of the twenty-four countries with high foreign conflict in the years 1955 to 1957 also had serious internal unrest, and both of these scored high on only one of the three foreign conflict dimensions. Rummel concluded that "the results . . . show that domestic peace occurs whether or not foreign conflict is present." [58]

Using different data (from their *Cross Polity Survey*) and the same basic technique as Rummel (factor analysis), Phillip Gregg and Arthur Banks confirmed that two measures indexing foreign conflict, expelling ambassadors and the number of foreign killed, fall on different factor dimensions than the measures of domestic conflict, indicating that countries high on expulsion will not necessarily be high on foreign killed.[59] Further, Raymond Tanter replicated Rummel's study for 1958 to 1960, and then combined both data sets to investigate the relationship over a six-year period.[60] He found almost no relationship between the two different phenomena. Tanter uncovered two dimensions of internal conflict (as opposed to Rummel's three) but there was little relation between the two and the existence of external conflict. Although when the variables of protests and severance of relations during the 1958-1960 period were correlated with internal demonstrations, revolutions, and guerrilla warfare between 1955 and 1957, some slight relationships emerged, nonetheless Tanter's study served for the most part as a general confirmation of Rummel's original findings.

Warren Phillips also illustrated the essentially secondary role that internal unrest plays. In an intriguing analysis, Phillips demonstrated that conflict received from the environment correlates with conflict sent to the environment. But an analysis of the deviations of conflict *sent* from conflict *received* showed that countries initiating levels of military violence higher than that which they received also had high levels of domestic violence that resulted in deaths. Other forms of domestic unrest such as unemployment and cost of living were also related, although less

[58] Rudolph J. Rummel, "Dimensions of Conflict Behavior within and between Nations," *General Systems: Yearbook of the Society for General Systems Research* 8 (1963), p. 23. Rummel's regression analysis also showed that foreign and domestic conflict were unrelated to each other. The dimensions of war and diplomacy correlated at .26, and belligerency at .31 with the three domestic dimensions combined, but the statistics showed that the predictions from domestic to foreign would be poor. For a critique of Rummel's basic research design, which may apply to many other empirical studies, see appendix, paragraph E.

[59] Phillip M. Gregg and Arthur S. Banks, "Dimensions of Political Systems: Factor Analysis of *A Cross-Polity Survey*," *American Political Science Review* 59 (September, 1965), pp. 602–14.

[60] Raymond Tanter, "Dimensions of Conflict Behavior within and between Nations, 1958–1960," *Journal of Conflict Resolution* 10 (March, 1966), pp. 41–64.

strongly, to higher levels of military violence and very moderately to other, non-violent forms of conflict.[61]

SINGLE COUNTRY: LONGITUDINAL

Robert Burrowes and Bertram Spector tested the hypothesis of a relationship between domestic and external conflict in a dynamic situation for Syria for the years 1961 to 1967.[62] Their overall results, however, were similar to earlier ones. Statistical correlations were low and generally negative: as conflict indicators in one domain were increasing those in the other were decreasing. Of five separate dimensions of foreign behavior, only two—indirect conflict (such as informal protests and threats) and minor agreements—related to the independent variables of domestic conflict.

Scholars of contemporary China have often argued that its belligerent foreign policy is a function of its internal problems. Andres Onate investigated the hypothesis for the People's Republic of China from 1950 to 1970 and discovered that both on an annual and a quarterly basis there was a very moderate relationship between total amount of weighted internal conflict and total amount of weighted external conflict (Onate did not deal with dimensions extracted from factor analysis for either domain).[63] Of most interest was the fact that in lagging each domain behind the other, he found that domestic conflict seemed more strongly associated with foreign conflict in *previous* time periods (yearly and quarterly) than the reverse. Nonetheless, the relationships, although significant statistically, were—as Onate noted—moderate.

MULTI-COUNTRY: LONGITUDINAL

Wilkenfeld investigated the relations between six Middle East countries, including Syria, for twenty years, beginning in 1948. He compared the strength of internal unrest in one country against the effect of other nations' behavior toward it. Domestic conflict was a significant factor, but it was secondary to the impact the conflictual actions of other coun-

[61] Warren R. Phillips, "The Conflict Environment of Nations: A Study of Conflict Inputs to Nations in 1963," in *Conflict Behavior and Linkage Politics*, ed. Jonathan Wilkenfeld (New York: David McKay, 1973), pp. 124–47.

[62] Robert Burrowes and Bertram Spector, "The Strength and Direction of Relationships between Domestic and External Conflict and Cooperation, Syria: 1961–1967," in *Conflict Behavior and Linkage Politics*, ed. Jonathan Wilkenfeld (New York: David McKay, 1973).

[63] Andres Onate, "The Conflict Interactions of the People's Republic of China, 1950–1970," *Journal of Conflict Resolution* 18 (December, 1974), pp. 578–94.

tries had on it. Of even greater interest, however, was the direction of
the effect. Prior governmental instability in Israel, for example, led to
a *decrease* in Israeli foreign hostility, whereas for the Arabs, prior and
current domestic violence led to an increase in foreign hostility. On the
whole, however, regardless of the direction of the effect, the impact of
internal instability was moderate and secondary.[64]

Treating countries over time in a dynamic sense, therefore, shows
some relationship between internal disturbances and foreign conflict,
although it is true that *changes* from time period to time period were
not examined. The negative correlations in the Burrowes and Spector
study of Syria may mean that the *trend* of one dimension is up while
the trend of the other is down. The positive correlations in some of the
other dynamic studies, on the other hand, may mean merely that both
dimensions were—for other reasons—moving up or down through time.
There is no way of knowing whether the fluctuations around the trends
are moving in tandem or not.[65]

INTERNAL CONFLICT AND TYPE OF GOVERNMENT:
THE AGGREGATION PROBLEM

None of these studies are highly supportive of the traditional hypothesis concerning domestic unrest and foreign conflict. In almost every
instance there were relations between the two dimensions, but they were
small. Further, these studies say little about the relationship as possibly
mediated by other variables. We will return later to more explicit testing of multiple attributes, but several studies should be noted here for
what they say about the basic internal-external relationship. Wilkenfeld,
for instance, argues that Rummel was facilitated in reaching his conclusion because he did not bother to "differentiate between the nations
under consideration." Wilkenfeld disaggregated the seventy-seven nations analyzed by Rummel by introducing the variable of type of government to "determine whether type of nation has any bearing on the
relationship between internal and external conflict behavior." [66] Wilkenfeld's grouping of countries into personalist, centrist, and polyarchic has
already been discussed. He analyzed each group separately and found
a small number of relationships. For instance, in the personalist group,
the dimensions of turmoil and subversive internal unrest were related

[64] Jonathan Wilkenfeld, Virginia Lee Lussier, and Dale Tahtinen, "Conflict Interactions in the Middle East, 1949–1967," *Journal of Conflict Resolution* 16 (June, 1972),
pp. 135–54.

[65] For further analysis of this problem, see appendix, paragraph D.

[66] Jonathan Wilkenfeld, "Domestic and Foreign Behavior of Nations," *Journal of
Peace Research* 5 (No. 1, 1968), p. 57.

to the dimension of diplomatic foreign conflict; in the centrist group, turmoil was related to both belligerency and diplomatic foreign conflict; and revolutionary internal unrest was related to war. In the polyarchic group, turmoil was related to war whereas revolutionary internal unrest was related to belligerent foreign conflict. The specifics of each of these relations are not particularly worth noting, because there seems to be no general pattern. The most important finding, however, was Wilkenfeld's conclusion that the relation between internal and external conflict was being partly hidden by aggregating all countries.

In subsequent analyses, Wilkenfeld and Zinnes pursued the subject with more and increasingly complex models.[67] On the whole the results confirmed that domestic conflict does not overwhelmingly relate to foreign conflict with all nations combined. The results did show that the foreign conflict dimension of belligerency—antiforeign demonstrations, severing relations, and negative sanctions—is moderately related to domestic conflict. Otherwise, foreign conflict seemed overwhelmingly related to previous levels of foreign conflict, with one exception: when there is no foreign conflict and no domestic conflict, the tendency will be to remain at the low level of foreign conflict; the same holds true for medium levels of each. When domestic conflict is at a high level, however, the situation changes:

When domestic conflict becomes extremely intense it would seem more reasonable to argue that there is a greater likelihood that a state will retreat from its foreign engagements in order to handle the situation at home. Given that a state had been involved in foreign conflict at level two, if the domestic conflict situation reaches level two one would expect an attempt to retreat to at least level one of foreign conflict behavior.[68]

Disaggregating all seventy-four countries into types, they again found some small and very particular relations. With only a simple one-year lag, domestic conflict in personalist countries seemed almost unrelated to foreign conflict, whereas belligerency related to turmoil for the centrist and to internal war for the polyarchic group.[69] Thus, of eighteen possibilities only two were significant. However, in later applying five other models, Wilkenfeld found that for centrist and polyarchic groups the best predictor by far of foreign conflict was the previous level of foreign conflict, whereas for the personalist group this relationship was less strong; to the contrary, domestic conflict did affect level of foreign con-

---

[67] Zinnes and Wilkenfeld, "Analysis of Foreign Conflict Behavior"; Jonathan Wilkenfeld, "Models for the Analysis of Foreign Conflict Behavior of States," in *Peace, War, and Numbers,* ed. Bruce M. Russett (Beverly Hills: Sage Publications, 1972).

[68] Zinnes and Wilkenfeld, "Analysis of Foreign Conflict Behavior," p. 184.

[69] Ibid., pp. 204–205.

flict in the personalist group, but this was limited almost entirely to belligerence, especially with a two-year lag between domestic and foreign conflict. In sum, as Wilkenfeld concluded, "domestic conflict in general appears to be only minimally related to foreign conflict behavior." [70]

John Collins pushed this research strategy one step further by looking at thirty-three African countries and utilizing a more extensive data-collection procedure to reflect more accurately both internal and external conflict within that one group.[71] He found very high correlations between several domestic and foreign dimensions. The best predicted foreign conflict variables were all nonviolent behaviors: negative communications such as complaints about subversive activities; antiforeign unofficial activity such as antiforeign riots, demonstrations, and boycotts; and negative behavior such as closing off borders and expelling foreigners. The worst predicted foreign conflict variables were "hostile policies" (such as complaints about threatening military moves or violations of air space) and "general criticism" (very generalized, vague criticism of another country, such as on ideological grounds).

The most consistent predictors to foreign conflict were the number of people killed in domestic violence and domestic suppression—both involving governmental action against the populace as opposed to citizen unrest directed against the government. This suggests that at least in this subset of African countries, the internal-external relation is a very narrow one where governments involved in domestic suppression will engage in only a specific kind of foreign conflict, namely, low-level violent or nonviolent activity.

INTERNAL STRESS AND STRAIN

As noted earlier, internal unrest, as reflected in physical acts of violence or disorder, constitute only one method of measuring the concept. A much broader conception would view overall societal stress and strain as promoting a more aggressive foreign policy. Haas investigated ten countries from 1900 to 1960, focusing primarily on war and preparation for war, and using independent measures such as unemployment, industrialization, homicide, suicide, and alcoholism death rates.[72] He found

[70] Wilkenfeld, "Models for Analysis," p. 298.

[71] John Collins, "Foreign Conflict Behavior and Domestic Disorder in Africa," in *Conflict Behavior and Linkage Politics*, ed. Jonathan Wilkenfeld (New York: David McKay, 1973).

[72] Michael Haas, "Social Change and National Aggressiveness, 1900–1960," in *Quantitative International Politics: Insights and Evidence*, ed. J. David Singer (New York: Free Press, 1968), pp. 215–45.

that suicide rates did correlate with war aggressiveness and that alcoholism correlated with military expenditures. More generally, he contended that suicide, homicide, and alcoholism related to the military arm of statecraft, though the relationships were again very small. As Haas noted, the overall theory of internal stresses and strains affecting external military behavior and aggressiveness is only very moderately supported.

To the two internal factors isolated by Tanter—turmoil and internal war—Louis Terrel added the measures of societal frustration and social cleavage, and related them to the defense budget (as a percent of GNP) and percent of the population under arms. His findings confirmed the earlier studies.[73] All four domestic variables combined, according to Terrel, accounted for only 13 percent of the variation in GNP devoted to the defense budget, and 11 percent of the variation in men under arms. In addition, one relationship was negative, the opposite of that expected: The greater the internal war, turmoil and social cleavage, the lower the military manpower levels.

Defining internal unrest or change in an even broader sense, Nazli Choucri and Robert North have investigated the effect of changes in population and technology on certain military patterns such as defense expenditure and men under arms. While the major powers showed strong linkages between internal pressures and external violence and changes in defense budget, examination of the same process for the Scandinavian countries and the Netherlands disclosed only weak links, primarily in the Swedish and Norwegian cases.[74]

CONCLUSION

In sum, conflict, unrest, or disorder within a state does affect its foreign policy, but the relationship is neither clear nor determined. It can safely be said, however, that their overall effect appears to be low. There are different kinds of both domestic and foreign conflict, and one potentially intervening variable appears to be the type of government. There has been a tendency for many studies to point out that "no" relationship exists between internal and external conflict when, in fact, they do report statistical correlations of, admittedly, very moderate proportions. However, Collins's study of African states reports very high relationships, but

[73] Louis Terrel, "Societal Stress, Political Instability, and Levels of Military Effort," *Journal of Conflict Resolution* 15 (September, 1971), pp. 329–46.

[74] Nazli Choucri and Robert C. North, "In Search of Peace Systems: Scandinavia and the Netherlands, 1870–1970," in *Peace, War, and Numbers*, ed. Bruce Russett (Beverly Hills: Sage Publications, 1972); Nazli Choucri and Robert C. North, "Dynamics of International Conflict: Some Policy Implications of Population, Resources, and Technology," *World Politics* 24 (Spring supplement, 1972), pp. 80–122.

once again these are limited to only a few of his several dimensions of domestic and foreign conflict. His findings would suggest that the relationship is stronger in the less-developed countries, a finding we will see confirmed in the next section with a further description of Terrel's study. Also, using Russett's factor scores on economic development [75] it becomes clear that *if* economic development is a crucial factor, the relationship should become stronger as we move from the polyarchic to the centrist to the personalist groups in Wilkenfeld's studies because we are dropping in overall levels of economic development.[76] The findings here are mixed, but they tend to support that assertion. Though Wilkenfeld and Zinnes found no relation between domestic and foreign conflict for the personalist group and very moderate links for the other two groups, Wilkenfeld later applied different time models and showed that past foreign conflict predicted better to present foreign conflict for the centrist and polyarchic group but less so for the personalist; for the latter, domestic did appear to relate to foreign conflict, especially with a two-year lag.[77]

Furthermore, in no case was violent foreign conflict a result of domestic unrest. In instances where relationships did show up, it was either some type of belligerent foreign conflict (severing relations, negative sanctions) or low-level violent conflict directed by citizens and not by the government. Nonetheless, even here, with the one exception of Collins's study of African countries, the relationships remained consistently low. Also, when compared with other variables, internal unrest invariably took a second place in importance.

Multiple Attributes

The obvious drawback of the above analyses is the implicit simple model which assumes that individual attributes of a nation should strongly predict differences in its international behavior. The usual reaction to studies showing a small relation between single attributes

---

[75] Russett, *International Regions and International System*, pp. 28–30.

[76] Using Russett's data, and making cutting points at scores of −1.00, .00, and +1.00, the countries distribute in the following manner (eight countries could not be categorized, but it is unlikely they could change the overall result):

Governmental Type	Economic Development		
	Low	*Medium*	*High*
Personalist	6	9	0
Centrist	3	14	1
Polyarchic	3	16	14

[77] Wilkenfeld, "Models for Analysis."

and foreign policy behavior is that *all* attributes must be considered, which implies the use of an *additive* model whereby variation in foreign policy is viewed as a result of a series of attributes. The results of using such a model show, however, that merely piling attributes on top of one another does not help much, and even complicating the relationships using multiple variables in nonadditive models also fails to account for much more of the variation in foreign policy.

SIMPLE ADDITIVE MODELS

Rummel, for example, tested eleven different hypotheses concerning relations between specific national attributes and foreign conflict behavior. He concluded that the eleven "hypothesized correlates of foreign conflict behavior acting singly *or in combination or with the effects of other variables controlled* are little related to a nation's foreign conflict behavior." [78] Rummel also cites two other studies supporting that general conclusion.

David Moore investigated the impact of attributes on seven generalized foreign policy behaviors, and while some differences occurred within different groups (categorized by size, wealth, and accountability), only simple patterns emerged. For instance, conflict (protests, threats, and accusations) was related only to size; and for participation, only size and development were potent predictors, and they were strong across all groups of countries. [79]

In Skrein's large study, the strongest predictors were development, size, type of political system, and internal political violence; with all attributes combined, the greatest amount of variation accounted for was 30 percent. [80] Salmore and Hermann found the multiple effects of size, development, and political system were not much greater than when each was taken separately. [81] Total numbers of actions were linked primarily to size (larger countries used more of almost every kind of behavior), but the variation accounted for by all three variables combined was small (12 percent). In considering types of behavior, they found that open, large, and developed systems used less offensive verbal conflict and more verbal cooperation than closed, small, and undeveloped systems. In each case, the type of system was the most important variable, but even all

[78] Rummel, "Relationship between National Attributes," p. 213. Emphasis added.

[79] David W. Moore, "Governmental and Societal Influences on Foreign Policy in Open and Closed Nations," in *Comparing Foreign Policies: Theories, Findings, and Methods,* ed. James N. Rosenau (New York: Wiley, 1974).

[80] Skrein, "National Attributes and Foreign Policy Output," p. 65; this applies only to behaviors other than gross levels.

[81] Salmore and Hermann, "Effect of Size."

three variables combined did not do much better in predicting foreign behaviors than the variables taken singly. The largest amount of variation explained was only 15 percent.

Kean and McGowan argue that size and modernization are mediated by the dimensions of *resources* and *needs*. Their argument is not entirely convincing, however, given the high correlations among their independent variables ("resources" correlates with both size and modernization, and "needs" correlates with modernization). What is of note is that in their numerous analyses only two of the four independent variables account for the majority of explained variation in the dependent variables, all representing participation behaviors.[82] While "resources" (gross domestic product) does appear to be the most potent overall explanatory variable, its high correlation with both size and modernization raises some doubt as to the theoretical import—or difference—between the three variables. The multiple effect of all four variables was always higher, but it was seldom extraordinary.

In a sense, even the additive model, which requires that numerous attributes be combined, is itself very simple because no specific linkages among the attributes and foreign policy are systematically spelled out. Leo Hazelwood postulated a two-step process wherein the attribute of unrest leads to governmental response and both then combine to produce various levels of foreign conflict. More specifically, rapid short-term economic growth, in addition to population, social, and ethnic diversity, represents a stress that will become manifested over time in turmoil— what Hazelwood refers to as "relatively unorganized, sporadic . . . low intensity, short duration, limited geographical" conflict.

Using Tanter's foreign conflict data for 1958-1960, Hazelwood formulated several models, and finally found population diversity, economic expansion, and turmoil consistently related to the responses of technological capacity to coerce, relative size of armed forces, and budget growth. In turn, budget growth and, especially, size of the armed forces were related to all three measures of foreign conflict. Hazelwood concluded that the method of governmental response makes a major difference in whether systemic stress will be externalized. In other words, the link from internal events to external events is not a simple one, but rather must work itself through various intervening variables. Changes in systemic stress, such as population diversity and turmoil, may be medi-

---

[82] Kean and McGowan, "National Attributes and Foreign Policy Participation." Their dependent variables—of a participation type—were: total number of event interactions as calculated by WEIS for each country, regional number of actions measured by WEIS, the number of headquarters and subsidiary offices of international governmental and nongovernmental organizations located in each state, and the number of targets toward which each state directed five or more event interactions for the 1966–1969 period.

ated by how much the government is able to put into capping that stress; if the size of the military is large, this will have a dampening effect on external belligerent conflict.[83]

Hazelwood's study illustrates the complexity involved in going beyond bivariate or even simple multivariate designs, both of which are too gross to capture the intricacies involved. The study also shows, however, the difficulty and complexity of trying to untangle the relationships. But perhaps the most important lesson from the multivariate analyses is that foreign policy cannot be much better understood even when several different clusters of attributes are combined. The argument that one must look at all the attributes of a nation to better understand its foreign policy is not particularly well-supported. In almost every instance, multiple attributes did little or no better than single attributes taken separately. This assertion rests, of course, on the supposition that size, wealth, type of political system, and internal conflict or unrest tap the primary attributes of nation-states, and that the present measurements of these dimensions have tapped the underlying phenomena.

Conclusion

THEORETICAL IMPLICATIONS

Simple theoretical linkages between internal attributes, or domestic sources, and external behavior do not exist. Rather, very specific linkages need to be formulated into the theoretical structure of national attribute theory, and even these—the research here strongly suggests—do not play a *large* part in differential foreign policy behavior.

Economic development (wealth) and size appear to be the strongest influences across more types of foreign policy, though the link is not one that many would have thought existed. To state the point in another way, while large and developed states contribute their share of tragedy to the world community, in terms of their total foreign policy output they tend to be proportionally more cooperative and less conflictual than small undeveloped states. When they do use conflict, they seem more likely to resort to its verbal rather than its physical form.

The second most consistently researched variable, after size and wealth, was internal disorder, conflict, or turmoil. The findings show that a *generalized* link between various measures of internal conflict and foreign policy is not supported. When linkages were *specified*—either in

[83] Leo A. Hazelwood, "Externalizing Systemic Stress: International Conflict as Adaptive Behavior," in *Conflict Behavior and Linkage Politics*, ed. Jonathan Wilkenfeld (New York: David McKay, 1973), pp. 148–90.

terms of types of conflict, types of countries, regions of the world, or when several variables of internal stress were combined—more significant relationships appeared with foreign conflict.

In this regard, several interesting observations can be made concerning the relationship between internal and external conflict. First, as Wilkenfeld and Zinnes point out, countries experiencing a *great* degree of internal instability seem to reduce their foreign conflict levels, a direct contradiction of the traditionally held theory. Second, when comparing the effect of internal instability with that of other variables on foreign conflict, Wilkenfeld found it consistently had much less impact; the actions of other countries aimed at a specific target country had a much greater influence on variation in that country's foreign policy than internal instability. East and Gregg also found that compared with certain "international situation" variables, internal instability was much less important. Third, although some minor contradictions to this conclusion have been pointed out, there seems to be a pattern whereby the relationship between internal and external conflict was greater and more consistent in the less developed countries. Even in the Wilkenfeld and Zinnes study, which contradicted this finding when using a one-year lag, the personalist group—primarily low developed—showed a slight link between turmoil and diplomatic conflict. This observation leads to a fourth observation, namely, that the type of foreign conflict most consistently linked to internal disruption was either verbal or low-level physical conflict; in no instance was war, warlike acts, or serious physical violence related to the internal situation. Finally, in addition to the evidence suggesting that *very high* levels of domestic unrest lead to decreased foreign conflict was the suggestion by Onate's study of China that in certain circumstances domestic unrest actually increases after the occurrence of external conflict, another direct contradiction of traditional theory. These studies, however, help to sort out the specific domains that different hypotheses are able to cover, and thereby make the theory more specific and applicable.

The role of the political system has not been as extensively researched as either size and wealth or internal conflict. Evidence that does exist lends credence to the argument of democratic theorists who see "good" flowing from open, democratic systems. For the most part the open systems engage in less overall conflict (of different types) than do closed systems, both in the long and short run.[84] Open systems are also much more positively disposed to international organizations.[85]

[84] Wright, *Study of War;* Salmore and Hermann, "Effect of Size"; Wilkenfeld and Zinnes, "Analysis of Foreign Conflict Behavior"; East and Gregg, "Factors Influencing Cooperation"; Skrein, "National Attributes and Foreign Policy Output."

[85] Alker, "Supranationalism in United Nations"; Clark et al., "National Attributes."

In sum, on all three dimensions, national attributes are related to foreign policy, and in numerous cases the findings dovetail to a remarkable degree, despite different data sources and numerical manipulation. Thus, theories relating national attributes and domestic sources to foreign policy carry some validity, but it cannot be emphasized too often that the consistency in the findings was also a consistency of very small relationships. Perhaps the most interesting finding to emerge, therefore, is not the strength of national attributes, but the similarity of the effects that national attributes have.

National attribute theory, it should be clear by now, is in reality a very simple one. The theoretical linkage drawn from attributes to foreign behavior is not difficult to understand or plot out. But perhaps it is this simplicity in the way attributes have been studied in the past that results in the small relations emerging from the empirical studies. It is possible that attributes conceived in slightly more complex ways might produce more significant findings.

One area of research is exemplified by Choucri and North, namely, the dynamic changes within societies and their impact on foreign behavior. Although they did find such internal changes to be important in some instances, they also discovered that changes in national attributes were secondary when compared with the importance of systemic variables such as alliance commitments.[86] No doubt data limitations have kept research in this dynamic area limited, for data on attributes across long periods of time are difficult to come by. Even so, many argue that such large-scale attributes as population and economic growth simply do not change that much, and therefore, their variation cannot have much effect on substantial changes in foreign policy. Nonetheless, theoretically the idea that *changes* in attributes will affect behavior is more pleasing than the simple, gross attribute-behavior linkage because it views national systems as changing, living entities.

But many authors have recognized that attributes of sources other than those investigated here may play a role. Burrowes and Spector, for instance, suggest that a "state of mind" variable might be useful.[87] David Wilkinson's concept of "will" might also be conceptualized as a national attribute.[88] Further, McGowan and Shapiro cite a study by Ivo Feierabend and Rosalind Feierabend showing a negative correlation between the "need for achievement" and foreign conflict for modern nations and

---

[86] Nazli Choucri and Robert C. North, "The Determinants of International Violence," *Peace Research Society Papers* 12 (1969), pp. 33–63.

[87] Burrowes and Spector, "Strength and Direction of Relationships," p. 316.

[88] David O. Wilkinson, *Comparative Foreign Relations: Framework and Methods* (Belmont, Calif.: Dickenson Publishing, 1969).

a positive correlation for middle- and low-modern nations.[89] Another potential attribute of importance might be the "density" (or "crowding") present in a national system despite one study indicating otherwise. Stuart Bremer, J. David Singer, and Urs Laterbacher found that no relation existed between density and war proneness from 1820 to the middle of this century, even controlling for technological development and other variables. They did find, however, that urbanizing nations tended to initiate wars more often, but suggested that the relation was most likely a function of industrialization (similar to development or wealth) and not density.[90]

Another intriguing possibility lies in the data suggested by Kal Holsti. Noting that the concept of "role" has not often been used in international relations—in spite of its wide popularity and utility in other social sciences —Holsti asks:

Are there gradations in the specificity and structure of policymakers' national role conceptions? If so, what are the likely consequences for foreign policy decisions and actions? Under what conditions will knowledge of national role conceptions permit us to explain or predict typical forms of diplomatic behavior? [91]

Holsti isolated a large number of role perceptions of states—faithful ally, protector, active independent, anti-imperalist agent—and suggests that one hypothesis emerging from his data (a content analysis of leader's statements from seventy-one countries) is that countries with a larger number of well-developed role conceptions tend to be more active in the international system or within regional groupings.[92] More active countries were more than likely to have a larger number of role conceptions, whereas less active nations had fewer role conceptions. This hypothesis is not unlike the one linking size and development with level of activity; unfortunately, the *pattern* of foreign activity is still left unexplained. In fact, relating the number of role conceptions for eighteen countries to

[89] Ivo Feierabend and Rosalind Feierabend, "Level of Development and International Behavior," in *Foreign Policy and the Developing Nation,* ed. R. Butwell (Lexington: University of Kentucky Press, 1969), pp. 150–51; cited in Patrick J. McGowan and Howard B. Shapiro, *The Comparative Study of Foreign Policy: A Survey of Scientific Findings* (Beverly Hills: Sage Publications, 1973), p. 128.

[90] Stuart Bremer, J. David Singer, and Urs Laterbacher, "The Population Density and War Proneness of European Nations, 1816–1965," *Comparative Political Studies* 6 (October, 1973), pp. 329–48.

[91] K. J. Holsti, "National Role Conceptions in the Study of Foreign Policy," *International Studies Quarterly* 14 (September, 1970), p. 236.

[92] Using McClelland's WEIS data and calculating the percent of actions that each country contributed to the world output, Holsti's weighted number of role conceptions does relate to each country's amount of action in the international system for 1966–1968.

the percentage of their conflict behavior for the year 1966 produced an insignificant and negative correlation.[93] Perhaps *type* of role is more important than number of roles held by a state.

These can be no more than suggestions as to potential attributes that are more difficult to measure but that may provide a greater payoff for linking domestic sources to foreign policy. A word of caution should be injected, however. As A. F. K. Organski points out in his discussion of national "power," many of the more nebulous concepts traditionally used to describe states are not necessarily independent dimensions.[94] National "morale," he notes, may be quite closely related to objective measures of power, and national unity might also be found related to other objective measures. Merely to propose "psychological" or "morale" variables as important national attributes, therefore, does not solve the question of whether they are not manifested in other variables. Nor does the enumeration of such variables imply necessarily that these variables—if they could be measured—would account for much of the variation currently left unaccounted for by present national attribute measures.

POLICY IMPLICATIONS

Direct policy implications are not easy to draw from attribute studies because large-scale attributes of nations are hard to manipulate. Gross national product, population, defense expenditures, literacy levels, domestic unrest, and other attributes and domestic sources are very difficult to change, especially within a short time. Policy implications, therefore, fall more into the category of intelligent reactions to existing situations. For instance, the consistent failure to find strong relations between the existence of internal unrest and external conflict in a large number of countries cautions against the too facile assumption that a country's foreign conflict is merely a function of its internal disruptions.

At the same time, the research suggests that there might be ways of distinguishing between "real" and "imagined" conflicts in the international system. Collins's findings, for example, that certain types of foreign conflict among African states was related to specific internal troubles could help national leaders viewing such conflict and attempting to decide what to do about it. If the foreign conflict in question were due to internal sources, then reaction to it would be of a different nature than if it derived from legitimate, honestly perceived interstate dis-

---

[93] Charles McClelland and Gary Hoggard, "Conflict Patterns in the Interactions among Nations," in *International Politics and Foreign Policy: A Reader in Research and Theory,* ed. James Rosenau (New York: Free Press, 1969), p. 720.

[94] A. F. K. Organski, *World Politics* (New York: Knopf, 1958), pp. 207–8.

agreements. For African states, military violence would most likely *not* result from internal disruption, according to Collins's findings, and therefore other states involved—or states concerned with resolving the dispute—would be well advised to use different tactics from those they would employ in situations where nonmilitary conflict was a factor. On the other hand, the foreign behavior labeled "internal interference" was a low-level, though emotional, verbal violence. It appears that this type of foreign behavior among African countries might be more likely meant for internal consumption, and therefore reaction to it should be cognizant of the probable source of the conflict.

Likewise, Holsti and Sullivan's findings suggest that reactions to hostile or negative communications and attitudes from other states should be different depending upon the type of government. Extensive conflict communications received from a closed system might not mean a desire on the part of such states to increase or escalate conflict, but merely be a result of the spillover of one individual's or group's attitudes into many decision-making areas.

Any hope for an effective future role for the United Nations does not receive much encouragement from research on differential attitudes toward that organization by developed and undeveloped countries. The large, developed countries, which provide most of the funding for it, are the most negative about its role. After the People's Republic of China was admitted to the United Nations, for example, the United States government in late 1971 held serious internal discussions about the size of its future economic contribution to the U.N. If more states move into the developed category in the future, there should be a concomitant increase in the number of countries sharing these negative opinions.

Given the findings that rather consistently showed open, democratic systems to be more cooperative and less conflictual, the support that countries such as the United States give to small, closed systems may in the long run be one factor adding to international tension. Consideration of moral or ethical questions aside, concern over the future path of international relations should lead countries—especially open systems—to a greater fostering of democratic processes and procedures in other states—assuming, of course, that "fostering" does not take the form of outright conflict. The same point applies to economic development. The findings again rather consistently showed that the larger, more developed states are more cooperative, most likely as a function of their greater need to interact with more nations and to do it cooperatively to get things from them. Concern for the future stability of the international system should lead larger states to pursue the further development of the smaller, currently underdeveloped states.

It might be argued, of course, that the greater proportion of physical conflict among the smaller, less developed states can be attributed to the fact that they are able to fight without annihilating one another with large-scale military hardware, including nuclear weapons. One would not want to push this implication too far—for other variables enter into the situation—but perhaps the way to a more stable international system is, in fact, for all states to possess large-scale weapons, including nuclear weapons.

The effect of national attributes on foreign policy behavior is limited, and thus the potential impact for decision-makers is also limited. It is very likely, however, that because many of the findings have been so consistent that refinement will produce more specific—and therefore more useful—theories. National attributes do provide information on the setting of international politics. They are limited, at least at the present time, in terms of how much of international behavior they can explain.

part II

The International System:

SYSTEM DYNAMICS

Introduction

The first part of this book focused on how man and the state affect international politics. It assumed that either of these two broad independent variables were the causal factors of international behavior. But other assumptions can be made about what causes international behavior.

The following chapters shift the focus rather drastically to the international system. They put man and the nation-state in a much broader framework. In other words, theories considered in earlier chapters make the assumption that individual and "small" elements—a person's values, his personality, his perceptions—influence very strongly the pattern of international relations. Had Richard Nixon been in John Kennedy's position, it is argued, the Cuban Missile Crisis might have turned out utterly different; had Clark Clifford never been appointed secretary of state in early 1968, the Vietnam war might have continued unabated. These are certainly plausible assertions, but the following chapters use as a starting point the assumption that a great deal of international behavior can be understood without considering these individual-level elements.

The International System

Is there any rhyme or reason to what happens in international behavior? Do events fall into any large-scale patterns? Can they be analyzed as part of a pattern, or system? To the layman, looking at his daily paper, crises just seem to erupt for no reason at all. Or two old foes are suddenly toasting each other at the head table. Or troops are being abruptly mobilized without warning and without seeming justification. There always seem to be new and unpredictable confrontations—or détentes. The layman has a tendency, understandably, to see these events as random, as basically unpredictable, caused by the multitude of idiosyncratic and individual- and state-level variables that often seem to be at work. But are they? Can they be considered from a systemic level? Can these seemingly random events be fit into overall patterns? Can they be understood and explained by other than individual-level theories?

Such an approach would suggest that random-appearing events are really part of large-scale systems, that they can be viewed as having a life of their own. A room full of people, for instance, can be described as "tense," "nervous," "relaxed." A crowd listening to a speaker or demonstrating in front of a building can likewise be described as "quiet" or "tense." Sociologists can learn a great deal about a society simply by tracing its demographic patterns and changes in those patterns. People do not move without rhyme or reason; there are *patterns* to and reasons for demographic changes.

The same argument applies to international systems. It is one thing, however, to assert that there is "organized complexity" and that organized international systems do indeed exist. It is something else to decide exactly how to visualize these systems or how to organize that complexity.

But what is an "international system" and how can international behavior be explained in terms of a system? Charles McClelland in his numerous writings has set out perhaps the best description of the system-level approach as well as its important underlying assumptions.[1] First,

[1] Charles McClelland, "Field Theory and System Theory in International Politics, mimeographed (Los Angeles: University of Southern California, June, 1968); "Acute International Crises," *World Politics* 14 (October, 1961), pp. 182–204; "International Interaction Analysis: Basic Research and Some Practical Uses," mimeographed (Los Angeles: University of Southern California, November, 1968); "Interaction Analysis and Foreign Policy Futures," mimeographed (Los Angeles: University of Southern California, October, 1968); "Action Structures and Communication in Two International Crises: Quemoy and Matsu," *Background* 7 (1964), pp. 201–15; "Access to Berlin: The Quantity and Variety of Events, 1948–1963," in *Quantitative International Politics, Insights and Evidence,* ed. J. David Singer (New York: Free Press, 1968), pp. 178–84; "The Beginning, Duration, and Abatement of International Crises: Comparisons in Two Conflict Arenas," in *International Crisis: Insights from Behavioral Re-*

McClelland argues, "organized complexity prevails" in international relations; [2] what often appears to the layman or casual observer to be complex, nonpatterned, and "crazy" behavior, in fact fits into certain organized—though complex—patterns. Second, "repetitive patterning and deterministic processes in the world are mixed with accidental, idiosyncratic, and random elements"; [3] that is, of all the events that occur every day in foreign affairs, some can be viewed as "random" in that they are a function of small-scale, idiosyncratic elements. However, says McClelland, "any specific phenomena, entity, trait, relationship, or process should be considered in its context or milieu rather than in isolation." [4]

The daily newspaper's concern with immediate events, of course, fosters the attention to specific events out of context. But viewed systemically, these events, however complex, do become part of large-scale patterns that cannot be understood or explained in terms of man and the state alone.

Types of International Systems

Several different research efforts can be used to illustrate system-level approaches. How should these complex international systems, then, be viewed? How can their complexity be organized?

Bruce Russett has investigated the patterns in the international system in terms of trade, U.N. voting, and membership in international organizations, and has found that over moderately long periods of time—thirteen years in some cases—the behavior of countries, grouped by regions, has exhibited strong patterns. In other words, despite what might have appeared as a drastically changing and dynamic period—1952 to 1963—the stability of U.N. voting was extremely high. As Russett found:

About four-fifths of the variation in one year's voting pattern can be predicted by knowing, for the same states, what that pattern looked like in one of the other years. It [the correlation] is not notably lower for the entire 11-year span than for either of the shorter periods. [5]

search, ed. Charles F. Hermann, New York: Free Press, 1972), pp. 83–105; and "Some Effects on Theory from the International Event Analysis Movement," *Sage Professional Papers in International Studies* 1 (1972), pp. 15–44.

[2] McClelland, "Field Theory and System Theory," p. 6.

[3] Ibid.

[4] Ibid., pp. 6–7.

[5] Bruce Russett, *International Regions and the International System, A Study in Political Ecology* (Chicago: Rand McNally, 1967), p. 88.

Similarly, membership groupings in international organizations also remained stable through the 1951-1962 period, although there were changes in alignment, especially for Japan. Finally, trading patterns between 1954 and 1963 also showed remarkable stability.[6]

Russett's main interest was in delineating the "regions" of the world. His research also indicated, however, that regions—we can just as easily call them "systems"—remain remarkably stable through a period of time even though on the surface they appear to be experiencing one abrupt change after the other. Shifts in behavior, Russett found, certainly did occur, most of them being long-run changes. But the overall pattern of behavior, as manifested through United Nations voting, co-memberships in international organizations, and trading patterns, remained comparatively stable. Sudden realignment in the international system—the "spastic" change—is a rare phenomenon. What Russett did was to isolate systems of behavior that can be considered and analyzed quite apart from the makeup of the individual countries within the systems or the individual leaders within the countries. The systems are defined in *terms* of the behaviors, and the behavior is *explained* in large-scale, systemic terms.

Another view of international behavior from the systemic level is contained in J. David Singer's and Melvin Small's Correlates of War Project. Singer and Small collected data on the number of wars begun at any time between 1815 and 1965 and the amount of war under way in any given period during those 150 years. Figure 2-1 in Chapter 2, which plotted the amount of war being waged at various intervals, showed quite clearly that war during that century and a half was not a completely random occurrence. If it had been, the table would have indicated sawtooth, up-and-down fluctuations. In fact, Singer and Small concluded that international war between 1815 and 1965 evidenced a certain periodicity. They note that their findings suggest "not so much that discrete wars come and go with some regularity, but that, with *some* level of such violence almost always present, there are distinct and periodic fluctuations in the amount of that violence."[7] They fixed this periodicity at between twenty and forty years. Frank Denton and Warren Phillips, in an earlier analysis using the data of Quincy Wright, Pitirim Sorokin, and Lewis F. Richardson, discovered that after 1680 an upswing in the incidence of war seemed to occur about every thirty years.[8]

[6] Ibid., pp. 119 and 153.

[7] J. David Singer and Melvin Small, *The Wages of War: 1816–1965: A Statistical Handbook* (New York: Wiley, 1972), pp. 212 and 215.

[8] Frank H. Denton, "Some Regularities in International Conflict, 1820–1949," *Background* 9 (February, 1966), pp. 283–96; Frank H. Denton and Warren Phillips, "Some Patterns in the History of Violence," *Journal of Conflict Resolution* 12 (June, 1968), 182–95.

War as an international behavior, therefore, is one way in which to look at the international system across long periods of time. To then find the element of periodicity in the amount of war is in line with the mode of thinking that, as Singer and Small put it, "postulates a high degree of order and pattern in both the physical and the social worlds." [9]

A final example of a way in which to regard the international system is offered by McClelland. It is McClelland's assertion that the *daily actions* that occur in the international system constitute what he calls the "flow of events." [10] States perform many acts in the international system, and the most important of these find their way into the history books. Histories of the Cold War, for instance, may describe the formation of NATO and the Marshall Plan, the Warsaw Pact, the Berlin blockade, the Korean War, the numerous East-West crises, and finally the Vietnam War. This sequence of events describes part of the international system for a certain period, marking the well-known high points of the Cold War. The descriptions of events are sometimes considered in conjunction with other information on trade, cultural exchanges, or changing alignments. McClelland's "flow" or "stream" of events, however, ignores this other type of information—what he calls "transactions" —and focuses rather on a chronology of events or "interactions." These descriptive chronologies are very similar to the diplomatic histories of certain periods, though unlike the histories the flow-of-events approach is not selective. The historian picks and chooses among events he thinks are important; the stream-of-events analyst describes all publicly recorded "event interactions" that occur between nations. By including all public events, a much more complete chronology of the flow emerges, and this constant stream then becomes a picture of the international system or smaller subsystems. This flow of events does not provide a perfect description of action in the international system, of course; rather, it offers a painting of the pattern and shift of world events.

To paint this picture, a method is necessary to organize what on the surface appears to be a hopelessly complex array of behaviors. Using a public source (usually the *New York Times*), McClelland's method is to place every state action into one of twenty-two different categories, such as promise, request, accuse, agree, consult, comment, deny, demand, warn, threaten, and force. By categorizing the daily events of nations in this manner, it turns out once again that what on the surface seems to be completely random unpredictable behavior is—if not predictable—at least, highly patterned, both in terms of volume and type of events. The international system is not a sporadic, spasmodic system, but an extremely organized one, depending on how it is viewed. Figure II-1a–1c present

---

[9] Singer and Small, *Wages of War,* p. 204.
[10] See McClelland citations in footnote 1, especially first four.

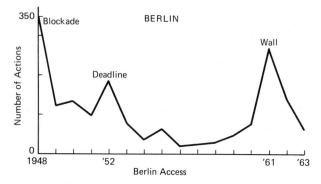

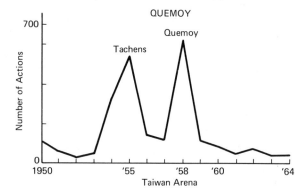

Source: Charles A. McClelland and Gary D. Hoggard,
"Conflict Patterns in the Interactions among Nations,"
in *International Politics and Foreign Policy: A Reader
in Research and Theory*, rev. ed., ed. James Rosenau
(New York: The Free Press, 1969), p. 723.

Figure II-1a. Fluctuations of international interaction, Berlin and Quemoy.

three different "pictures" of three different "systems" solely in terms of volume of events: the Berlin crisis system from 1948 to 1963, and the Quemoy-Matsu crisis system from 1950 to 1964 (1a); the entire world system as recorded by McClelland's scheme from 1966 through 1970 (1b); and from 1969 through March, 1974 (1c). The three big events in the Berlin situation—the blockade (1948), the "Deadline" crisis (1952), and the Berlin Wall (1961)—show up clearly; the crises between Mainland China and Formosa over off-shore islands—Tachens in 1955 and Quemoy in 1958—are also quite prominent. Finally, when the entire world is looked at in the late 1960s and early 1970s (II-1b and II-1c), the Middle East

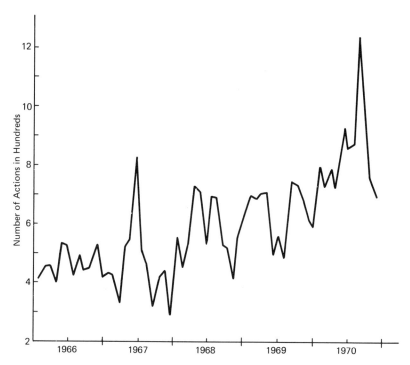

Source: Gary A. Hill, "The Flow of International Events: 1970; A General Survey and a Look at the Jordanian Crisis," mimeographed, Interim Technical Report (Los Angeles: University of Southern California, 1971), p. 2.

Figure II-1b. Total number of international actions of all countries in the world, monthly, from January, 1966–December, 1970, as reported in the *New York Times.*

War of June, 1967, the Civil War between Jordan and Arab guerillas in 1970, and the India-Pakistan War of 1971 clearly take precedence in terms of volume of actions.[11]

These data—as noted—are not particularly revealing in terms of any immediate theory. That is not their purpose; rather, they show patterns, they present a picture. For one thing, there was obviously an increasing upward trend in the sheer volume of international events from late 1967

[11] McClelland's basic scheme and data have been utilized here because they were the first extensive ones to be developed; in more recent years, numerous other data-collection systems have been developed. See Edward E. Azar, *Probe for Peace* (Minneapolis, Minn.: Burgess Publishing, 1973); and Phillip M. Burgess and Raymond W. Lawton, *Indicators of International Behavior: An Assessment of Events Data Research* (Beverly Hills, Calif.: Sage Publications, 1972).

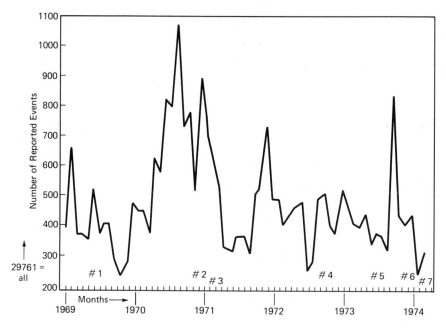

Source: Charles A. McClelland, "Warning Signs Under the International Threat System," mimeographed (Los Angeles: University of Southern California, 1974), p. 20.

Figure II-1c. Total number of international events reported in the *Times* of London, January, 1969–March, 1974.

to late 1970 (Figure II-1b). That trend was then reversed for eleven months, at which point the volume was at its lowest point in almost three years. The next peak, in November, 1971, was not as high as that attained in the PLO-Jordanian conflict. Was the upward trend broken? Figure II-1c is data taken from the *Times* of London, and suggests that the international system in the early 1970s did shift from an increasing level of interactions to a somewhat lower level.

These data can be used, in other words, to "describe" the international system merely in terms of volume of actions. Much more interesting descriptions, however, occur when we break down the actions into types. Figure II-2 shows that the increasing trend in interactions between 1966 and 1970 was accounted for primarily by one type of action: force. By force we mean to take something through physical possession or military engagement, or to destroy it militarily. As actions involving force were expanding, other actions—such as defensive verbal conflict, cooperation, and indulgence were all on the decline. Although Gary Hill, in deleting the conflict occurring in Cambodia and Vietnam in late 1969 and 1970

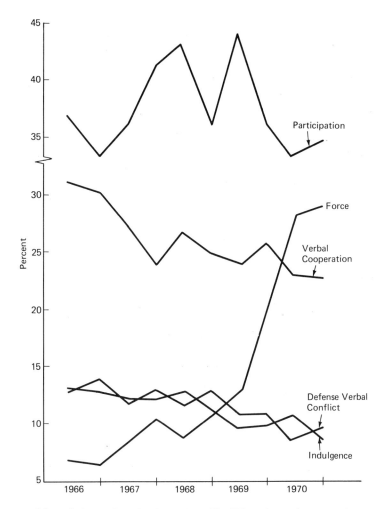

Adapted from data in Gary A. Hill, "The Flow of International Events: July–December, 1970: A General Survey and a Look at the Jordanian Crisis," mimeographed (Los Angeles: University of Southern California), 1971, p. 1.

Figure II-2. Types of international actions, 1966–1970.

showed that the "general conflict" indicator dropped,[12] it is unlikely that the entire behavioral change pictured in Figure II-1c is accounted

[12] Hill's data are not shown here; see Gary A. Hill, "The Flow of International Events: July–December, 1970: A General Survey and a Look at the Jordanian Crisis," Interim Technical Report, mimeographed (Los Angeles: University of Southern California, 1971).

for by conflict occurring solely in Cambodia and Vietnam. The trend is present throughout the entire five years, and accelerates only during the last eighteen months, primarily as a function of the drop in participation behaviors. The figure does suggest that world diplomacy during that five-year period was undergoing a rather subtle shift from less to more physical conflict, and a corresponding decline in low-level verbal conflict and cooperative behaviors. McClelland has also shown that interesting patterns occur when smaller sub systems in the international system are investigated, and that an analysis of mere frequency of actions over time can often signal upcoming international crises.[13] The important point here is that state actions do exhibit some patterns. These actions taken by themselves—either for large systems or for smaller dyadic systems—can be treated in isolation from any other evidence and provide a great deal of information about those systems.

System-Level Behavior

Another way of elucidating the idea of the international system as shown in the research of Russett, Singer, and McClelland,[14] among others, is to note that the behavior is of a different type than that encountered in earlier chapters. The behavior previously discussed was usually

[13] McClelland, "Access to Berlin," "Beginning, Duration, and Abatement," and "Warning Signs."

[14] It should be understood that these three research strategies merely scratch the surface of "systemic" approaches. Others would include R. J. Rummel, "A Social Field Theory of Foreign Conflict Behavior," *Peace Research Society Papers* 4 (1966), pp. 131–50; Richard Rosecrance, *Action and Reaction in World Politics* (Boston: Little, Brown, 1962); Morton Kaplan, *System and Process in International Politics* (New York: Wiley, 1957); Johan Galtung, "A Structural Theory of Aggression," *Journal of Peace Research* 1 (No. 2, 1964), pp. 95–119; P. Terry Hopmann, "International Conflict and Cohesion in the Communist System," *International Studies Quarterly* 11 (September, 1967), pp. 212–36; Dina Zinnes, "An Analytical Study of the Balance of Power Theories," *Journal of Peace Research* 4 (No. 4, 1967), pp. 270–88; Barry Hughes and Thomas Volgy, "Distance in Foreign Policy Behavior: A Comparative Study of Eastern Europe," *Midwest Journal of Political Science* 14 (August, 1970), pp. 459–92; Barry Hughes and John E. Schwarz, "Dimensions of Political Integration and the Experience of the European Community," *International Studies Quarterly* 16 (September, 1972), pp. 263–94; Steven Brams, "The Structure of Influence Relationships in the International System," in *International Politics and Foreign Policy, A Reader in Research and Theory*, ed. James Rosenau, rev. ed. (New York: Free Press, 1969); Paul Smoker, "Fear in the Arms Race: A Mathematical Study," in *International Politics and Foreign Policy;* Karl Deutsch, Sidney Burrell, Robert Kann, Maurice Lee, Jr., Martin Lichterman, Raymond E. Lindgren, Francis Loewenheim, and Richard Van Wagenen, "Political Community and the North Atlantic Area," in *International Political Communities: An Anthology* (Garden City, New York: Doubleday and Company, 1966).

confined either to one nation, one individual, or one group (decision-making).[15] Here the behavior changes to the system level: Singer's data on war constitutes the aggregated behavior of many nations; McClelland's "flow of events" is also usually system-level behavior of many states or of a few states over time. Understandably, looking at large-scale behaviors —patterns of war, trade, or the flow of events between countries—we lose a great deal of specific information. Treating U.S.-German trade similar to the way in which we treat French-British trade may hide differences between the two phenomena. A "threat" from the U.S.S.R. to the U.S. is not the same as a "threat" from the U.S. to Kuwait. However, the assumption is made that *at a certain level* and *for certain purposes* these differences may not be important, which brings us back to several intro-ductory remarks made in Chapter 1. The way a research question is posed dictates the data that are needed. Thus, the majority of theories to be discussed in the remaining chapters are dependent upon an interest in certain kinds of system-level behavior, and with rare exceptions can-not be readily applied to nonsystem-level behavior. This distinction is quite important for the discussion of various theories and an evaluation of their potency. As noted in Chapter 1, in order to truly evaluate a theory, we must know the behavior it is meant to encompass, and whether that behavior is actually what the theory is being applied to.

Conclusion

Several summary comments are now in order. First, the following chapters assume that international systems *exist* and that these systems *behave*. What often appears as unrelated complexity and perhaps even random behavior does, in fact, take on shape and form when viewed from system perspectives. Second, the basic assumption of the systemic approach is that states behave as a function not of internal attributes, individuals, or decision-making processes, but rather as a function of their position in the international system or subsystems, or as a function of how other states behave toward it.

Third, what first appears as a serious drawback for explaining this complexity is in fact a real advantage. The assumption that individual-or state-level variables are not important, that personalities, images, belief systems, and decision processes can be assumed to have a random effect on international behavior means that our theories may become

---

15 Although this is not true in every case (recall, for example, the type of behavior utilized in several stimulus-response studies in Chapter 2), the general tendency was to confine the analysis as noted.

much more parsimonious, namely, that the number of variables needed to explain international behavior is smaller. A final underlying element of these theories is that by looking at large-scale, aggregated behavior, or at the sequences of international behaviors demonstrated by states as *patterns*, we are not beholden to the momentary interests and attention spans of crisis-oriented daily newspapers. Events come and go, crises erupt and decline, and too often the scholar of international relations is corralled into focusing on these events until—of course—they become stale and old, and other events hover on the horizon, at which time he must turn his attention to them. The theories here foster a longer run perspective that places passing events into larger patterns.

Chapter 5 discusses the crucial variable of "power." It sorts out the contending approaches and definitions of the concept of power, and it weeds out the real from the pseudo problems involved with power. Its key point is that in spite of the many disputes and arguments about the role of power, there is in fact a small body of hypotheses to be derived from power concepts, hypotheses that can—and have been—tested. Chapter 6 presents theories on the variable "integration," using the very general concept of "social distance," that is, that nations' behavior is a function of their proximity to other nations on variables such as values, ideology, and similar perceptions and ideological systems. It thus continues the theoretical argument begun in Chapter 5 that a central method of viewing theories at the systemic level is through the concept of "distance" between states. Chapter 7 is distinct from the others. It proposes that behavior in international politics is a function of the *bargaining* or influence attempts that states use in their relations with one another, and that states in interaction form bargaining systems that very often take on a life of their own. Various bargaining approaches are analyzed, including brinkmanship, learning theory, and stimulus-response.

Chapter 8 incorporates different variables considered in the earlier chapters, especially 5 and 6, into multivariate approaches. Much emphasis is given to forms of "field" theory, and the different types of research carried out using field theory models. The chapter also illustrates several ways in which different levels of analysis can be unified into fuller multivariate research designs, with several suggestions for combining different levels of analysis. Chapter 8 does not constitute a separate approach; the theories it covers are almost without exception contained—in a simpler form—in earlier chapters.

chapter 5 Power and Rank:

Distance

and Systems

"Power," "power theory," and "balance of power"—these are the concepts that form the core of this chapter. Their close similarity to the concepts of "rank" and "status," however, demand that they be considered together. After a preliminary investigation of power and balance of power, two concepts will be presented to distinguish between different views of power: "Distance" will be used to analyze dyadic relationships, and "system" or "distribution" will be used to study system-wide relationships —two frameworks similar in their measurement of power, but different in the fashion in which they explain behavior.

Power

Hans Morgenthau's theory of power politics probably goes the longest way toward accounting for the popularity of power as an analytic tool in the study of international relations. Very briefly, Morgenthau contends that man possesses an inherent "lust for power," that he desires control over his fellowmen, and that men aggregated into states behave as a function of this basic drive:

It is sufficient to state that the struggle for power is universal in time and space and is an undeniable fact of experience. It cannot be denied that throughout historic time, regardless of social, economic, and political conditions, states have met each other in contests of power.[1]

To Morgenthau the problems of the world, far from being a result of depravity that can be fixed or evil that can be abolished, result simply from "forces inherent in human nature," which consist of the "drives to live, to propagate, and to dominate," [2] and in the satisfaction of these drives, power is centrally important. Morgenthau goes one step further. In his view, individual-level variables, such as motivation and ideological preferences, are unimportant:

Even if we had access to the real motives of statesmen, that knowledge would help us little in understanding foreign policies. . . . It is true that the knowledge of the statesman's motives may give us one among many clues as to what the direction of his foreign policy might be. It cannot give us, however, the one clue by which to predict his foreign polices.[3]

International politics in Morgenthau's view, therefore, is "a struggle for power . . . whenever [nations] strive to realize their goal by means of international politics, they do so by striving for power." [4] He sees three basic patterns in a state's behavior, and these, moreover, can be understood in terms of how they relate to power. First, nations try to retain their power by adopting policies that support the status quo. Second, nations low in the international pecking order attempt to increase their power, most usually through some sort of imperialistic, outward movement. Finally, countries satisfied with their level of power and not concerned about either losing it or gaining more—at the moment—feel obliged to demonstrate that power, which they do through policies of prestige, including diplomatic ceremonies and displays of military force. All three patterns of international behavior have power as a central component.

Morgenthau is far from alone in focusing on power. Organski, for example, maintains that "one of the most important characteristics of a nation is its power, for power is a major determinant of the part that the nation will play in international relations." [5] World politics for Organski consists of the "doings" of America and Russia, Britain and China, "and of the other great nations. It is not much concerned with relations between Iceland and Liberia or with the latest twist of foreign policy in Paraguay." Why? "They are simply less powerful. What they or

---

[1] Hans Morgenthau, *Politics among Nations: The Struggle for Power and Peace,* 3d ed. (New York: Knopf, 1965), p. 33.

[2] Ibid.

[3] Ibid., p. 6.

[4] Ibid., p. 27.

[5] A. F. K. Organski, *World Politics,* 2d ed. (New York: Knopf, 1968), p. 101.

their governments do does not have much effect on the rest of the world.
. . . The importance of power is obvious." [6] Deutsch would agree. Says
he:

Who is stronger and who is weaker? Who will get his way and who will have to
give in? Such questions as these, when asked about actual or possible encounters
among a limited number of competitors, lead to rank lists, such as the rankings
of baseball clubs in the pennant races, of chickens in the pecking order, and of
great powers in world politics.[7]

Argues German:

Thoughout history the decisive factor in the fates of nations has usually been the
number, efficiency, and disposition of fighting forces . . . national influence
bears a direct relationship to gross national strength; without that, the most ex-
quisite statesmanship is likely to be of limited use.[8]

"States depend for their existence upon power," says John Burton, "and
achieve their objectives by power, thus making the management of power
the main problem to be solved." [9]

From these and other authors flow several assumptions forming the
basis of the so-called power framework. First, there exists something
called "power." Second, it is central to international politics because
power equals bigness and bigness equals influence and influence means
affecting other people. Third, violence and force are central to international relations, and because power equals the ability to be violent and
impose one's will on others, then power is important. Fourth, the linkage
between power and violence means that power must be controlled in the
era of devastating nuclear weapons. Furthermore, because the international system is basically anarchistic, with no central authority, every
state must fend for itself, and states can only get what they want, or
even survive, by utilizing their power. If a violent power struggle does
break out, the world would again become fascinated with winners; in
international relations, the obvious interest would center on who will be
the victor. In Deutsch's terms, who will be at the top of the pecking
order? More often than not, the powerful countries will win, and therefore power seems totally relevant.

6 Ibid.

7 Karl W. Deutsch, "On the Concepts of Politics and Power," in *International
Politics and Foreign Policy,* ed. James N. Rosenau, rev. ed. (New York: Free Press,
1969), p. 257

8 F. Clifford German, "A Tentative Evaluation of World Power," *Journal of Conflict Resolution* 4 (March, 1960), p. 138.

9 John W. Burton, *International Relations: A General Theory* (Cambridge: At the
University Press, 1967), p. 46.

But just how much of international behavior consists in the use or threat of force? Does the focus on force simply result from an interest in the larger, more powerful countries, and if so, then does it apply only to a subset of the international system? Some data suggest, for instance, that for the year 1966 only 33 percent of the behavior in the international system consisted of conflict—threats, accusations, protests, and forceful acts—and an even smaller percentage of the conflict was made up of *violent* acts.[10] Hill's study, described in the Introduction to Part II, also showed that "general conflict" accounted for anywhere from 28 to 38 percent of all actions in the international system from 1966 to 1969, and that by 1970 it had reached about 45 percent. Physical conflict acts, however, accounted for anywhere from 7 to 18 percent for the years 1966-1969, and one fourth (27 percent) for 1970.[11] By far the largest amount of interaction in any time period came under the heading "participation"—meaning general "comment" or consultations—and it ranged from 33 to 44 percent. In other words, conflict actions—especially of the physical as opposed to verbal—constituted a very small percentage of interstate interactions in those five years.

Few of the statements thus far presented about power, or the assumptions underlying power, show how power *explains* international behavior, however. It would be fallacious to equate the great interest in power with the assertion that power thereby "explains" nation-state behavior. If we consider power as an attribute and that it *might* be measured in such terms as population size, GNP, and so on, then national attribute theory (Chapter 4) does provide some insight and some evidence; the more powerful states, we found, did act differently from the less powerful states. Yet it seems clear already from the citations of those writing about power that something else is involved than mere hypotheses concerning national attribute theory. We turn to the question of what power is—and whether that "something else" found in so much of the literature on power helps to really explain international behavior.

Two Conceptions of Power

Many of the problems encountered with the concept of power derive from confusion over what power is. The most widely utilized definition

[10] Charles McClelland and Gary Hoggard, "Conflict Patterns in the Interactions among Nations," in *International Politics and Foreign Policy: A Reader in Research and Theory*, ed. James N. Rosenau, rev. ed. (New York: Free Press, 1969), pp. 711–24.

[11] Gary A. Hill, "The Flow of International Events, July–December, 1970: A General Survey and A Look at the Jordanian Crisis," Interim Technical Report, mimeographed (Los Angeles: University of Southern California, 1971).

of power is that of strength, implied in Deutsch's questions: Who is the strongest? Who is the biggest? Hence, strength implies the possession of items or "attributes" of power. Any introductory textbook on international politics can be called upon here to provide a list of such attributes: geography, natural resources, industrial capacity, military capability, and population usually form the core of "power attributes."

Most authors also recognize, however, that such tangible attributes may not necessarily equate with power. Morgenthau, for instance, argues that because Germany and Russia have always had a high regard for standing armies, compulsory military service, and other militaristic traits, they possess an advantage because they can more easily transform their resources into instruments of war. At the same time, Britain and the United States have suffered for their aversion to such values.[12] Although more elusive still, national morale—"the degree of determination with which a nation supports the foreign policies of its government in peace and war" [13]—is yet another "element of power." Morale also relates to the quality and type of government, for if segments of the population feel deprived of their rights, they will have a lower morale. To Morgenthau:

A government that is truly representative, . . . above all in the sense of being able to translate the inarticulate convictions and aspirations of the people into international objectives and politics, has the best chance to marshal the national energies in support of those objectives.[14]

Lists of elements of power could go on forever, but those mentioned above provide a sense of what constitutes a "powerful" country. Unfortunately, many analyses do not go much beyond the mere listing of such elements equated with power; and listing attributes of power is really nothing more than listing attributes of power. A very important equation is normally only implicit, namely, that countries high on such power lists have predominance in international affairs, and therefore can influence other states. Even more implicit, however, is the basic notion that states are constantly involved in a "struggle for power" and that once they have attained it they do their best to maintain it. The exact linkage between those two behaviors and power attributes, however, is somewhat hazy. In fact, findings under national attribute theory contended that, when looked at from one perspective, powerful nations seem to do less "struggling"—proportionately—than less powerful countries.

To consider international relations in terms of "power attributes," then, is clearly insufficient. Scoring high or low on power does not neces-

---

12 Morgenthau, *Politics among Nations*, p. 131.
13 Ibid.
14 Ibid., p. 138.

sarily link systematically to using power effectively or productively. Nor can we go much beyond the findings of attribute theory in the last chapter. Yet a careful reading of the main theorists on power indicates that somehow the theory involves power relations, and the ability of a nation to produce a desired effect in international affairs by using its power. But supposedly powerful countries don't always act powerfully, nor always get their way. Something, therefore, seemed to be wrong with the power theory stated in terms of gross attributes of power. This has led scholars to a different approach, that power is more than simply the possession of attributes, that it pertains to the exercise of influence over others. Morgenthau has described it as "man's control over the minds and actions of other men." [15] K. J. Holsti's extensive analysis of the power concept quite clearly relies on this view, seeing power primarily as the act of influencing others and the use of capabilities to wield that influence.[16]

Power may not only be distinguished from sheer capabilities, it can also be differentiated from the use of force. Power can be present in situations where force is not used. Indeed, some argue that such instances are illustrations of ultimate power—when one party influences the other to act without even possessing the supposed necessary capabilities. "Power," then, can become *psychological control* over others. The driver who meets another at an intersection and signals, by gunning his engine and roaring ahead, that he intends to go through the intersection—thus forcing the other driver to stop—has exercised power over the other's behavior. The neutralist leader of a small, "powerless" country exerts great power if through his international appeal he can force larger countries to agree to a cease-fire or negotiate a treaty.

In sum, there are essentially two general perspectives on power. The first sees power as involving attributes, the second sees power as involving the ability to influence. The important question now becomes what each perspective can tell us about explaining variations in the actions of states.

Power Theory

If power is *simply* a commodity or attribute, how can it explain variations in foreign policy? Attribute theory showed that more powerful states (large and wealthy) tend to be more active in the international

15 Ibid., p. 28.

16 K. J. Holsti, "The Concept of Power in the Study of International Relations," *Background* 7 (February, 1964), p. 182.

arena and to possess different patterns of behavior. The relationships were small, however, and, as noted, power theorists usually see something *more* to power than attributes.

In considering power as an influence phenomenon, however, a crucial problem arises that is primarily methodological. The measurement of power in terms of influence must usually be done post facto, which means that more often than not the explanation turns out to be tautological. For instance, this perspective might "explain" the Cuban Missile Crisis of 1962, by noting that the United States was able to convince the Soviet Union that it possessed sufficient power, and the will to use it, to back up its blockade of Cuba. The Soviets backed down, then, because of the United States's ability to influence the Soviet leaders. In this instance, the United States was then the more "powerful" country, and the important role of "power" becomes clear. Unfortunately, we don't know whether the United States convinced the Soviets of anything nor that the Soviets backed down because of that reason; we can only infer it. If the United States had retreated, then the explanation would have been that the Soviets were more powerful because they influenced the United States. The explanation must always await the outcome of the event, which means that one can always find some "power" reason for the outcome.

Hence, the concept of power, whether seen as a simple attribute or as influence, has certain built-in, serious problems in terms of exactly how much it explains foreign policy. A first step toward untangling these problems is to deal here with power as an attribute and reserve a discussion of power as influence, as a process of interstate "bargaining," for Chapter 7.

But even considering power as an attribute, it has been the center of disputes. The crux of the problem has been the failure to outline what behavior the concept or theory of power is supposed to explain. That is, though much attention has been given to power as an independent variable—somehow affecting something else—little attention has been given to what it is supposed to affect. An example should illustrate this. Morgenthau suggests numerous possible questions that revolve around the role of the power of states:

What effect will the use of atomic energy have upon the industrial capacity of the United States and of other nations? . . . How has political independence influenced the national morale of India? What is the significance of the revival of a German army for the national power of Germany? . . . In what ways does the advancement of the Russian sphere of influence to the Elbe River affect the geographical position of the Soviet Union? . . . What will the industrialization of Brazil, China, and India signify for the military strength of these countries? . . . To what extent does the quantitatively and qualitatively superior industrial capacity of the United States compensate for its probable inferiority in over-all military effectiveness? . . . What is the significance, in terms of the respective power positions, of the operation in the United States of groups subservient to Russian foreign policy, and of the enforced homogeneity of Russian public opinion? [17]

All of these questions must be asked, Morgenthau insists, if we are to understand international processes.

The relative influence of the different factors upon national power must be determined with regard to all nations . . . one ought to know whether France is stronger than Italy and in what respects. One ought to know what the assets and liabilities in terms of the different power factors of India or China are with respect to the Soviet Union, of Japan with regard to the United States, of Argentina with regard to Chile, and so on.[18]

In addition to this, Morgenthau suggests numerous other questions, each one piled on in ever-more complicated tiers. First would be those concerned with the elements in one country that influence that country's power in what ways. On top of these, and more difficult to answer, are the questions concerning the "influence of changes in one factor upon other factors, and here the difficulties increase and the pitfalls multiply." [19]

Third, a set of questions, even more difficult to answer than the above, concern "the comparison of one power factor in one nation with the same or another power factor in another nation." [20] Fourth, such power computations must be assessed at one point in time and projected into the future. Finally, as if the chore was not already hopelessly complicated, "there would be unknown factors to spoil (the) calculations":

. . . such natural catastrophes as famines and epidemics, such man-made catastrophes as wars and revolutions, as well as inventions and discoveries, the rise and disappearance of intellectual, military, and political leaders, the thoughts and actions of such leaders, not to speak of the imponderables of national morale.[21]

At this point, of course, the analyst interested in a systematic treatise on the *role* of power throws up his hands, for it is a hopeless chore. The questions are too numerous and hopelessly complex.

Three observations should be made, however. First, it is not quite

---

[17] Morgenthau, *Politics among Nations*, pp. 149–51.

[18] Ibid., p. 151.

[19] Ibid., p. 149.

[20] Ibid., p. 150.

[21] Ibid., p. 153.

clear *why* one should focus on certain attributes, certain assets or liabilities relating to the power of countries. What do we expect to find, for instance, if certain power factors in India relate in specified ways to certain power factors in China? Do we want to know which country is the *most* powerful? These questions have *not* set out the role or effect of power, but rather have merely sought a list of attributes. Second, the prolonged focus on delineating every conceivable aspect or attribute of power tends to overshadow concern about the specific *role* of power, for by the time all the complicated elements are outlined, no extended attention can be given to systematic analysis of their import. Finally, by making power appear so complex that it becomes all-encompassing, power theorists are assured of successfully explaining any action in international relations, for from the large grab bag of the attributes of power surely one can be plucked to account for any given situation.

Power theory, then, withers away as a valid *explanatory* theory of international behavior if it only says that (1) some states with certain attributes are powerful and others with other attributes are not; (2) states seem to have the goal of increasing their power; (3) power is needed for force, and force seems to be a prevalent mode of international behavior; (4) states are constantly influencing one another, and although powerful states can often wield more influence, they often buckle under to the influence of others; and (5) national power is so complex that no single measurable entity or index can possibly embrace it.

Furthermore, general theories that purport to explain all international politics as "power politics" are extremely limited. Morgenthau has asserted concerning his own theory that behavior of a cooperative nature is outside the theory because the motivation of that behavior—such as signing an extradition treaty or agreeing on exchange of cultural events —does not have power as a basis and is not meant to increase any nations' power.[22] But as we have already said, most actions in international affairs are of a cooperative nature, and therefore any such theory that international affairs are the workings of power politics, as Morgenthau proposes, is highly limited.

Two options seem possible at this point: one, to discard the entire concept of power because of its complexity, and rely on other explana-

---

[22] If Morgenthau is correct and people always think in terms of power as a goal, then the question arises: why have not whole "power" theories been established to explain domestic politics or interpersonal relations? Any such theories that do surface are as tautological as many explaining international behavior through the single variable of power. Second, Morgenthau himself admits that states do not always think in terms of power, and the decision-making models reviewed earlier suggested strongly that in some cases even national decision-makers quite clearly do not have "power" as their goal when they act. Very often their behavior can be quite adequately explained by saying they simply wanted to "get by" or "muddle through" a difficult situation.

tions for state behavior; or, two, to reduce the complexity of the concept by linking each element of power singly or in combination to international behavior. We turn in the next section to such linkages as implied in the literature on power. To organize that vast literature, however, we must think in terms of power *relations* or *distances* (not influence relations), and power *distributions* or *systems*.

Power as Distance

Power considered as distance between countries utilizes the basic idea of power as an attribute, but casts it in terms of a relation of one power to another, and it is from that perspective that the power explanation of state behavior derives. Traditionally, power as distance has been one aspect of the larger "balance of power" theories, but the overemphasis on the normative aspects of the theory has served to hinder development of the causal hypotheses imbedded within the theory. Because so much of international affairs appears to be a succession of alliances and balancing tactics, attention has focused on these empirical phenomena. And because this balancing seems to occur so consistently, the empirical phenomenon somehow came to be equated with balance of power "theory." Moreover, the tendency has been to transfer the empirical phenomenon into a normative one: states *should* play the balancing game. One focus of attention then becomes the success with which a state (or group of states) carries out its balancing chores. The results are either descriptive or normative, or both. But merely describing a series of balancing acts, or the success or lack of success in balancing, says little about the *effect* of various balance systems. The more important questions, then, are: When, under what circumstances, do states act in a balancing fashion? Under what circumstances do they *not* act in a balancing manner? What impact on international behavior do various balancing systems have?

Ernst Haas's and Inis Claude's critiques of the multiple meanings for the term "balance of power" illustrate the failure to outline the effect of balance of power.[23] According to Claude, balance of power has been used as a *situation,* as a *policy,* and as a *system;* in Haas's review, balance of power has been used to describe a process of "power politics," to

---

[23] Ernst B. Haas, "The Balance of Power: Prescription, Concept, or Propaganda," in *International Politics and Foreign Policy: A Reader in Research and Theory,* ed. James N. Rosenau (New York: Free Press, 1961); Inis Claude, Jr., *Power and International Relations* (New York: Random House, 1962).

describe equilibrium, hegemony, or to describe a universal law. But balance of power as description or situation implies only that nations may be "balanced" or "unbalanced" toward each other on the dimension of power. Saying states will always balance each other—that is, some power relationship will always exist—is, as Claude remarks, "like saying that there will always be *weather* (good or bad, hot or cold) on the earth, or that Mr. X and Mr. Y are inevitably either identical or different in age." [24] Such statements give no hint as to which of the different situations will have what effect on state behavior.

The same critique applies to balance of power as "policy." To argue that the United States "balances" or partakes in a "balance of power policy" in the Western Hemisphere—in order to maintain unchallenged supremacy in the area—says nothing about *when* the United States will act, with whom it will act, or in *what way* it will act. If the retort is that the United States will act when the balance is not in its favor, it is not sufficient to point out, once the United States acts, that it did so because the balance was not in its favor. Such explanations are tautologies.

The same critique applies also to balance of power as a "system," that is, that some type of *automatic* balancing mechanism operates regardless of the individuals or states involved. If balance of power means (1) that states relate to one another, (2) that these relationships often change, and (3) that the changing relationships seem to occur across time regardless of the specific individual states involved, then descriptive content may be high, but explanatory content is very low.

One final problem with the balance of power theory is that it implies states *must act* in power-political terms. As Claude has so succinctly demonstrated with Morgenthau's theory of balance of power, what starts out as an iron law of politics, that states act in terms of power politics, turns out to be Morgenthau's prudent rule of diplomacy, for he admits that some states, at some times, do *not* act in power-politics terms.

Balance of power as "equilibrium" or "hegemony," however, does contain linkages between specific balancing situations and state behavior. For instance, Haas, citing Harold Lasswell, notes that under certain conditions (which need not be specified at the moment), a state will act to increase its power when another increases its potential:

Further increases on the part of one side will always bring corresponding increases on the part of its competitors, so that in effect a rough equality of power potential will always prevail, a factor which may make for either open conflict or induce fear of refraining from hostilities, depending on circumstances.[25]

[24] Claude, *Power and International Relations*, p. 28.
[25] Haas, "The Balance of Power," p. 325.

In other words, "power equality" would more likely lead to a situation of outright conflict than, for instance, situations where the power ratio between the two units was quite great. Here then is a linkage between "balance of power" and behavior: equality of power is more likely to be associated with war or conflict and inequality with peace or the absence of war. Equality means each side thinks it may win; it is also likely to mean each side fears what the other may do. Or as Claude argues, "if an equilibrium means that either side may lose, it also means that either side may win" [26] and therefore that a nation interested in conquest is perhaps likely to undertake that conquest when it has an even chance of winning and not a grossly unfavorable chance of winning. As Dina Zinnes and her associates point out:

A state will not go to war (i.e., commit aggression or allow itself to be drawn into an avoidable war) if it perceives its power (or the power of its coalition) as "significantly" less than that of the enemy at the time that such a decision must be made.[27]

It can also be argued, of course, that "confrontation with approximately equal power will deter a state from undertaking aggressive adventures." [28] And Claude's argument can be used again: If either side has an equal chance of winning, it also has an equal chance of losing. Any potential aggressor is more likely to be deterred when his potential opponent has power equal to his own, for his probability of losing is roughly fifty-fifty. These hypotheses take on much more than academic interest when we realize that military strategists very often contend that the other side must not be allowed a military superiority, an argument constantly employed for the upgrading of military capabilities.

These two hypotheses—that power equality tends to lead *to* conflict, and that power equality tends to *prevent* large-scale conflict—go beyond mere description. They suggest conditions that should lead to specific behavior. Even though contradictory, they can be tested. In fact, a third hypothesis combines the two and partially takes care of the contradictions: the relationship between power equality or inequality and war may be curvilinear. The more equal two countries are, the greater the probability of conflict, *except* that at some point the opposite process, as suggested by Claude, begins to operate: high equality stifles ag-

---

[26] Claude, *Power and International Relations*, p. 56.

[27] Dina A. Zinnes, Robert C. North, and Howard E. Koch, Jr., "Capability, Threat, and the Outbreak of War," in *International Politics and Foreign Policy: A Reader in Research and Theory*, ed. James N. Rosenau (New York: The Free Press, 1961), p. 470.

[28] Claude, *Power and International Relations*, p. 56.

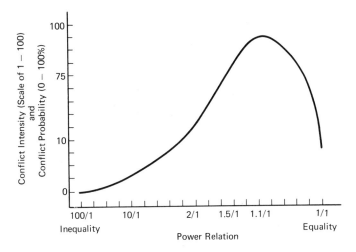

Figure 5-1. Hypothesized relation between power equality or inequality and level of conflict within a dyad.

gressive tendencies because of the fifty-fifty chance of losing. Figure 5-1 presents one possibility of the curvilinear pattern suggested by this hypothesis. Gross inequality would have either low probability of conflict or low conflict; the greater the equality, however, the greater the chance of conflict and, if conflict does break out, the greater the chance of high levels of conflict. When two powers are exactly equal, however, the probability of conflict drops off and if conflict does occur, it will be low level.

These three hypotheses are basically static. They treat the power relationship among states at one point in time. Because the power of states changes, what happens when these relationships change? Organski's "power transition" theory proposes that conflicts are more likely in periods when power transition is under way, when a second party is gaining on the first.[29] He categorizes countries into three groups: those with potential power where productivity is low and industrialization has not begun; those in the transitional growth stage, where industrialization is moving along rapidly, urbanization is occurring, and overall power is growing; those that have reached power maturity, having become fully industrialized and where no large spurts in industrialization take place.

Organski focuses on the second stage, the transitional, because sudden changes in power tend to upset the previous distributions, or balances,

[29] Organski, *World Politics,* chap. 14.

of power. He then introduces the variable of satisfaction, and, combining it with power, categorizes states into four groups:

1. Countries that are powerful and satisfied.
2. Countries that are powerful and dissatisfied.
3. Countries that are weak and satisfied.
4. Countries that are weak and dissatisfied.

As long as all countries fall into categories 1, 3, or 4, war, large-scale war, is unlikely, for the countries are either satisfied and have no reason to wage war or they are weak and therefore cannot wage it successfully. When *power transition* occurs, however, and dissatisfied countries begin to increase their power, they become a threat to those in a position of dominance. War is then more likely to occur because (1) the dissatisfied country may feel its newfound power permits it to take on the predominant power, or (2) the dominant power, viewing the growing power potential of the dissatisfied nation may decide on pre-emptive aggression.

Expanding the proposition even further, if a situation wherein one country is increasing its power over a lead country is likely to produce war, then a situation wherein a lead country is losing its power—even if the second nation is not increasing its power, or at least not noticeably —is also likely to lead to war. The dominant country fears its losing status, and strikes out before running the risk that the second country will wait until its power has become diminished. A third hypothesis would be that any unstable power relation—either where the parties are converging *toward* equality or diverging *from* equality—is more likely to erupt into war than a stable situation, and that if war does occur in an unstable power situation, it will more likely be of high intensity.

There are, therefore, numerous hypotheses linking power relationships or distances between two countries to their warlike behavior. But it should be noted that the dependent variable—war—can take on many forms: "war" as opposed to "no war" is different from "levels of war," which in turn is different from the probability of the outbreak of conflict. Thus, for instance, while Figure 5-1 assumed that increasing parity would have the same effect on both the probability of conflict as well as the intensity of any conflict that did occur, that assumption may be incorrect. It is also plausible to reason that parity may deter the probability of hostilities between any two countries, but if war does break out, the more equal countries may have more intense conflict. Thus, the same hypothesis concerning parity may produce contradictory findings, depending on what behavior is to be explained. As a hypothetical example, one might argue that parity between the superpowers during the Cold War prevented direct conflict between them; at the same time, it is not illogical to conclude that had the improbable actually occurred—namely superpower war—it would be their very parity which would have caused that war to be quite intense.

In sum, power as distance is certainly nothing new. Hypotheses can be found scattered throughout the power literature which reflect those noted here, but there is so much emphasis on peripheral problems such as the definition of power that the hypotheses themselves are very often not the central focus. The hypotheses presented here have offered a beginning framework; however, at a later point, either logic or contradictory findings may force reformulation or suggest new, more complicated hypotheses.

Power as System

Any dyad can be considered analytically as a "system." Our concern now is not with dyadic behavior, however, but with larger, system-wide behavior. The concept of power remains central, but the way in which power is used to explain behavior is quite different. For one thing, power from the systemic perspective will be used in two senses. First—similar to our analysis of it in the preceding section—it will be considered a national attribute, which implies certain behavioral capabilities. Second, it will be considered as a *pole* within a given system. From the perspective of attribute, power is important as a quantity; from the perspective of poles, power is important as a unit of distribution.

Morton Kaplan's classic work on international systems is a convenient starting point for our discussion of power as system. Kaplan proposed six types of international systems based on the distribution of power in terms of potential: the balance of power, loose bipolar, tight bipolar, universal, hierarchical, and unit-veto systems.[30] Only the balance of power, tight bipolar, and loose bipolar systems have actual historical referents. Each system requires that certain rules be followed to perpetuate it; if they are not followed, the system will break down and be transformed. The balance of power system, for instance, requires that nations continually increase their capabilities and negotiate rather than fight. For a nation to violate either part of this rule would mean that it was running the risk of being overpowered, or of destroying the system with all-out war. A second rule requires that nations stop fighting before destroying an essential participant in the system. Again, failure to follow this rule would reduce the probability of maintaining the system because one of

[30] Morton A. Kaplan, *System and Process in International Politics* (New York: John Wiley, 1957), ch. 2.

the fulcrum points would be eliminated. A third rule is that the participants in the system must oppose the predominance of one particular actor or bloc lest "balancing" cease and another international system take its place. As Brian Healy and Arthur Stein note, Kaplan alternates between description and prescription in setting out these rules,[31] saying that not only does the balance of power system describe a given situation but also that in order to retain that system the nations involved must act in certain ways. That is, the system exists because states behave in certain specified ways, and states behave in these patterns because the system exists and therefore constrains them.

But the important question involves *what constraining effect* different systems have on system-wide behavior. Kaplan's rules, for instance, predict that the balance of power system is likely to result in short-term and very specific alliances, which will "shift according to advantage and not according to ideology (even within war)."[32] In addition, balance of power will tend to produce limited wars because people do not want to eliminate an essential actor. Waltz suggests that a rather tight bipolar system, such as that manifested after World War II, would permit second- and third-rate countries more freedom of action, producing, most likely, numerous so-called brush-fire wars as the major countries continued their conflicts with each other on the peripheries.[33] The loose bipolar system, on the other hand, will result in alliances that "tend to be long-term, to be based on permanent and not on shifting interests, and to have ideological components." Kaplan feels that wars under such circumstances, except for the fear of nuclear devastation "would tend to be unlimited."[34]

These propositions in no way exhaust the linkage between power distribution and general conflict, warlike behavior, or alliances, but they do give a general flavor for the kinds of linkages that have been proposed. The most common denominator has been concern over which of the many possible international power distributions is the most *stable*.

The vast majority of balance of power or power theorists tend to view power in terms of capabilities. Deutsch and Singer and later Singer and Small take a slightly different approach when they revert to the notion of *number* of actors in the system and the effect of that distribution on

[31] Brian Healy and Arthur Stein, "The Balance of Power in International History: Theory and Reality," *Journal of Conflict Resolution* 17 (March, 1973), p. 40.

[32] Morton A. Kaplan, "Variants on Six Models of the International System," in *International Politics and Foreign Policy: A Reader in Research and Theory*, ed. James N. Rosenau, rev. ed. (New York: The Free Press, 1969), p. 295.

[33] Kenneth Waltz, "International Structure, National Force, and the Balance of World Power," in *International Politics and Foreign Policy: A Reader in Research and Theory*, ed. James N. Rosenau, rev. ed. (New York: The Free Press, 1969).

[34] Kaplan, "Variants on Six Models," p. 297.

stability. Moreover, their logical link from number of actors in the system to stability is slightly different. Deutsch and Singer argue that "as the system moves away from bipolarity toward multipolarity, the frequency and intensity of war should be expected to diminish." [35] Citing the "pluralistic" model as a basis for their argument, they note that incompatibilities between states will tend to be amplified if they all run along the same lines or divisions. To resort to the traditional domestic example by way of explanation: if a dispute occurs along racial lines, conflict may occur; the more divisions that occur along the same racial lines, however, the more likely will conflict occur. If cross-cutting pressures are present—that is, if some divisions do not run along racial lines —then the conflict will not be amplified. However, if union members, for instance, dislike all nonunion members, and if union members also happen to be Catholic and dislike all Protestants, who happen to be nonunion members; and if this situation is further aggravated by the fact that the union members are not only Catholics but predominantly black, whereas the nonunion members are Protestants and white, then all three divisions are pitting the same people against each other on each dispute. This theory contends that such numerous divisions along the same lines should result in few interaction opportunities between the opposing groups. The contrary situation, of course, would be one of many interaction opportunities, one that "would seem to favor social stability and to inhibit social cleavage." [36]

Greater numbers of interaction opportunities require the parties to pay attention to more states, which means they will be less able to pay attention to a state with which they might be in an escalating conflict. Thus, if we assume that some minimal level of interaction is needed between two states before they can have anything to conflict about, and if the number of actors increases and thereby decreases the amount of attention any one actor can pay to any other actor, "such an increase [in the number of actors] is likely to have a stabilizing effect upon the system." [37] The type of international system—in this case the "number of poles"—should explain some of the variation in the existence and intensity of warlike behavior in the system.

Dina Zinnes has elaborated upon and clarified these propositions.[38] Zinnes noted that there are really two *dependent* variables: international

35 Karl Deutsch and J. David Singer, "Multipolar Power Systems and International Stability," in *International Politics and Foreign Policy: A Reader in Research and Theory*, ed. James N. Rosenau, rev. ed. (New York: The Free Press, 1969), p. 315.

36 Ibid., p. 317.

37 Ibid., p. 321.

38 Dina Zinnes, "An Analytical Study of the Balance of Power Theories," *Journal of of Peace Research* 4 (No. 3, 1967), pp. 270–88.

peace and the status quo, the latter being a circumstance in which all states are held in check. This critique takes on particular importance because of the earlier observation that much of the problem with power and balance of power theories is an unwillingness to state exactly the behavior to be explained. Predicting peace from a balance of power situation is quite different from predicting simple maintenance of the status quo.

Zinnes's more important contribution focuses on the *independent* variable of balance of power. What exactly is *the* or *a* balance of power? After citing eleven different definitions, Zinnes comments that all, except for differences in expression, exhibit "almost complete agreement on the defining characteristic of a balance of power world." The phenomenon involves a distribution of power among states such that no single state or alliance has an overwhelming preponderance of power. "Any distribution is permissible," says Zinnes, "as long as the power of each unit—state or alliance of states—in the system is less than the combined power of all the remaining units." [39] To Zinnes, the theory ultimately being tested by Singer and Small is not so much a "balance of power" theory as it is a "polarity" or "cross pressure" theory. First, the traditional definitions allow only for dichotomous measures of the independent variable, namely, that there can be either balance of power systems or nonbalance of power systems. To Singer and Small balance of power is a continuous variable; it changes simply by increasing the number of nations having alliance commitments. Second, the Singer-Small study does not posit the independent variable as a function of *power* as a measureable attribute but as a function of the distribution of alliances. Finally, the definition of the alliance variable differs in the Singer-Small study from the traditional formulations of balance of power reviewed by Zinnes; in the latter the *number of alliances in the system* (two or none; balance of power or nonbalance of power) is the important factor, whereas in the Singer-Small study *the number of nations having at least one alliance commitment* is the crucial factor.

This critique of one notion of balance of power is important for its emphasis on outlining the independent and dependent variables. It takes particular cognizance of the fact that the theory may have nothing to do with "power" as normally defined. This "balance of power" theory, then, is more accurately a "polarity" theory, one in which the number of poles is the independent variable rather than the levels of attribute power. The distinction made at the beginning of this section should now be clear, and is important to keep in mind: two views of balance

[39] Ibid., p. 272.

of power on the systemic level are: that (1) power involves attribute strength and that (2) power involves polarity regardless of strength.

As we have mentioned, balance of power theorists do not speak with one mind. Singer and Small see instability resulting from a bipolar world. Waltz notes that the post-World War II system—a fairly tight bipolar world—was in fact very stable, despite the crises and disruptive periods. Healy and Stein present yet a slightly different hypothesis in citing Arthur Lee Burns's proposition that the closer two or more countries are bound by an alliance, the greater the pressure between one or both of those and any third power or group of powers.[40] Thus in a three-nation system, mutual reduction of arms by two powers will change their relationship with the third; cooperation between the first two will be offset by conflict between one or both of those, on the one hand, and the third power, on the other. In this example, the balance of power between that single power and the other two has changed, and the prediction is for greater conflict.

These hypotheses may not be exceptionally complex, at least as presented here in preliminary form. They do, however, become somewhat more complicated when it is recognized that what appear to be similar hypotheses are very often quite different. For instance, in asking "Which system is more stable?" Kaplan and Waltz appear to be on opposite sides. Kaplan is contending that the multipolar system has greater stability and Waltz is arguing that the bipolar is the more stable. What Waltz may in fact be maintaining, however, is that the specific bipolar world of the Cold War was stable insofar as a big-power war—nuclear or nonnuclear—did not ocur. But that hypothesis is quite different from one contending that bipolar systems are more stable than other systems, because in fact on many measures the Cold War era was highly unstable.

Although the vast majority of "power theory" has been applied to *conflict* behavior as the dependent variable, power distribution has also been related to cooperative behavior. Many writers lump the propositions that follow regarding cooperation under something called "alliance theories." They properly belong, however, to the domain of power theory. The manifested behavior may be an alliance, but the *explanations* of that behavior rest on power. Balance of power, in other words, plays a role in the formation of alliances. Morgenthau's general statement that "alliances are a necessary function of the balance of power operating within a multiple-state system" [41] does not present a theoretical proposi-

---

[40] Healy and Stein, "Balance of Power in International History," p. 36.

[41] Morgenthau, *Politics among Nations*, p. 181.

tion linking the two phenomena. Nonetheless, he does observe that alliances will form when several countries are threatened by one large country, or when a group of countries feels it must come together to confront another alliance. Unfortunately, no *general* form of the relationship is proposed.

William Riker's formulation concerning coalition behavior—later generalized by Bruce Russett to international alliances—can be viewed as an extension of Morganthau's hypothesis in that a general statement can be used to propose what nations are likely to align with what other nations. Although Russett limits his formulation to situations where a threat of war either exists or is likely to exist shortly, with a little imagination the theory can be generalized beyond that. Russett uses Riker's "size principle" to suggest that (in gaming terms) "the players will form that grouping which is the smallest winning coalition, that contains just enough power to gain the decision, but no more than is necessary for the purpose." [42] Because the rational decision-maker has no desire to squander payoffs derived from the coalition on needless members, he will favor coalitions that constitute the smallest number capable of winning, and at the same time provide the largest payoffs per member.

To illustrate, assume four countries each with the following power potential: $A = 7$; $B = 9$; $C = 2$; $D = 1$. The "size principle" predicts that countries B and D will form into a coalition, because their combined power $(9 + 1 = 10)$ is sufficient to defeat the other possible coalition $(A + C = 9)$, and yet B will be required to pay out less to D than it would to any other member. This formulation assumes, of course, that payoffs are closely related to the respective country's power potential, to their power input in a given situation. Although the assumption may not always apply, Morgenthau argues that "the distribution of benefits is . . . likely to reflect the distribution of power within an alliance, as is the determination of policies." [43]

The coalition situation mentioned above does *not,* of course, meet the requirements set down by Zinnes for a balance of power system, namely that "the power of every unit in the system—state or alliance of states—is less than the combined power of all the remaining units in the system." [44] Clearly, if B and D align, their power is greater, and the balance of the

[42] Bruce M. Russett, "Components of an Operational Theory of Alliance Formation," *Journal of Conflict Resolution* 12 (September, 1968), p. 286; William Riker, *The Theory of Political Coalitions* (New Haven, Conn.: Yale University Press, 1962).

[43] Morgenthau, *Politics among Nations,* p. 185.

[44] Dina A. Zinnes, "Coalition Theories and the Balance of Power," in *The Study of Coalition Behavior: Theoretical Perspectives and Cases from Four Continents,* ed. Sven Groennings, E. W. Kelley, and Michael Leiserson (New York: Holt, Rinehart, and Winston, 1970), p. 353.

system is thereby lost; this is a crucial point to which we will return. Even so, the balance—defined now as distribution—provides predictions about what alliance will be formed. Power distribution, therefore, predicts alliance formations—based on certain postulates of rational man.

Other predictions from power distribution can be derived by making slightly different assumptions. Here both Zinnes's and Russett's reviews are helpful.[45] First, if stronger nations usually control weaker ones, as Morganthau states—certainly a reasonable assumption—and if a prime desire for any strong country is to control as many other nations as possible—again a reasonable assumption—then for each power distribution, predictions can be made about the most probable coalitions to occur, all other things being equal. For instance, if the distributions were: $A = 7$; $B = 5$, $C = 2$, $D = 1$; $E = 1$, then the most general prediction would be for A to align with someone else, for if aligned with almost any other member A could defeat the remaining countries combined. The size principle alone predicts that A would align either with C, or with D and E. The alternative theory presented here, however, would predict a definite alignment with C, because, the A-C coalition would then control three other countries, whereas if A aligned with D and E, that coalition would control only two other countries. Other variables will influence alliance formation; nonetheless, the question at hand is how distributions of power differentially affect the formation of alliances.

But what of the problem, cited a moment ago, concerning the definition of balance of power? According to Zinnes, Riker's propositions about alliance formation involve a contradiction. Because states play a rational game, they want to maximize their payoffs, and inasmuch as Riker is working in a zero-sum situation the actors can only maximize their payoffs by taking something from the other players. To do that, a state must join a coalition because—as the definition for balance of power states—no single individual state or alliance is stronger than any other state or alliance. And that's the rub: coalitions do form; therefore, a winning coalition can only occur by violating Zinnes's criterion for a strict balance of power, namely, that the coalition obtains enough power to defeat other countries or coalitions, in which case there is no longer a balance of power. As Zinnes remarks, "By definition, a balance of power ceases to exist at that moment at which Riker's winning coalition emerges." [46] A balance of power, then, can be very unstable, and it ends since coalition formation is a constant process. That conclusion is of secondary concern here, however, since our primary concentration is on

45 Zinnes, "Coalition Theories"; Russett, "Components of an Operational Theory," pp. 285–301.

46 Zinnes, "Coalition Theories," p. 359.

what effect different balance systems or configurations have on *other* behavior in the international system.

Power conceived quite explicitly therefore as "distance" or as "system" presents several propositions predicting state action, both cooperative and conflictual. All of this has been an attempt to move beyond common-sense notions of power as a "goal" (and therefore somehow "important" theoretically) or as a mere description of a situation, to actually considering propositions about power's effect.

Rank and Status Theories

In recent years a slight variant on theories of power has emerged, called rank theory. Its operational indicators are often the same as those of power theory, it also considers behavior either dyadically or system-wide, and, ultimately, rank theory is also really talking about power. But its *explanation* of behavior has a slightly different twist.

Only a brief overview of rank theory can be presented here: many formal expositions have been presented elsewhere.[47] The basic supposition of the theory is that social systems become stratified and that certain types of stratification, combined with certain assumptions about how human beings behave, then lead to predictions about their behavior based on their rank or status in the system. Assuming that there may be numerous dimensions of rank or status, the equilibrated nation would be one that is high (called "topdog" by Galtung) on all dimensions or low ("underdog") on all dimensions; if there are five dimensions, the topdog and underdog nations would be designated TTTTT and UUUUU. Neither of these situations is likely to cause trouble. When a nation (or person) becomes disequilibrated, when it becomes, say, a TTTUU, it means it is going to receive differential treatment (esteemed because of its TTT dimensions, but not esteemed because of its UU dimensions), and it is going to have the totally topdog nations as a reference point.

Clearly, such a hypothesis edges fairly close to Morganthau's notion of struggle for power. The TTTUU nation is obviously trying to replace its two underdog dimensions with topdog ones. To think in terms of two

---

[47] Galtung, *Journal of Peace Research* 1; Johan Galtung, "Rank and Social Integration: A Multi-Dimensional Approach," in *Sociological Theories in Progress*, eds. Joseph Berger, Morris Zelditch, and Bo Anderson (Boston: Houghton Mifflin, 1966); Rudolph J. Rummel, "U.S. Foreign Relations: Conflict, Cooperation, and Attribute Distances," in *Peace, War, and Numbers*, ed. Bruce Russett (Beverly Hills: Sage, 1972); Nils Gleditsch, "Rank and Interaction," *Proceedings of International Peace Research Association* 2 (1970).

dimensions of status, for instance, "achieved" and "ascribed," a nation that has a very large population and land mass may have high ascribed status (China, India, Brazil) but very low achieved status, meaning other countries do not treat it as important even though it has many of the parameters that make nations "important." The theory then suggests that these countries will attempt to upgrade their underdog categories.

Aggression is more likely to be committed, therefore, by states that are disequilibrated. While the causal factors—the perception that one's nation is disequilibrated—may exist on the individual level with individual perceptions—nonetheless the theory is considered systemic because rank can only be defined relative to other nations, and the theory makes the assumption that by and large individuals will react to disequilibrated situations in similar ways. When nation-state rank is not in equilibrium, therefore, aggression is more apt to take place than when a nation-state is equilibrated. Moreover, the greater the degree of disequilibrium, the greater the likelihood of aggression.

Rank—or "status"—theory has, of course, the greatest implications for international behavior such as aggression. But it also makes predictions concerning simple raw interaction as well as cooperative behavior. Higher rank states will interact more with other higher rank states than with lower rank states. In addition, lower rank states will tend to aim their interaction more often at the higher rank nations than at their fellow underdogs. Finally, nations more similar in economic status (as opposed to other types of status) will be more cooperative toward one another than states distant from one another in economic development.

Rank or status theory bears striking resemblances to power hypotheses, but its explanations are distinct. With rank, nations are not particularly concerned about the possible aggression of another party; rather, the causal factor is an internal one of "frustration" or "dissatisfaction" with one's position in the system. Like the power hypothesis, however, rank theory can be conceptualized on both a dyadic as well as a systemic level: predictions regarding aggression can be made about dyads as the unit of analysis, as well as about overall systems, using the overall level of rank disequilibrium in the entire system.

Measurement

An extraordinary amount of attention has been given to the problems of measuring power, and the normal conclusion is that it cannot really be measured effectively. The difficulties of measurement arise from two tendencies: the first is an insistence on measuring every conceivable aspect of power, and the second is an unwillingness to separate power as attribute from power as influence, for the latter truly does present formidable measurement problems. As noted already, we will consider power as influence in Chapter 7, where it is treated as influence theory. The task of measuring power as attribute, however, must now be confronted.

Our solution to the supposedly insuperable problem of measuring power is deceptively simple, and therefore will not satisfy purists who insist that power is ultimately nonmeasurable. It requires at least one assumption: if gross, objective yardsticks of power—population, GNP, energy production, size of the military, or a combination of these—do *not* measure it accurately, then the results of research on power based on these indicators should be inconclusive. Confirmation of hypotheses using these gross measures should, therefore, apart from lending credence to the underlying theory, also serve as partial validity of the power measure.

Perhaps even more important, however, is the fact that although many pay extended lip service to the more nebulous aspects of power—morale, will, character—few researchers have used these aspects in any systematic sense. Even those who advocate their consideration and inclusion in studies of power fall back on gross, observable measures. Organski, for instance, suggests six determinants of power—population, political development, economic development, national morale, resources, and geography—but admits the impracticability of using all six. "We must limit ourselves to those that can be measured with some exactness," says Organski, "but even with this limitation we can construct an index that will be of use." [48] He concludes that GNP or GNP per capita constitute perhaps the best overall index of power.

Even the failure to measure the nebulous items, as Organski points out, does not mean that a useful index cannot be constructed. Geography and resources make little contribution to power by themselves, but they do contribute as they are developed and used in industrial production. It is almost impossible to assess national morale, rated fourth in importance by Organski, yet its influence shows up in the workings of the government. In other words, the determinants of power are related to one another and affect one another.

Furthermore, some research suggests that people's perceptions of national power correspond closely with these observable attributes. Norman Alcocke and Alan Newcombe found that the perceptions of thirty-eight people regarding the power of 122 nations correlated highly with the GNP and military expenditures of those countries. They concluded that "power is some function of GNP . . . and the function is identified as military expenditures in purchasing power-equivalent dollars." [49]

[48] Organski, *World Politics,* p. 207.

[49] Norman Alcock and Alan G. Newcombe, "The Perception of National Power," *Journal of Conflict Resolution* 14 (September, 1970), p. 339.

With the above arguments we have legitimately bypassed some of the great mystery that has for so long surrounded the question, "What is power?" Admittedly, power is complex and objective measures cannot hope to reflect all of its possible nuances nor perfectly reflect each country's power. But the indicators do show the different aspects of power, and they offer some valid suggestions on how it can be assessed.

Power Analysis

POWER DISTANCE: CROSS-SECTIONAL

The effect of the distance between countries in power on their behavior towards each other has received a substantial amount of research attention. One method of investigating that relationship is to use the dyad as our unit of analysis, and make comparisons across numerous dyads on both their power distance as well as their behavior towards each other. Most of the findings regarding power distance are abstracted from larger studies not specifically related to that subject. The relationships, therefore, may be very small because the other variables in the larger studies have not been included (see Chapter 8).

As part of his larger field theory studies, Rummel tested the "equality" hypothesis that countries equal in power are more likely to engage in conflict than countries unequal in power. He determined, however, that for ninety-one dyads between the years 1955 and 1957 the role of power distance was not significant, though verbal conflict (threats, protests, accusations) was very moderately related to power distance.[50] Michael Sullivan extracted from Rummel's data only those dyads with conflict, contending that power distance may be more important for the *level* of conflict rather than the conflict-no conflict dichotomy, which, of course, would make it a much more limited theory. The relationships again turned out to be very small. For a different set of fifteen conflicts, power distance taken alone was also unrelated to the level of conflict.[51]

In a later reanalysis of his data for 1955, however, Rummel investigated a different dependent variable for his equality hypothesis. He found that

[50] Rudolph J. Rummel, "A Social Field Theory of Foreign Conflict Behavior," *Peace Research Society Papers* 4 (1966), pp. 131–50. The partial correlation, however, which means the effect of power on the communication dimension of conflict once all other effects have been controlled for, was only .15.

[51] Michael P. Sullivan, "Escalatory and Nonescalatory 'Systems,'" *American Journal of Political Science* 18 (August, 1974), pp. 549–58. The second set of fifteen conflicts was drawn from Barbara Fitzsimmons, "The Role of Violence in International Conflicts," Mimeographed Support Study No. 1 (Los Angeles: University of Southern California, 1969).

differences between nations on energy consumption per capita and national income can account for sixty-three percent of the variation in one nation's behavior towards another in terms of translations, tourists, treaties, and co-joining international organizations.[52]

These findings relate to power distance because power capability is equated with the ascribed status concept of rank theory; the more dissimilar in ascribed status the object nation and the actor, the more likely are there to be high levels of cooperative behavior. Thus, the equality hypothesis receives support only in terms of its relation to cooperative and not conflictual behavior.

Rummel later included the variables of cooperative as well as conflict behavior in his investigation of actions of the United States toward eighty-one other countries. The distance between America and the others, he found, contributed "positively to the magnitude of cooperative actions." [53] Power parity did not, however, explain much of the *net* co-operation-conflict behavior, though it did correlate highly with another behavior labeled by Rummel "Western European Cooperation and Deterrence." Even so, his conclusions are quite straightforward:

Were we to consider the hypotheses (1) U.S. conflict behavior is a result of power parity, (2) Cold War behavior or deterrent behavior is a consequence of the closeness in power of the object, (3) U.S. conflict is dependent on power, or similar hypotheses, then they also find little confirmation in the results [of his investigations].[54]

Tong-Whan Park, on the other hand, found support for the power parity hypothesis in the Asian subsystem for both 1955 and 1963, but his findings were quite limited. For both years power parity correlated with "net conflict" (conflict minus cooperation) at a statistically significant level but the amount of net conflict variation accounted for was extremely small.[55] Furthermore, Sang-Woo Rhee's analysis of only China's conflict behavior toward eighty-one nations for 1955 and 1963 found "that the more powerful the object nation, the more hostile China's communica-

[52] R. J. Rummel, "Field Theory and Indicators of International Behavior," Research Report 29, Dimensionality of Nations Project, University of Hawaii (Paper delivered at the Annual Meeting of the American Political Science Association, New York, September, 1969), pp. 30–31.

[53] Rummel, "U.S. Foreign Relations," p. 102.

[54] Ibid., p. 109.

[55] Tong-Whan Park, "Asian Conflict in Systemic Perspective: Application of Field Theory (1955 and 1963)," Research Report 35, Dimensionality of Nations Project (Honolulu: University of Hawaii, December, 1969). With 342 observations, the correlation of .15 for 1955, for instance, while statistically "significant" at the one percent level, still only shows a common variation between power parity and net conflict of two percent.

tion." [56] Clearly this finding is contrary to the power parity hypothesis, for in this case the more China was the underdog, the more hostile was its communication, whereas the power parity hypothesis would predict the opposite. Even though the United States—with its large power level—is accounting for much of the high linear correlation Rhee discovered (see appendix, paragraph A.1 for an analysis of the effect of such "outliers"), nonetheless the scatterplot that Rhee presented showed that states less powerful than China received less negative communication, and those higher in power received more. A confirmation of the power parity hypothesis would have shown a *curvilinear* pattern with countries that were very close to China on power measure (such as India, South Korea, Japan, Italy, and Egypt) receiving the greatest amount of negative communication.

Wayne Ferris tested the hypothesis on the forty-two international wars drawn from the Singer-Small Correlates of War Project, spanning the 1850–1965 period, as well as conflicts taken from Holsti and Wright.[57] He did find a very small relationship, indicating that the greater the power disparity, the less the devastation of the war; conversely, therefore, the smaller the disparity, the longer and more devastating the war. One view of the parity hypothesis, therefore, is confirmed, although the strongest relation explains only 7 percent of the variation in war devastation.

However, upon investigating the data visually, it turns out the relationship might be slightly more complex—and interesting—than the linear hypothesis would suggest. There appears to be a very slight curvilinear relation with the casualties data, however (Table 5-1a), whereby those dyads with the greatest parity run the greatest risk of severe wars, those

Table 5-1a. Casualties and Power Ratios in 41 International Wars

	Power Disparity Ratios			
Casualties	*1.00-1.99*	*2.00-3.99*	*4.00-7.99*	*8.00 +*
600 +	6 (40%)	3 (27%)	4 (40%)	0 (0%)
100-599	8 (53%)	3 (27%)	2 (20%)	4 (66%)
0-99	1 (7%)	5 (45%)	4 (40%)	2 (33%)

[56] Sang-Woo Rhee, "Communist China's Foreign Behavior: An Application of Field Theory, Model II," Research Report 57, Dimensionality of Nations Project (Honolulu: University of Hawaii, 1971), pp. 140–41.

[57] Wayne H. Ferris, *The Power Capabilities of Nation-States* (Lexington, Mass.: Lexington Books, 1973); the additional data were taken from K. J. Holsti, "Resolving International Conflicts: A Taxonomy of Behavior and Some Figures on Procedures," *Journal of Conflict Resolution* 10 (September, 1966), pp. 272–96; and Quincy Wright, *A Study of War*, 2nd ed. (Chicago: University of Chicago Press, 1965).

with "almost equal" power have a much lesser risk, while those with even less parity have a slightly higher risk of severe wars. However, in terms of war duration (Table 5-1b), there is a much more linear rela-

Table 5-1b. Nation-Months of War and Power Ratios for 41 International Wars

Duration in Nation-Months	Power Disparity Ratios			
	1.00-1.99	*2.00-3.99*	*4.00-7.99*	*8.00 +*
30 +	4 (27%)	2 (18%)	1 (10%)	1 (17%)
10-29	2 (13%)	2 (18%)	1 (10%)	0 (0%)
0-9	9 (60%)	7 (64%)	8 (80%)	5 (83%)

tionship, with countries close to one another in power more likely to have longer wars than the other groups. (However, it should be noted that these cut-off points for parity are to some degree arbitrary and placing them elsewhere changes the relationships somewhat.)

Some very partial confirmation of the curvilinear relation is presented in Table 5-2, showing Wright and Holsti data with Ferris's power disparity

Table 5-2. Power Disparity Ratios in Hostile and Nonhostile Conflicts

Hostilities		Power Disparity Ratio			
		1.00-1.99	*2.00-3.99*	*4.00-9.99*	*10.00-39.99*
Wright	YES	7 (16%)	1 (4%)	5 (23%)	5 (19%)
	NO	38 (84%)	26 (96%)	17 (77%)	21 (81%)
Holsti	YES	6 (26%)	3 (19%)	5 (42%)	5 (31%)
	NO	17 (74%)	13 (81%)	7 (58%)	11 (69%)

Figures in this table are based on data contained in Wayne H. Ferris, *The Power Capability of Nation-States* (Lexington, Mass.: Lexington Books, 1973).

scores. The percentages bear out the curvilinear relation, where the "most equal" and the "not very equal" powers have more of a chance of experiencing hostilities with the other party than the "almost equal" group (ratio of 2.00 to 3.99). However, it should again be noted that despite the same curvilinear trend in both tables, the percentage differences are *not* very great, and only one of the tables (the Wright data) even comes near statistical significance.

But the dependent variable has been either level of war (duration and severity from Singer and Small) or hostilities versus no hostilities (Wright and Holsti data). The conclusion therefore seems to be that there is indeed a slight relation in which, *for all power situations,* parity or something very close to it is the most dangerous.

The parity theory does not seem to work, however, when evaluating which situations are likely to move from *no conflict* to *conflict.* Tables 5-3a and 5-3b present data comparing the Holsti and Wright conflicts to 105 nonconflict situations between adjacent states randomly drawn from the international system by Ferris.[58] Reading across Table 5-3a shows that in comparing conflict to nonconflict groups across categories of

Table 5-3. Power Disparity Ratios in Conflict and Non-Conflict Situations

Table 5-3a. Percentage of Conflict and Non-Conflict Situations in Six Different Power Disparity Categories

				Power Disparity Ratio							
	1.00-1.99		*2.00-3.99*		*4.00-9.99*		*10.00-39.99*		*40.00 +*		*Total*
	(H)	(W)	(H)	(W)	(H)	(W)	(H)	(W)	(H)	(W)	(H) (W)
Conflict Situations	32%	37%	23%	21%	17%	18%	23%	21%	6%	2%	101% 99%
Nonconflict Situations	58%		19%		16%		7%		0%		100

Table 5-3b. Percentage of Conflict and Non-Conflict Situations in Each of Six Power Disparity Ratios

				Power Disparity Ratio					
	1.00-1.99		*2.00-3.99*		*4.00-9.99*		*10.00-39.99*		*40.00 +*
	(H)	(W)	(H)	(W)	(H)	(W)	(H)	(W)	(H) (W)
Conflict Situations	27%	43%	45%	56%	41%	56%	70%	79%	100% 100%
Nonconflict Situations	73	57	55	44	59	44	30	21	
Total	100%	100%	100%	100%	100%	100%	100%	100%	100% 100%

Figures in these tables are based on data contained in Wayne H. Ferris, *The Power Capability of Nation-States* (Lexington, Mass.: Lexington Books, 1973).

[58] Ferris's analysis is somewhat confusing on this count. While he hypothesizes "the greater the power capabilities disparity prior to the initiation of war, (1) the less devastation resulting from war, and (2) the shorter the duration of war," yet he concludes that "all of the coefficients are in the opposite direction of that predicted, suggesting that as power capabilities disparity increases, war devastation and war duration diminish." Ferris, *The Power Capabilities of Nation-States,* p. 65. However, as noted in the text, Ferris's findings *do* appear to confirm at least one version of the parity (disparity) hypothesis.

power ratios, a greater percentage of nonconflict situations fall into the low-disparity group (58 percent), than is the case with conflict situations. The conflict situations are much more evenly distributed, although still the majority do tend to fall into the lower power ratio groups. Comparing the percent conflict to nonconflict situations within each of the power disparity categories (Table 5-3b) shows that the majority of parity situations (1.00–1.99) are in the nonconflict group. Likewise, the majority of those in the unequal groups (disparity ratio of 10.00 and above) are conflict situations. The parity groups in between these extremes exhibit a trend whereby as we move toward greater disparity there are more situations falling into the conflict category, starting earlier with the Wright than with the Holsti data. These data must, of course, be interpreted with caution, because the group of conflict situations was not chosen in the same way in which the nonconflict group was, and therefore some variable common to each of the former but absent from the bottom group (i.e., different ideologies—see Chapter 6) may be causing the pattern illustrated.

The power distance between countries does not appear to be a singularly strong predictor of the conflict behavior within given dyadic situations. Measures of cooperative behavior, on the contrary, do appear to be related to power distance. It is possible, however, that a curvilinear relation describes the power distance-conflict hypothesis more accurately, and that power distance relates differently to the level of conflict than to the presence or absence of conflict.

POWER DISTANCE: LONGITUDINAL

Power parity as a static variable seems to be only a moderate predictor to international behavior. Power distance, however, may play a dynamic role where a *changing* distance might cause more conflict if two powers are becoming more equal—the superior country fearing the rising power of a second nation, and the second nation becoming bolder as its power increases. On the other hand, any *unstable* power relation—regardless of which country is gaining or losing—might also be more likely to produce more violence than a very stable situation.

Sullivan considered both hypotheses in his re-analysis of the Rummel conflict dyads, but found no consistent pattern in this respect.[59] Ferris also investigated the effect of changed power ratios on the occurrence of military hostilities and likewise found no significant relations in four different sets of conflicts. All of his correlations were negative. Plotting

[59] Sullivan, "Escalatory and Nonescalatory 'Systems.'"

the Singer-Small war duration data against Ferris's power ratio shows why: The longest conflicts had the smallest percent change in power disparity (Figure 5-2). A rather interesting finding emerges from Figure 5-3, however, which shows that a closing of the gap (negative changes) is more likely to result in wars than a broadening of the gap (positive changes). Of the eight wars of more than twenty nation-months duration, six were situations of a closing gap.

The Sullivan and Ferris studies are longitudinal only in that they consider dynamic changes in power before the outbreak of conflict. Jeffrey Milstein's analysis of the Middle East illustrates a longitudinal design investigating the effect of *changing* power on *changing* conflict levels in which both variables are measured across time. Milstein hypothesized that the military power of an enemy is a potential threat, and

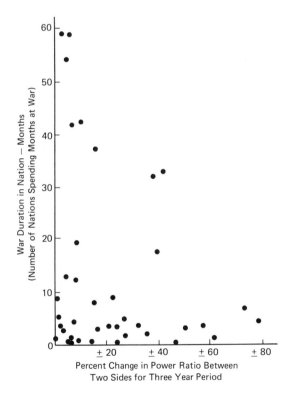

Source: This table is based on data presented in Wayne H. Ferris, *The Power Capability of Nation-States* (Lexington, Mass.: Lexington Books, 1973).

Figure 5-2. Change in power ratio and war duration.

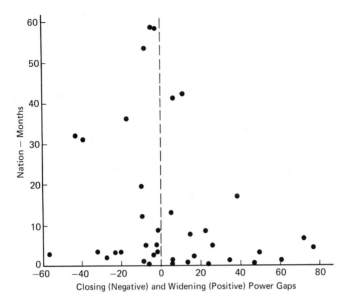

Source: Ferris, 1972.

Figure 5-3. Direction of power change and war duration.

that in the Mideast "we would expect a gap in military capabilities to put stress on the leaders to decrease the gap or, in more traditional terms, to return the balance of power." [60] He first investigated the relationship merely across time. The difference or gap in military expenditure (plus military aid received) between Israel and the Arab countries, he felt, should explain the differences in violence. Only one behavior was affected in the Egyptian-Israeli dyad, and only in terms of Israel's actions; more specifically, the greater the Egyptian military superiority, the more encounters between government forces Israel initiated. Similarly, in the Israeli-Syrian dyad, the greater Israel's superiority, the more Syria initiated encounters between government forces. No relations occurred between Israel, on the one hand, and Jordan, Iraq, and Lebanon, on the other.

Dynamic hypotheses, however, ultimately imply rates of change between power distance rather than merely the gross distance itself. If the opponent's rate of power change is increasing, or a nation's own power

[60] Jeffrey Milstein, "American and Soviet Influence, Balance of Power, and Arab-Israeli Violence," in *Peace, War, and Numbers,* ed. Bruce Russett (Beverly Hills: Sage, 1972), p. 158.

is decreasing, it might be motivated to resort to violent action. In Milstein's study the relationships changed slightly: the more superior Egypt was in terms of *levels* of power *and* yearly *increases,* the more mobilizations and alerts *it* initiated; and, as just noted, the greater the increment of Israeli power change, the more Syria initiated encounters between government forces. Even investigating the differences in changes between two countries—comparing country A's power change with country B's power change—the same dyad behaves in a relatively similar fashion: the more superior Israel is relative to Syria, the more Syria initiates confrontations. Milstein is correct in concluding that "the balance of military power does not in any systematic way affect the initiation of violence between Arabs and Israelis." [61]

Inasmuch as the main antagonists in the Middle East have been Egypt, Syria, and Israel, Milstein's findings say more about violence in that sector of the world than he infers. About one-third of the variation in Israeli and Syrian encounters between government forces are accounted for by the military gap with the other side. Furthermore, roughly one-fourth of Egypt's mobilizations and alerts are accounted for by Egypt's superiority: the more superior Egypt is, the more it will go on alert, emergencies, and mobilizations.

The findings reported in this section in no way firmly supported the distance hypotheses. Nevertheless, they clearly showed that power disparity as a single variable plays at best only a minor role in accounting for several types of behavior. But the findings, especially Ferris's, may prove quite helpful on two counts: first, the suggestion that a curvilinear relationship exists between power disparity and conflict or war, and second, the hint that power parity plays a different role depending on whether the analyst is interested in the level of war, in hostilities versus no hostilities, or in major moves from no conflict to conflict. Some questions can be raised concerning the design of the Ferris study in this regard, but it appears that parity is much more successful in keeping dyads from engaging in conflict than it is in keeping them from escalating a conflict to severe proportions.

It is difficult to reconcile the several findings concerning dynamic changes. The Ferris study indicated that small changes in power ratios and changes that closed the power gap (as opposed to widening it) were slightly more prone to produce longer (and more severe) wars. The Milstein study did not necessarily confirm these findings, but his unit of analysis was not numerous different dyads but only a few dyads considered over time. If the data were to show Egypt closing the gap between

[61] Ibid., p. 162.

itself and Israel, and Israel closing the gap between itself and Syria, then the findings would confirm that closing gaps tend to produce more violence.

RANK, OR STATUS

Though the rank, or status, theory has been more concerned than other theories with simply predicting overall interaction, the type of interaction is often of a cooperative nature. Galtung, for example, finds that in almost all instances involving governmental initiative (diplomatic visits, trade agreements, tourist restrictions, tourist volume, airline connections) between NATO and the Warsaw Pact countries, the greatest amount of interaction went from topdog to topdog, with the second largest moving up in rank from underdog to topdog.[62] Nils Gleditsch found that in terms of airline flights, International Governmental Organizations (IGO) and International Nongovernmental Organizations (INGO) ties, and diplomatic bonds (number of diplomats sent or received), the greatest interaction was between nations with the highest *total* rank, followed by those with rank profile similarity, meaning that they were topdog and underdog on the same types of ranks.[63] Maurice East, however, in using IGO data taken from Russett, determined that the greatest amount of interaction was *not* necessarily between those with highest rank.[64] Finally, W. R. Thompson concluded that no relation existed between status and state visits in the Middle East in 1965.[65]

Concerning cooperation and conflict, Gleditsch found that rank theory seemed to predict once again the overall level of interaction, but, contrary to the study just mentioned, he also discovered that overall rank profile *dissimilarity* seemed to be related to *positive* interaction. Disequilibrium did not—contrary to the theory—appear to be very strong.[66] Testing similar rank propositions on China's behavior toward thirty-two nations, Sang-Woo Rhee found that the higher the object nation on power, the more cooperation China aimed at it, although "economic" status was not

[62] Johan Galtung, "East-West Interaction Patterns," *Journal of Peace Research* 3 (No. 2, 1966), pp. 146–77.

[63] Gleditsch, "Rank and Interaction."

[64] Maurice A. East, "Rank-Dependent Interaction and Mobility: Two Aspects of International Stratification," *Peace Research Society Papers* 14 (1970), pp. 113–28; data on IGOs from Bruce Russett, *International Regions and the International System: A Study in Political Ecology* (Chicago: Rand McNally, 1967).

[65] W. R. Thompson, "The Arab Sub-system and the Feudal Pattern of Interaction, 1965," *Journal of Peace Research* 7 (No. 2, 1970), p. 158.

[66] Gleditsch, "Rank and Interaction."

very important.[67] For conflict behavior, hypothesized to increase as the target had more power and less economic status, it was confirmed only for the first part: the more powerful the object nation, the more verbal conflict (negative comments) China aimed toward it. Rummel tested rank propositions on United States foreign behavior and likewise found them to be not particularly strong; conflict as well as net cooperation-conflict were unrelated to the status dimensions, although, as noted above, power parity was related to "deterrence" (military violence and negative communication). The closer the country was to the United States on power, the more deterrent behavior did the United States direct toward it. Thus while power parity appears to affect United States foreign behavior, rank disequilibrium does not.[68] In a later analysis, Vincent and his co-workers tested the status propositions, and though they found support for the cooperative behavior propositions—more cooperation will be directed toward nations with a higher status in power and economic development—little consistent confirmation was found for the conflict propositions.[69] In sum, tests on rank or status propositions do not seem to be overwhelmingly supported, except in the cooperative area. In the conflict area, those findings supporting rank theory are also consistent with propositions from power theory.

BALANCE OF POWER "SYSTEMS"

As we move from a consideration of dyadic relationships to that of larger systems, behavioral changes will, understandably enough, be observed. We will be taking into account all behavior in an international system at different points in time. It is also here in the international system that the more traditional balance of power concepts can be utilized. Given the confusion in the basic theory about dyadic systems noted in an earlier section, it is not surprising that quite different results manifest themselves in what turn out to be quite different perspectives in the larger systems.

Claude reviews some of the historical findings, citing John Herz, for instance, who contends that although the "balance of power system" has managed to prevent one-power hegemony, it has failed to prevent

[67] Sang-Woo Rhee, "China's Cooperation, Conflict, and Interaction Behavior, Viewed from Rummel's Status-Field Theoretic Perspective," Research Report 61, Dimensionality of Nations Project (Honolulu: University of Hawaii, 1972), p. 40.

[68] Rummel, "U.S. Foreign Relations."

[69] Jack Vincent, Roger Baker, Susan Gagnon, Keith Hamm, and Scott Reilly, "Empirical Tests of Attribute, Social Field, and Status Field Theories on International Relations Data," *International Studies Quarterly* 17 (December, 1973), pp. 405–44.

war.[70] Claude also cites Morgenthau, for whom the balance of power system after the sixteenth century safeguarded the independence of countries because they could then join together in alliances and counter-alliances. Morgenthau argues in numerous places that the system helps the small states retain their independence, but Claude points out that even Morgenthau sees different patterns emerging:

Morgenthau notes that "the two periods of stability (in the operation of the balance of power system), one starting in 1648, the other in 1815, were preceded by the wholesale elimination of small states and were interspersed, starting with the destruction of Poland, by a great number of isolated acts of a similar nature." [71]

Claude further observes that Morgenthau admits that the balance of power system "has a poor record in terms of either the prevention of war or the safeguarding of the independence of weak states." [72] It appears, then, that the "balance of power" system—according to Herz and Morgenthau—does not necessarily serve a stabilizing function; it does not prevent war or aggression.

British Prime Minister Harold Macmillan once argued that the century from the Treaty of Vienna until the outbreak of the First World War was one "in which the peace of the world as a whole was maintained virtually unbroken" and was "achieved by the Balance of Power and the Concert of Europe." [73] Henry Kissinger suggests a slightly different interpretation: the century was really an era of small wars rather than absolute peace.[74] E. H. Carr insists, says Claude, that it was British supremacy, rather than equilibrium, that kept Europe stable during that century.[75]

These citations illustrate that evidence on the effect of balance of power can be interpreted in many ways, and one outstanding reason for this is the failure to clearly define power, balance of power, and the dependent variables of peace, war, and aggression. There is also the additional failure to note that these concepts often constitute distinct types of behavior, and that the utilization of different theories may therefore be required. Most of the studies discussed below have tried

[70] John Herz, *Political Realism and Political Idealism* (Chicago: University of Chicago Press, 1951), pp. 211, 220–21; cited in Claude, *Power and International Relations*, p. 67.

[71] Ibid., p. 68.

[72] Ibid., p. 69.

[73] Ibid., p. 70.

[74] Henry Kissinger, *Nuclear Weapons and Foreign Policy* (New York: Harper and Row, 1957), p. 142; cited in Claude, *Power and International Relations*, p. 71.

[75] Claude, *Power and International Relations*, p. 71.

to investigate the role of power not through citation of specific historical examples but through the investigation of a large number of cases. Most of them have also tried to be more specific in their definitions of the variables involved.

Singer and Small tested what they called "balance of power" theory, although as explained earlier their theory comes closer to "polarity" or "cross pressures" than strict, traditional balance of power. Using as their measure of polarity the number of alliance formations in the international system, they contended that "nations in the same alliance are less free to compete with their allies in such spheres of incompatibility, and less free to cooperate with outsiders in areas of overlapping interests." [76] If each alliance reduces interaction to some degree, then *increases* in alliance formation should reduce these opportunities, and, more importantly, if more and more alliance commitments show less and less overlap, "and they instead increasingly reinforce a tendency toward a very few (but large-sized) coalitions, the system's loss of interaction opportunities becomes even more severe." This movement could ultimately result in a strict bipolar system.

Singer and Small tested the proposition on their list of forty-two wars, and early findings showed that alliance commitments did relate to several measures of war between 1815 and 1945. Breaking down the entire 130 years into two shorter periods, 1815-1899 and 1900-1945, the relations turned uniformly negative in the first and positive in the second. Singer and Small concluded, therefore, that alliance aggregation (loss of interaction opportunities) and bipolarity covaried with the occurrence of war, but the relation was dependent on time. In the nineteenth century, bipolarity was moderately related to less war (accounting at best for 9 percent of variation in war), whereas in the current century it seems unrelated to war. The interaction opportunity hypothesis was confirmed: the greater the number of nations in alliances (less interaction opportunity), the greater the war. They admit, however, that "national decision-makers will tend to step up their alliance-building activities as they perceive the probability of war to be rising." [77] In a causal chain, therefore, the rising perception of the possibility of war might have to be explained in order to understand the outbreak of war. Alliance aggregation, then, might serve as a possible intervening variable or perhaps as a "signal"—but not necessarily a cause—of impending war. Manus Midlarsky attempted to measure the concept of uncertainty (using the log transformation of the basic alliance measures), and found that it

[76] J. David Singer and Melvin Small, "Alliance Aggregation and the Onset of War, 1815–1945," in *Quantitative International Politics: Insights and Evidence*, ed. J. David Singer (New York: Free Press, 1968), p. 249.

[77] Singer and Small, "Alliance Aggregation," p. 284.

correlated more highly with frequency of wars than did the basic alliance indicators. Further, when statistically controlling for the basic measures, the correlations between his measures of uncertainty and war remained high. He claims that "uncertainty" occurs after alliance formation, which is then followed by war.[78]

A later test by Singer, Stuart Bremer, and John Stuckey framed the research question somewhat differently and used actual power measures rather than number of alliances. Their findings, though, are remarkably similar.[79] The research question was: What effect do different power distributions have on the incidence of violence? They proposed two models: a "preponderance-stability" model, which argues that war will increase as a system moves away from a highly concentrated and stable system; and a "parity-fluidity" model, which argues that war will decrease as a system moves away from such a highly concentrated and stable system, and approaches the more ambiguous state of approximate parity. The variable of uncertainty—again unmeasured—is important; by it they meant the uncertainty "foreign policy elites experience in discerning the stratifications and clusters in the system, and predicting the behavior of the other members of that system." [80] Uncertainty may lead to war because of "misjudgment, erroneous perception, and poor predictions"; it may also inhibit war. Because "coalition bonds are ambiguous, outcomes are more in doubt, and it is that very uncertainty which helps governments to draw back from the brink of war." [81] Singer and his colleagues argue that uncertainty will rise when capabilities are more equally distributed and not concentrated, when the direction of change is further away from such concentration, and when there is a great deal of fluidity, rather than stability, in such capability distributions.

They found that generally from 1820 to 1965 the predictions of the "preponderance and stability" school were more accurate, though the fit of the predictions to the data on interstate war was not "impressive." However, they concluded that for the nineteenth century the parity-fluidity school was more accurate; that is, in the nineteenth century, the more concentrated the system the greater the incidence of war. In the twentieth century, on the other hand, the greater the concentration the

[78] Manus I. Midlarsky, "Power, Uncertainty, and the Onset of International Violence," *Journal of Conflict Resolution* 18 (September, 1974), p. 418. Some doubt must be registered about these findings, however, given the fact that the measures of uncertainty correlate with the respective alliance measures from which they are drawn, at .92, .95, and .97.

[79] J. David Singer, Stuart Bremer, and John Stuckey, "Capability Distribution, Uncertainty, and Major Power War, 1820–1965," in *Peace, War, and Numbers*, ed. Bruce Russett (Beverly Hills: Sage, 1972).

[80] Ibid., p. 23.

[81] Ibid., p. 24.

less the war. Again, contradictions in the hypothesis depend on the time period.

Singer, Bremer, and Stuckey fall back on historically accepted descriptions of the differences in diplomacy during the two centuries to explain the variant findings. The nineteenth century was marked by certainty regardless of power distributions because the leaders knew one another, rules of the game were relatively well-established, and therefore even if the system was fluid, it did not necessarily raise uncertainty levels. In the twentieth century, however, with many newly independent nations and the so-called democratization of international diplomacy, it was only through clearly delineated status and power distributions that war would decrease. Departure from certain and clear power distribution—toward less concentration and more fluidity—would bring about war. In a sense, they are only explaining why war *did not* occur while the situation was fluid in the nineteenth century, not why war *did* occur when concentration was high. In other words, their conclusions explain why fluidity did not produce war, not why concentration did.

But their study shows an amazing convergence with the earlier Singer-Small findings which indicated that increased alliance activity in the nineteenth century led to a downturn in war. In the subsequent study the data show that the greater the concentration in the system, the more war. But both independent variables—alliance formation and power concentration—can be seen as measurements of the number of poles: more alliances mean more poles; less concentration means more poles; and both empirically predict the same phenomenon in the system.

Likewise, for the twentieth century: more alliance activity and less concentration both mean more poles; and the empirical predictions are similar. Despite the use of two different measures and two rather distinct theoretical bases, the same empirical results occur. These might be combined in a more general way by the theory of polarity or the structure of poles in the system. Still unanswered, however, is whether interaction opportunities or uncertainty is the causal factor.

Ferris, also using the Singer-Small war data, at first found a relation between the average amount of power change system-wide during five-year periods and the amount of war under way in the system. The change within the system on power, however, may have been a result of the war itself, and when correlating war under way during the five-year periods with the mean change system-wide immediately prior to the period, all correlations dropped. General system-wide instability, therefore, does not seem related to the amount of war system-wide.[82]

Healy and Stein raise some doubt about the Singer-Small findings

---

[82] Ferris, *Power Capabilities of Nation-States*, p. 85.

when they measured the variable of interaction, left unmeasured by Singer-Small, by the number of international events culled from diplomatic histories for the 1870-1881 period.[83] Isolating one decade, they note that "two major examples of alliance cooperation" occurred: the Three Emperor's League of 1873 and the Dual Alliance of 1879. In the former, Germany, Austria, and Russia formed a pact generally directed against France, whereas in the latter Austria and Germany created a defensive alliance aimed at Russia. First, Healy and Stein found that with neither alliance did interaction among the parties increase after its formation; rather, it actually *decreased,* at least in the case of the 1873 League, therefore logically increasing the amount of interaction outside the system. Concerning system-wide behavior along the conflict-cooperation dimension, however, they narrowed the original Singer-Small proposition down to saying that "system-wide cooperation would decline following an important coalition of previously uncommitted nations." [84] Contrary to that proposition, however, their data show that system-wide cooperation *increased* after the formation of those two alliances. The difference between the Healy-Stein and Singer-Small studies, of course, is that the former focus on one decade isolated from the rest and use one "important" alliance, whereas Singer and Small focus on the relationship between the variables across *several* time periods.[85] If one decade, for instance, had been high in alliance activity followed by the 1870-1881 period of low activity, then the increase of conflict behavior in the Healy-Stein data of that latter decade would confirm Singer-Small.

Returning to the original Singer-Small data does in fact confirm their original hypothesis, although to a very limited degree. Table 5-4 shows six different time periods, the number of alliances formed, countries in alliances, battle deaths, and nation-months of war, as well as the percentage increase or decrease from the previous time period.[86] Of note is the fact that the 1858-1869 period showed an increase in alliance formation over the eleven-year time span preceding it, and that it was followed by a gigantic increase in casualties and nation-months at war during the

---

[83] Healy and Stein, "Balance of Power in International History,"; 982 international events for 23 nations were collected during the 11-year period, scaled on a cooperation-conflict continuum.

[84] Ibid., p. 46.

[85] Healy and Stein cite Singer and Small to the effect that the "formation of a significant alliance" will, "because of the loss of interaction opportunities," lead to a decrease in cooperation and an increase in conflict; Healy and Stein, "The Balance of Power in International History,": p. 36. It becomes quite clear, however, that their interpretation of the Singer-Small hypothesis is open to question when one compares that hypothesis to the original linkage between alliances and war; see Singer and Small, "Alliance Aggregation," p. 249.

[86] All of these data have been calculated from raw data presented in J. David Singer and Melvin Small, *The Wages of War, 1816–1965: A Statistical Handbook* (New York: Wiley, 1972).

Table 5-4. Frequencies and Percentage Change of Alliances, Battle Deaths, and Nation-Months of War, 1834-1907

	Alliance Formation		Battle Deaths (in thousands)	Nation-Months At War
	Number of	*Countries in*		
I 1834-1845	3	11	0	0
II 1846-1857	2 (− 33%)	4 (− 36%)	302 (+ 302%)	211 (+ 211%)
III 1858-1869	9 (+ 350%)	20 (+ 400%)	97 (− 60%)	184 (− 13%)
Healy-Stein analysis				
IV 1870-1883	9 (0%)	20 (0%)	487 (+ 400%)	215 (+ 9%)
V 1884-1895	5 (− 44%)	11 (− 45%)	1 (− 100%)	1 (− 100%)
VI 1896-1907	12 (+ 140%)	24 (+ 118%)	161 (+ 161%)	98 (+ 98%)

These data were compiled from raw data contained in J. David Singer and Melvin Small, "National Alliance Commitments and War Involvement, 1818-1945," in *International Politics and Foreign Policy: A Reader in Research and Theory*, rev. ed. (New York: Free Press, 1969), pp. 513-42.

Healy-Stein period. Time period II also shows the same pattern whereby a decrease in alliance formation is followed by decreasing casualties (1858-1869). The relation does not hold across all time periods, as witness the decreasing alliance formation in period V, followed by increasing war in period VI. It is quite possible that immediate cooperation of the type Healy and Stein talked about occurs after important alliances, but that long-term violence in the system is affected negatively. In other words, the theory makes different predictions, depending on the behavior to be explained.

Haas broadened the investigation somewhat further by looking at twenty-one different international systems that were more narrowly geographic and time-bound. Using new data, as well as data from Lewis Richardson and Quincy Wright, Haas notes that in both data sets unipolar systems not surprisingly had more extraregional wars (the one power would fight with those outside); bipolar systems were associated with *longer* wars in Richardson's data, but not associated with war in the Wright data. Finally, tripolar and multipolar systems seemed highly related to several indexes of war.[87] Haas suggests that the traditional faith in "benign operations within multipolar systems" is not upheld: bipolarity, tripolarity, and multipolarity consistently showed greater adhesion to the war variables than unipolarity. Further, the war variables are much more closely related to multipolarity than to bipolarity or tripolarity. But even in these three types of systems, war behavior differs: bipolar systems have few, localized, but prolonged wars, whereas tripolar and multipolar systems contain the highest number of wars and war casualties. Even utilizing the same measure as Singer-Small, Haas also contends his findings contradict the Singer-Small results:

A tight subsystem with many alliances, members and minor powers allied to major powers is very likely to have many powers actively engaged in wars; the wars will be long, often spilling over into adjacent eras, with many lives lost. In larger systems, there will be many outbreaks of warfare, especially among major powers and the wars are likely to result in destabilization . . . The . . . interaction opportunity hypothesis, in short, is completely inconsistent with the findings . . . we should look for smaller systems, with less so-called interaction potential, to bring about a more peaceful state of affairs.[88]

Much more indirect evidence of the possible differential effect of polarity systems can be seen in data calculated on outcomes of fifty-three conflicts as presented in Table 5-5. Note that the more strictly bipolar

---

[87] Michael Haas, "International Subsystems: Stability and Polarity," *American Political Science Review* 64 (March, 1970), p. 121; Lewis F. Richardson, *Statistics of Deadly Quarrels* (Pittsburgh: Boxwood Press, 1960); Quincy Wright, *A Study of War* (Chicago: University of Chicago Press, 1942).

[88] Haas, "International Systems," pp. 114–15.

Table 5-5. Outcome of 53 Conflicts, 1919-1965

	Conquest	Forced Submission	Compromise
1919-1939	16	8	5
1945-1965	6	8	10

Based on data in Kal Holsti, "Resolving International Conflicts: A Taxonomy of Behavior and Some Figures on Procedures," *Journal of Conflict Resolution* 10 (September 1966), pp. 293-96.

world of the Cold War era showed many more instances of conflicts ended through compromise, whereas during the previous twenty-year interwar period, the vast majority of conflicts ended in either conquest or forced submission.

The question again presents itself on whether polarity theory works differentially in different empirical domains. Singer and Small dealt with world wide systems over lengthy periods of time; Haas concentrated on geographically and time-bound systems of a much smaller nature. Moreover, much doubt has been raised concerning the measure of bipolarity utilized by Singer and Small (see appendix, paragraph E), though Zinnes, in her partial retest of the Singer-Small initial study, showed that at least one of their original findings was substantiated.[89] Whether all of the data, if retested, would support the "polarity" or cross-pressures theory must, of course, await a full reexamination of the theory, taking into consideration all of Zinnes's criticisms.

In the light of earlier findings that a curvilinear relation may better describe the effect of power distance on war, it is not surprising that further research has also uncovered that same possibility concerning polarization. Michael Wallace, using a very complicated series of techniques, discloses a curvilinear relation between polarization and war, with war more probable at very *low* and very *high* levels of polarization and minimized at moderate levels of polarization.[90] His findings, however, can have no bearing on the stability of bipolar as opposed to multipolar systems because his measure was conceived only to differentiate systems from low to high polarity, and high polarity cannot be equated with multipolarity. In this regard, Midlarsky's findings are of interest here. Relating the number of international poles in the system to the frequency of war from Singer and Small, he shows a logarithmic relationship, where the move from one to two poles increases the frequency of war in the system much more drastically than the larger jump from

[89] Zinnes, "An Analytical Study."

[90] Michael D. Wallace, "Alliance Polarization, Cross-Cutting, and International War, 1815–1964: A Measurement Procedure and Some Preliminary Evidence," *Journal of Conflict Resolution* 17 (December, 1973), p. 597.

two to five poles (Figure 5-4).[91] Midlarsky's findings suggest that the danger point, at least in terms of frequency of war, rests on the movement from one to two poles; any further multipolarization, though increasing the frequency of war, does so at much smaller increments.

In a sense, Paul Smoker's research on big-power defense spending also supports—albeit very indirectly—the effect of greater polarization.[92] If the addition of more countries to an existing big-power alliance indicates a move toward polarization in the system, and if changes in defense budgets represent—to some degree, at least—hostile behavior, then the German entry into NATO at the end of 1954, and the signing of the

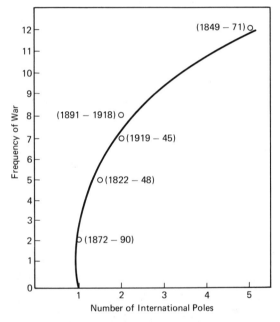

Source: "Power, Uncertainty, and the Onset of International Violence," by Manus I. Midlarsky is reprinted from *Journal of Conflict Resolution* Vol. 18, No. 3 (September, 1974), 427 by permission of the author and the publisher, Sage Publications, Inc.

Figure 5-4. Observed logarithmic relationship between polarity and international warfare (1815–1945).

[91] Midlarsky, "Power, Uncertainty, and Onset," p. 427.

[92] Paul Smoker, "Fear in the Arms Race: A Mathematical Study," in *International Politics and Foreign Policy, A Reader in Research and Theory*, ed. James N. Rosenau, rev. ed. (New York: The Free Press, 1969).

Treaty of Friendship, Cooperation, and Mutual Assistance between the Soviet Union and its East European allies can be used as evidence in favor of the theory. Smoker's analysis showed that the annual arms expenditures of the major powers in the post-World War II era exhibited rather straight linear patterns, with the two exceptions noted above: The greatest Russian deviation from the pattern occurred after Germany joined NATO, and the largest American deviation occurred after the Treaty of Friendship. *If* both cases polarized the system, then the change in defense expenditures might have been a result of that increased polarization.

STATUS AND RANK

Rank on the systemic level provides a quite different explanation for international behavior compared with power distributions. On the systemic level, rank theory contends that the greater the status discrepancy system-wide, the greater the chance of more violent or conflictual international behavior system-wide.

Unfortunately, the evidence on rank propositions for the entire system is very sparse. Wallace found that in using the Singer-Small war data for the 1920-1964 period and measuring status inconsistency as the total differential scores in rank for the entire international system (on three measures of population, armed force size, and diplomatic missions received), status inconsistency was related to both armed forces expansion and battle fatalities for the entire period as well as for subperiods within it.[93] Even when taking into account other variables, status inconsistency remained important. He also found that these relationships were stronger when the war data was lagged approximately fifteen years.[94]

Maurice East, however, using the Singer-Small data for a shorter period of time (twelve wars for the period 1948-1965), uncovered only very moderate relations between the amount of status discrepancy in the system and several measures of violence. Though East reports the hypothesis confirmed, this conclusion rests on correlations that—although all moving in the same and predicted direction—are not particularly high.[95] Using another set of interstate conflict data, the relationships

[93] Michael D. Wallace, "Status, Formal Organization, and Arms Levels as Factors Leading to the Onset of War, 1820–1964," in *Peace, War and Numbers,* ed. Bruce Russett (Beverly Hills: Sage, 1972).

[94] Michael D. Wallace, "Power, Status, and International War," *Journal of Peace Research* 8 (No. 1, 1971), pp. 23–36.

[95] Maurice East, "Status Discrepancy and Violence in the International System: An Empirical Analysis," in *The Analysis of International Politics: Essays in Honor of Harold and Margaret Sprout,* ed. James N. Rosenau, Vincent Davis, and Maurice East (New York: The Free Press, 1972), p. 309.

were even less strong, wherein the conflict data related to only one of four measures of status discrepancy. However, as with Wallace's data, lagging both sets of conflict behind status discrepancy showed that the relationships increased, and in the predicted direction. This finding suggests that while changes in status discrepancy may not be related to changes in violence one or two years hence, the trend of the former is related to the trend of the latter, which makes sense given the supposed time-lag effect that such systemic processes must take.

Conclusion

THEORETICAL IMPLICATIONS

Power has served as a focal point for much description of international politics as well as explanations of and predictions concerning international behavior. Unfortunately, there has been just as much focus, if not more, on the descriptive aspects as on explanations and predictions, thus drawing attention away from legitimate theoretical concerns. This chapter has tried to filter out of the multitude of writings on power the descriptive and the peripheral and to concentrate on the theoretical. As a result, power as a "drive" or "lust" or automatic "balancing" system in international politics, which forces states into coalitions and alliances, and the problems of "managing" power in the international system have not been given attention here. As a consequence, a great deal of discussion normally considered under "power" has been passed over. And by passing it over, we have highlighted the real theoretical concepts of power: how, and in what ways, power influences international relations. Conceptualizing power as *distance* and power as *system* showed that the central questions concerning power, that is, the theoretical questions, are in fact not as extensive as is often suggested.

The empirical studies cited throughout this chapter have indicated the need to investigate carefully the manner in which the questions about power's role are answered. The research designs, the way data are handled and manipulated, and the implications of measuring the variables in different ways are all vitally important. For instance, Healy and Stein's conclusion that their data contradict the findings of Singer-Small is correct if we limit the original Singer-Small study to the argument that an alliance, or even an important alliance, should be followed by less interaction opportunities (and thus war). Singer and Small's proposition, however, is clearly imbedded in a larger context of the entire system's alliance structure, and of cross-time analysis. Healy and Stein take only one twelve-year period out of the context of system changes *over time*. John Sullivan's comments sum up the dilemma in attempting to digest contradictory findings. The difference, he says, may result from different research designs and conceptual schemes, as well as from the sample of nations used and the statistical tests employed. Singer and Small, for example, rely largely on correlation coefficients, whereas Haas uses the data-reduction techniques of smallest space and cluster analysis. As Sullivan suggests:

> It may be that the findings of each are valid but that the *range* of findings does not cover the same phenomena. . . . It may be that the Singer and Small findings are valid for the European system in the last century and a half but that Haas' work points to the possibility these findings may not hold up for different time periods or different international systems.[96]

Despite these problems, however, the number of theories and the amount of writings on power and balance of power continue unabated. The amount of empirical research, though, has been comparatively sparse. It should be clear by now that the concept "balance of power," for instance, does not have one meaning, nor does "balancing system," nor any of the other concepts that are part and parcel of the "power" literature. It may be for this reason that so many of the findings seem to contradict one another. But as Sullivan points out, these contradictory findings indicate that the role of polarity or "distribution of power" in the international system is far from simple, and may not be applicable to several different empirical domains. The different results may also be due, of course, to different research designs, which means that different questions were asked.

Nonetheless, there are some consistencies and some rather interesting findings. Almost no study, for example, gave much support to the basic hypothesis that power distance affects the occurrence or outcome of conflict in a dyad. One possible suggestion did emerge from Ferris's study of a curvilinear relation; the curve, however, is more complex than originally proposed. It showed that the least conflictual dyads were those both very distant on power and those only moderately distant, and that those dyads falling in between these two categories as well as those *very close* to each other on power were the most conflictual. Even this curvilinear relation differed, depending on whether the dependent variable was *level* of war, hostilities versus no hostilities, or conflict

---

[96] John D. Sullivan, "Cooperation in International Politics: Quantitative Perspectives on Formal Alliances," mimeographed (August, 1970), p. 41; a revised version appears in *International Systems: A Behavioral Approach*, ed. Michael Haas (New York: Chandler, 1974).

versus no conflict. Comparing nonconflict with conflict showed that parity did seem to deter countries from *becoming involved* in conflict, but once involved in hostilities, those with large and small power ratios had a greater chance of escalating the conflict into war, at least in Wright's inventory of wars. Power parity, therefore, may play a different role depending on what is to be explained. While power parity does appear to deter states from engaging in hostilities, once hostilities do occur, the intensity is likely to be greater among nations more equal to each other. Note, however, that these findings can only be applied to hostilities versus no hostilities, and level of actual physical hostilities; other conflict behavior such as verbal conflict or severing relations or mobilizations seem unrelated for the most part to parity.

Change in power distance seems to have little systematic effect, although Ferris's data once again suggested that smaller changes appeared to have a greater impact than larger changes, and those that closed a gap between two countries were a little more likely to produce very intense conflicts than changes that opened up a gap.

The consequence of balance of power in terms of system distribution seemed to change in relation to the century being investigated and the empirical domain. All polarity systems witnessed wars, but a larger number of poles seemed to bring about greater amounts of violence. Very high and very low polarized systems also seem to witness more war, although systems of medium polarization seem to be moderately free of war. It is difficult to weave these findings together with Singer's results and those gleaned from Smoker's study of arms races because of the differing empirical domains and definitions of the independent variable of polarity or polarization. Increasing the polarity in an already polarized system, however, appears to be dangerous—Smoker and Wallace both support this hypothesis—and Singer's study noting that lower concentration in the twentieth-century system seems to be associated with war may also support it.

One final note concerns the differing levels of analysis studied and the different findings. System-level studies seem to show consistently stronger relations than dyadic studies; their correlations on the average have been higher and explained variation is greater. This fact should not lead to the conclusion that system-level theories are therefore "better," only that the behaviors they describe are different. Large-scale systemic behavior has fewer fluctuations and is less likely to be shaped by the multitude of forces involved in dyadic behavior. Dyadic behavior, because it is on a smaller scale, is more difficult to explain. When numerous dyadic behaviors are aggregated into systemic behavior, some of that variation, some of that information, is lost. It is not surprising, therefore, that the analyst's ability to predict systemic behavior is somewhat better.

POLICY IMPLICATIONS

All of the above theoretical arguments and empirical findings become more than interesting historical facts, however, if knowledge of the role of power aids in understanding not only the contemporary but also future international systems and the relations between states in those systems. While immediate, day-to-day policy relevance may not be gleaned from system-level research, nonetheless, it may provide information about the large, overall picture of international politics. Events and behavior conceptualized at the system level may be a function of large-scale systemic phenomena, and analysis of power systems helps to sensitize the analyst to those potential effects.

Though the distance propositions were not overwhelmingly supported, it must be recalled that several of those studies were pulled out of context—thereby eliminating other variables that may work in combination with power distance. Until the combination of all variables is investigated (Chapter 8), we must conclude that the hypothesis that power parity is a primary influence on international behavior is a somewhat overrated one, for if it were, the relationships would have been much stronger.

However, taking the results of distance studies at face value, and recognizing that they neither overwhelmingly confirm nor disconfirm the various propositions, it is still not at all clear that those arguing for power parity were shooting at stars. As Haas suggested in reference to the entire system, it depends on what the policy-maker is willing to put up with. Parity may very well deter countries from becoming involved in conflict situations, but if conflict does erupt, it appears that the more equal the countries the more intense the conflict. For policy-makers, then, it depends on what they are willing to risk, the chance of deterring hostilities, or the chance of keeping hostilities at a low level. Certainly these considerations are crucial for large powers contemplating aid to smaller powers, aid which can shift the power balance among them. The answer unfortunately is not simple. In addition, the suggestion that closing a power gap is more dangerous in terms of greater hostilities than widening a gap would certainly be a consideration for decision-makers contemplating aid to a smaller country to make it more equal to its adversaries. Similar questions can be raised concerning the constant attention of the big powers themselves to maintaining parity with their counterparts. Perhaps the most ideal situation—suggested by research here but not definitely confirmed by it—would be to maintain as equal power as possible, but to make sure that one large power does not *widen* the gap between itself and another large power, which would then push the second power into closing the gap—the slightly more dangerous situation.

On the systemic level, the entire international system (as well as numerous subsystems) are constantly undergoing change in terms of number and distribution of power poles. This flux provides a constant laboratory for further refinement and testing of the "power as system" notions. This opportunity for further refinement is especially great, given the strong relationships between power distribution and international behavior, particularly the interesting findings showing the sharp differences between the nineteenth and twentieth centuries. How similar is the post-World War II system—and now the post-Cold War system—to the rest of the twentieth century, and to the nineteenth? To which system does it show the greatest similarities, or is it yet changing to some new structure? What would time-series plots of alliance formation, power distribution, and number of power poles predict as to the changing level of conflict or cooperation, system-wide, during the next half-decade or decade? Can we take findings on power and extrapolate to the future?

More specifically, one intriguing study would be to assess the effect of changed big-power relations during the 1971-1973 period under President Nixon. The strict bipolar system of the Cold War years had slowly been breaking down for some time, but U.S.-Chinese actions toward détente finally moved the system to a more truly tripolar one. Taking into account Japan, the system might be moving beyond just a tripolar setup to a multipolar system. If so, Haas's findings suggest that the prolonged wars of the bipolar system—Korea and Vietnam—will give way to more war and more devastating wars, with more casualties. Wallace's interpretation is slightly different: polarization has declined from its high point in 1954, and further moves toward breaking down the polarity could result in less war. However, his last data point was 1970, prior to the Sino-American détente. Measurements after 1970 might indicate a more precipitous drop in polarity, past that medium range that Wallace found to be the most stable and toward either extreme multipolarity (Haas) or extremely low polarization (Wallace), where the result—war—would be the same.

Pushing these implications somewhat further, however, Midlarsky suggests that "beyond a certain number of actors in the system . . . the addition of several more will have a relatively small impact on the frequency of war, when compared to the earlier formation of bipolar and tripolar systems." [97] The question for the policy-maker, therefore, is whether he should oppose the emergence of a new actor, or actors, and the decision on that question would hinge largely on the "number of

[97] Midlarsky, "Power, Uncertainty, and Onset," p. 429.

polar actors found in the system at that time." [98] While the increased number of actors or poles—beyond that "certain number" of five or six— is going to increase the probability of war, that increase would not be as devastating as the move *up to* those five or six.

Even if Haas's findings are applicable only to subsystems of the larger international system, they might equate with A. Doak Barnett's prediction in terms of great-power relations in the Asian system.[99] He contends that big-power conflict would be reduced in that system if polarity were lessened. Barnett admits, however, that should big-power polarity be reinstituted—if, for instance, the Chinese and the Soviets were to end their conflict with each other—that would raise the probability of large-scale conflict again. (It is rather difficult to work with Barnett's formulation in more than rough form, however, because he does not establish operationally what he means by "stability" and "instability.")

In terms of recent United States foreign policy, it is interesting to speculate what an analysis of John Foster Dulles's penchant for alliance formation would show. Many have criticized the former secretary of state for overextending the United States, for putting too much emphasis on alliances made with small, out-of-the-way countries. The issue is usually viewed ideologically. But more important is the impact his activity had on the structure of the international system, on United States foreign policy, and on the level of conflict and cooperation in the system as a whole. Proponents of the interaction opportunity thesis—more alliances lead to less interaction which leads to more war—would contend that structural changes might have been linked to the increased violence in the international system, such as the Vietnam War. A full analysis of this question is beyond our interest here. Even so, it might be noted that Singer and Small's data show a moderate increase in the amount of war being waged in the late 1950s (after the decline following the Korean War) and that Kjell Goldmann found East-West tension in Europe dropping from its peak in 1947-1948 to a low in 1953, and then rising again to peak in 1958 and again in the 1961-1963 period.[100] Neither of these data-sets confirm that Dulles's alliance-formation behavior resulted in that observed violence or later resulted in the Vietnam War. Nevertheless, they do point out one method of investigating an ideological question by using a theoretical formulation.

About a decade ago, many thought that power and balance of power were dead issues in the contemporary study of international politics.

[98] Ibid.

[99] A. Doak Barnett, "The Changing Strategic Balance in Asia," in *Sino-American Détente and Its Policy Implications,* ed. Gene T. Hsiao (New York: Praeger, 1974).

[100] Kjell Goldmann, "East-West Tension in Europe, 1946–1970: A Conceptual Analysis and a Quantitative Description," *World Politics* 26 (October, 1973), pp. 106–25.

They had reached that conclusion partially because of the surviving definitional view of power as something involving *lust* or inherent *drive,* and partially because of disagreement about whether power was an attribute or a matter of influence. There was the troublesome problem of how to measure it. Treating power solely as *distance* and *system* is not a new perspective, but doing so permits a central focus on propositions that can be researched. Some simple notions of power parity have been discarded for somewhat more complex formulations that depend on the behavior being explained. Likewise, system-wide stability depends on what kind of stability is meant—fewer wars or shorter wars; no system is free of conflict. Power distributions appear to be fairly accurate in explaining conflict system-wide, though power parity propositions were not so successful in doing so in terms of dyadic behavior. No doubt more complex designs will provide stronger relationships between power and dyadic behavior.

chapter 6 Integration, Distance, and Balance Theories

In a figurative sense, the theoretical subject matter of this chapter stands halfway between the power hypotheses outlined in the previous chapter and the field hypotheses of Chapter 8. Integration, distance, and balance theories share an underlying postulate: that distances between countries affect their behavior. Chapter 5 considered the effect of *power* distance; here we shall be concerned with a somewhat broader concept of distance: *social* distance. Social distance is markedly different from power distance not only in terms of measurement, but also in terms of the way in which it explains behavior. People are not viewed as being swayed by their power differential or by power distributions in the system, but rather by their social and value similarity to people in other countries, or by the system of behavioral relations among other countries. It is hoped that this very general conception of social distance will allow us sufficient compass to discuss many of the traditional writings on international integration as well as other theoretical perspectives—such as balance— that have certain elements in common with integration.

We shall first offer a brief overview of the notion of integration, together with several traditional problems with the concept itself. The broad concept of social distance will then be linked both to integration and to balance theory, and problems of measurement will be outlined. We shall then turn to the difficult task of assessing the research on social distance.

Integration

The integration of nation-states has held the interest of scholars for centuries, and the two major wars of the twentieth century have drastically increased that interest, not only among scholars but among national leaders as well. The League of Nations and the United Nations have been seen by some as the first step toward a "united" or "integrated" world. Most observers have by now concluded, however, that those early hopes were naïve, that a worldwide community has an extremely slim probability of success, at least in the foreseeable future.

Nonetheless, several common-sense assumptions still remain to serve as the starting point for theories of integration, and despite the limited success of world government movements, these assumptions still command a good deal of attention. A common theme in philosophical as well as empirical literature in the humanities and social sciences is that hostility between men would cease if we were all alike. Wars, this argument runs, are prompted by dissimilarities between men and the conflicts of interests, fears, and jealousies arising from those dissimilarities. If men could get to know one another and understand one another's beliefs and goals and problems, their natural rationality and empathy would override, or at least dampen, their mutual hostility. As Haas notes, through international integration, "bridges can be built and preventive measures can be taken in the relations between nations and humans long before the outbreak of tensions, disputes, conflict, or violence itself." [1]

A related but slightly different assumption regarding integration pertains to the cross pressures thought to result from numerous and high levels of transactions between many units. As we saw in Chapter 5, cross pressures constitute barriers to the buildup of conflicts because they prevent two sides from being pitted against each other on many issues, a process that tends to intensify disputes. A third common-sense assumption serving as a basis for studying integration is that an integrated international system (or subsystem) will resemble the nation-state insofar as violence would be controlled by an elected or appointed group within the system. Conflicts could then be settled much more amicably than in situations of anarchy. A final basis for studying integration as a hopeful goal is the "neofunctionalist" view which maintains that people who cooperate on a small, nonideological, noncentral issue-area are very likely to build up, over time, patterns of cooperation that will carry over to matters of rather crucial concern.

Thus, there are numerous different perspectives on the question of

---

[1] Michael Haas, "International Integration," in *International Systems, A Behavioral Approach*, ed. Michael Haas (New York: Chandler, 1974), p. 204.

integration, relating to both process and domain. On the one hand is the institutional approach, which views integration primarily in terms of the formation of a political body. Other approaches use the same basic assumptions about integration, but their perspective is rather different. One such approach, less organizational, sees the modern world as moving very slowly but very surely toward a type of world community, if not an actual worldwide government. Increased communications, as well as greater travel and tourism should, this argument goes, bring the world closer together. Increased transactions and communications heighten knowledge about and understanding of other people, their ideas, and their problems. But in this view, despite the same basic assumption, man is not necessarily seen as the causal agent producing the institutions that will bring about a unified or communal world. Rather, the large-scale processes occurring throughout the world—over which no individual or country has control—are autonomously working toward a unified community.

These perspectives concern the process of integration or community formation. Yet another distinction relates to the domain. Though integration or community in either sense can take place system-wide, it also may occur on a smaller level, such as the thirteen colonies joining together to form the United States, efforts at European unification, or the repeated attempts to confederate the many Arab countries in the Middle East. In this view, world community or world government efforts are naïve and impractical, and integration must take place on a regional level.

But despite the differences, all perspectives still utilize the underlying hypothesis that countries "integrated" with one another are going to behave differently toward one another than less integrated nations. Or, to put it another way, international systems that are integrated are going to be—on the whole—more peaceful. The entire basis of the research by Karl Deutsch and many others begun in the 1950s utilizes that assumption. As spelled out in one of the earliest works, which has been cited ever since, Deutsch began with a series of nominal definitions. First, a *security community* is a group of people who have become integrated. Second, *integration* is the attainment of a "sense of community" and of institutions that can assure dependable, peaceful change. Third, a *sense of community* consists at a minimum of agreement on at least one point: that common problems must be solved by "peaceful change." Finally, *peaceful change* consists in the resolution of social problems, normally by institutionalized procedures, without resort to large-scale physical force. As Deutsch notes:

A political community is not necessarily able to prevent war within the area it covers. . . . Some political communities do, however, eliminate war and the expectation of war within their boundaries. . . . A security-community, therefore, is one in which there is real assurance that the members of that community will not fight each other physically, but will settle their disputes in some other way.[2]

Ernst B. Haas, whose perspective on integration in Europe differs in some respects from Deutsch's, nonetheless also views the ideal type of "political community" as one in which there are limitations on the violence of group conflict.[3] J. S. Nye contends that one of the functions of regional organizations is to control intraregional conflict.[4] Robert Angell has studied "trans-national participation," such as student and business exchanges, contending that increased interaction through such participation may carry the world over the "threshold of peace."[5]

Two central points regarding the concept of integration must be made. First, our concern is not necessarily with *explaining* the formation of supranational organizations or communities, but with how the concept itself—or others closely allied with it—can explain *either* the formation of such units *or* other kinds of international behavior.

Second, integration need not necessarily be equated with the actual formation of an international body. Perhaps one of the most insightful suggestions that Deutsch and his colleagues made in their studies of integration was that truly integrated communities may not necessarily be those that declared they were integrated by means of a formal agreement. Rather, using concepts from communication theory, Deutsch contended that those nations that retain high and consistent levels of communications and transactions with each other may be more integrated than those that have signed agreements. On the personal level, for instance, two married people who no longer communicate with each other remain united—integrated—in a formal sense, but outside observers may come to quite different conclusions by investigating the number and kind of transactions they have with each other. The same circumstance may occur with groups and with nation-states. Thus, as Deutsch puts it, "transaction flows first establish mutual relevance of actors."[6] And

---

2 Karl Deutsch, Sidney Burrell, Robert Kann, Maurice Lee, Jr., Martin Lichterman, Raymond E. Lindgren, Francis Loewenheim, and Richard Van Wagenen, "Political Community and the North Atlantic Area," in *International Political Communities: An Anthology* (Garden City, New York: Doubleday and Company, 1966), pp. 1–2.

3 Ernst B. Haas, *The Uniting of Europe: Political, Social, and Economic Forces, 1950–1957* (Stanford, Calif.: Stanford University Press, 1958), p. 6.

4 J. S. Nye, *Peace in Parts: Integration and Conflict in Regional Organization* (Boston: Little, Brown, 1971).

5 Robert C. Angell, *Peace on the March: Transnational Participation* (New York: Van Nostrand Reinhold, 1969), pp. 28 and 156.

6 Karl Deutsch, "Communication Theory and Political Integration," in *The Integration of Political Communities,* ed. Philip E. Jacob and James V. Toscano (Philadelphia: Lippincott, 1964), 67.

though numerous transactions do not necessarily equate with a lack of conflict, nonetheless, "the one thing which is unlikely to accompany a high level of transaction is continued high tension and conflict." [7]

Among the many disputes in studies of integration, this hypothesized linkage between transactions and conflict has probably caused more debate than any other. To understand the logic of Deutsch's linkage, we shall outline a series of steps, (using Roger Cobb and Charles Elder's description of the process [8]):

1. Communication of some type must exist. As noted already, units having absolutely no communication with each other cannot be considered social systems or communities. Even hostile or negative communications represent a type of system, though normally we think of communities as those with positive interactions. Some form of communication, in other words, must be taking place.

2. Something of interest must be present for two parties to communicate about. Not only does this mutual interest presume the physical capability to communicate—talk, transmit information, trade—but also an identification of interests to allow meaningful communication to occur.

3. Nations that interact a great deal have relevance to each other. They are important to each other, and therefore, their basic relationship (to a great extent defined by the communication) is different from those with whom they do not interact.

4. High interaction between nations along certain dimensions is unlikely to be accompanied by high tension and conflict. In cases of high interaction, behavior becomes institutionalized, and patterns of interaction develop. These patterns may soon develop into standard procedures which very often culminate in formal organizations.

This four-step process suggests that as communication increases between units, the complexities inherent in such activity increase, and that to handle these complexities the units formalize their interactions, one result of which is greater collaboration. From mutual cooperation might flow actual, formal institutions to further simplify relationships or to make decisions for the units involved as *one* unit. Once that stage has been reached, integration of previously separate units into one becomes more likely. Deutsch, of course, has not been alone in proposing this theory. Wright suggests the same process, but in slightly different terms:

In proportion as men in different groups *communicate* with each other regularly and abundantly they tend to form a public opinion. This in the long run synthesizes the values and technologies of the communicating groups into a *common culture* and value system. . . . The participants in a common culture tend to

7 Ibid.

8 Roger W. Cobb and Charles Elder, *International Community: A Regional and Global Study* (New York: Holt, Rinehart, and Winston, 1970), pp. 8–9.

become aware of that culture . . . to formulate in legal rules the standards, interests, and goals that culture implies, and to *co-operate* for the realization of these rules. Such co-operation stimulates the acceptance of common policies and an *organization* to enforce the law and to achieve the policies.[9]

Related theoretical perspectives alluded to already are the "functional" and "neofunctional" or "spillover" theories. Functionalist theory contends that "conflict among states is the result of social inequality, arising primarily from the maldistribution of economic benefits." [10] Because political problems between states are often intractable, social inequities can only be dealt with on a social and economic level; joint problems of disease and hunger can be dealt with cooperatively whereas political matters cannot. Theoretically, such cooperation results in a working relationship between states rather than a political one, and these relationships can only be established through international organizations. The transference of functions to these organizations is supposed to lead to a transference of loyalty and support from the national to the supranational unit, thus effecting a political community.

The neofunctionalists do not view this process in such strictly automatic terms. They argue that political variables cannot be extracted completely from the process. Although the individuals involved in solving problems may be technocrats, they nonetheless are aware that politics cannot be entirely divorced from the relationship.[11] Neofunctionalists also expand the number of variables involved in bringing about a community through the functional process, and they realize that the process, not being automatic, may in fact need a "political push" at times. At the core of both approaches, however, is the process of spillover, wherein certain procedures and behaviors occurring in the communication process spill over into others; cooperative processes in the matter of trade, for example, may affect relations between the parties in the matter of extradition. As James Caporaso notes, "Spillover is commonly thought of as a process whereby integrative activity in one societal sector leads to integrative activity in other related sectors." [12] Communication and spillover approaches resemble each other to some degree in that, as Susan Welch and Cal Clark note, spillover is similar to a "learning pro-

[9] Quincy Wright, "Toward a Universal Law for Mankind," in *Toward a Theory of War Prevention,* ed. Richard A. Falk and Saul H. Mendlovitz (New York: World Law Fund, 1966), pp. 84–85.

[10] Jack C. Plano and Robert E. Riggs, *Forging World Order: The Politics of International Organization* (New York: Macmillan, 1967), p. 514.

[11] James A. Caporaso, *Functionalism and Regional Integration: A Logical and Empirical Assessment* (Beverly Hills: Sage Publications, 1972), p. 30.

[12] James A. Caporaso, "Encapsulated Integrative Patterns vs. Spillover: The Cases of Transport Integration in the European Economic Community," *International Studies Quarterly* 14 (December, 1970), p. 365.

cess in which the occurrence of benefits in certain situations leads to the 'learning' of certain types of behavior connected with these situations." [13]

All of these approaches to integration—from the institutional to the spillover—constitute one quite distinctive approach. Another—not considered here specifically in terms of integration—views the formation of supranational units as the result of a decision-making process. Under this hypothesis states come together because individual leaders have decided that they should, that their self-interest is enhanced by joining together instead of staying apart. In these cases, concepts of self-interest, or "national interest," and power might operate as explanatory variables: states see their interests taken care of through amalgamation, or they force others (or are forced by others) into a union. One part of Amitai Etzioni's model of the formation of international communities, for instance, concerns the locus of power, and he contends that "a new community is formed . . . when a nation more powerful than the other potential member 'guides' the unification process." [14]

We have for the most part opted for the transaction or communication approach, but since research in both the transaction-communication and decision-making areas use many similar starting points and similar variables, our decision in no way closes off the latter approach. It is probably safe to say, however, that those utilizing the decision-making approach have been more concerned with the actual formation of political or economic union. We are interested here in integration not as an *end result* nor solely as *a process,* but rather as a way of explaining behavior. As we will argue in the next section, though the majority of writers on international integration seem to have focused on the prerequisites or processes leading *to* actual amalgamation—a legitimate concern, and one that will be considered here—nonetheless integration as an explanatory theory will still be the primary concern.

Integration: Definition and Measurement

There are, as might now easily be imagined, conceptual problems concerning integration. As widespread as the concept of integration is in the study of international politics, it has drawn much criticism. The

[13] Cal Clark and Susan Welch, "Western European Trade As a Measure of Integration: Untangling the Interpretations," *Journal of Conflict Resolution* 16 (September, 1972), p. 375.

[14] Amitai Etzioni, "The Epigenesis of Political Communities at the International Level," in *International Politics and Foreign Policy: A Reader in Research and Theory,* ed. James N. Rosenau, rev. ed. (New York: The Free Press, 1969), p. 348.

most basic problem is the definition of integration: some view it as a level or situation that nation-states reach and then maintain, others view it as an ongoing process that ultimately is never-ending. As a result, for some the state of integration is a well-defined "point" that can be empirically established, usually by the formation of a union. For others, there is no "point." They concentrate on the process of integration, believing—as Deutsch did—that integration may not necessarily equate with formal union. For them, integration is the fluctuation of numerous indicators thought to represent union, and, therefore, states can be constantly oscillating in their process or level of integration.

Is integration, then, an independent or a dependent variable? Some consider it as dependent, and therefore investigate what causes *it;* others see it as an independent force causing other phenomena. While each of those linkages may be correct, the problem here arises when the distinction is not made clear. For instance, scholars have used the communications theory outlined above, predicting *to* integration from high transactions or communications levels; but integration is very often defined *as* high communications or transactions. Hence, as we will find, especially in studies of Western Europe, the level of integration is seen to be directly correlated with levels of transactions. Such a correlation only means that (1) we are merely investigating the changes in indicators *thought* to be related to integration (which means we may only be studying changes in indicators); and (2) if transactions cause integration but integration is measured in terms of transactions, then nothing but perfect relationships between transactions and integration are going to occur.

These problems lead, then, to a consideration of the measurement of integration and whether it is a unidimensional or multidimensional phenomenon. Is integration to be equated with "high" levels of transactions? Where does "community formation" fit in? Certainly integration was originally thought of in terms of political union. The Deutschian communication approach, however, raised questions about the dimensions of integration. It was largely the emphasis in the 1950s and 1960s on trade that caused many to suggest other components of integration. Recent research has delved into the question of multidimensionality of integration. Barry Hughes and John Schwarz, for instance, suggest three different types of integration: mass community, political amalgamation, and intergovernmental cooperation.[15] Mass attitudes toward other political units constitute the measure of mass community: Do Frenchmen have positive attitudes toward people in other countries? What about Italians? Germans? Masses are considered to be integrated if they have

[15] Barry Hughes and John E. Schwarz, "Dimensions of Political Integration and the Experience of the European Community," *International Studies Quarterly* 16 (September, 1972), pp. 263–94.

a high recording of mutual "good opinions" about other countries. The second type of integration, political amalgamation, is measured by the number of decisions made by supra-national organizations within the European context—the European Economic Community, the European Coal and Steel Community, and EURATOM, a measure taken from W. E. Fisher.[16] Their final type is "intergovernmental cooperation," measured by events—agreements, state visits, notes—occurring between European governments, excluding actions taking place within the framework of an international organization.[17] Thus integration is high when intergovernmental cooperation is high, mass feelings about other people are positive, and many decisions are made by supranational organizations.

Leon Lindberg and Joseph Nye also contend that there may be different types of integration.[18] Nye, for instance, suggests economic, political, and social variations. Economic integration would constitute high trade; social integration would include the unification of masses, special groups, or elites; political integration would encompass a wide array of phenomena, including more decisions on the international level, international bureaucracies, and attitudinal similarity among nations. Robert Bernstein, using Lindberg and Nye's original data on decisions made in different arenas, contends that integration is a unidimensional phenomenon. Investigating decisions made in both the EEC and two additional systems in Central America and East Africa, he shows that their decisions increased in a linear fashion through time toward more supranational decision-making. While Lindberg and Nye might establish, using a priori categories, different types of decisions (economic, political), and then show that centrality is occurring at different rates in the different categories, Bernstein argues that these types are imposed on the data by the researcher and that if the simple measure of *number* of decisions is used, all three organizations exhibit a unidimensional increase toward centrality over time.[19] While Hughes and Schwarz show that their three indicators change differentially through time and that some seem to precede others (their findings are discussed below), Martin Abravanel and Barry Hughes present data partially contradicting the direction of the Hughes-Schwarz findings, and Bernstein as well as Caporaso and Alan

[16] W. E. Fisher, "An Analysis of the Deutsch SocioCausal Paradigm of Political Integration," *International Organization* 23 (Spring, 1969), pp. 254–90.

[17] Hughes and Schwarz, "Dimensions of Political Integration," p. 285.

[18] Leon Lindberg, "Political Integration As a Multidimensional Phenomenon Requiring Multivariate Measurement," *International Organization* 24 (Autumn, 1970), pp. 649–732; Joseph S. Nye, "Comparative Regional Integration: Concept and Measurement," *International Organization* 22 (Autumn, 1968), pp. 855–80.

[19] Robert A. Bernstein, "International Integration: Multidimensional or Unidimensional?" *Journal of Conflict Resolution* 16 (September, 1972), pp. 403–8.

Pelowski argue that some indicators of "integration" move very much in tandem.[20]

The question of whether integration is a single, simple process or a much more complex, multidimensional one remains open. The reams of research on integration in Europe—where the vast majority of attention has been focused—further illustrate the problems. There is general agreement that integration increased in Europe after World War II, particularly through the early 1950s. The formation of the EEC, ECSC, and other organizations are only the most pronounced evidence of the supranational process taking place. Yet a somewhat revisionist description of European integration has set in with evidence later compiled, especially by Deutsch and his colleagues, which showed that trade in Europe had reached the "highest level of structural integration it has ever reached" in the 1957–1958 period. While Europe is more integrated now than between the wars or before World War I, "from about 1957–1958 on, there have been no further gains." [21]

Trade, however, is not the sole indicator undergoing change. An analysis of elite newspapers indicated that interest in an Atlantic Alliance decreased in French, German, and British newspapers, remaining high only in the *New York Times*. Furthermore, concern in the newspapers with internal as opposed to external supranational questions was the same in the mid-1960s as it had been a decade earlier.[22]

Similar trends occurred in mass opinion. There had been an increase between 1954 and 1962 in the importance of an "image" of a united Europe in French and German opinion, and the idea that European unity would be a good thing, and should be strengthened and pushed. By 1966, however, Deutsch was reporting that "there seems to be no clear image in mass opinion as to what these steps should be, or how far they should go, nor is there any sense of urgency about them." [23] Deutsch's general conclusion in his 1966 report is that the phenomenon that looked so promising ten years earlier for bringing Europe together was undergoing a change. Deutsch, be it noted, equates measures of mass opinion, elite attitudes, and trade with integration; his argument is that because these indicators were not increasing, integration was flagging.

[20] Martin Abravanel and Barry Hughes, "The Relationship between Public Opinion and Governmental Foreign Policy: A Cross National Study," in *Sage International Yearbook of Foreign Policy Studies*, ed. Patrick McGowan, Vol. 1 (Beverly Hills: Sage, 1973); Bernstein, "International Integration"; James Caporaso and Alan L. Pelowski, "Economic and Political Integration in Europe: A Quasi-Experimental Analysis," *American Political Science Review* 65 (June, 1971), pp. 418–33.

[21] Karl Deutsch, "Integration and Arms Control in the European Political Environment: A Summary Report," *American Political Science Review* 60 (June, 1966), p. 355.

[22] Ibid., p. 356.

[23] Ibid., p. 357.

Hayward Alker and Donald Puchala present extensive analysis of trade data on Europe that support Deutsch's argument. According to their analysis, "the period of all-western European partnership is over. . . . There has been as much economic *dis*integration in Europe since 1951 as there has been integration." [24] Despite changes elsewhere using other indicators, Alker and Puchala argue that members of the Common Market were no closer economically in the early 1960s than they were in the early 1950s.

Puchala also contends that Franco-German integration has not always been one marked by increases. Confidence, amity, and cooperation between the two countries did expand from 1954 to 1965; the 1963–1965 period, however, showed a drop in cooperation, and the establishment of bilateral institutions generally leveled off after 1959. At the same time, amity among the public in both countries, which had declined from 1960 to 1962, rose during the 1963–1965 period. Puchala contends that by that time a "strain" or "load" had been put on Franco-German relations.[25]

Ronald Inglehart argues that despite Deutsch's findings, survey data from Western Europe indicates a potential movement *toward* integration. He maintains that the important data to investigate are not current mass opinion or elite newspaper perceptions of the desirability of integration in Europe, but rather European youths' perceptions of that goal.[26] For instance, Table 6-1 shows the percentages favoring European integration in four different countries: the youth percentages are consistently higher than the adult. On other questions, the youth group answered more in favor of integrative steps—abolishing tariffs, common foreign policy—than did the adults; the differences between the generations

Table 6-1. Overall Percentages "Strongly For" or "For" European Integration

	Netherlands	France	Germany	Britain
Adults, 1962	87	72	81	65
Youths, 1964-1965	95	93	95	72

Ronald Inglehart, "An End to European Integration?" *American Political Science Review* 61 (March, 1967), p. 92.

24 Hayward Alker and Donald Puchala, "Trends in Economic Partnership: The North Atlantic Area, 1928–1963," in *Quantitative International Politics: Insights and Evidence,* ed. J. David Singer (New York: Free Press, 1968), p. 315.

25 Donald Puchala, "International Transactions and Regional Integration," *International Organization* 24 (Autumn, 1970), pp. 732–63.

26 Ronald Inglehart, "An End to European Integration?" *American Political Science Review* 61 (March, 1967), pp. 91–105.

ranged from a low of 5 percent in the Netherlands to 16 percent in France and Germany. Inglehart notes that the youth sample was born between the mid-1940s and the mid-1950s. The full effect of their political influence will not come for some time—Inglehart suggests not before the 1990s.

Another problem with the Deutsch and the Alker and Puchala findings is their reliance on using a specific measure of trade interactions, termed the "relative acceptance" (RA) score, perhaps the most widely used on trade and other transaction data. The underlying model of that measure, however, is a "null" model which assumes complete randomness of trade; an RA score is a measure of the deviation from that randomness. The larger the trade over what would be expected randomly, the larger the RA score, and the more integrated two countries are. The assumption is that such deviations from randomness represent decisions made by one or both sides to increase trade, which in turn represent higher mutual relevance and interest, and thus higher integration.

As Barry Hughes has shown, however, other measures—using other assumptions, equally valid—provide quite different results. He compared the RA model to two others, the "export percentage model," and the "GNP model." The export model makes a ratio of country A's transactions with country B to all of A's transactions, whereas the GNP model uses country A's gross national product as the denominator.[27] Hughes illustrated the effect of measurement decisions by comparing the three models on trade data for the EEC for the 1958–1963 and 1958–1966 periods, and for Eastern Europe for the years 1958 to 1966. Integration increased in every case with the exception of the RA model for Eastern Europe, but also in every case the variable-sum measure, the GNP model, showed drastically higher integration than the other two models. Moreover, the null-model—the widely-used RA scores—showed the least amount of integration. Finally, as Hughes notes, the RA scores he presents are higher than those provided by Alker and Puchala. They are high because he added several East European countries to his pool, thereby decreasing the expected values for Western European nations and increasing the RA scores.

These findings question Deutsch's contention that integration in Europe has ceased, a conclusion that rests on a specific manipulation of the trade data. Fisher insists, however, that the entire "social assimilation" framework is empirically incorrect insofar as Western Europe is concerned. These conclusions again are dependent not only on a strict interpretation of what he calls the "Deutsch Sociocausal Paradigm of

[27] Barry Hughes, "Transaction Analysis: The Impact of Operationalization," *International Organization* 25 (Winter, 1971), pp. 132–45.

Integration," but also on certain interpretations of indicators of integration. Says Fisher:

The sociocausal paradigm contends that a process of *social assimilation* leads to or causes a process of *political development* to occur. In the paradigm social assimilation is conceptualized as a learning process during which peoples, in response to mutually rewarding transactions, adopt habits that they perceive as conducive to further rewarding transactions.[28]

If these processes continue, then common perceptions of ways to solve common problems emerge; to solve these problems effectively supranational organizations often arise and are given power to make binding decisions: "Social assimilation causes political development and therefore that social assimilation must exist before political development can start." [29]

Using Deutsch's conclusion that rates of social assimilation in Europe ceased in the 1957–1958 period, Fisher concludes that the utility of the paradigm then rests on political assimilation also having ceased during the same period. He analyzes data on "decisional output" from the EEC, ECSC, and EURATOM, and concludes that contrary to the Deutsch paradigm, political assimilation *increased* in Europe at the point that Deutsch claims social assimilation decreased. That is, the *number of decisions* made by the three organizations increased, especially during the 1958–1959 and 1961–1964 periods. Taking the paradigm as a *deterministic* one, therefore, it proves to be incorrect *if* Deutsch's assertion of decreasing social assimilation is correct. However, it may very well be that despite the decrease in social assimilation throughout the late 1950s and early 1960s, its increase prior to 1958 might have set the stage for the later increase in political assimilation that Fisher finds, especially for the 1961–1964 period. In sum, Fisher's critique of the Deutsch paradigm rests on (1) accepting Deutsch's interpretation of his own data, (2) accepting Fisher's deterministic view, and (3) assuming no time lag.

Caporaso and Pelowski's approach to the question of European integration is somewhat different, and they reach both similar and dissimilar conclusions. Regarding types of integration, they suggest "system linkages" as an alternative to supranational organizations. Contending that "if the behavior of a given political structure is indifferent to other political structures or to economic structures, then we may speak of that 'system' as poorly integrated."[30]

They investigated the effect of three potentially strong changes within

28 Fisher, "Analysis of Deutsch Paradigm," p. 257.

29 Ibid., p. 258.

30 Caporaso and Pelowski, "Economic and Political Integration," pp. 421–22.

Europe: the formation of the EEC in January, 1958; the adoption, by the European Council of Ministers, of the first agricultural "package" decision in January, 1962; and the Common Market agricultural crisis between June, 1965, and January, 1966. Hypothetically, other components should be affected by these events, such as the number of European Commission Regulations and Decisions, Council of Minister Regulations, intra-EEC trade, and so on. On the whole, they found not only that the EEC is a "weakly integrating social system" because there is limited responsiveness on the part of "major components or subsystems [political and economic] of the EEC,"[31] but that the three experimental changes, introduced into the European system as quasi-experimental events, produced few effects on other components in the system. As they point out, however, "there is another way to view integration—in terms of the growth and development of structures and functions at a new level. In these terms, the EEC (as a positive growth system) is rapidly integrating. Almost without exception, all the variables we dealt with are and have been rapidly increasing.[32] Thus, indicators such as Germany's exports to the EEC and the number of political decisions and regulations adopted by the EEC have become greater.

Investigation of some of Caporaso and Pelowski's evidence, presented in Figures 6-1, 6-2, and 6-3, show why they came to such conclusions. Figure 6-1 shows German exports to the EEC as a proportion of its total world exports. Clearly, Germany's exports between 1955 and 1965 are on the increase, especially after 1960; in that sense, therefore, the system is integrating. However, whether it was the formation of EEC at timepoint 12 that caused that increase or not is unclear; it certainly had no immediate impact on the trend, and it seems reasonable to conclude that the next thirteen quarterly observations were unaffected by the formation of the EEC. The January 14, 1963 decision by the Council of Ministers laying the basis for common agricultural decisions appears to have a very clear effect on Commission Regulations and Decisions (Figure 6-2) although their statistical analysis shows that this is not true for several other variables. The effect of the 1965 Agricultural Crisis (Figure 6-3), in which several representatives in the Council of Ministers walked out, appeared to have almost no effect, especially when taking possible trend effects out of the data. Thus, changes in the time series of these indicators of integration did not uniformly respond to experimental events, with some exceptions that they note. Caporaso and Pelowski's

31 Ibid., p. 432.
32 Ibid.

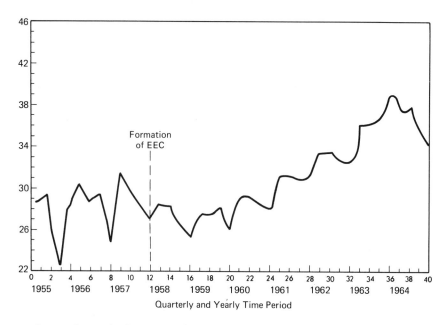

Source: James A. Caporaso and Alan L. Pelowski, "Economic and Political Integration in Europe: A Quasi-Experimental Analysis," *American Political Science Review* 65 (June, 1971), p. 425.

Figure 6-1. Ratio of Germany's EEC exports to total exports.

findings, therefore are circumscribed: European integration is increasing in terms of growth of intra-EEC trade and decisional outputs, but not in terms of responsiveness of one component to another.

Clearly, the dispute arising from all these studies is theoretical as well as methodological. Deutsch as well as Alker and Puchala are correct if transactions and attitudes represent integration and if their manipulation of these measures is valid. They are not correct, however, if institutional decisions more accurately reflect integration, as Fisher suggests, or if attitudes must be given a time-lag analysis, as Inglehart suggests. These studies show why it is so difficult to separate out what integration seems to be a function of, and what, in turn, integration is thought to cause. It is not entirely satisfactory, either, to simply contend that all of these phenomena are factors or elements of integration and then to be solely concerned with the interaction among them, for that leaves aside the entire question of what causes them, and again, what in turn they cause —both central concerns of traditional integration literature.

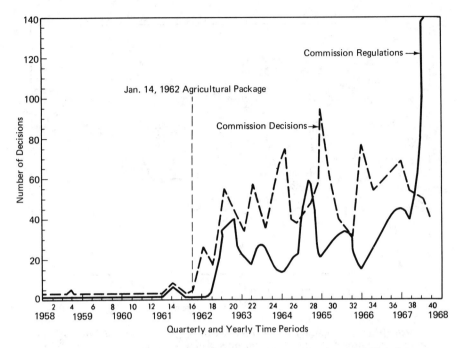

Source: James A. Caporaso and Alan L. Pelowski, "Economic and Political Integration in Europe: A Quasi-Experimental Analysis," *American Political Science Review* 65 (June, 1971), p. 428.

Figure 6-2. Effect of council of ministers' decision concerning common agricultural policy on trend in EEC regulations and decisions.

Distance

In order to reduce some of the confusion generated by the above problems, to separate out the many components of integration, and to cast that concept into a broader theoretical framework, we here suggest for heuristic purposes a set of models. These models, though simplified, nonetheless reflect the central thrust of much of the integration literature and ways of explaining international behavior. We employ the concept of "distance," which is a somewhat more neutral term than "integration" and does not carry along with it the intellectual baggage that "integration" does. It should be noted that these are heuristic devices to be tested and used as a beginning framework. They rely heavily on the communication framework outlined above concerning the importance of transactions and communications, and they interpret these phenomena broadly as constituting a type of distance between parties.

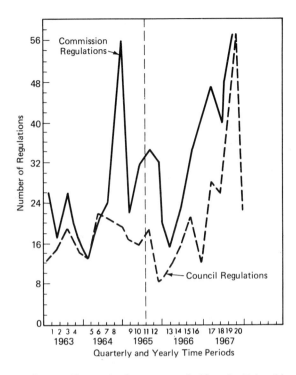

Source: James A. Caporaso and Alan L. Pelowski, "Economic and Political Integration in Europe: A Quasi-Experimental Analysis," *American Political Science Review* 65 (June, 1971), p. 430.

Figure 6-3. Effect of ministers' walkout from EEC on trend in commission regulations and decisions.

Transactions and communications between social units say something about the system, and we reinterpret that here to mean that distance between parties along certain social, transactional or communication dimensions will say something about the relationship among units within the system. First, distance between parties may say how integrated they are or are likely to become in terms of the "we-feeling" of community. Second, distance between parties may also indicate whether the formation of organizations is a highly probable event. Finally, the combination of distance (integration) and community formation should also provide some predictions about general behavior to be expected within a system. This reasoning leads to the three-step model which, despite its simplicity, sets out the components of contemporary integration theory as effect. Yet it also reflects what we referred to above as the traditional view of the phenomena of integration and integrative processes as cause. The first formulation of the model posits two links:

distance/integration ⟶ community formation ⟶ cooperative/ behavior

One of the central problems with the integration literature, however, as we have already noted, is its tendency to mix these three components, so that measures of distance, such as communications or transactions, are equated automatically with whether states are integrated or not, which in turn is often equated with whether states behave peacefully with one another. For this reason, distance and integration have here been equated but yet kept somewhat distinct, leaving open the possibility that distance, in fact, does not equate with integration.

With that in mind, therefore, three alternative models might be proposed:

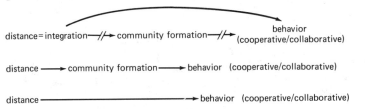

distance=integration ⟶//⟶ community formation ⟶//⟶ behavior (cooperative/collaborative)

distance ⟶ community formation ⟶ behavior (cooperative/collaborative)

distance ⟶ behavior (cooperative/collaborative)

In the first model, while community formation does occur, it is not necessarily linked with distance or integration nor with the cooperative behavior. The model indicates that social distance is the causal factor bringing about the cooperative behavior as an end result. The second model implies that we really do not know what integration means, but that we can measure social distance, and from that flows community formation and cooperative/collaborative behavior. The final alternative suggests that social distance is the primary operative variable for predicting behavior, regardless of whether community formation occurs or whether the units are truly integrated (implying once again that integration may not necessarily equate with distance variables).

Further variations of the model would take the first two components (social distance and integration) and note that there may in fact be different types of integration—a question we turn to in a moment—and that each of them may have differential effects on the validity of the model. Thus, for each of the four possibilities here, several subalternatives could be postulated.

These models are far from perfect, but they do try to forestall treating integration as both a dependent and independent variable, and equating integration automatically with changes in distance indicators.

They also try to set out clearly what the dependent variable or variables might be. Using the concept of distance in this fashion does not eliminate the problems in the area of integration, but it at least reduces some of them by keeping the concepts separated from each other. Other distinct processes—which appear to be distinct—can actually be seen as types of "distance." One such process is that of "polarization," a common process in many conflict situations. James Coleman utilizes it in analyzing community conflicts:

> As controversy develops, associations flourish *within* each group, but *wither* between persons on opposing sides. People break off long-standing relationships, stop speaking to former friends who have been drawn to the opposition, but proliferate their associations with fellow-partisans.[33]

This process is really one of communication: individuals begin communicating more with those on their own side and less with those on the opposite side. In that sense, the communication structure has an influence on the behavior of the units in the conflict. In international politics, Ole Holsti suggested that the higher the stress the greater the proportion of intracoalition communication as compared with intercoalition communication.[34] In other words, communication patterns describe the system, whether we are talking about a community controversy or an international conflict, much the way alliance aggregation described the system for Singer and Small. But the *explanation* here is different. Singer and Small focused more on the sheer number of poles in the system and what that might say concerning the level of uncertainty in the system; distance theory as conceptualized here views the pattern of communication as important. If communication is decreasing, then the distance between the parties is increasing. If distance along the communication dimension is increasing between opponents on opposite sides of a conflict, and yet increasing among allies, the system is polarizing. Increased distance measured by amount of communication implies less information, less accurate information, and perhaps less empathy with the other party and his problems. Through this rather circuitous path, distance becomes hypothesized as being related to a greater likelihood of prolonging or intensifying a conflict situation. On the contrary, situations of decreasing distance will be more likely to set opposite tendencies in motion, and the conflict is more likely to de-escalate or cease to exist.

The concept of distance, therefore, is a very broad one. It can include

[33] James Coleman, *Community Conflict* (New York: The Free Press, 1957), p. 11.

[34] Holsti, "The 1914 Case," *American Political Science Review* 59 (June, 1965), pp. 365–78.

several seemingly disparate theoretical perspectives. Deutsch's communication and transaction notions, the polarization of communication patterns—along with many others—merely illustrate the wide compass of the distance theory. Although specific elements may differ, they are similar in that they describe the structure of a system usually along communication or transaction dimensions, and that very structure is going to affect other behavior in the system.

Structural Balance Theory

In addition to the "integration" perspective on distance, yet a second perspective is contained in structural balance theory, which, simply put, says: "An enemy of my friend is my enemy; a friend of my friend is my friend." The hypothesis can be illustrated in two different domains. First, as Terrence Hopmann notes, citing both Georg Simmel and Lewis Coser, the relations *within* a system are directly related to that system's relations with the outside world.[35] It will be recalled that we first encountered this hypothesis under national attribute theory, part of which suggested that conflict with an external enemy produced internal cohesion. Translated to an international system, the hypothesis reads: greater interalliance conflict will produce greater intra-alliance cohesion. Thus, behavior between nations within an alliance is a direct function of the relations between that alliance and an outside object.

The second domain applies more strictly to dyadic and triadic behavior. Hopmann utilizes Newcombe's well-known A-B-X model of interpersonal communication, in which actors A and B have some orientation toward an external actor, X (Figure 6-4). The relations between the three

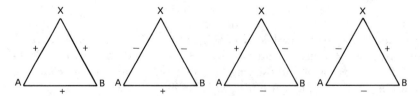

Figure 6-4.   Four possible balanced A-B-X systems of communication.

    [35] P. Terry Hopmann, "International Conflict and Cohesion in the Communist System," *International Studies Quarterly* 11 (September, 1967), pp. 212–36; Lewis Coser, *The Functions of Social Conflict* (New York: Free Press, 1956), p. 88; Georg Simmel, *Conflict* (Glencoe, Ill.: The Free Press, 1955), pp. 92–93.

actors carries a "charge," either positive or negative. "Balance among these points," Hopmann points out, "is achieved only when the number of negative bonds connecting them is even or zero." [36] For the three nations, then, if both A and B have a "symmetrical" relation to X (both either positive or both negative), then the relationship between A and B must be positive for the system to be in "balance." If their relationship to X differs, however, with A being positive and B being negative, their relationship with one another should be negative. As Hopmann notes, "With any other combination the system is in a state of imbalance with pressures to restore balance." [37]

These models are, of course, nothing new, for common sense tells us the same thing. If a person is extremely friendly with someone, it is very unlikely that he will have extreme negative relations with a third person who is also friendly with his friend. On the other hand, if the person's friend has extreme dislike for a third person, it is unlikely—if he is close to his friend—that he will have strong positive relations with that third person. Although such unlikely relations do happen, the probability is less for imbalanced situations to occur than for balanced.

The rationale for considering balance as a distance theory should be clear. Says Hopmann:

> The implications . . . for the study of international cohesion are thus apparent. If cohesion is defined in terms of co-orientation toward salient external objects or events, then symmetry of orientations may be assumed to be a valid indicator of cohesion.[38]

Further, he notes, "Similar evaluations, by enhancing mutual responsiveness, tend to enhance cohesion." In addition, the "co-orientations" within the A-B-X model are, in fact, distances "measured in terms of differences in orientations toward X." [39] For instance, if country A perceived X as 80 percent negative and country B perceived X as 70 percent negative, then the "distance" between A and B would be 10 percent. However, if A perceived X as 80 percent negative and B perceived X as 30 percent negative, the distance would be 50 percent. It is these dis-

[36] Hopmann, "International Conflict and Cohesion in the Communist System," p. 219; Theodore M. Newcombe, "An Approach to the Study of Communicative Acts," in *Small Groups*, ed. E. F. Borgatta and R. F. Bales (New York: Knopf, 1955); and Theodore M. Newcombe, "The Study of Consensus," in *Sociology Today: Problems and Prospects*, Vol. II, ed. Robert K. Merton, Leonard Broom, and Leonard S. Cottrell (New York: Harper and Row, 1965).

[37] Hopmann, "International Conflict and Cohesion in the Communist System," p. 219.

[38] Ibid., pp. 219–20.

[39] Ibid., pp. 220, 223.

tances that, according to the model, will tell us something about the relation between A and B. Hypothetically, the greater the distances, the more likely the A-B relation will be negative.

Healy and Stein use Arthur Lee Burns's balance of power hypothesis in a somewhat similar fashion, although the conception of "power" differs considerably from power seen as distance and system in Chapter 5. They use Burns's analogy with economic price-fixing behavior. If three firms are in competition, each producing the same product, and two of them decide on a price-fixing policy, then the third suffers. In this sense, closing distance between the two results in a greater distance between them and the third company. In international relations, they suggest that mutual arms reduction between two nations places a third country in a less secure position. "If two nations reduce their arms vis-à-vis each other, the newly created surplus of weapons and men is now available for use against the third power." [40] In terms of dyadic behavior, the reduced distance between the two arms-reducing nations should produce increased distance between each of them and the third country, predicting a tougher time for that third country in its relations with the other two. In terms of *system* behavior, the decreased A-B distance, according to Healy and Stein, would "severely limit the possibilities of drastic conflict resolution in the system."

In summary, then, balance theories are exceptionally simple and understandable, and yet they have several real advantages. Because of their simplicity, they satisfy the criterion for parsimony. Furthermore, they bear striking resemblance to theories of integration and communication, and yet are distinct in terms of the *way* in which behavior is explained. The balance approach and the integration approach can be seen as competing theories, and because of their distinctiveness can be evaluated in terms of respective potency. And finally, as with integration theories, the basic notion of balance corresponds to our everyday perception of the world.

Measurement

No extended discussion need be given to the question of measuring integration or distance; it has been discussed at some length earlier. Moreover, many of the operational indicators noted earlier as measures of distance or integration can also be used to assess balance. Even so, it

[40] Brian Healy and Arthur Stein, "The Balance of Power in International History: Theory and Reality," *Journal of Conflict Resolution* 17 (March, 1973), p. 37; Arthur Lee Burns, "From Balance to Deterrence: A Theoretical Analysis," *World Politics* 9 (July, 1957), pp. 494–529.

is well to reiterate several of these basic indicators, or variables. Cobb and Elder suggest three major types of interaction or transaction variables: communication, involving the interchange of messages; trade, involving the exchange of goods and services; and mobility, involving the movement of persons.[41] In each case, we would argue, the greater the transactions, the less the distance between the units. Other measures of distance between parties might be similarity of mass attitudes toward an external object (as described, for instance, in the A-B-X model in the previous section), feeling of amity among mass publics in respective units toward those in other units, and so on. These measures constitute operational indicators for distance, but they are also very often equated with integration. As the models proposed earlier suggest, we don't necessarily have to agree with that assertion—or disagree—to use them as indicators of distance.

For the variable of community formation, the clearest measure, of course, is the formation of an international organization that takes over at least some decision-making authority from the respective national units. Another measure, somewhat more controversial because it has also been used as a measure of other variables in the model, is common membership in international organizations, especially governmental. Here the units would be seen as integrated because of their expressed desire, through joining the organization, to solve mutual problems amicably and internationally rather than nationally.

The final link in the models constitutes the end result of almost all the traditional work in integration, namely, the behavior among or between the integrated or "united" countries. This behavior might take two forms: one quantitative—ongoing events measured through specific time periods (weeks, months, quarters, years), the other qualitative—the presence or absence of major war or conflict measured over long periods of time. Though the two overlap to some degree, it has been noted on several occasions that what often appear to be similar phenomena are in fact quite distinct, and therefore may be a function of quite dissimilar theories. Most of the integration literature tends to focus on the second, qualitatively measured variable.

Measurement in the case of balance theory does not present serious problems, nor are they as intimately tied into theoretical concerns. In the limited empirical research in this area, distance has usually been measured as similarity or dissimilarity in general orientation (usually along the familiar positive-negative or hostility-cooperation dimension) toward some external object, ether in terms of perceptions of the object or actual behavior toward that object.

[41] Cobb and Elder, *International Community*, p. 72–73.

Distance and Integration: Empirical Linkages

We shall deal here with the many relationships proposed in the several models already presented. Presentation of this evidence is difficult because of the theoretical and methodological fuzziness previously referred to. Nonetheless, some attempt will be made to separate out the different linkages.

DISTANCE-INTEGRATION
AND POLITICAL COMMUNITY

What leads to the formation of a community? Karl Deutsch went so far as to question the importance of investigating the formation of political communities. Contrary to much common belief after the Second World War, he felt that the world was not making headway toward "coming together." It was widely assumed by mid-century that "modern life, with rapid transportation, mass communications, and literacy, tends to be more international than life in past decades or centuries and hence more conducive to the growth of international or supranational institutions." [42] Deutsch concluded to the contrary that there seemed to be no "unequivocal trend toward more internationalism and world community." Furthermore, the closer to modern times, "the more difficult it is to find any instances of successful amalgamation of two or more previously sovereign states." If formation of political communities is not a particularly common phenomenon, then in terms of the models, the component of a political community takes on less interest—which, of course, suggests concentrating on the relationship between distance and forms of interstate behavior other than community formation. Deutsch also found, contrary to what had been expected, that the formation of "pluralistic security communities" (in which states retain some national independence) was more easily attained than "amalgamated security communities" (in which units sacrifice independence to the new supranational organ).

In terms of the correlates of pluralistic security communities, Deutsch and his colleagues found several variables, viewed traditionally as important, to be relatively unimportant, or at least overrated. A previous administrative union, ethnic or linguistic assimilation, strong economic ties, and foreign military threats seemed not to carry as much weight as other essential requirements. One variable that he did find crucial was the very difficult-to-define notion of sense of community or "we feeling,"

[42] Deutsch, *et al.*, "Political Community," p. 4.

not so much in terms of an outward verbal attachment to a set of values as in terms of "identification," "self-image and interests." What was important, in other words, was a "perpetual dynamic process of mutual attention, communication, perception of needs, and responsiveness in the process of decision-making." [43] A second and third set of variables discerned by Deutsch revolved around the need for (1) a strong "core area" or country capable of playing a leading role in the community, and (2) growing "capabilities" within the units to enable them to respond to the other units in necessary ways. Thus, for units that would retain their original independence, many of the distance-integration concepts from the communication school (linguistic assimilation, strong economic ties) do not appear particularly important, whereas certain decision-making clusters (core areas) and national attributes (capabilities to respond) are essential.

For an amalgamated security community, however, where the units give up their independence to the new community, several requirements were isolated that coincide more closely with the distance-integration concepts. First, a compatibility of values held by the politically relevant elite was vital: the closer the respective elites were to each other on central values, the more likely community would occur. Second, increasing capabilities of the units, along with improvements in the communication process, enabled the level of transactions to rise. Third, ease of population mobility would also ease the movement toward community formation. Fourth, the transactions between the units must be multiple and balanced: they must occur over a wide range of issues and be so balanced that neither side is dominating the other nor totally responsive to the other. Finally, mutual predictability of behavior between the units is assurance against "treachery" by one side or the other.

DISTANCE-INTEGRATION
AND COLLABORATIVE BEHAVIOR: DYADIC

Numerous studies can be cited reflecting the concern noted above about whether integration is a unidimensional or multidimensional phenomenon. They can be viewed, therefore, either as analyses of the relationships among various indicators of integration, or as support for one or more of the links in the models. Cobb and Elder, for instance, present data on these questions in their study of the North Atlantic area (with two sets of 65 and 210 dyads) and a global domain (1,176 dyads). They found that certain transactions, such as tourist and student exchanges, relate fairly strongly to later intergovernmental collaboration,

---

[43] Ibid., p. 17.

such as treaties, but they also found that collaborative behavior in the 1958-1960 period correlates strongly with transactions in 1964. In their global analysis, transactions such as trade, common membership in nongovernmental organizations, and telegraphic communications proved to be the strongest predictors of collaboration in the legal, cultural, and technical domains.[44] Because of the strong correlations that go each way, however, it is next to impossible to ferret out which is the stronger causal linkage.

Cobb and Elder's findings for mass attitudes is somewhat different, however. Although none of their correlations are exceptionally high, transactions relate to attitudes at a later point in time, whereas the opposite is not true. Transactions in 1952 correlated with attitudes in 1955 and 1964 at a higher level than mass opinion correlates with transactions two years later. Abravanel and Hughes correlated cooperative events data with favorable public opinion for seventeen dyads (primarily European and almost all large), and determined that changes over time correlated when attitudes were lagged behind events by six months. They found that the relationship was strongest with France, Britain, and West Germany.[45] Both studies indicate that the distance-integrative measure of mass attitudes follows cooperative or collaborative behavior.

Hughes and Schwarz present even further data supporting that finding. They investigated the relations among (1) mass community, measured by survey data on how populations in the European community view one another; (2) political amalgamation, using the data on decisional outputs of the various European community organizations collected by Fisher; and (3) intergovernmental cooperation, measured by daily events among the original six members of the Common Market. They found that intergovernmental cooperation affects political amalgamation and mass community, and that political amalgamation also influences mass community. Thus, high-level intergovernmental cooperation (*exclusive* of actions of political amalgamation) constitutes the first part of the chain, not an entirely surprising relationship: governments should be cooperating exclusive of their amalgamating behavior prior to their decisions to unite or amalgamate. Even though Hughes and Schwarz's analysis of the data involved one subjective judgment (the assignment of years to high and low institutional growth in the EEC), the causal paths they noted most likely do *not* run in the opposite direction.[46] In fact, using the data they present and looking at the relation-

[44] Cobb and Elder, *International Community*, pp. 124–27.

[45] Abravanel and Hughes, "Relationship between Public Opinion and Governmental Foreign Policy," pp. 120–21.

[46] Hughes and Schwarz, "Dimensions of Political Integration."

ship between changes in variables over time, the correlation becomes even stronger than they report when changes in mass attitudes are lagged two years behind intergovernmental cooperation. Lagging intergovernmental cooperation produces a smaller relation.

These data tend to contradict the models proposed earlier if we assume that mass attitudes constitute a type of distance or integration. As Hughes and Schwarz observe, however, they do not account for the first variable in their study—intergovernmental cooperation—and one can argue that other distance variables might change prior to that phenomenon.

It is possible, however, to interpret intergovernmental cooperation not as the final link in the model but as the first, viewing it as representing transactional distance between countries rather than as the outcome variable at the end of the chain.[47] In this formulation, the dependent variable would then become actual community formation or long-range cooperation more clearly reminiscent of Deutsch's work: the probability of outbreak of war, or resolution of a specific conflict by violent as opposed to peaceful means. Unfortunately, this linkage steers dangerously close to the tautological argument cited already, in which intergovernmental cooperation—peaceful interaction—causes conflicts to be resolved peacefully, a not entirely astounding proposition. If intergovernmental transactions constitute only one of many distance variables, however, then the final outcome of resolution of conflict by peaceful means becomes a function of that multitude of variables, and not just one.

Russett also investigated the relationship among components of distance or integration. Comparing U.N. voting groups in the early 1950s with mutual membership in international organizations in the 1960s and then reversing that analysis, he found that earlier U.N. voting patterns correlated at .88 with international organizations, whereas, the reverse relationship was .81. He concluded that "behavior was leading institutions rather than the opposite; countries first came to have similar positions on the major issues of international politics and *then* joined international organizations in common."[48] He also showed that early U.N. voting was more closely related to subsequent trade distance ($r = .84$) than the early trade patterns were to later U.N. voting (.78). However, trade in the 1950s was more highly related to organizations in 1962 (.91) than the reverse (.89). From these relationships Russett infers that similar political orientations "lead to the growth of trade between

[47] Barry Hughes and Thomas Volgy, "Distance in Foreign Policy Behavior: A Comparative Study of Eastern Europe," *Midwest Journal of Political Science* 14 (August, 1970), pp. 459–92.

[48] Bruce Russett, *International Regions and the International System: A Study in Political Ecology* (Chicago: Rand McNally, 1967), p. 206.

countries, and the trade, along with the similar political outlooks, leads on to the growth of international organizations.[49] Given the fact, however, that *all* of the relationships are exceptionally high, and that the largest change when reversing direction drops the correlation from .88 to .81, we must conclude, contrary to Russett, that all three of the components correlate with each other.

But how do distance or integration variables relate to warlike behavior? Russett claims to show from one set of data that contrary to the expectation of integration theorists, distance (a term Russett does *not* use) does not relate to the warlike behavior of states. Russett grouped countries (using the data reduction technique of factor analysis—see appendix, paragraph C) along several dimensions, such as International Organization (I.O.) membership, geography, trade, sociocultural similarity, and U.N. voting. In the forty-one conflict dyads he examined, those within the same "region" were *more* likely to engage in conflictual activity than those in separate regions. Social assimilation theory would predict that those within similar regions—IO membership, trade, and sociocultural harmony—would be less distant and therefore less likely to resolve conflicts violently. Russett's forty-one cases show this not to be the case (Table 6-2). A large proportion of his cases, though, involve colonial situations, a potential intervening variable. Removing most of these from the analysis, the influence of geography and sociocultural

Table 6-2. Cluster Memberships and Warlike Behavior

	I O Member-ship	Geo-graphical Similarity	Trade	Socio-cultural Similarity	U.N. Voting
Percentage of all warring pairs that shared membership in the same cluster	32	63	53	24	16
Percentage of all pairs that shared membership in the same cluster in 1960s	14	26	25	21	16
Percentage of all warring pairs exclusive of colonial situations	37	74	40	47	27

Rows 1 and 2 are taken from Bruce Russett, *International Regions and the International System: A Study in Political Ecology* (Chicago: Rand McNally, 1967), p. 198.

[49] Ibid., p. 207.

similarity becomes stronger. Some 74 percent and 47 percent of all warring pairs shared the same geographical and sociocultural region as opposed to 63 percent and 24 percent when all forty-one dyads were
considered. Trade, however, becomes less important, with 40 percent of
all the warring dyads sharing the same trade regions as opposed to 53
percent when analyzing the entire sample. Nonetheless, the data still
strongly suggest that membership in the same cluster on these dimensions
in no way prevents war. That conclusion is reinforced further if we
investigate the second line in the table, which shows what would
normally be the case with any random sample drawn from the entire
population. In each instance, except for the U.N. cluster, the percentages
there are less. On the whole it appears that nations in the same region
geographically are the most prone to violent conflict, with trade and
sociocultural similarity being next in importance.

Russett's data, however, only refer to membership in the same cluster,
not *how close* each member is to other members within the region. His
conclusion that "this finding demands a reformulation of some assumptions about international integration and conflict" is somewhat pre-
mature, especially inasmuch as he later points out that "very *major* wars
involving over 5,000 fatalities between states that cluster together by
all five of the criteria are rare." [50] Of eleven such cases of major international conflict since World War II, only the Hungarian revolt against
the Soviet government was one in which both parties occupied the same
region in all five respects. As Russett notes, Hungary was forcibly placed
in the region by the actions of the Soviet government, and the conflict
was over its attempt to extricate itself from that region. Distance on
social assimilation variables may relate to *extent* of conflict rather than
to the conflict-no conflict dichotomy.

Another study lends moderate support to these conclusions. In one
set of fifteen dyads, the high level of inter-trade before conflict between
the two countries was moderately related to low verbal violence, high cooperative interactions, and a scaled measure of escalation. [51] In a second
set of twenty-nine dyads, a communication dimension was moderately
related to high trade. The dynamic trade ratios, which record changing
trade distances over time, were all insignificant. Common INGO membership was likewise related to four measures of violence in the first set
of conflicts (using *only* INGOs founded ten years before the outbreak
of the conflict), but not in the second set. These findings, then, tend to

[50] Ibid., pp. 199, 205.

[51] Michael P. Sullivan, "Escalatory and Non-Escalatory 'Systems,'" Mimeographed:
University of Arizona, 1972, p. 21; the correlations were −.60, .62, and .47, all in the
predicted direction.

support Russett's suggestion that the *extent* of conflict as opposed to whether there is a conflict or not, might be related to distance within the dyad. In this study the greater the trade and the larger the number of common INGO memberships (as a percentage of both countries' total membership), the less the verbal violence and general overall escalation and the greater the number of cooperative interactions. Of perhaps more than passing interest is the fact that one of the distance measures used in the study was *non*governmental organizations, as opposed to the governmental organizations in Russett's analysis. It is possible these institutions more clearly represent the broad social distance between parties; data will be reported below on the systemic level supporting this assertion.

Hughes and Volgy used trade, state visits, and diplomatic contacts (embassies and legations) as measures of distance in East European-Soviet relations.[52] They investigated the Hungarian revolution and surrounding events in 1956, the Polish revolution of about the same time, and the Albanian deviation during 1960–1961. A fourth case, somewhat different from the other three, was Cuba's shift to the Soviet orbit during the 1960–1961 period. In each case, where data were available, they found that change in distance occurred between the respective countries and the bloc, and that in several cases—especially with Hungary—the distance indicators changed *prior* to the recorded change in behavior. More specifically, trade and diplomatic distance between Hungary and the Soviet bloc increased in 1954; trade distance increased even more in 1956. Similarly, Poland's trade and diplomatic distance rose in 1955–1956. Czechoslovakia's distance from the bloc began to increase on all three indicators in 1966–1967, one to two years before the Soviet invasion of Czechoslovakia in 1968. Albania's distance on trade and state visits increased in 1960–1962. The only other marked change was with Romania, whose distance increased on trade and diplomatic contacts during the 1960–1962 period and later during the 1965–1967 period.

Hughes and Volgy conclude only that the three distance indicators accurately *describe* East European-Soviet behavior. However, given the juxtaposition of changes in their distance variables to important events in East European-Soviet behavior, their evidence roughly corroborates the notion that distances may *lead to* behavior. In the cases of Albania, Czechoslovakia, Hungary, and Poland, important shifts in distances between them, on the one hand, and either the entire bloc or the U.S.S.R., on the other, were followed by rapid shifts—and usually to the more violent end of the spectrum—in the Soviet Union's behavior toward these countries. The fashion in which Hughes and Volgy present their data

[52] Hughes and Volgy, "Distance in Foreign Policy Behavior."

disallows conclusions of *correlations,* but the linkage is fairly clear nonetheless.

Distance in terms of communication patterns also finds some secondary support for its impact on the behavior of nations. Neither Coleman nor Holsti [53] drew the link between these communication patterns and greater violence, but it is plausible that conflicts in which parties are polarized are much more likely to have violent than nonviolent outcomes—because each has less information about the other and his motives, and therefore less empathy. In Holsti's data on the crisis leading to World War I, the number of inter-alliance versus intra-alliance communications decreased as the stress became higher. In a later analysis, Holsti reports the same pattern: 32 percent of all communications during the low-stress period were between alliances, whereas only about 26 percent were inter-alliance during the high stress.[54] In both instances, the pattern, though not a strong one, shows a shift toward greater polarization (see appendix, paragraph A.3).

Paul Smoker's dyadic analysis of Chinese-Indian trade and defense expenditures also supports the effect of trade distance and subsequent state behavior, here defined as defense expenditures.[55] He found a negative relation between the Chinese-Indian trade and yearly letter rate and defense expenditures. Again the causal relationship, however, is extremely difficult to ferret out.

Numerous other studies have also been cited relating various kinds of distance measures to conflict behavior. McGowan and Shapiro review several, pointing out, for instance, that Rummel found high transactions (mail from country A to B, as well as translations by one country of another country's works) related to lower conflict.[56] Michael Haas reported data showing that states undertake war against other states that are culturally dissimilar, whereas an earlier study by Rummel found that countries already in conflict would be unaffected by the level of cultural similarity in terms of the *level* of conflict.[57] Finally, L. F. Rich-

[53] Coleman, *Community Conflict;* Holsti, "The 1914 Case."

[54] Ole Holsti, *Crisis, Escalation, War* (Montreal: McGill-Queens University Press, 1972), p. 102.

[55] Paul Smoker, "Sino-Indian Relations: A Study of Trade, Communication, and Defense," *Journal of Peace Research* 1, No. 2 (1964), pp. 65–76.

[56] R. J. Rummel, "Some Empirical Findings on Nations and Their Behavior," *World Politics* 21 (January, 1969), p. 239; cited in Patrick McGowan and Howard Shapiro, *The Comparative Study of Foreign Policy: A Survey of Scientific Findings* (Beverly Hills: Sage, 1973), p. 127.

[57] Michael Haas, "Communication Factors in Decision-making," *Peace Research Society Papers* 12 (1969), p. 86; and R. J. Rummel, "Dimensions of Dyadic War, 1820–1952," *Journal of Conflict Resolution* 11 (June, 1967), p. 182. Both cited in McGowan and Shapiro, *Comparative Study of Foreign Policy,* p. 127.

ardson found that while similarity in religion has not necessarily made for peaceful relations, dissimilarity seemed to be related to war; similarity in language, however, seemed to have little effect.[58] As with the findings on power, the contradictions that seem to flow from these many studies might very likely be a function of both different independent as well as dependent variables, suggesting that distance measures do not uniformly relate in the same way to all types of conflict or cooperative behavior.

DISTANCE-INTEGRATION/
COLLABORATIVE BEHAVIOR: SYSTEMIC

As with power, social distance or integrative measures exist on the systemic as well as the dyadic level. In his analysis of regional organizations, Nye presents data showing that of twenty-five interstate conflicts, eight were between fellow members of regional organizations. Furthermore, in only three of those eight did the regional organization play a role in dampening the violence, although it did not resolve the issue. The U.N. was found to be even less effective than the regional organs: it dampened violence in only six out of twenty-three conflicts.[59] Nye also claims to show that macroregional organizations helped isolate conflict among members in 74 percent of the cases he investigated, brought about an abatement in 58 percent, and ended the fighting in 44 percent; there was a lasting settlement in 32 percent of his cases. When Nye weighted the conflicts in terms of seriousness, however, the successes were shown to be primarily cases of low intensity.[60] The assessment of these data is confounded by the fact that there was no control group of countries involved in conflicts but *not* in regional organizations. As Cal Clark and Steve Ropp suggested concerning the Central American Common Market and the war between Honduras and Nicaragua, the very presence of regional organizations may foster conflict.[61] Systemic data presented by Singer and Wallace show, according to them, that "at the close of very warlike periods, the creation of new IGO (intergovernmental organizations) is high, and at the close of peaceful ones, that creation is low," but they found no relation between the number of IGOs during one period

[58] L. F. Richardson, *Statistics of Deadly Quarrel* (Pittsburgh: Boxwood Press, 1960), pp. xi–xii; cited in McGowan and Shapiro, *Comparative Study of Foreign Policy*, p. 127.

[59] Nye, *Peace in Parts*, p. 131.

[60] Ibid., pp. 171, 175.

[61] Cal Clark and Steve C. Ropp, "Disintegrative Tendencies in the Central American Common Market: The Limits of Integration Theory," Research Series 23, Institute of Government Research, mimeographed (Tucson: University of Arizona, 1974).

and the beginning of war during following periods.[62] However, only one of their many variables (a "weighted" score for IGO membership) was concerned with change over time; recomputing correlations for their data indicated that the correlations, although not becoming rather significant, changed from positive to negative, in the predicted direction.

Furthermore, Michael Wallace, in a later study using very similar data, showed that for the 145-year period, 1820–1964, there was a fairly high negative relationship between the change in the number of intergovernmental organizations and the change in armed forces levels and battle casualties, a relationship that became stronger in the last 114 years of the period. Wallace notes that the relation is not a direct one; rather, IGO formation rate appears to have an effect by lowering arms levels in the system, which then tends to dampen war.[63]

James Harf and his colleagues, using the same data but restricted to the 1900–1964 period, found negative relations at this systemic level for the European and Asian systems for all periods, including wartime. Thus, a slight tendency exists for the number of wars to vary inversely with the average number of IGOs that nations belong to in any given five-year period.[64]

Smoker investigated the 1900–1960 periods with different data, and arrived at rather similar conclusions. Figure 6-5 shows Smoker's data: three profiles of arms races (before World War I, World War II, and the Cold War); the formation rate of new international nongovernmental organizations (INGOs), and the net INGO formation rate.[65] The years 1902 to 1911 and 1918 to 1928 clearly exhibited increasing numbers of international organizations. Following each of these periods was a decline in the formation rate of INGOs, at the same time that the respective arms races were accelerating. After another rise in the net INGO formation rate from 1945 to 1951, a drastic falloff was accompanied by the third arms race spiral, from about 1948 through 1953. In the mid-1950s both variables began to drop, but while the arms race profile continued to decline until about 1960, the net INGO formation rate began increasing again about 1956 until the end of the series. Conclusions from

[62] J. David Singer and Michael D. Wallace, "Intergovernmental Organization and the Preservation of Peace, 1816–1964: Some Bivariate Relationships," *International Organization* 24 (Summer, 1970), p. 540.

[63] Michael Wallace, "Status, Formal Organization, and Arms Levels as Factors Leading to the Onset of War, 1820–1964," in *Peace, War, and Numbers,* ed. Bruce Russett (Beverly Hills, Sage, 1972), p. 66.

[64] James E. Harf, David G. Hoovler, and Thomas E. James, Jr., "Systemic and External Attributes in Foreign Policy Analysis," in *Comparing Foreign Policies: Theories, Findings, and Methods,* ed. James N. Rosenau (New York: Wiley, 1974), p. 240.

[65] Paul Smoker, "Nation-State Escalation and International Integration," *Journal of Peace Research* 4 (No. 1, 1967), pp. 61–75.

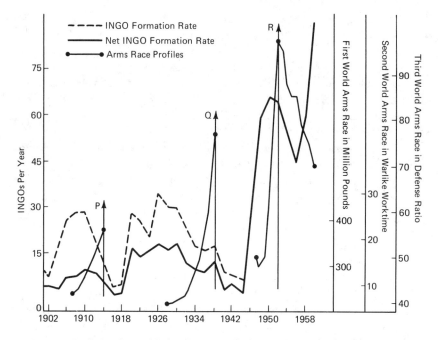

Source: Paul Smoker, "Nation-State Escalation and International Integration,"
Journal of Peace Research 6 No. 1 (1967), p. 66.

Figure 6-5. INGO formation rate and arms races, 1902–1960.

this data are difficult to draw with certitude, but the overall pattern
seems to show an inverse relation between INGOs and arms races. We
certainly cannot say that increasing distance here *caused* the spiraling
arms races, for the relationship may have gone the other way around.
Nevertheless, changes in large-scale systemic distance may say something
about the potential extent and intensity of other behavior in the system,
such as ongoing arms races.

Several different components of the models linking distance or integration to either dyadic-level or system-level behavior have now been
illustrated. Overall theoretical conclusions and implications will be left
to the conclusion of the chapter, but two points might be emphasized
here. First, the findings reiterate our point about the complexity of the
concept of "integration." There are not only different types of integration, but also many different ways in which to manipulate indicators
thought to reflect integration, and these manipulations have an enor-
mous impact on conclusions concerning either the integrative process or
the potential effect of integration. Second, in spite of the extensive interest and writing on the subject of integration, very few tests have been

devoted to the issue of whether integrated or "low distant" states behave differently from nonintegrated states. A wealth of research has gone into investigating the interaction among various indicators of integration. Given the infrequency of actual political assimilation, it is not surprising that we are left almost solely with the task of inter-relating indicators of integration. Yet, while that may prove interesting, such a task is in a sense rather restricted.

Balance as Distance

The system-level explanation in terms of balance predicts that states behave toward one another as a function of their respective orientation to outside elements. Hopmann has conducted a rather thorough investigation of this linkage in NATO-Communist bloc relations, and his findings for the most part support the hypothesis, but primarily in terms of interbloc-intrabloc hostility. In one study, he isolated four years, 1950, 1955, 1963, and 1965, as representative of high and low levels of East-West tension: 1950 (Korean War) and 1965 (bombing in Vietnam) were defined as times of high tension, whereas 1955 (U.S.-Soviet détente) and 1963 (Test Ban Treaty) were low-tension periods.[66]

The findings for the entire eleven members of the Communist system showed that the high-tension years of 1950 and 1965 exhibited much greater agreement on attitudes toward the Western bloc (less distance among the Communist bloc countries) than the low-tension years. The same finding holds true if the United States is taken singly as the "target" or object. The results are confirmed when analyzing intra-NATO "distance" but only when the Soviet Union is the object, as distinct from the entire Communist bloc. Thus, using the nominal definition of high and low tension, the attitudinal distance within the blocs conforms for the most part to the hypothesis.

Relating that distance to intra-alliance behavior, however, changes the picture slightly. Hopmann's data on intra-NATO behavior is so similar for all four years that no real variation exists, and therefore differences that may exist in NATO countries' perception of the Communist bloc— their distance from each other—has nothing to explain.[67] For the Communist bloc, though, as Table 6-3 shows, the hypothesis is not confirmed —in fact, the relationship goes in the opposite direction. Hypothetically

---

[66] See Hopmann, "International Conflict and Cohesion," p. 226.

[67] Ole R. Holsti, P. Terrence Hopmann, and John D. Sullivan, *Unity and Disintegration in International Alliances: Comparative Studies* (New York: Wiley, 1973), pp. 118–19.

Table 6-3.   Intra-Communist Bloc Behavior

High Tension	1950	10.46
	1965	10.33
Low Tension	1955	7.9
	1963	8.8

Data in this table have been extracted from table 5 in Ole Holsti, P. Terry Hopmann, and John Sullivan, *Unity and Disintegration in International Alliances: Comparative Studies* (New York: Wiley, 1973), pp. 118-119. The scale runs from 1 (cooperative) to 30 (conflict).

during the high-tension years, when the average distance among the Communist nations was consistently lower, their intrabloc behavior should have been more cooperative. Yet the opposite is true. Even when it is graphed over time to account for possible behavioral trends, the two East-West low-tension years showed high cooperation within the Communist bloc.

An analysis of events instead of attitudes as a measure of distance, however, shows that only intra-NATO behavior can be explained by changes in behavior between NATO and the Communist bloc. When intercoalition conflict is high, intra-NATO behavior will be more cooperative; the reverse relationship also is true. Further, the effect seems to be greatest when intra-NATO behavior is lagged twelve months behind the intercoalition behavior. The balance hypothesis, then, is supported only minimally.

Ole Holsti used the same research strategy to investigate Soviet and Chinese attitudes toward the West during periods of high and low tension.[68] Premier Khrushchev's visit to the United States in 1959, the bargaining period of the Cuban Missile Crisis in late 1962, and the signing of the Test Ban Treaty in July-August, 1963, represent low-tension periods; the Bay of Pigs invasion of April, 1961, and the crucial period of the Cuban Missile Crisis (October, 22–25, 1962) were the high-tension periods. Perceptual data again show that for the three détente periods the two Communist countries were farther apart from each other in their positive attitude toward United States policy than during the two high-tension periods. The hypothesis, therefore, that high intercoalition conflict increases intracoalition unity is supported in terms of differences in Chinese and Soviet perceptions of an external enemy. However, the use of Hopmann's data for 1959, 1961, and 1963 for conflict

[68] Ole Holsti, "East-West Conflict and Sino-Soviet Relations," *Journal of Applied Behavioral Science* 1, No. 2 (1965), pp. 115-30.

Table 6-4. Intra-Communist Bloc and China-Albania Behavior

		Intrabloc Tension	Chinese-Albania versus Bloc
Low Tension	September, 1959	8.27	9.78
	July-August, 1963	8.40	12.70
High Tension	April, 1961	11.11	11.79

Data for this table have been extracted from Ole Holsti, P. Terry Hopmann, and John Sullivan, *Unity and Disintegration in International Alliances: Comparative Studies* (New York: Wiley, 1973), pp, 118-119 and 124-125.

between China and Albania on the one hand and the rest of the Communist bloc on the other does not confirm the hypothesis (Table 6-4). For the entire Communist bloc, the two low-tension periods between the East and West resulted in less internal conflict; for the Chinese-Albanian conflict with the rest of the bloc, the findings are somewhat mixed, but do *not* definitely support the hypothesis. (Of course, these findings are heavily qualified because the Hopmann conflict data cover six-month periods, whereas Holsti's cases are of much shorter duration).

The basic hypothesis is also not confirmed by French actions toward the United States, a co-member of NATO, and toward the Warshaw Pact nations between 1950 and 1967 (Figure 6-6).[69] Of seventeen year-to-year changes, only three are in agreement with the hypothesis, that is, where French-United States actions became more cooperative as NATO-Warsaw Pact behavior became more conflictual. Eleven of the changes clearly contradict the hypothesis. The first six changes, between 1950 and 1956, were all in disagreement with the hypothesis, though the later years appear to be more in line with it—suggesting that in a strict bipolar world the hypothesis is less likely to work.

Healy and Stein also contradict the hypothesis that intercoalition conflict causes intracoalition cooperation or cohesion. They investigated the effect of the Three Emperors' League of 1873 (Germany, Russia, and Austria aligned in a pact generally directed against France) on behavior among the three signers and between those three and other members of the international system. The hypothesis predicts an increase of conflict between the three and the rest of the system; that was confirmed (Table 6-5), but note that *conflict* among almost all the signers themselves increased after the pact. The fact that Germany received the greatest increase may indicate a systematic intervening variable; certainly something must explain that nearly across-the-board increase. In any event, the

[69] Holsti, *et al., Unity and Disintegration,* p. 118.

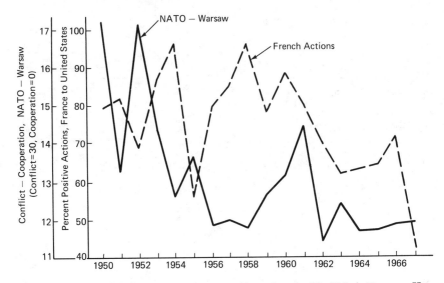

Source: These figures have been calculated from data in Ole Holsti, Terrence Hopmann, and John Sullivan, *Unity and Disintegration in International Alliances: Comparative Studies* (New York: Wiley, 1973), pp. 118–19 and 184–85.

Figure 6-6. NATO-Warsaw conflict-cooperation and percent of positive French
actions toward the United States.

Table 6-5. International Interaction before and after the Establishment of the Three Emperors' League in 1873

Actor-Target	Before	After	Change
Germany-Russia	59.08	54.49	− 4.59
Germany-Austria	54.77	52.80	− 1.97
Russia-Germany	59.89	47.60	− 12.29
Austria-Germany	57.41	47.80	− 9.61
Austria-Russia	54.18	56.39	+ 2.21
Russia-Austria	61.37	57.10	− 4.27
Germany, Russia and Austria—rest of system	53.08	50.87	− 2.21

*Scores over 50 mean a cooperative balance; those below 50 indicate a con-
flictual balance. The range is from 0 (perfect conflict) to 100 (perfect cooperation).

This table from "The Balance of Power in International History: Theory
and Reality," by Brian Healy and Arthur Stein is reprinted from the
Journal of Conflict Resolution, Vol. 17, No. 1 (March 1973), p. 38
by permission of the authors and publisher, Sage Publications, Inc.

hypothesis itself is not confirmed. Healy and Stein also tested the hypothesis using the Austro-German Alliance of October, 1879, directed against Russia. In this case Austria and Germany stepped up their hostile behavior toward each other, while actually advancing their cooperation with Russia.[70]

In testing a much stricter version of "structural balance" theory, Healy and Stein found support for the contention that balance within a system can explain state action. Between October, 1873, and August, 1875, relations among Germany, Austria, and Russia underwent a change. Russia and Austria turned against Germany, and system-wide cooperation declined. Austria improved relations with Russia. Healy and Stein contend that situation was unbalanced, in that the behavior of Austria and Russia toward Germany is much more negative than the reverse. Although balanced in that the Austria-Russian dyad is the highest in cooperation, and both aim negative behavior toward Germany, the imbalance arises because Germany's positive behavior toward those two is not reciprocated. Something must "give," and it does. Between August, 1875, and April, 1877, all behavior patterns turn positive: Austria and Russia modify their behavior toward Germany, and the system is again "balanced." The period from April, 1877, to May, 1878, shows the system again unbalanced, with almost all three major powers positive to one other major power but negative to the second. As Healy and Stein explain: "Bismarck cannot be an ally of both Austria and Russia while they are so hostile; likewise, the Tsar cannot trust Bismarck while he is so close to Austria; Austria must also feel tense about Germany's support of Russian moves in the Balkans." [71]

In addition to historical interpretations (substantiated by interaction data), however, Healy and Stein also assess what happens to the system at large depending on how many of the triads and dyads are in balance. If the entire 1871–1881 period can be subdivided into smaller periods, all of which can be viewed as centering on the relations between Germany, Austria-Hungary, and Russia, then the more unbalanced dyadic and triadic relations present during one period, the more likely will the system undergo change, and likewise any given dyad is more likely to undergo change. They report that seven out of nine dyads that were unbalanced underwent change, while only nine out of the twenty balanced ones did. Hence they concluded that international systems undergo changes as a result of their structural balance: the more unbalanced the system, the more likely a change in behavior by one or more parties will occur.

[70] Healy and Stein, "Balance of Power in International History," pp. 38–39.
[71] Ibid., p. 54.

The dramatic and intriguing shifts in large-power relations during the late 1960s and early 1970s are also amenable to interpretation in balance terms. The following discussion, it should be noted, is not as systematic as we would like; a much more complex model of big-power relaionships, and much more sophisticated techniques, would be needed to confirm the effect of balance on these relations. Nonetheless, some of the shifts are certainly in line with predictions of the theory, and suggest that contemporary relations between the big powers might be partly a function of structural balance in the system. The United States' move toward détente with the Chinese in 1970 and 1971 can be seen as affecting the structural balance in the system. On the basis of data from Herbert Calhoun on East-West tension levels, Figure 6-7a shows the balance configuration for 1967 and 1968.[72] The United States-China dyad is extremely

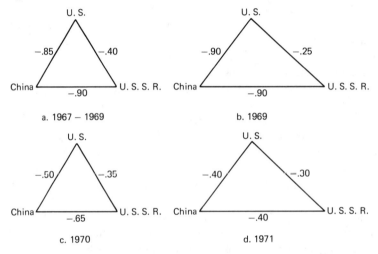

Source: These conflict-cooperation scores (the more negative, the more conflict; the less negative, the less conflict) were adapted from year-long trends presented in Herbert Calhoun, "Exploratory Applications to Scaled Event Data" (Paper delivered at the Annual Meeting of the International Studies Association, Dallas, March 15–17, 1972).

Figure 6-7. Levels of dyadic conflict and cooperation between the United States, U.S.S.R., and China, for four time periods.

[72] Because these data are extrapolated from year long trends, and therefore represent rough averages for the year, this analysis is not as precise as we would like. More complex analysis which would consider monthly or quarterly data—and the effect of changes in the behavior of two parties on the behavior of the third in later months or quarters—would be needed to confirm the rough interpretations presented in the text; data has been extrapolated from Herbert L. Calhoun, "Exploratory Applications to Scaled Event Data," paper prepared for delivery at the Annual International Studies Association meeting, Dallas, Texas, March 15–17, 1972, pp. 31–32.

negative and the China-U.S.S.R. dyad is extremely negative also; the United States and the Soviet Union are only moderately negative toward each other. This is a roughly balanced system, and we might further interpret the slight shift in the U.S.-U.S.S.R. dyad in 1969 toward a less negative stand as a further balancing off of the other two highly negative dyads (Figure 6-7b). In 1970, however, the United States and China shifted behavioral gears. While there can be different interpretations given the looseness of the data, one possibility consistent with the data is that such a dramatic turn toward a more positive stance forced another change, namely, the reduction in hostility between China and the Soviet Union (Figure 6-7c). If from 1967 to 1970 the Soviet Union was befriending the United States, and the latter suddenly befriended China, then the prediction would be for a changed China-U.S.S.R. relationship, which does show up. However, there is also a slight shift upward in hostility in the U.S.-U.S.S.R. dyad, concomitant with the Sino-American rapprochement, which is countermanded, however, the following year (Figure 6-7d) when all three dyads move even further toward less negative interactions.

These interpretations of an interesting historical era are, to be sure, tenuous. Some of the data changes are slight, the designation of "negative" and "positive" is open to interpretation, and the scores and time periods involve some estimates. Even so, the data do provide rough evidence of what one would expect to find if balance theory is operative in big-power relations. At least in terms of interpreting large-power shifts over six- or twelve-month periods, balance provides an understanding of certain general behavioral changes.

Despite their intuitive and common-sense appeal, balance notions have not received an excessive amount of testing. The small number of findings reviewed here are certainly not definitive, and in several instances the basic proposition is not supported. It is possible, therefore, that if balance theory does explain international behavior, its application is to a restricted empirical domain, although these findings cannot isolate that area at present. Unlike some findings in national attribute theory and power theory, *broad* and systematic confirmation of balance has not been achieved.

Conclusion

THEORY

This chapter has tried to present the notion of integration in a slightly different way than traditionally, and has tried also to link it to other theories. One of its goals has been to reintroduce into discussions of the broad question of integration the concerns that spawned the research in the first place, but that in recent years have been too often relegated to secondary importance.

Distance not only encompasses several disparate approaches, it also contains an explanatory basis. Perhaps one of the most severe criticisms that can be made about recent integration literature is its failure to focus clearly on what is to be explained. Haas has noted, for instance, that one of the basic problems in discussions of regional integration is a lack of understanding of exactly what the dependent variable is.[73] For example, proponents of what he calls "federalist theory" are thinking in terms of the achievement of a federal union among the units being studied. Communications theorists see the end product as a security community, either of the amalgamated or pluralistic type. Neofunctionalists, finally, view the end product as a political community or a political union. But as Haas observes, "One of the more bothersome aspects of these efforts at specifying a dependent variable was the tendency to mix its imputed characteristics with those of independent and intervening variables." [74] Haas rightly notes that we should do away with what he calls the "fudge variables"—he mentions "functional equivalents," "catalysts," "federalizers" "high politics," and "similar mythical animals." Unfortunately, he himself perpetuates the practice when he calls for *multiple* dependent variables, suggesting "regional state," "regional commune," and "asymmetrical regional overlap." [75]

Traditionally, integration has been thought of as a situation that would bring about cooperation as opposed to conflictual relations among nation-states. Integration, therefore, was often thought of as a positive goal to be achieved because it would produce cooperative interstate relations. In recent years, however, especially within the transactions or communications approach to integration, the interests have shifted more to describing than explaining integration. As Puchala comments after extensively describing Western European integration: "It cannot be underlined too strongly that there is a major difference between *describing* regional integration and explaining it." [76] He admits that transaction flows do not cause integration, and because "it is not entirely clear, either theoretically or empirically, exactly what causes, accelerates, or reverses transaction flows, there is some risk in using transaction analysis *predictively* in integration studies." [77] Few would dispute these words, but then

[73] Ernst Haas, "The Study of Regional Integration: Reflections on the Joy and Anguish of Pretheorizing," *International Organization* 24 (Autumn, 1970), p. 630.

[74] Ibid., p. 630.

[75] Ibid., p. 634.

[76] Puchala, "International Transactions," p. 762.

[77] Ibid.

Puchala turns around and says that if used in a "cautious and critical" way, and when care is taken, "transaction flow analysis may shed light upon the causal dynamics of regional integration." Unfortunately, no clear and specific suggestions are set out as to how that goal is to be achieved.

We have tried in this chapter to rectify some of these problems, both by setting out clearly what the dependent variables are and by linking clearly measured independent variables to them. On the one hand, we looked at what influence many distance or integration measures had on the formation of organizations, and on the other hand we considered what affect either or both types of variables had on state behavior in other domains, either long-term or short-term. The early findings by Deutsch and his colleagues in a general sense set the stage for considering communication or distance variables. However, conditions such as the "we feeling" or "sense of community" have lost their potency among scholars because they are so nebulous. The transactional conditions, like high trade and personal mobility, have played a significant role in the communications school, but all too often they have been equated automatically with an integrated state or the process of integration. Thus, the models proposed to deal with these problems were only partly successful because—as Haas noted—the same indicators were often used in different studies to measure different parts of the model. Moreover, because so many possible indicators of integration exist, it becomes a grave problem when so many of the studies show the indicators moving in tandem, in which case no assessment of causal paths can be made. Data presented in Russett and in Cobb and Elder show that U.N. voting, membership in international organizations, mass attitudes, and such other indicators as translations, tourist patterns, and treaties are closely related. Caporaso and Pelowski likewise found a long-range upward trend in several indicators.[78] Hughes and Schwarz, however, are able to separate out time sequences between intergovernmental cooperation, institutional growth, and changes in mass attitudes.[79]

But few studies have investigated that last link in the model. Both Russett and Sullivan present some evidence that the extent of conflict in dyadic situations is related to distance measures.[80] Wallace also found a link between the establishment of IGOs and war (mediated by other variables, to be sure), and Smoker's evidence can be interpreted as sup-

---

[78] Russett, *International Regions and the International System;* Cobb and Elder, *International Community;* and Caporaso and Pelowski, "Economic and Political Integration."

[79] Hughes and Schwarz, "Dimensions of Political Integration."

[80] Russett, *International Regions and International System;* and Sullivan, "Escalatory and Non-Escalatory 'Systems.'"

porting that link also.[81] Numerous other studies were cited, and a relation does seem to prevail between these measures and warlike behavior, but it is a moderate one. Balance theories have received less support, however; indeed, in some cases they were directly contradicted by the evidence.

Given these moderate findings, it would appear logical that the theories need both more clarification as well as additional complications to make them more isomorphic with the real world. Distance as integration probably needs the greatest clarification. In terms of balance, it could most probably use one important intervening variable, namely, the state of the international system or power distribution; states are likely to react in a balancing sense much differently in bipolar and multipolar worlds.

POLICY IMPLICATIONS

Distance is a phenomenon conceptualized here on the systemic level, and as we have noted in earlier chapters such systemic-level variables are not readily manipulated. Implications for the policy-maker therefore will be general and are unlikely to shed much light on specific, day-to-day moves he might want to make. Some findings in distance theory suggest that certain types of systems—in which countries are similar on several dimensions or those in which polarization on distance attributes is low— are less likely to erupt into large-scale violence, even though some kind of conflict seems likely.

As an illustration of one possible systemic-level policy implication, decison-makers might focus on highly abstract and general international changes. Long-term plottings of distance variables, such as the formation rate of INGOs, may inform the decision-maker about trends within the international system. A decline in the formation of international nongovernmental organizations may mean many things, but if it occurs when an arms race is escalating, it may signify a continual escalation of the arms race. While some countermeasures sound naïve—such as form more INGOs—and certainly would be questionable in terms of their potential for halting the arms race, the concatenation of decreasing INGO formations and escalating arms races should nonetheles be a forewarning to decision-makers about the potential effect of those changes on the international system.

Structural balance likewise constitutes a high-level systemic perspective. Policy-makers aware of the balance hypothesis would react to increasing conflict with allies quite differently depending on the relation

---

[81] Wallace, "Status, Formal Organizations, and Arms Levels"; Smoker, "Nation-State Escalation."

between themselves and an external enemy, as well as the ally's relationship to that enemy. The small number of studies testing the hypothesis suggested, however, at least for the Cold War era, that the effect of structural balance is primarily on attitudinal behavior and not on events. In general terms, as Healy and Stein found, unbalanced systems were more likely to undergo change than balanced systems. In more particular terms, balance does allow for some predictions about where change is going to occur in an unbalanced system, although we know of no research on assessing which of two or more potential changes is more likely.

Knowledge of balance, nevertheless, can provide information about which systems are likely to undergo change. The balance approach, however, requires a long-range, large-scale, systemic perspective. As such, the predictions it makes are likewise systemic. Another drawback of balance theory, of course, is that the behavior predicted, being large-scale also, is considerably affected by other variables. Though it is unlikely that the decision-maker would find results from distance or balance studies useful for the everyday crisis, or for understanding specific events, they can sensitize him to the effects his actions might have on relations among other powers in the intermediate and long term. Such a perspective helps place the decision-maker in a larger framework, and may even foster less ad hoc thinking.

These policy implications can only be suggestive. They are further circumscribed by the fact that balance theory itself has not been well worked out, as the contradictions between it and several studies are witness. But certain findings do confirm the hypothesis, and others confirm the basic hypothesis of distance (or integration) theory. Research differentiating the scope and domain of both simply has not been done. Such research would attempt to reconcile the conflicting findings and refine both concepts. In the meantime, however, it is unlikely, given some findings that confirm the theories and the intuitive appeal of both—plus the fact that diplomats have historically thought in terms of balance (often construed to mean only balance of *power*), that either of these theories will be discarded in the rubbish heap.

chapter 7 The Bargaining Approach to International Politics

The analysis of international behavior as a process of bargaining cannot be represented by a well-formulated, single theory. Rather, such an approach to the study of international politics involves many theories, hypotheses, and propositions. Deterrence, brinkmanship, diplomatic negotiations, along with influence strategies, are related to the bargaining approach. We shall first consider the basic orientation and underlying assumptions that set this approach apart from others; subsequently, we shall examine more specific examples of bargaining.

Behavior as Bargaining:
The Game of International Politics

Given the stakes, it may seem improper to call international politics a game—like chess or Monopoly. Yet the term "game" is helpful for suggesting the sense of the "bargaining" approach. Many would view this approach as a realtively new one, born of the post–World War II interest in game theory and strategic military thinking. In reality, however, it has a long tradition in international politics. Nor is it limited—as many would think—to strategists utilizing methods such as computer simulations or game theory. William Carleton clearly relies on the bargaining perspec-

252

tive throughout his book on American foreign policy.[1] For instance, he describes the deadlock in the Cold War at the beginning of the Kennedy administration in terms of a game, as though Kennedy and Khrushchev were playing poker, each raising the ante in turn. Each side, says Carleton, was "seeking to convince the other that it had the willingness to fight, with nuclear weapons if need be, if pressed too far. Provocation was piled on provocation. Both were caught in a vicious cycle." [2] Carleton even sees specific decisions in that light:

Kennedy returned home [from the Vienna summit of 1961], called up reserves, and exhorted the nation to build bomb shelters. In August, [East German leader Walter] Ulbricht built a wall of concrete and barbed wire between East and West Berlin, and incidents multiplied. The Americans increased their counterforce capacity and their Polaris deterrent. The Russians broke the truce on nuclear-weapons testing and in September began their atmospheric explosions. The Americans resumed underground testing. The Russian tests continued. The Americans, in the Spring of 1962, resumed tests in the atmosphere. Then the Russians began another round of tests, which were followed by more American tests, which were followed by still more Russian tests. Then Khrushchev built his sneak missile bases in Cuba and the Americans reacted sharply.[3]

Carleton never once uses the terms "bargaining" or "game." Nonetheless he clearly views both the overall trend of the Cold War as well as specific U.S.-Soviet actions during the 1961–1962 period as a reciprocal tit for tat.

Nor is this perspective merely the creation of action-starved academicians. Decision-makers quite clearly see their own behavior in these terms also. In many ways, they probably possess a better feel for the bargaining process because they are involved in it. The 1962 Cuban Missile Crisis has become perhaps the classic case where decision-makers on both sides realized they must make absolutely clear to their opponent exactly what they desired, because each side's moves were highly dependent on the other side's moves. Robert Kennedy quotes his brother, the president, as saying:

They, no more than we, can let these things go by without doing something. They can't, after all their statements, permit us to take out their missiles, kill a lot of Russians, and then do nothing. If they don't take action in Cuba, they certainly will in Berlin.[4]

1 William G. Carleton, *The Revolution in American Foreign Policy* (New York: Random House, 1963).

2 Ibid., p. 287.

3 Ibid., p. 288.

4 Robert F. Kennedy, *Thirteen Days: A Memoir of the Cuban Missile Crisis* (New York: Norton, 1969), p. 14.

Robert Kennedy himself noted that "during the crisis, President Kennedy spent more time trying to determine the effect of a particular course of action on Khrushchev or the Russians than on any other phase of what he was doing." [5]

Bargaining is by no means reserved for crisis situations, however. Former Secretary of Defense Robert McNamara testified in 1968 concerning the deployment of the Nike-X missile as a suitable defense system for American cities:

Any attempt on our part to reduce [the Soviets'] "Assured Destruction" below what they might consider necessary to deter us would simply cause them to respond with an offsetting increase in their offensive forces. It is precisely this process of action and reaction upon which the arms race feeds.[6]

Likewise, President Nixon, shortly after taking office in 1969, defended the limited ABM effort of the United States by noting that there should be no reason for the Soviets to perceive it as an offensive move, that it was strictly defensive, and thus should not prompt the Soviets to respond by further missile development of their own. The very fact that he made the statement indicates he felt the Soviets might indeed respond in kind to the U. S. move, perhaps through further Soviet missile increments.

To bargain with an adversary is an attempt to influence him. Thus we return to an issue left hanging in Chapter 5, namely, the "power" that countries possess by virtue of their ability to influence other nations. As noted in Chapter 5, scholars dissatisfied with measuring power solely in terms of national capabilities have turned to the notion of the psychological power one nation has over another. In Robert Dahl's formulation, this means that country A has power over country B if it can influence B to do something B would not normally do.[7] Unfortunately, as Lloyd Jensen has noted, no attempt has been made to operationalize this formulation in international relations.[8] Furthermore, our contention here is that there is no need to carry over any of the power concepts from Chapter 5 into the current discussion on bargaining and equate attempts to influence with the exercise of power. If analysts want to do so, fine, but it is unnecessary. For here the theory that will explain be-

[5] Ibid., p. 102.

[6] Statement by former Secretary of Defense Robert S. McNamara, introduced by Secretary of Defense Clark Clifford, Hearings on Military Posture and an Act (S. 3293), before the Committee on Armed Services, House of Representatives, 90th Congress, 2d Session, April 30, 1968, p. 8510.

[7] Robert A. Dahl, "The Concept of Power," *Behavioral Science* 2 (July, 1957), pp. 201–15.

[8] Lloyd Jensen, "Foreign Policy Calculation," in *International Systems: A Behavioral Approach*, ed. Michael Haas (New York: Chandler, 1974), p. 89.

havior is one of "influence" or "bargaining," which may or may not have anything to do with the attributes of power or the psychology of power.

The diplomat is at the center of international bargaining. Traditionally, the behavior of diplomats has always seemed to involve such a large complex of both physical and psychological interactions that systematic analysis was impossible. For this reason the romantic world of diplomacy has always held a certain fascination. The diplomat is viewed as a mix of so many skilled attributes that the awed layman can only sit back and marvel. If we are to believe Harold Nicolson, the diplomat must, among other things, be truthful ("not merely abstention from conscious misstatements, but a scrupulous care to avoid the suggestion of the false or the suppression of the true"); precise ("the negotiator should be accurate both in mind and soul"); and calm ("not only must (he) avoid displaying irritation when confronted by the stupidity, dishonesty, brutality or conceit of those with whom it is his unpleasant duty to negotiate; he must eschew all personal animosities").[9]

Normally the study of diplomacy breaks down into two general perspectives: first, its characteristics are mysterious; it is an area in which intelligent, suave, crafty protagonists work their "art," an area only vaguely understood by the uninitiated; second, its characteristics are institutional. The institutional characteristics receive no attention here, for they shed little light on *why* states behave the way they do. Excellent treatises exist on the function of the diplomat, the difference between "classical" and "modern" diplomacy, the role and history of the consulate, embassy, legation, and so on.[10] Important as these matters may be in some contexts, they are secondary to an understanding of the ongoing *process* of diplomacy.

But even in considering the art of diplomacy we must broaden the inquiry to include all state actions and not merely the official, public actions of specified diplomats. Furthermore, we must try to break away from the stereotype that diplomacy is somehow unfathomable. One way in which to do that is to outline the basic assumptions that set bargaining apart from other approaches. The first assumption relates to the introductory remarks to Part II, where we argued that large-scale systems exist in international politics. The bargaining approach assumes that one type of analytical system that can be created is the system of *interactions* made up of the behavior of states toward one another. National leaders,

[9] Harold Nicolson, *Diplomacy* (New York: Oxford University Press, 1963), pp. 110-16.

[10] Kal Holsti, *International Politics: A Framework for Analysis*, 2d ed. (Englewood Cliffs, N.J.: Prentice-Hall, 1972), pp. 174ff; Werner Levi, "International Statecraft," in *International Systems: A Behavioral Approach*, ed. Michael Haas (New York: Chandler, 1974), pp. 156ff.

in other words, do not act completely independently; they know that their actions are likely to produce counteractions by other leaders, who in turn, of course, calculate the actions of the national leaders in terms of how they feel the national leaders will react. And so on. Decisions are not made in a vacuum. Nor do they depend entirely on the results the decision-maker may *want* (the intrinsic motivational element) or on large-scale national goals. The bargaining perspective realizes that behavior is dependent on what an actor thinks his action will bring forth from the other party. "In general," says J. C. Harsanyi, "each player's strategy will depend on his expectation about the other player's strategies." [11] Nations therefore often become "locked in" to other nations through their interactions, and that fact alone has a bearing on their behavior. The layman may not like to think that such is the course of events, but the behavior of decision-makers is often independent of goals and motivations. Consequently, we must look at the behavior—the type, pattern, trend, or strategy—to understand why decision-makers act the way they do.

A second underlying assumption is that despite the complexity that does exist in ongoing diplomatic maneuvers and despite the high danger especially in superpower diplomacy, nonetheless "solutions" are found, there are "rules of the game," and somehow the complex interplay itself works out. Thomas Schelling, perhaps the most innovative thinker in this area, summarizes much of what has been said so far in terms of the strategies players use in the game of international politics:

Each party's strategy is guided mainly by what he expects the other party to accept or insist on; yet each knows that the other is guided by reciprocal thoughts. The final outcome must be a point from which neither expects the other to retreat; yet the main ingredient of this expectation is what one thinks the other expects the first to expect and so on. Somehow, out of this fluid and indeterminate situation that seemingly provides no logical reason for anyone to expect anything except what he expects to be expected to expect, a decision is reached. These infinitely reflexive expectations must somehow converge on a single point, at which each expects the other not to expect to be expected to retreat.[12]

Even the way Schelling has phrased the situation indicates the potential complexity, but nonetheless we still asume that at some level there are patterns in the way states interact. If there were *no* predictable patterns, then diplomats would be at a loss as to how to act.

A third assumption of the bargaining approach relates to our view

11 J. C. Harsanyi, "Bargaining and Conflict Situations in the Light of a New Approach to Game Theory," *American Economic Review* 75 (May, 1965), p. 450.

12 Thomas Schelling, *The Strategy of Conflict* (New York: Oxford University Press, 1963), p. 70.

of conflict and conflict resolution, namely that conflicts do not necessarily end because someone loses, or because one of the parties resolves, "I shall end this conflict because I am losing, or because I don't like it, or because I am tired of it." As Schelling notes, the outcome may result not from the "logic of the situation" but from the "tactics employed." [13] Schelling's observation undescores two points about the bargaining perspective: first, conflict is not viewed as something total. There are few situations of *pure* conflict, in which both parties are interested in wiping out the other. Some mutual interest is always present, perhaps at a cost beyond which neither side is willing to go. Second, conflict is not viewed as something deviant or evil, or a passing fancy of statesmen that will end in some future millennium. Rather, conflicts are recognized as a form of behavior that will *always* occur—between allies as well as between enemies, between lovers as between rivals. For these reasons, we need to understand the process of conflict. With some exceptions, therefore, the bargaining perspective implies a *dynamic* as opposed to a *static* model, a model concerned with the *process* of interaction, with how people work out their disputes, with what types of action and reaction patterns are used, with which type is more likely to resolve disputes and which is more likely to prolong them.

The bargaining perspective can be illustrated in the study of the "acute" international crisis. Charles McClelland was one of the first to suggest that crises could be plotted or mapped in terms of the behavior of the states. His early interest in the subject was triggered by the acute international crises that erupted in the post-World War II period between the major powers. McClelland was concerned with the central question of "accounting for the differences which would explain why many crises are begun and then abated while some lead on into war." [14] Crises in the international system may not necessarily result from either a clash of ideologies or from conflicting power interests. Instead, they may develop from an increase in interactions, from the "piling on of provocations," or as McClelland would have it, from unexpected inputs and new outputs. When, says McClelland, a "succession of extraordinary inputs begetting new outputs begetting new inputs, etc., passes some point in volume and intensity, the whole phenomenon begins to be called an international crisis." [15] But these actions may be far from rationally thought out ploys indicating that one party is trying to "make trouble"

[13] Ibid., p. 22.

[14] Charles McClelland, "The Beginning, Duration, and Abatement of International Crises: Comparisons in Two Conflict Arenas," in *International Crises: Insights from Behavioral Research*, ed. Charles F. Hermann (New York: Free Press, 1972), p. 84.

[15] Charles McClelland, "The Acute International Crisis," *World Politics* 14 (October, 1961), p. 199.

or "get something" from another party. Rather, mistakes are made and behavior can be misinterpreted. Each move contributes to a series of moves that becomes each side's attempt to elicit information from the opponent: How will he react to this? What happens if I change my behavior pattern? What will his reaction indicate about his motives? Each move may be motivated as much by a desire to feel out the opponent and find a way to end the confrontation as by a desire to gain something. The high degree of uncertainty in imputing motives to actions, however, keeps the crisis from moving toward resolution in a straight, linear, rational fashion. This "feeling out" process takes time, and two important questions concerning crises are: (1) Do they exhibit similar traits? and (2) Is there anything in the interactions of the crisis itself that might give a hint as to the direction it will take?

Crises, however, are only the most apparent examples of bargaining in international relations, primarily because of their intensity and high visibility. But all actions of one state directed at another are really bargaining in the most general sense.

To summarize, bargaining implies a dynamic situation of states in interaction, each acting partly because of what it thinks its action will produce in the opponent, and also reacting to the opponent's actions. Of course, the opponent is acting with the same thoughts in mind. Two parties so involved create a *system* in which there are rules for action and strategies to follow and utilize. The clearest noninternational analogy familiar to all is the youthful dating situation, in which each party is acting at least partly in terms of how he or she thinks the other will respond; in which clear strategies exist for prompting desired behavior from the other party; in which maneuvers, ploys, feints, assaults and counterassaults are all made with neither party ever—or rarely—admitting that such behavior is going on. A moment's reflection will show that such behavior is by no means restricted to interpersonal situations. In a very general sense, the same strategies are used in international situations—although the goals are somewhat different. A nation's decision-makers think in these terms, and they operate quite clearly with bargaining propositions in mind.

Bargaining in international politics, then, is not restricted to *negotiations* that take place across a table over a specific issue or question. Such behavior is certainly within the bargaining framework, but it is only one aspect of it. Some of the concepts developed regarding negotiations, however, can be used to understand bargaining behavior more broadly conceived, and it is that extension of negotiation concepts that often causes problems. Many object that by using concepts and propositions common to other fields of human interaction, such as labor-management negotiations, gaming, or interpersonal relations, the "political" element of international diplomacy is lost. Just exactly what these political elements are, however, is not clear, nor whether international relations has an exclusive monopoly over them. If they do not, that is, if political elements may be just as much present in labor-management and interpersonal bargaining—then they are a constant and not a variable and need not concern us here.

A somewhat more potent objection to the approach might be that bargaining is merely another word for image analysis because so much of the explanation *seems to* depend on perceptions. Perceptual data are sometimes used in the bargaining approach, but the explanations do not come from that data alone. Instead, they emanate from the process that is occurring between countries and to the imputed motivations behind that process. Furthermore, in cases where perceptual data are not used, even though the explanation might come from inferences about how decision-makers *probably* perceived a situation or action, nonetheless since we are not dealing with perceptual data, the explanation cannot accurately come on that level.

Theoretical Considerations

With these broad parameters and assumptions concerning the bargaining approach to international politics in mind, let us begin a theoretical evaluation of this method of explaining international politics. As with the question of power, we must first establish what we mean by a bargaining theory. A great deal of bargaining or influence literature is descriptive or primarily illustrative in nature. It often skirts the more general, theoretical concerns. Herman Kahn, for instance, has been helpful in shedding light on definitions, categories, and types of bargaining, all of which are ultimately useful in developing theories of bargaining. It is important to understand, though, that definitions, typologies, and illustrations do not in themselves constitute theories. Kahn defines bargaining as "the attempt by one side in a controversy to convince the other that a given solution is in both their interests." He lists seven bargaining positions:

"It is in your interest
"Somebody has to be reasonable"
"My partner won't let me"
"This is my last demand"

"Your own friends don't agree with you"
"It is unfair to complicate (or simplify) the problem"
"Put yourself in my place." [16]

Each position is familiar to us all, even from experience in inter-personal "negotiation" with friends. Helpful as they are as illustrations of common bargaining positions and strategies, each position says nothing about a potential expected outcome. Nor do they say anything about what strategies should or could be used most successfully in what situations, or how to counter their use by an opponent. The failure to link descriptions of bargaining strategies to the dynamics of actual bargaining, as we will see, has plagued everyone analyzing the bargaining, or influence, approach to an understanding of international relations. It is one thing to *recognize* a bargaining position, in a static sense, and quite another to predict its effect, to determine what positions should be used in conjunction with it, and to assess under what specific situations it is likely to be most successful, all implying the dynamic sense of bargaining.

Likewise, Kahn's device of an "escalation ladder" helps to sort out where, along a continuum of violence, a given bargaining "system" currently resides, from "subcrisis disagreement" to all-out war. It is also true that "at . . . times there is a tendency for each side to counter the other's pressure with a somewhat stronger one of its own." [17] Yet this observation is not the same as pointing out the conditions under which a "subcrisis disagreement," for example, will move up the escalation ladder, and under what conditions it won't, or what bargaining strategies will force parties up the ladder.

As with Kahn, Oran Young has also shed light on the bargaining approach primarily from a descriptive perspective, with post facto interpretations of four international crises. While his interpretation of those crises provides some insights into the bargaining approach, nonetheless serious questions can be raised about his generalized propositions on bargaining, one of which is:

HYPOTHESIS: Conditions of crisis raise incentives both to demonstrate resolve clearly and to react in a prudent fashion to the dangers of destructive outcomes. The resultant cross-pressures tend to produce bargaining patterns among the principals which are unpredictable and subject to erratic oscillations.[18]

[16] Herman Kahn, *Thinking about the Unthinkable* (New York: Horizon Press, 1962), pp. 178ff.

[17] Ibid., p. 185.

[18] Oran Young, *The Politics of Force: Bargaining during International Crises* (Princeton: Princeton University Press, 1968), p. 177.

Several elements stand out in this hypothesis. First, no clear independent and dependent variables are presented; common sense tells us that crises produce prudent behavior because of possibly destructive outcomes. Second, it is not clear exactly how one acts "prudently" and with "resolve." Young, in the analysis of the four crises, points to certain acts as indicative of resolve, but a theory of bargaining would demand a general statement rising above the particular. Third, crises are seen as erratic and unpredictable. This viewpoint is illustrated in Young's discussion of how to convince an opponent that he must initiate force even though political disadvantages will befall him for doing so—which is, of course, one's goal in the first place. Young suggests that "efforts to cut off a garrison from essential provisions without overwhelming it by force or to block critical land or sea passages in such a way that an opponent would have to launch a violent attack in order to advance on a territorial objective" are examples of a strategy that forces the opponent to initiate violence. Unfortunately, the "complexity of crises" can play tricks, a strategist may "overlook or miscalculate certain contingencies," and thus may find the tables turned with the opponent forcing *him* to initiate violence.[19] Thus we come away from Young's study of crises with the perception of them as being almost completely intractable, with each one possessing idiosyncratic differences and innumerable "contingencies." With that perspective, no truly theoretical analysis is likely.

A final illustration of the tendency in bargaining literature to focus on definitions and categories is Paul Gordon Lauren's careful description of the elements, types, and purposes of ultimatums. The classical ultimatum must contain specific demands, a time limit, a threat of punishment for failure to comply, and may contain "carrots" as well as "sticks." Different types of ultimatums can be distinguished by their threat, such as to break off discussions, terminate agreements, or use force. And finally, ultimatums have the purpose of bringing issues to the fore and manipulating opinion.[20] Ultimatums, however, are by nature escalatory; they "may" catalyze a process of escalation that cannot be controlled, are often in contradiction to "prudent crisis management," and thus "increase" the possibility of an unfavorable response from an adversary. He concludes, therefore, that "practical as well as ethical considerations" suggest their "very infrequent employment . . . in the strategy of coercive diplomacy."[21] But the definitions and categorizations of different elements, types, and purposes of ultimatums do not answer the question

[19] Ibid., pp. 338–39.

[20] Paul Gordon Lauren, "Ultimata and Coercive Diplomacy," *International Studies Quarterly* 16 (June, 1972), pp. 131–66.

[21] Ibid., p. 163.

of when or how they might be used, nor do they outline more than only "probable" responses of an adversary.

To summarize, bargaining theories as explanations require more than mere assertion that in fact international relations *is* bargaining behavior, and that in such situations "anything" might happen. They also require more than illustrations and categorizations of international interactions that can be construed as the give-and-take of bargaining. To say that it is *possible* to bargain does not spell out the conditions of success—the crucial question, especially to the practitioner—or the primary variables involved in explaining bargaining. Even so, to criticize Kahn, Young, Lauren, and others does not imply that research analyzed here will be capable of answering these questions. Rather, the critique is by way of establishing the important questions and parameters of the research. As we will see, theorists—for very good reasons—have not been able to isolate the conditions for success in a general sense. Yet the goal is still to go beyond categorization.

Deterrence, Brinkmanship, and Commitment

Bargaining in its broadest sense is popularly associated with the Cold War behaviors of deterrence and brinkmanship. In many circles there is the assumption that the advent of modern weaponry, especially nuclear weapons, created the necessity for deterrence. Although very often deterrence takes the specific form of a threat to use nuclear weapons, to equate the two is a superficial and parochial view of recent and past international politics. The specific *type* of deterrence in the post-World War II era—eyeball to eyeball, nuclear blackmail—differs, of course, from anything the world has known before. But the general strategy of deterrence has been known for as long as men have interacted; indeed, one of the delightful attractions of Schelling's *Strategy of Conflict* was his illustration of the broad generality of deterrence behavior, on the international as well as interpersonal level. (Schelling points out, for instance, that children are extremely adept at bargaining.) The popularly recognized military or nuclear types of deterrence, therefore, are secondary in importance to the more general question of deterrence. Too many discussions of military deterrence are reduced to questions of military balance or tactical military maneuvers; they demonstrate little recognition of the fact that these are subtypes of a large class of strategies.[22]

Three basic issues are at the center of any discussion of deterrence,

22 James E. Dougherty and Robert L. Pfaltzgraff, Jr., *Contending Theories of International Relations* (Philadelphia: J. B. Lippincott, 1971), pp. 254ff.

and they are of interest both to the policy-maker and to the theorist: What is it? When is it used? When is it successful? Deterrence is the ability to *prevent* someone from doing something they ordinarily would do. As with all influence attempts, deterrence may have nothing to do with innate ability or attributes. The obverse of deter is compel, to *make* someone do something. Because neither action necessarily implies military force or action, they should not be equated with defense which concerns military capabilities in the event deterrence fails. Deterrence and defense are, of course, not completely distinct either, because deterrence involves the posing of grave costs for an opponent if he does not come through with what is wanted. At that point military capability certainly comes in handy, but it in no way assures the success of deterrence.

The "calculus" that Glenn Snyder suggests is inherent in a deterrent situation illustrates clearly why deterrence involves a system of bargaining.[23] The aggressor, for instance, first evaluates his own objectives, or what he wants. Second, he evaluates the costs likely to be incurred from any response by his opponent who is trying to deter him. Third, and most important, he evaluates the probability of each response by that opponent, including the possibility that there will not be a response at all. Finally, he considers the probability of achieving his own objectives with each of the responses he thinks his opponent might make. The opponent, of course, attempting to deter the potential aggressor from his action, is going through the same calculus: how important to him are his objectives, and the objectives associated with each of his responses; what the costs are of fighting; and, in turn, what the probability is of the aggressor responding to his action, and what the probability each of his actions has of forcing a return response of a specified type. George and Smoke use similar categories in analyzing such influence situations. Their "commitment" theory concerns the defender's attempt to establish deterrence, their "initiation" theory pertains to the initiator's decision on how to respond to that deterrence, and, finally, their "response" theory focuses on how the defender then responds to the situation he faces.[24]

This calculus describes what probably goes on in the mind of those in deterrent or compellent situations. One important characteristic of this calculus is that it presents a rational picture, not unlike the rational process models outlined earlier (Chapter 3). For example, of the seven basic assumptions of traditional deterrence thought outlined by George

[23] Glenn Snyder, *Deterrence and Defense: Toward a Theory of National Security* (Princeton: Princeton University Press, 1961).

[24] Alexander George and Richard Smoke, *Deterrence in American Foreign Policy: Theory and Practice* (New York: Columbia University Press, 1974), chaps. 17, 19, and 20.

and Smoke, two are primary: each side in a deterrence situation is a unitary, purposive actor; the payoffs and choices of the actors can be deduced by assuming an overall "rationality." [25] Traditional deterrence theory, therefore, implies that some such "rational process" is used, and the answer to the question, When is deterrence utilized?, rests heavily on the validity of that assumption. The most obvious and superficial answer is that deterrence will be used when one side calculates that his objectives can be achieved or that there is a high probability of achieving them.

Unfortunately, it is this very type of proposition that plagues the influence and deterrence theories. For instance, deterrence will fail—in other words, the initiator will be successful—if the initiator believes that his risks are calculable and that any risks that are unacceptable can be controlled and avoided. On the other hand, when the initiator believes that his risks are not calculable nor controllable, then the defender is more likely to be successful.[26] Likewise, deterrence is more likely to be successful when the initiator believes the defender has adequate capabilities, high motivation, and is free from internal constraints, and by "the defender's supplementing deterrence with appropriate inducement policies vis-à-vis the potential initiator." [27]

It is exactly here where a theory of deterrence would attempt to answer certain crucial questions, or would at least incorporate them into a complex analysis. For instance, what has been the defender's record of reactions to aggression in the past? Has he bluffed more often than not? Has he *ever* responded to aggression? Or is the record fifty-fifty? In addition, what kinds of public "policy declarations" or statements has he made? Do they suggest an immediate and strong reaction, or are they nebulous and weak? Finally, what capabilities does he possess: what is the size of his military establishment, its deployment and so forth?

These are still only questions and very broad ones at that, however; even knowing the answers would not provide a theory suitable for specific action. To say, for instance, that the aggressor should investigate the defender's past responses to aggression is one thing; but investigate in what way? Is a defender who has *never* responded in the past to be assumed never to respond in the future? What about the defender who has responded 20 percent of the time? Or 40 percent? 50 percent? 80 percent? What exactly can one conclude from these data? Similarly, how do we evaluate a defender's policy declarations? Along what dimensions? Finally, how much weight should be given to the capability variable, and in what way? How should all three of them be combined?

---

[25] Ibid., p. 504.

[26] Ibid., p. 529.

[27] Ibid., pp. 530–31.

Singer's model of internation influence illustrates this complexity. In this model, the influencer must consider three variables in deciding how he will behave: (1) the perceived present behavior of the other party, (2) the predicted future behavior of the other party, and (3) the preferred future behavior of the other party [28] Singer combines these with three broad options open to the influencer: reinforce or modify the behavior, threaten or promise the opponent, and punish or reward him. Table 7-1 shows how Singer meshes the three elements of the calculus with the types of behavior.

Two illustrations will flesh out the model and its logic and possible implications. In every case, the behavior in the bottom five rows of the figure flows directly from the specified situations above. In persuasion situation number 2, for instance, where country A prefers the other country to do "X" at some future time, we find that the predicted future behavior is indeed "X" although the present behavior is not. In that case country A does not reinforce the other country but tries to modify its current behavior. There is some question as to whether country A should punish or not, but it definitely should not reward because the other country is doing the opposite of what it wants. The same reasoning would lead it to use some kind of threat as well as a promise. In dissuasion situation number 8, where country A prefers "O," the other side is neither acting that way at present nor is predicted to do so in the future; country A then attempts behavior modification, punishes, threatens, and promises, but does not reward.

Singer's model systematically sets out the basic elements of almost

Table 7-1. Influence Techniques

	Persuasion Situations: A Prefers X				Dissuasion Situations: A Prefers O			
	1	*2*	*3*	*4*	*5*	*6*	*7*	*8*
Preferred future behavior	X	X	X	X	O	O	O	O
Predicted future behavior	X	X	O	O	O	O	X	X
Perceived present behavior	X	O	X	O	O	X	O	X
Reinforce or modify	R	M	R	M	R	M	R	M
Punish?	No	P	No	Yes	No	P	No	Yes
Reward?	Yes	No	Yes	No	Yes	No	Yes	No
Threaten?	P	Yes	Yes	Yes	P	Yes	Yes	Yes
Promise?	Yes	Yes	Yes	Yes	Yes	Yes	Yes	Yes

J. David Singer, "Inter-Nation Influence: A Formal Model," *American Political Science Review* 57 (June, 1963), p. 427.

[28] J. David Singer, "Inter-Nation Influence: A Formal Model," in *International Politics and Foreign Policy: A Reader in Research and Theory*, ed. James N. Rosenau, rev. ed. (New York: Free Press, 1969), pp. 383–84.

any persuasion and dissuasion situation in a formalized way as distinct from a loose verbal model. It remains a *general* model, however, and therefore cannot be applied specifically. This drawback was not lost on Singer, who observed:

> The central problem . . . is that of developing, pre-testing, and applying measures or indices of an operational and unambiguous nature. Until we have devised a means for recognizing and recording perceived, predicted, preferred, and actual outcomes, such experimental research is impossible.[29]

It may be true that one should reward, but what does "reward" mean? And how does one "punish"? In what ways can one "reinforce"?

Knowledge of deterrence, therefore, can be viewed as applying to two levels: (1) general statements resembling—and assuming—a rational process and a great deal of information, and (2) specific operational statements that flesh out the general statements. The literature is replete with the former, but very light in the second area. The same judgment applies to brinkmanship, a type of deterrence. Brinkmanship is a strategy involving moving toward the "brink"—forcing the opponent to consider the loss he will incur unless he backs down. John Foster Dulles, secretary of state during the Eisenhower administration, is most often associated with this ploy. To Dulles, opponents in the international system could walk all over any adversary not willing to go to the brink to defend its territory and way of life. Going to the brink means showing the opponent that one's goals are highly valued and that one is willing to risk serious destruction in order to achieve them. For Schelling, it also means that the situation is a little out of control:

> Brinksmanship is thus the deliberate creation of a recognizable risk of war, a risk that one does not completely control. It is the tactic of deliberately letting the situation get somewhat out of hand, just because its being out of hand may be intolerable to the other party and force his accommodation. It means harassing and intimidating an adversary by exposing him to a shared risk, or deterring him by showing that if he makes a contrary move he may disturb us so that we slip over the brink whether we want to or not, carrying him with us.[30]

Whereas deterrence seems to work when as much information as possible is available, successful brinkmanship depends on the uncertainties of exactly where the danger point lies. Assuming the opponent does not want to risk danger to himself, and that the uncertainty of being "on the brink" is intolerable to him, brinkmanship is likely to be successful.

But the same operational problems plague brinkmanship as they did

29 Ibid., p. 389.
30 Schelling, *The Strategy of Conflict*, p. 200.

deterrence. If some information is helpful, then what kind? Where exactly is the danger point on the "brink," and how specifically does one signal this to the opponent? The Cold War, the stewardship of John Foster Dulles, and the rise to prominence of the military strategists have all combined to publicize contemporary deterrence—balance of terror—and crisis diplomacy. Many decision-makers possess the naïve view, however, that a threat backed up with a "strong will" is sufficient to deter or coerce an opponent. But seldom have those who advocate such behavior bothered with the more specific questions: What *kind* of threat? What *kind* of action? The difficulty of answering these questions is largely attributable to the slipperiness of a central concept about inter-nation influence. The bargainer in international politics must show that he is *committed* to a certain goal or behavioral outcome; simultaneously, he must make that commitment *credible* to the opponent. As Schelling puts it: "The threat is ineffectual unless the threatener can rearrange or display his own incentives so as to demonstrate that he would, *ex post,* have an incentive to carry it out." [31] What is involved here, of course, is the rather sticky question, as Schelling notes, of how a person can "commit himself in advance to an act that he would in fact prefer not to carry out . . . in order that his commitment may deter the other party?" [32]

Illustrations of how to establish a commitment are easy to draw from areas other than international politics. Schelling, for instance, suggests the buyer-seller relationship. How, he asks, can we convince a seller of a house which is worth $20,000 that we will pay no more than $16,000, even if we desire the house very much? The buyer might make an enforceable bet with a third party that he, the buyer, will pay no more than $16,000 for the house, or else forfeit to the third party $5,000, and the seller can take or leave the $16,000 offer. The buyer thereby commits himself to that $16,000 price; to go higher would cost him more in the final analysis than even the $20,000 asking price.

There is another strategy beside brinkmanship associated with the bargaining approach and it is known as the "last clear chance" (a second strategy of committing oneself). At an intersection, if one driver speeds up, knowing the other driver is aware of the increased speed and has a chance to stop himself, then the onus is on the second driver; the first has already committed himself to getting through the intersection. In the constant interchange of influence attempts in international affairs, the role of commitment is equally important but much more nebulous because we are no longer dealing with tangible elements such as dollars or clearly understood actions such as zooming through an intersection.

[31] Ibid., p. 36.
[32] Ibid.

For country A to threaten another nation with harm is merely a communication of intent, and very easy to carry off; the hard part is convincing country B, through bargaining moves and tactics, that the threat will be carried out unless country B gives in, even though it may constitute behavior country A would prefer not to carry out.

A gruesome illustration of this tactic used by Schelling relates to the credibility of the "massive retaliation" policy of the Eisenhower years. One way in which to make that policy completely credible would be to install a trip wire at the most vulnerable parts of Europe; if Soviet soldiers crossed the wire, it would set off the entire Western retaliation system *automatically*. If installed in such a way that the defender had no control over it, the aggressor would then know for sure that if he moved across that trip wire retaliation would occur—no ifs, buts, or maybes.

Such mechanical operations are not only unavailable in a fail-safe way, but if they were they would take too much control away from the decision-maker. The national leader must use much more nebulous strategies, which still involve commitment. In international affairs, however, more often than not this commitment means using continuous strategical moves rather than specific actions. Alexander George and Oran Young have both used the term "asymmetries" to describe such strategies. In any conflict, motivations are central for assessing which party will succeed and which will fail. The *intrinsic level* of motivation, however, is less important than the *relative levels* of each party. According to George and his colleagues:

> In devising a coercive strategy the defending power must calculate the strength of the opponent's motivation to resist what is demanded of him. . . . The coercing power's own motivation is also an important factor that must enter into the calculus of a coercive strategy. . . . The chances that coercive diplomacy will be successful will be appreciably greater if the objective selected—and the demand made—by the coercing power reflects only the most important of its interests that are at stake, for this is more likely to create an asymmetry of motivation favoring the coercing power.[33]

Of course, both sides are involved in this process, each trying to show the other that he is more highly motivated, more committed to his objective.

Young distinguishes between different types of asymmetries and the possible trade-offs. He points to the "classic case in international bargaining" in which "intensity of feeling or strength of resolve" is substituted

---

[33] Alexander L. George, David K. Hall, and William E. Simons, *The Limits of Coercive Diplomacy: Laos, Cuba, and Vietnam* (Boston: Little, Brown, 1971), p. 26.

for "deficiencies in numerical strength or physical capabilities." [34] In other words, convincing an opponent that one is *truly* resolved to see a confrontation through to a favorable end counteracts one's own lack of physical strength. The opponent, it is hoped, will perceive the intensity of feeling, though he may consider it a bit irrational. Assuming the opponent's motivation is not as intense, the ploy is likely to work.

A common method of making a threat or promise more credible is to put one's "honor" at stake, so that one simply "cannot" lose. This gambit will serve to impress upon the aggressor that a particular objective is valued highly. As Snyder suggests, it raises the credibility of the threat "by increasing the cost of not responding in the threatened way, by implicating additional values beyond the bare value of the territorial objective, values which would be lost if the threat were not carried out." [35] To truly persuade an opponent, two other analysts suggest, you must make him know that "your commitment is not only to a piece of territory, a resource, or some similar object, but to a principle . . . so that in the very marrow of your existence you would risk everything to maintain it intact." [36]

Young also elaborates on this proposition. The party, he maintains, "that can effectively demonstrate that the underlying issues at stake in a crisis are of more fundamental and far-reaching importance to itself than to its opponent" [37] is more than likely to carry the advantage. Thus in a crisis situation between two parties in which one holds the *tactical* advantage and the other must respond, the side with the tactical advantage (the Soviets in the 1948 and 1961 Berlin crises, the United States in the 1962 Cuban Missile Crisis) is more likely "to seek a rather narrow definition of the proximate issues to emphasize the pointedness and credibility of its offensive moves." [38] Because this side holds the tactical advantage, Young argues, it wants issues defined specifically. The responding actor, however, is likely "to formulate the proximate issues of the crisis in considerably broader terms in order to achieve defensive credibility by turning the clash into a *symbolic* test of its general pattern of international *commitments*." [39] Young goes on to say that "an explicit move to stake a country's *reputation as a power* in international politics on the outcome of the proximate issues of a crisis sometimes serves to

[34] Young, *The Politics of Force*, p. 33.

[35] Snyder, *Deterrence and Defense*, p. 23.

[36] Thomas M. Franck and Edward Weisband, *Word Politics: Verbal Strategy among the Superpowers* (New York: Oxford University Press, 1972), p. 140.

[37] Young, *The Politics of Force*, p. 216.

[38] Ibid., p. 390.

[39] Ibid., p. 391, emphasis added.

create an asymmetrical advantage affecting the overall clash." [40] The "symbolic commitment" referred to earlier (Chapter 2) as a possible image affecting a decision-maker's behavior, therefore, can also be viewed as a conscious influence attempt to create an asymmetry by citing one's prestige or status as a world power.

Yet another strategy, potentially of use to both sides in the dispute but more likely to be used by the side with the tactical advantage, is to "emphasize physical links that establish the importance of the issues in question. . ." [41] That is, if one structures the situation so that you are physically tied to territory, to a treaty, or a person, that *commits* you, and likewise can be a powerful asymmetry in one's favor. Roger Fisher illustrates further strategic ploys at a level somewhat below reliance on "honor" or "status." He argues that "specificity increases the credibility of an offer," [42] that a specific offer shows that a nation has thought about the issues involved in more than a vague way. A specific offer is also much more difficult to turn aside. In terms of the Vietnam conflict, he contends that greater credibility would have flowed from a statement that United States forces would be out of Vietnam "six months" after a peace had been signed rather than one saying they would be removed "in due course."

An offer can be made more credible, says Fisher, by showing that detailed plans have been established for its implementation. An offer of free elections in Vietnam supervised by a "strengthened" International Control Commission carries little credibility if no detailed plans are announced for *how* the ICC would be strengthened, or the specifics of how the election would be held. The more work one puts into specifics of an offer, Fisher argues, transmits to the adversary the willingness to carry it out.

A final way to make an offer credible is to "keep one's reputation high." "If the adversary discovers that we never had any intention of keeping the promise—that there was deliberate deception—then our ability to exert influence will be seriously weakened for an indefinite future." [43] In this connection, Fred Ikle cites Khrushchev's promises regarding an East German peace treaty:

Khrushchev spoiled his bargaining reputation by repeating again and again his threat to sign a peace treaty with the Communist regime in East Germany, each

---

[40] Ibid.

[41] Ibid.

[42] Roger Fisher, *International Conflict for Beginners* (New York: Harper & Row, 1969), p. 119.

[43] Ibid., pp. 122–23.

time specifying the period within which he would do so but doing nothing each time his bluff was called.[44]

In spite of these seemingly clear suggestions for generating credibility, uncertainties remain momentous. The very act of threatening an opponent may have negative effects on his ability—forgetting for the moment his willingness—to react in the desired manner. Singer notes that a "threat often exercises a negative influence on B's capacity to recognize signals and communications accurately." [45] Threat may also produce "cognitive rigidity," in which the responding nation's capability to assess incoming information and to solve problems decreases. Singer further illustrates the very difficult nature of bargaining by pointing out that

B must be provided with two categories of information. One is the precise nature of the action which A prefers to see B take. . . or avoid . . . ; without this information B is unable to respond in a mutually advantageous fashion. The other is the availability of alternatives, and this is particularly relevant in the dissuasion situation. For A to try to dissuade B from a given action (to induce O, a given action) when B must clearly do X or something similar to X, without helping B to ascertain which O acts are available to B and acceptable to A, is to call for a probable showdown. If B is completely thwarted, he has little choice but to resist.[46]

In a way, our knowledge of the important concept of commitment is similar to our knowledge of the more general notion of deterrence. On one level we intuitively know that commitment is important, and that in order to make our threat credible, we can call on symbolic, status, or reputational commitments, or emphasize physical linkages with a threatened party. But on another level it becomes very difficult to set out moves or tactical ploys to carry this off. *How* does one stake his reputation in a given issue? *What kinds* of physical linkages will be truly convincing to an opponent? What is needed is a *broad* theory of bargaining. Internation influence is not merely the *making* of general threats, but rather encompasses a large array of coordinated efforts and events that—in the aggregate—result in a bargaining posture. The foregoing has attempted to set out some parameters of such a posture through strict consideration of deterrence. The following sections consider more generalized and formal models of bargaining behavior.

---

44 Fred Ikle, "Negotiating Skill: East and West," in *Dynamics of World Politics: Studies in the Resolution of Conflict,* ed. Linda B. Miller (Englewood Cliffs, N.J.: Prentice-Hall, 1968), p. 24.

45 Singer, "Inter-nation Influence," p. 390.

46 Ibid., p. 391.

Bargaining Models

Martin Patchen has proposed several models for the analysis of bargaining theory that clearly capture its various perspectives.[47] Patchen first distinguishes between models of "negotiation" and what will be called here strict models of "bargaining." Negotiation models, in Patchen's view, focus primarily on the bids and counterbids that ultimately end with a solution, and do not give explicit attention to the interaction between the parties; such models are restrictive because they are concerned only with the trading of bids until a settlement is reached.[48] Patchen cites the experimental work of Sidney Siegel and Leon Fouraker as an illustration; [49] their major concern was predicting the price and quantity of an item that a buyer and seller would agree on. As Patchen notes, such experiments, although providing insights into numerous bargaining situations, nonetheless are restrictive: no costs and no risks are involved, so that the status quo does not cause suffering or advantage for either party, and therefore no true incentive exists for striking a bargain. Because a war or strike cannot break out, few risks are involved. Patchen does note, however, that some of these theories do discuss coercion and other tactics, but the "formal, basic theoretical models do not help us to predict the types of 'tactics'—for example, the use of coercion—which will be used on the way to agreement." [50] Excluding for the moment, then, such negotiation models, Patchen distinguishes between *cognitive, learning,* and *reaction process* models.

COGNITIVE MODELS

Cognitive models view a nation's actions as dependent upon its perception of the results of its own actions, which often depend on the estimate of the other country's future reactions. Cognitive models rely heavily on implicit decision theories to account for behavior. Patchen cites Singer's work on influence and Russett's analyses of deterrence.[51]

---

[47] Martin Patchen, "Models of Cooperation and Conflict: A Critical Review," *Journal of Conflict Resolution* 14 (September, 1970), pp. 389–408.

[48] Ibid., p. 395.

[49] Sidney Siegel and Lawrence Fouraker, *Bargaining and Group Decision-Making* (New York: McGraw-Hill, 1960).

[50] Patchen, "Models of Cooperation and Conflict," p. 394.

[51] Singer, "Inter-Nation Influence"; Bruce Russett, "The Calculus of Deterrence," *Journal of Conflict Resolution* 7 (June, 1963), pp. 97–109; Bruce Russett, "Pearl Harbor: Deterrence Theory and Decision Theory," *Journal of Peace Research* 4, No. 2 (1967), pp. 89–106.

Russett's interest was in what *situations* would give rise to successful deterrence, in which a potential aggressor failed to carry out aggressive acts against another country. He investigated three-nation situations composed of a small or "pawn" country, a potential aggressor, and a defending country. He suggested that the situation the aggresor found himself in vis-à-vis the two other countries would be an important factor. More specifically, and reminiscent of Young's concept of asymmetry, Russett suggested that the ties between the pawn country and the defender might serve to deter the aggressor. This situation, then, represents a cognitive model because the situation works on the aggressor's calculus. It is is a two-step model that can only *infer* an effect. Patchen notes that the model does not take into account the process of interaction between the parties, and how that phenomenon may bring about agreement: "Russett's formal model is concerned with the decisions of each party at a given point in time and not with interaction between them over time." [52]

LEARNING MODELS

Learning models see a country's actions as dependent upon the previous results of its interactions with the other country. The focus, therefore, is on the interaction patterns themselves. Harsanyi, for instance, analyzes two methods for reaching agreement when both parties' upper and lower bargaining points are unknown.[53] The bargainers may assume certain high and low utility points based on past bargaining behavior (indicating learning), or they may proceed through a process of mutual adjustment in which each tests out the other through bids and counterbids. Rejection of bids—and perhaps the speed or intensity of rejection—constitutes information for the bargainer. It indicates where the true settlement point might be. One *learns* that a specific bid is no good simply because it has been consistently turned down.

Fred Ikle and Nathan Leites likewise view political negotiations as a process of mutual modification of one another's goals.[54] Through bargaining moves, one discovers the other's position; a sham bargaining position, for instance, can be helpful even if it is almost a totally unacceptable proposal. One's estimate of the opponent's minimum disposition is often uncertain, and the sham move may modify or soften that position.

[52] Patchen, "Models of Cooperation and Conflict," p. 397.

[53] J. S. Harsanyi, "Bargaining in Ignorance of the Opponent's Utility Function," *Journal of Conflict Resolution* 6 (March, 1962), pp. 29–38.

[54] Fred C. Ikle and Nathan Leites, "Political Negotiation as a Process of Modifying Utilities," *Journal of Conflict Resolution* 6 (March, 1962), pp. 19–28.

It may also make it more difficult for the opponent to estimate one's own minimum disposition.

Anatol Rapoport's experimental work on what he calls "prisoner's dilemma" also illustrates learning. Two players are told they have been taken prisoner and are accused of a capital crime. However, the evidence against them is so weak that if they don't confess they can only be convicted of a lesser crime. Each is interrogated separately with no communication and are told that if they don't confess to the capital offense, they will both get five years; if one confesses and implicates the other, he will go free while the implicated party gets the gas chamber; and if both confess they will both get life sentences. Figure 7-1 illustrates the payoffs numerically. If both confess to the crime they both lose, and likewise if neither confesses, they both lose but to a lesser degree. However, the highest payoff goes to the player who confesses and implicates his nonconfessing compatriot, who would then be the highest loser. The player therefore who is contemplating implicating his partner must realize that his partner may be thinking the same thing, in which case they would both lose. Because they cannot communicate, neither one knows how his partner is going to behave in any given "play" of the game. As Rapoport and Albert Chammah point out:

much of the variance [in behavior] is accounted for not by inherent propensities of the players to cooperate or not to cooperate, but rather by the characteristic instabilities of the dynamic process which governs the interactions in Prisoner's Dilemma.[55]

Prisoner 2

		Confess	Don't Confess
Prisoner 1	Confess	−5 / −5	−10 / 10
	Don't Confess	10 / −10	5 / 5

* The figures in each box represent the payoffs, with those in the upper right-hand part of each situation applying to Prisoner 2 and those in the lower left to Prisoner 1. The payoffs are mythical, although in the gaming situation money is often used; the figures have been established by the experimenter to illustrate the true dilemma.

Figure 7-1. Payoffs in Prisoner's Dilemma Game.*

[55] Anatol Rapoport and Albert M. Chammah, *Prisoner's Dilemma* (Ann Arbor: University of Michigan Press, 1965), p. 199.

Thomas Harford and Leonard Solomon found evidence of different kinds of outcomes depending on which pattern of cooperative or noncooperative behavior was used in a game. They concluded that "a strategy of initial noncooperation followed by unconditional cooperation and then conditional cooperation (reformed sinner) is more effective in eliciting cooperation from a subject than is an initial cooperative strategy followed by conditional cooperation (lapsed saint)." [56] The reformed sinner—initially uncooperative—communicates his willingness to fight and brings about mutual losses in early plays of the game, but then communicates his willingness to cooperate, at first unconditionally and then only if the other player is also cooperative. The other strategy of initial cooperation may be viewed by some opponents as a "set up" for exploitation, and they proceed to exploit the cooperative party. Harford and Solomon conclude that opponents learn cooperative strategies more readily in the former than in the latter situations.

In other words, one's behavior is a function of having learned in past plays of a game. Few people, for instance, are likely to continue cooperating if their cooperation is consistently met with noncooperation by the other player, which for them results in the lowest possible payoff. One learns that such behavior does not pay off, and the behavior then changes.

John Raser illustrates learning theory with the specific example of United States-Chinese relations. He posits two general behavior syndromes: reward-satisfaction-hope on the one hand, and punishment-frustration-fear on the other. States are more likely to associate reward-satisfaction-hope with friendship, and punishment-frustration-fear with hostility:

Learned behavior, stemming from hope, resulting in goal achievement and satisfaction, seems likely to result in the system's perception of the outside environment (in this case, the other national actor) in friendly terms. This perception will in turn increase the hope affect, behavior will be characterized by a friendship loading, and a self maintaining cycle will tend to emerge, with the dominant behavior-determining element being what we might refer to as the friendship-hope affect.[57]

One continuing problem in United States-Chinese relations during the Cold War was that each perceived the other in a completely hostile

---

[56] Thomas Harford and Leonard Solomon, " 'Reformed Sinner' and 'Lapsed Saint' Strategies in the Prisoner's Dilemma Game," *Journal of Conflict Resolution* 11 (March, 1967), p. 108.

[57] John Raser, "Learning and Affect in International Politics," in *International Politics and Foreign Policy: A Reader in Research and Theory*, ed. James N. Rosenau, rev. ed. (New York: The Free Press, 1969), p. 438.

fashion. If the United States had isolated the possible goals motivating Chinese leaders (Raser suggests world domination, military expansion in Asia, economic-cultural hegemony in Asia, and a stable, prosperous regime at home, free from threat), and then decided which were legitimate and rewarded those goals, the Chinese environment should have ceased to be completely hostile. Through a little probing, Chinese leaders might have discovered which actions on their part would bring forth the friendship syndrome from the United States. The same would apply, of course, to the United States. Raser sums up this learning approach quite well by observing that "behavior can be altered by the conscious manipulation of reward and punishment . . . that will tend to establish a milieu in which further behavior will take place." [58]

The use of case studies—where one can plausibly illustrate one or two situations of "learning" by the parties involved—or the use of experimental and gaming research—in which learning strategies are easy to manipulate—are much easier than plotting out systematic patterns of interactions with real-world international behavior. To some degree Young is correct in saying that the intricacies involved in any such interactions seem completely unpredictable. What sequence of behavior by party A will "teach" party B that his behavior is undesirable? The very nature of the question suggests the difficulty of the task. Learning models for the most part have been used in situations where the same parties face each other time and time again, which makes it difficult to extrapolate to new or novel situations, where "behavior is usually not based primarily on past learning but on such factors as the present perception of possible outcomes and present perceptions about the other party's likely behavior." [59]

REACTION-PROCESS MODELS

This set of models view a country's behavior as an almost automatic reaction to another country's previous action. It closely approximates a strict stimulus-response model. One example of the reaction process model involves Lewis Richardson's research on arms races. [60] Richardson was concerned with predicting the change in armaments of one party based on the change in armaments of the other party, and argued that certain variables (the opponent's level of strength, one's incentive to accumulate arms because of opponent's strength, fatigue and cost, and the level of grievance against the opponent) could be combined to pre-

58 Ibid., p. 440.
59 Patchen, "Models of Cooperation and Conflict," p. 399.
60 Lewis F. Richardson, *Arms and Insecurity* (Pittsburgh: Boxwood Press, 1960).

dict one's own change in armaments level.[61] Party A's arms level would be a direct result of party B's arms level; increases in one's own strength would be a function of increases in the opponent's strength. In a more general sense, action begets reaction: hostility begets hostility and co-operation begets cooperation; states will react in accordance with what they receive. This model appears on the surface to be much too over-simplified, but it has many adherents among practitioners in interna-tional politics. Moreover, although Patchen is correct in noting that this rather mechanical model is unlikely to account for a vast amount of international behavior, nonetheless numerous studies present data very consistent with the stimulus-response model.

Everyday international behavior can be viewed as the give-and-take of bargaining, and strategies such as deterrence and brinkmanship are only two illustrations of broader theoretical perspectives. Patchen's three models provide perhaps the best organizing device for investigating those strategies and other international bargaining behavior. We shall now take up the crucial question of measuring international bargaining before turning from the theoretical to the empirical to see what type of evidence exists for the several models.

Measurement

In experimental studies of bargaining between individuals the infor-mation needed consists of their bids and counterbids. The same require-ment holds for analyses of bargaining between countries. In international affairs most studies of bargaining (with the exception, to some degree, of the cognitive models) utilize the actions, events, bids, counterbids or "influence behavior" of the parties involved. Bargaining implies actions or events. But many people contend that everyday actions of nation-

---

[61] The equation Richardson proposed is:

$$\frac{dx}{dt} = ky - a\chi + g,$$

in which the letters correspond to the following variables:

$$\frac{dx}{dt} = \text{rate at which one increases arms}$$

$x = $ one's own strength
$y = $ opponent's strength
$k = $ readiness to accumulate arms
$a = $ fatigue and cost
$g = $ grievance.

states are the result of so many forces that their behavior becomes un-predictable, unpatterned. At the same time, however, few people find difficulty in explaining actions or finding patterns or trends after the fact.

In a sense, scholars analyzing bargaining behavior are plagued by the diplomatic historians and the journalists. While the historian tends to focus on what in his judgment appear to be the "important" events—relegating all others to the back of his file cabinet—the journalist can see only the immediate, daily events, with a resultant loss of context. Much of the research into bargaining theories has placed the recording of dip-lomatic events somewhat beyond the realm of the traditional diplomatic historian. The technique of "events data" analysis makes the assumption that the important events in the international system can be "seen" be-cause they are reported by the news media.[62] Furthermore, these events, when categorized through the use of coding schemes, should show "pat-terns" as opposed to merely random behavior. It is only through a sys-tematic and careful recording of events, therefore, that we can attain the information necessary to test theories of bargaining. While it is true, as Young has argued, that conditions of crisis "tend to produce bargaining patterns among the principles which are unpredictable and subject to erratic oscillations," [63] it should be pointed out, first, that bargaining theories apply to more than just crisis situations, and second, that such a perspective derives partly from the journalistic emphasis on the impor-tance of specific daily events as opposed to each event in terms of a pat-tern or context.

One final note of caution on the use of event data. No scholar believes that the picture of the international system he draws with event data is the perfect replica of the world; he is quite cognizant of the fact that events do happen that are not recorded—and thus fail to be included in his analysis—and that relying on publicly reported events introduces the variable of censorship or news worthiness. These data, therefore, should be considered only as *indicators* of the real world.[64]

[62] McClelland, "Acute International Crisis"; Barbara Fitzsimmons, Gary Hoggard, Charles McClelland, Wayne Martin, and Robert Young, "World Event/Interaction Survey Handbook and Codebook," mimeographed; Technical Report No. 1 (Los An-geles: University of Southern California, 1969); Edward Azar, *Probe for Peace: Small State Hostilities* (Minneapolis, Minn.: Burgess Publishing Co., 1972); Charles Her-mann, Maurice East, Margaret Hermann, Barbara Salmore, and Steven Salmore, *CREON: A Foreign Events Data Set* (Beverly Hills: Sage Publications, 1974).

[63] Young, *Politics of Force*, p. 177.

[64] For an analysis of the problems of event-data research, see Robert A. Young and Wayne A. Martin, "A Review of Six International Event Interaction Category and Scaling Methods," mimeographed (Los Angeles: University of Southern California, 1968); R. F. Smith, "On the Structure of Foreign News: A Comparison of the New York Times and the Indian White Papers," *Journal of Peace Research* 6 (No. 1, 1969),

Cognitive Models

Brinkmanship—and the more general category of behavior called deterrence—can be considered in Patchen's cognitive model. It relies neither on assuming an automatic response from the opponent to an action nor on his learning, through a succession of moves, how to behave. Rather, it involves working on the opponent's "cognitive map," where he is convinced of the desirability of acting in a certain way or of ceasing to act as he has in the past.

There have been no systematic "tests" of the strategy of brinkmanship, and very few of deterrence—a circumstance that in no way has prevented people from using either strategy. The "proof" of both usually rests in anecdotal material. In the case of brinkmanship, John Foster Dulles cited three instances during his tenure as secretary of state which in his mind showed that brinkmanship was not only possible, but highly successful. In Korea in 1953, South Korean President Syngman Rhee released North Korean prisoners in South Korea, and the North Koreans broke off the peace talks. Dulles later claimed that the United States let it be known to the North Koreans through intermediaries that unless the talks were started again, widescale bombing would occur. The talks continued. The second instance was the Chinese involvement in the Indochina War in 1954. Here Dulles claimed the United States informed China, again through intermediaries, that the United States would invade and become fully involved if the Chinese continued backing the Vietminh. Chinese support decreased. The final instance concerned the Formosa Straits: Dulles let the Chinese know that the United States would intervene if China attacked the offshore islands of Quemoy and Matsu. The attack did not occur.

Dulles always referred to these three cases as instances of successful brinkmanship. His thinking was quite simple: if the opponent was left in no doubt that he would suffer by undertaking a given action or by

pp. 23–36; Edward Azar, Stanley Cohen, Thomas Jukam, and James McCormick, "The Problem of Source Coverage in the Use of International Event Data," *International Studies Quarterly* 16 (September, 1972), pp. 373–88; G. A. Hill and P. H. Fenn, "Comparing Event Flows—the New York *Times* and the *Times* of London: Conceptual Issues and Case Studies," mimeographed (Los Angeles: University of Southern California, 1972); John H. Sigler, "Reliability Problems in the Measurement of International Events in the Elite Press," in *Sage Professional Papers in International Studies,* Vol. 1 (Beverly Hills: Sage, 1972) pp. 9–29; Gary D. Hoggard, "Differential Source Coverage in Foreign Policy Analysis," in *Comparing Foreign Policies: Theories, Findings, and Methods,* ed. James N. Rosenau (New York: Wiley, 1974); Patrick J. McGowan, "A Bayesian Approach to the Problem of Events Data Validity," in *Comparing Foreign Policies: Theories, Findings, and Methods,* ed. James Rosenau (New York: Wiley, 1974).

not ceasing an action he was already engaged in, and if the United States showed it clearly had the will to back up its deterrent threat, the opponent would acquiesce. While the linkage between a threat and an adversary backing down may sometimes hold true, several questions can be raised that illustrate the problems in taking such evidence at face value. First, are there similar instances where the aggressor failed to back down? Second, can we be sure that the will to move toward the brink was the actual causal factor in bringing about the desired result? Finally, how can we know what specific *types* of action produced the positive results?

Russett's early analysis of deterrence relates closely to Dulles's brinkmanship.[65] In fact, he also utilizes the case of Quemoy-Matsu. Russett isolated seventeen historical instances where an aggressor, in his estimation, was likely to undertake action against a small, pawn country, and where a third country was seen as the defender or at least potential defender of that pawn. When would the third country be able to deter the aggressor? Was a verbal commitment to the pawn sufficient? What role did strategic or military superiority play? Or, as Young would ask, were the relations between the pawn and the defender the most crucial? On the basis of all seventeen cases, Russett concluded that strong and visible pre-existent ties (military, political, and economic) between the defender and the pawn are more likely to result in successful deterrence of the aggressor ("successful," of course, from the perspective of the defender) than situations where mutual interdependence is either minimal or nonexistent (see Table 7-2). As Russett argues: "Where visible ties of commerce, past or present political integration, or military cooperation exist, an attacker will be much more likely to bow before the defender's threats—or if he does not bow, he will very probably find himself at war with the defender." [66]

As examples, Russett refers to the successful deterrence of Communist forces by the United States in the cases of Iran in 1946 and Berlin in 1948. In both cases the United States either had troops stationed on the pawn country's territory or an American mission in the country at the time of the crisis. Russett found that in all cases of successful deterrence, the defender supported the pawn with military assistance in the form of arms and advisers; in only seven of the eleven *failures* were such ties evident. Four of the seven instances of successful deterrence also exhibited recent political ties between pawn and defender whereas in the unsuccessful instances only four of eleven situations showed preexisting political ties. Western advisers, for instance, participated in the government of

[65] Bruce Russett, "The Calculus of Deterrence," in *International Politics and Foreign Policy: A Reader in Research and Theory*, ed. James N. Rosenau, rev. ed. (New York: The Free Press, 1969).

[66] Ibid., p. 364.

Table 7-2. Presence or Absence of Factors Alleged to Make Deterrent Threats Credible

Factor	Attacker Presses On — Defender Does Not Fight									Attacker Presses On — Attacker Holds Back					Defender Fights		
	Iran	Turkey	Berlin	Egypt	Quemoy-Matsu	Cuba	Ethiopia	Austria	Czechoslovakia (1938)	Albania	Czechoslovakia (1939)	Romania	Guatemala	Hungary	Poland	South Korea	North Korea
Pawn 20% + of defender's population	*						x		x		x	x			x		x
Pawn 5% + of defender's G.N.P.		x	x				x	x	x		x	x		?	x	?	?
Formal commitment prior to crisis	?	x	x	?	?	?	?	x	x	?	?	x		?	x		
Defender has strategic superiority	x	x	x	x	x	x	x	x	x	x	?					?	?
Defender has local superiority		x	x	x	x	x	x	*	?	?	?					?	?
Defender is dictatorship				x	x	x							x				x
Pawn–defender military cooperation	x	x	x		x	x			x		x	x	x		x	x	x
Pawn–defender political interdependence	x	x	x	x	x	x						x	x		x	x	x
Pawn–defender economic interdependence	*	x	x	x	x	x		*				x				x	x

Key: x Factor present
? Ambiguous or doubtful
* Factor present for one defender

This table from "The Calculus of Deterrence," by Bruce M. Russett is reprinted from *Journal of Conflict Resolution* Vol. 7, No. 2 (June 1963), p. 109 by permission of the author and publisher, Sage Publications, Inc.

Berlin; the United States and Nationalist China had been allies (the Quemoy crises); and Turkey, threatened by the Soviet Union in 1947, had become allied with the Big Three toward the end of the World War II. Yet a few failures also showed interdependency: Romania, threatened by the Soviets in 1940, had had Britain as an ally during World War I, and the Guatemala government, successfully ousted by U.S.-backed rebels in 1954, had been allied during World War II with the Soviet Union; likewise, strong ties had existed between the United States and South Korea after World War II. Nonetheless, the pattern seems to be in the direction of interdependence working toward successful deterrence.

As with Dulles's explanations of his "successful" brinkmanship, however, there are a good many unknowns in "successful" deterrence. Clinton Fink, for example, questions whether it is valid to equate an observed event—the effectiveness of the defender's threat—with the unobserved phenomenon of his credibility, and whether it is correct to assume that in the absence of the defender's threat the aggressor would have attacked the pawn.[67] To infer that the aggressor will attack the pawn every time he threatens to do so is to impute perfect credibility to his threat. But in fact, his threat may be a diversionary tactic, or even a gambit to get concessions from the defender in some other area. For instance, the most strongly related variable to successful deterrence is the economic interdependence between the pawn and the defender. The aggressor, however, may make threats only to pawns strongly associated with the defender in order to harass the defender; thus the economic interdependence between pawn and the defender may be the reason for the threat in the first place, but since the aggressor had no intention of carrying out the threat, the interdependence is spuriously related to "successful" deterrence. Fink notes that all "no attack" situations occurred after 1945, whereas seven out of the eleven "attack" situations occurred before 1940. This switch suggests that a crucial factor affecting the decision to "attack" or "not to attack" is the changed post-World War II international system, a system in which world political pressures surfacing through the United Nations can work more on the aggressor's calculus.

Russett later applied his basic cognitive model to the Japanese attack on United States bases at Pearl Harbor.[68] If strong ties existed between the United States and the East Indies, an area of interest to Japan, then Japan's option to attack the East Indies was unpalatable because of the

---

[67] Clinton Fink, "More Calculations about Deterrence," in *Readings on the International Political System,* ed. Naomi Rosenbaum (Englewood Cliffs, N.J.: Prentice-Hall, 1970), p. 191.

[68] Russett, "Pearl Harbor."

potential United States response. Yet the "no attack" option was likewise a low-payoff one for Japan because of the loss of the East Indies. Russett suggests the aggressor had three options: to attack the pawn, to leave the pawn alone, to attack the defender. Again the important variables were the strong ties between the defender (the United States) and the pawn (the East Indies), and the strength of the defender, although the additional variable of the defender's vulnerability to attack might come into play. In the case of Japan's attack, the necessary variables were present: strong ties between the defender and the pawn were not sufficient to deter because of the vulnerability of the defender. Although much dispute exists about United States behavior prior to the Japanese attack, many observers contend the United States failed to take action that might have prevented the attack. Full-scale alerts, wide-ranging patrols, and public acknowledgment of possible attacks on Pearl Harbor (based on the sheer existence of the three-nation situation and knowledge of Japan's desire to move into the East Indies) might have signaled to the Japanese that Pearl Harbor was in fact *not* vulnerable. Japan's options would then have been to attack the East Indies or not attack at all, and the United States-East Indies ties would have then become the crucial variable.

The cognitive model takes on a slightly different explanation when applied to a two-nation, large-power, nuclear situation. During the debates over deterrent strategy in the 1950s and 1960s, a "capacity to delay response" (CDR) was proposed. Under this system, a country would have the capacity to withstand a first nuclear strike by the other side—in a sense, the capacity to "delay" its response. Regardless of how heavily the other side attacked, the possessor of CDR could then retaliate so extensively that he could destroy the aggressor. Knowing that, the argument went, the "pre-emptor" would be deterred.

Obviously, real-world testing of such a system is impossible. Crow and Raser, therefore, simulated the deterrent system. For data they used a questionnaire given to simulation participants to determine their perceptions of CDR and of the country possessing it.[69] The possessor of CDR was seen as the stronger and the more threatening. Accidental or pre-emptive wars were perceived as less likely under conditions of CDR, but wars were not necessarily less limited. In simulations where a specific "aggressive minded" country possessed CDR, strategic wars were *more* likely—a result, however, that may have been a function of that nation's character.

Other simulation data provides some support for the effect of a de-

[69] John R. Raser and Wayman J. Crow, "A Simulation Study of Deterrence Theories," in *Theory and Research on the Causes of War*, ed. Dean G. Pruitt and Richard C. Snyder (Englewood Cliffs, N.J.: Prentice-Hall, Inc., 1969).

laying mechanism. Charles Hermann and his colleagues found that 71 percent of those nations with no weapons or only a few weapons defended opted for an immediate counterattack, whereas 71 percent of the countries with all their nuclear forces defended delayed their response.[70]

Given the problems of generalizing from simulation data, these results can be little more than suggestive. Even so, Crow and Raser concluded that deterrence was not necessarily stabilized under conditions of CDR. Hermann, on the other hand, though admittedly addressing a different problem, found that further escalation of violence was at least temporarily alleviated under conditions of weapons survivability. One crucial element, of course, is that CDR may affect the perceptions of the country possessing it, perceptions that may run counter to either the stabilization or success of deterrence.

All of these findings concerning the cognitive model are dealing essentially with a structural situation. George, Hall, and Simons's innovative research on "coercive diplomacy," however, focuses on cognitive variables that are much more easily manipulated—even in the short-term—by the decision-maker.[71] One of their primary variables has been referred to already: asymmetry of motivation, which refers to the differing motivational levels on both sides. It is cognitive in the sense that the decision-maker is trying to work on the other's decision-making calculus by making him believe that his—the decision-maker's—motivation is much greater. The decision-maker can manipulate this variable because there are strategies—suggested by George and his colleagues as well as by Young—to convince the opponent of that asymmetry. Likewise, a "sense of urgency" is cognitive in that the decision-maker is trying to convince the adversary that the situation is on the "front burner," and that he intends to act; any weak action allowing the enemy to stall puts the situation into his hands. A final cognitive variable is the defender's attempt to arouse fear of unacceptable escalation on the enemy's part, while showing that he himself does not fear such escalation.

George's variables were inductively arrived at after investigating three cases of coercive diplomacy: the move by President Kennedy in 1961 to keep the Communist forces from overrunning all of Laos, the Cuban Missile Crisis in 1962, and President Johnson's attempt in early 1965 to force North Vietnam into backing away from the struggle in South Vietnam. George contends that six of the conditions for successful coercive diplomacy were present in Laos and Cuba and not present in Vietnam, thus pointing to the greater possibility of success in the first two than in the third. The test of the theory illustrates a central problem in evaluat-

[70] Charles F. Hermann, Margaret G. Hermann, and Robert Cantor, "Counterattack or Delay: Characteristics Influencing Decision-makers' Responses to the Simulation of an Unidentified Attack," *Journal of Conflict Resolution* 18 (March, 1974), p. 95.

[71] George et al., *Limits of Coercive Diplomacy*, pp. 215ff.

ing the cognitive model, for an extensive analysis of the study by George and his colleagues has shown that the presence or absence of the independent variables—the conditions—was in almost every case measured by the presence or absence of the dependent variable of coercive diplomacy.[72] The reasoning then becomes: if the enemy was successfully dissuaded, the conditions for successful coercive diplomacy *must* have been present, but no independent measure shows that motivational asymmetry favored the North Vietnamese. No indication is made of how the sense of urgency was conveyed nor exactly what constituted an arousal of fear of unacceptable escalation.[73]

George's analysis illustrates quite well the difficulty of testing the cognitive model of bargaining in international politics, and the problems in measuring cognitive elements. In this case, George equated their presence with the presence of successful coercive diplomacy; Russett equated the assumed occurrence of deterrence with supposed credibility of the defender's threat. Just as George had no clear independent measure of the three cognitive variables—asymmetry of motivation, sense of urgency, and arousing fear of escalation—Russett had no measure of the defender's credibility. Russett's analysis, however, does not depend on post facto reconstructions as explanations. Despite the absence of a measure for credibility of threat, the structure of the situation, one could argue, works on the potential aggressor's calculus. In George's case, almost the entire argument rests on such post facto explanations, which represents a real stumbling block to testing propositions of the cognitive model.

Stimulus-Response Model

Tests of the stimulus-response model are much more straightforward than those of the cognitive model because the model itself is simpler. Yet we will find it is difficult to differentiate between stimulus-response and learning models in many cases. One popularized version of stimulus-response is Osgood's Graduated Reduction in Tension (GRIT), in which he suggests that large powers locked into a mutual interaction process of increasing hostility might break out of that pattern by one side unilaterally reducing the tension as a signal to the other side.[74] Osgood formulated numerous criteria and suggestions whereby each side might monitor the other's behavior for signs of reciprocation in tension reduc-

---

[72] Michael P. Sullivan, "The Question of 'Relevance' in Foreign Policy Studies," *Western Political Quarterly* 26 (June, 1973), pp. 314–24.

[73] George et al., *Limits of Coercive Diplomacy*, pp. 221–23; 225–26.

[74] Charles E. Osgood, *An Alternative to War or Surrender* (Urbana: University of Illinois Press, 1962).

tion. Etzioni's analysis of East-West tensions during the last months of Kennedy's term in office (June to November, 1963) illustrate this approach.[75] Etzioni claimed that the subsequent thaw in 1963–1964 was to some degree a function of a series of cooperative actions beginning in June, 1963, which were reciprocated in kind by the other side. On June 10, Kennedy outlined his "Strategy for Peace" in a speech at American University, calling attention to the dangers of nuclear war and taking a generally conciliatory tone toward the East. Furthermore, he took the unilateral initiative of stopping nuclear tests in the atmosphere. That move did not constitute an important strategic action but rather a psychological one, for it was generally conceded that the United States was ahead in that area anyway.

The Soviets for their part first allowed the speech to be published in the Soviet Union. Khrushchev then followed up that action with a halt on the production of strategic bombers, once again mostly a psychological move. Both sides followed these actions with simultaneous moves at the U.N. in which they respectively moved away from long-held positions, suggesting further conciliation. In early August the Test Ban Treaty was signed. There followed other moves including the Soviet call for a nonaggression pact between the Warsaw Pact and NATO, and Kennedy's call for cooperative ventures in space. Hence, although admittedly unsystematic in terms of data collection and analysis, nonetheless this case certainly hints that cooperative behavior can result from the stimulus-response propensity of nation-states.

Somewhat more systematic data of numerous sorts also supports—or at least is consistent with—the stimulus-response model. Both Richardson's as well as Paul Smoker's data on arms races show each side exhibiting behavior in terms of arms level that is almost a mirror of that exhibited by the other side; to that extent, a great deal of the variation in level of arms expenditure—viewed as a foreign policy behavior—is a function of similar behavior by the other side.[76]

Tables 7-3a and 7-3b and Figure 7-2 show the patterns of big-power behavior from 1946 through 1963, presented in two different formats.[77] The tables illustrate how the refractory or conciliatory actions generated periods of either belligerency or accommodation on the part of the other side. Refractory actions by one side were more than not met with a belligerent reaction by the other side; conciliatory actions, on the other

[75] Amitai Etzioni, "The Kennedy Experiment," *Western Political Quarterly* 20 (June, 1967), pp. 361–80.

[76] Richardson, *Arms and Insecurity;* Smoker, in Rosenau, ed., *International Politics and Foreign Policy*, rev. ed.

[77] These data have been calculated from figures 7.1 and 7.2, and from the data presented in appendix E in William A. Gamson and Andre Modigliani, *Untangling the Cold War: A Strategy for Testing Rival Theories* (Boston: Little, Brown and Company, 1971).

Table 7-3a. United States Actions During Belligerent and Accom-modative periods of Soviet Activity			Table 7-3b. Soviet Actions During Belligerent and Accomodative Periods of U.S. Activity		
	Refractory	**Conciliatory**		**Refractory**	**Conciliatory**
Belligerence	68%	43%	Belligerence	79%	20%
Accomodation	32	57	Accomodation	21	80

Percentages computed from data in William Gamson and Andre Modigliani, *Untangling the Cold War: A Strategy for Testing Rival Theories* (Boston: Little Brown, 1971).

hand, were met with a high percentage of accommodative responses. Figure 7-2 is restricted to the *major* actions of each side as outlined by Gamson and Modigliani, and the percent conciliatory actions by each side for each year exhibit a very high level of correspondence. Goldmann also shows that the trend of behavior in Europe by both sides in the Cold War corresponds to what we would expect from a stimulus-response model.[78]

Likewise, Table 7-4 demonstrates that in three different studies a

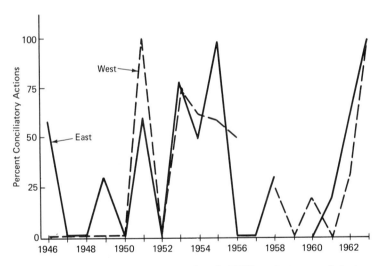

Source: Data computed from raw data in William Gamson and Andre Modigliani, *Untangling the Cold War* (Boston: Little-Brown, 1971).

Figure 7-2. Percentage of major East-West conciliatory actions, 1946–1963.*

* No major Eastern actions were recorded for 1959 and none for the West for 1957.

[78] Kjell Goldmann, "East-West Tension in Europe, 1946–1970: A Conceptual Analysis and a Quantitative Description," *World Politics* 26 (October, 1973), pp. 118–19.

Table 7-4. Correlations of Stimulus, Perception, and Response, in Three Historical Situations

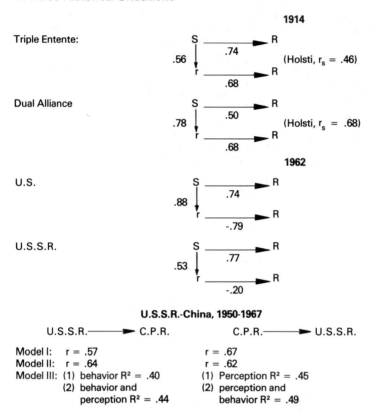

U.S.S.R.-China, 1950-1967

U.S.S.R.⟶ C.P.R.	C.P.R.⟶ U.S.S.R.
Model I: r = .57	r = .67
Model II: r = .64	r = .62
Model III: (1) behavior R² = .40	(1) Perception R² = .45
(2) behavior and	(2) perception and
perception R² = .44	behavior R² = .49

strict stimulus-response model does equally well or better than the perception-response model tested in Chapter 2.[79] For the 1914 case, both S⟶R linkages are moderately strong, and for the Triple Entente that linkage is even stronger than the perceptions⟶Response link. That is, the *rank* of the other side's level of hostile response during one period could be explained at least partially by the rank of the acting side's hostile action during the preceding period. The same holds for the Cuban Missile Crisis, although here the relations are even stronger (but less significant because the number of observations is smaller). Of par-

[79] Data for 1914 are actions measured on an interval scale; those for the 1962 Cuban Missile Crisis consist of the days of the crisis rank-ordered from least-to-most hostile days; data in the Mogdis study are both action and verbal data for both sides in the dispute. The correlations in parentheses for the 1914 case are those reported by Ole Holsti, *et. al.*, in *Quantitative International Politics: Insights and Evidence*, ed. J. David Singer (New York: Free Press, 1968). They are quite different from those computed from the data presented in that article.

ticular note is that Soviet perceptions of the other side do not correlate very well with its own reactions and therefore in this case the S⟶ R model is clearly the superior one. But even for the United States, the relation between the stimulus and response, on the one hand, and between the perception and response, on the other, are almost identical.

Because the hostile behavior of both alliances was increasing during the crisis in the 1914 case, it is not particularly surprising that their behaviors showed a high correlation with each other. It is also possible to investigate the correlation between *changes* from one period to the next.[80] The change in one side's behavior during one period *cannot* account for the change of the other side during the *following* period ($r_s = -.05$). However, if we forget the time-lag factor, Figure 7-3 shows the two sides' respective changes along the scale of hostility move fairly well in tandem with each other ($r_s = .46$).

For the Mogdis study,[81] three models were used: the first tries to account for the variation in the action of the Soviet Union or the Chinese People's Republic by looking at *their perception* of the other side during the previous year; Model II uses the *action* during the previous time period to account for action during the next one; and Model III combines the two. In both cases Model II is fairly accurate, and in the U.S.S.R.⟶C.P.R. case it is stronger. In sum, knowing actions during one

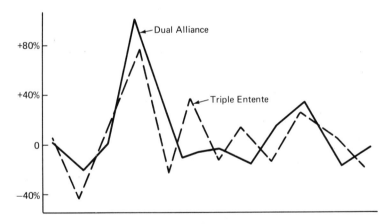

Figure 7-3. Percent change, level of hostility, across twelve time periods, Triple Entente, and Dual Alliance, June–August, 1914.

[80] Such an analysis cannot be done for the Cuban Missile Crisis because the data in that case, as noted in the text, were *ranked* hostility for the stimulus and response variables; obviously, percentage change could not therefore be computed.

[81] Franz Mogdis, "The Verbal Dimension in Sino-Soviet Relations: A Time Series Analysis," mimeographed: Paper Delivered at the Annual American Political Science Association Meeting, Los Angeles, September, 1970.

period allows us to predict actions during the next period moderately well.

There is a consistency across all three studies. If the basic stimulus-response model was inaccurate, then the correlations would not be significantly different from zero; in almost every case, however, they *are* different, lending some credibility to the S⟶R model in a very approximate sense: while specific actions cannot be predicted, large-scale differences in behavior could have been.

Milstein's study of the Arab-Israeli dispute has already been analyzed in Chapter 5 from the perspective of power theory. He also investigated the "hostile reaction" theory, however, and found it to be far superior either to the power balance or the influence of the superpowers.[82] Regardless of whether annual or quarterly data were used, the correlations between Israeli and Arab actions were uniformly high. As Milstein put it: "The violent actions of Israel and each Arab country can best be explained by the violent actions of that country's enemy." [83]

Wilkenfeld's analysis of the Middle East during almost the same time period lends further support to the stimulus-response propositions.[84] In fourteen out of fifteen different equations describing Middle East activity, the strongest predictor of one nation's action was the action directed at it by the other nations during the same time period. In more specific terms, the best explanations statistically for Israel's hostility (verbal conflict, mobilization, and troop movements) were, in order of importance, Egypt's and Iraq's "active" hostility toward Israel, and Jordon and Iraq's "verbal" hostility toward Israel. For Israel's military actions, the best explanations were the corresponding military actions of Jordon, Syria, and Egypt. Egypt's "active" hostility is best accounted for by active hostility toward it; Egypt's military action is accounted for by Israel's military action toward it and the level of Egyptian military action in the last year.

There were some differences, however. Israel's foreign conflict behavior seemed to be formulated more on the basis of the immediate situation, namely, the conflict behavior aimed at it by other countries. For the Arab states both domestic conflict and prior levels of their own

82 Jeffrey S. Milstein, "American and Soviet Influence, Balance of Power, and Arab-Israeli Violence," in *Peace, War, and Numbers,* ed. Bruce Russett (Beverly Hills: Sage, 1972). Milstein's data were somewhat different from much of the conflict data we have discussed so far; it measured the *pervasiveness* of conflict, the number of weeks in a time period in which a given action occurred. Thus Milstein is not talking about an absolute level of hostility.

83 Ibid., p. 165.

84 Jonathan Wilkenfeld, Virginia Lee Lussier, and Dale Tahtinen, "Conflict Interactions in the Middle East, 1949–1967," *Journal of Conflict Resolution* 16 (June, 1972), pp. 135–54.

foreign conflict affected their behavior toward Israel. Furthermore, for the Arab states, conflict among themselves entered into the situation. In several instances the strongest variables for understanding their foreign conflict was the hostility received from other *Arab* states. Regardless of these differences, in general the stimulus-response model was not only strong, but stronger than other explanations.

Raymond Tanter investigated the proposition on the opposing alliances of NATO and Warsaw Pact nations for the Berlin crisis of May-December, 1961.[85] With one exception he found that in no case did levels of action by one side relate highly to later levels of action by the other side. The one exception: when NATO behavior was lagged four days behind WTO behavior, it had some effect on the Warsaw Pact group. Tanter's data can be used to disconfirm the stimulus response model, though Tanter admits that his exclusion of several elements (unimportant for present purposes) could have affected the results.

Warren Phillips correlated the conflict that sixty-five nations received with the conflict they themselves exhibited during the same and the following month for the year 1963. The S-R proposition would predict a high correlation between the two, and that in fact occurred; using both concomitant time periods as well as lagging "conflict sent" by one month, the proposition was moderately supported, although less strongly with the time lag.[86] Ivo Feierabend and Rosalind Feierabend also found that aggression expressed is highly related to aggression received.[87]

These several studies lend rather strong support to the basic stimulus-response theory. With the exception of Tanter's analysis of opposing alliances, most studies show at least moderate support for what in essence is a very simple explanation of behavior. It bears repeating, of course, that these findings do not equate with predicting specific actions, nor do they account for all variation in state action. Moreover, in several studies the concern was with trends or with rank orders of hostility. Nonetheless, differences in international behavior along the conflict dimension were found to be, to some degree, a function of the behavior of other actors, a finding that scholars prefer to shy away from—as too

[85] Raymond Tanter, "International System and Foreign Policy Approaches: Implications for Conflict Modelling and Management," *World Politics* 24 (Spring, 1972 Supplement), pp. 7–39.

[86] Warren R. Phillips, "The Conflict Environment of Nations: A Study of Conflict Inputs to Nations in 1963," Dimensionality of Nations Project Research Report 42, mimeographed (Honolulu: University of Hawaii, 1970).

[87] Ivo and Rosalind Feierabend, "Level of Development and Internation Behavior," in *Foreign Policy and the Developing Nation,* ed. R. Butwell (Lexington: University of Kentucky Press, 1969), p. 146; cited in Patrick McGowan and Howard Shapiro, *The Comparative Study of Foreign Policy: A Survey of Scientific Findings* (Beverly Hills: Sage, 1973), p. 149.

deterministic—but that quite clearly permeates both the writing on international relations and foreign policies and the thinking of decision-makers concerned with the actions of other nations.

Learning Models

The "learning" models of international bargaining in a sense correspond to and complement the stimulus-response model, and some research considered under the latter model can also be analyzed from the learning perspective. The difficulty with some learning models, however, is their complexity. Whereas the "structure of the situation" in the cognitive models is relatively easy to construct, and stimulus-response even easier, learning models rely on interaction *patterns,* and these are not only difficult to reconstruct empirically but they also resemble closely the patterns in stimulus-response situations. In Milstein's Middle East study, for instance, he tried to test learning notions in addition to stimulus-response in the following way.

Learning theory suggests that national leaders can respond to attacks in two ways. On the one hand, if counterattacks against the enemy led to his decreasing his attacks, their counterattacks might be increased, but if they led to increases in enemy attacks they would be reduced, since punished behavior tends to be extinguished. This version would be supported with negative statistical relationships. On the other hand, if counterattacks led to punishment by an increase in the enemy's attacks, the counterattacks might still be increased, leading to a spiral of violence. For this version, positive statistical relationships would be supportive. As noted already, Milstein did find high positive relationships, which would hypothetically support this second version of learning theory—that when a nation's behavior fails to elicit the response it wants from the enemy, it becomes more hostile. Unfortunately, as pointed out, there is no way to distinguish between this theoretical explanation and the one derived merely from the stimulus-response model.

Barry Blechman's analysis of the Middle East does not contain these pitfalls, and therefore has more to say concerning the learning explanation.[88] He was interested in the effect of Israeli reprisals on future Arab behavior. Stimulus-response would predict that Israeli reprisals against the Arabs—a response itself to past behavior—would have a perpetuating effect, in which the Arabs would then respond with greater

[88] Barry M. Blechman, "The Impact of Israeli Reprisals on Behavior of the Bordering Arab Nations Directed at Israel," *Journal of Conflict Resolution* 16 (June, 1972), pp. 155-82.

hostility. Learning theory, however, would predict that the Arabs would "learn" from the Israeli reprisal and *not* react, because their original aggressive action resulted in the reprisal. Blechman's specific test was to ask what the probability would be of Arab action after Israeli attacks compared with all other times. If the probability was less than 50 percent, then Israeli reprisals would have had a dampening effect. If, however, Arab action was *more* probable after reprisals, then they would not have the desired effect from the Israeli standpoint, and stimulus-response explanations would be more accurate.

Overall, Blechman found that with the exception of Jordan, Syria, Lebanon, and Palestine during the two-year period, 1967–1969, the probability of Arab attacks was *less* after Israeli reprisals than at other times. It varied from a low probability of 5 percent for Syria (1964–1967) to 35 percent for Egypt and Jordan (1956). Where the reprisals did not dampen Arab response, the probability was 56 percent, 65 percent, and 70 percent respectively at ten, twenty, and thirty days after Israel acted (Table 7-5). The overall immediate effect of Israeli reprisals was therefore a dampening one. However, expanding the time period to twenty and thirty days shows the probability of Arab action increasing; the effect of Israeli reprisals apparently wears off with time.

Learning theory might also predict that there would be increased cooperative action by the Arabs after reprisals. Blechman shows that with one exception, the probability of cooperative action after reprisals is just about the same as it normally would be. The exception was Egypt and Jordan between 1954 and 1956, where cooperative actions had a probability of occurrence of anywhere from 61 to 79 percent, depending

Table 7-5. Effect of Israeli Reprisals with Regard to the Number of Arab-Initiated Physical Conflict Events

Reprisal category		Time lag		
Target nation(s)	*Time frame*	*10 days*	*20 days*	*30 days*
Jordan	1950-54	.34	.44	.40
Egypt	1954-56	.20	.28	.38
Egypt and Jordan	1955-56	.35	.42	.45
Syria	1964-67	.05	.08	.11
Jordan, Lebanon, Palestine	1965-67	.19	.20	.18
Egypt	1967-69	.20	.29	.05
Jordan, Lebanon, Syria, Palestine	1967-69	.56	.65	.70

This table from "The Impact of Israel's Reprisals on Behavior of the Bordering Arab Nations Directed at Israel," by Barry M. Blechman is reprinted from *Journal of Conflict Resolution* Vol. 16, No. 2 (June 1972), p. 171 by permission of the author and publisher, Sage Publications, Inc.

on the length of time considered after the Israeli reprisals. As Blechman concludes, the effect of Israeli reprisals is rather immediate, supporting learning theory, but erodes over time. In that sense, stimulus-response theory in the short run is not confirmed, for the Arabs were less likely to respond with greater hostility.

Conclusion

THEORETICAL IMPLICATIONS

Perhaps more than any other approach, bargaining is the most potentially fascinating because of its proximity to the everyday world of diplomacy. But diplomacy has traditionally been considered an "art," open only to the understanding of "the few." The diplomat must work his magic daily—successfully threatening an adversary, coaxing other countries into an agreement, convincing an opponent that his continued actions will bring a forceful response—and attachment to the "daily" view of the diplomat's world constitutes a basic stumbling block to systematic research on models of bargaining. While we may glean some helpful bargaining "truths" from memoirs, diaries, and reminiscences, we still lack systematic observations of influence attempts to make an accurate judgement as to whether the situations (cognitive models) or the interaction patterns (learning models) followed similar paths in those cases of successful deterrence or brinkmanship. Moreover, it is not quite clear how many situations occur where attempts at influencing failed, and what conditions or interaction patterns existed in these cases.

In other words, we have a great deal of common-sense knowledge about how states can exert influence, and a large number of general propositions or suggestions, but little hard, systematic evidence on these propositions. Indeed, the research that has been done indicates that many popular notions—two specifically: one, that states are not *determined* in their interactions, and the other that states will back down from a threat—can be seriously questioned. Certainly that would be the implication from the research by Zinnes in Chapter 2 on the perception of hostility resulting in the expression of hostility, and the studies here—particularly by Holsti, Mogdis, Milstein, and Wilkenfeld—that states react to other states' actions *in kind*.

Evidence for stimulus-response models seems to be the strongest, but that is very likely a function of the ease with which such models can be tested. Further, as noted in the analysis of Milstein's study of the Middle East, evidence of a learning process could just as easily be seen in his results: each side learned that a small counterattack was not sufficient and responded with a larger one. Only by breaking down such data more finely could some distinction be made between the models, which shows not only the complexity of learning models, but also the similarity between learning and stimulus-response models. Figures 7-4 and 7-5 illustrate these two points. Assuming that we can accurately scale nation-state action on an ordinal scale, with 1 being least conflictual, Figure 7-4 depicts two possible stimulus-response situations: 7-4a shows that nation B responds to nation A's hostility by increasing its own hostility, which in turn prompts A to increase its hostility, and so on; 7-4b is a variant, showing A and B responding to each other merely in kind, with neither side necessarily upping the hostility in the short-term although that does occur in the longer term.

Figure 7-5 shows two different learning situations. In 7-5a the first four time periods resemble the stimulus-response model in Figure 7-4b: increasing hostility is correlated with increasing hostility. The broken line in Figure 7-6 (Y to Y') shows that relationship. However, one could also argue that both A and B in Figure 6a are "learning" because when their increased hostility is not met with decreased hostility by the other side,

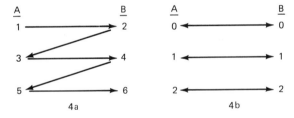

Figure 7-4.   Stimulus-response models.

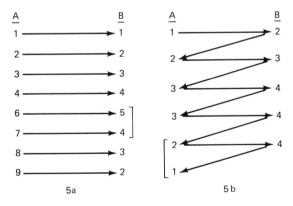

Figure 7-5.   Learning models.

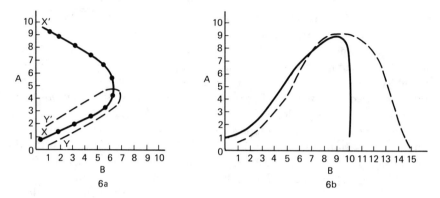

Figure 7-6. Hypothetical patterns of data illustrating both stimulus-response and learning-models.

they become even more hostile. There is no way of knowing whether the parties are learning or merely responding to each other in kind. The bottom part of Figure 7-6a, though, shows that B is learning, for as A keeps increasing its hostility, B begins to reduce its own hostility. The line X to X' in Figure 7-b shows this relationship. Of interest here is the fact that although the line Y to Y' may indicate learning, the learning cannot be assessed merely from a plot of the data. The X-to-X' line is much more clearly a learning situation, but, interestingly enough, it would show up in linear correlation techniques as a relatively low correlation.

Another possible learning situation is described in Figure 7-6b, although here it is on A's part. As A increases its hostility, B responds by increasing its own; at the fifth time period, however, A begins to drop its hostility, while B's remains very high. Figure 7-6b illustrates two other possibilities: as A begins to drop off in hostility, B continues higher, creating the curvilinear situation of Figure 7-6a (dotted line), or B merely remains at a high state of hostility while A backs down (straight line). Again simple statistical analysis may not uncover these learning relationships.

Yet another problem, not confined certainly to bargaining theories but very clearly present in them, has been the tendency in many studies to use fairly simple and gross conflict-cooperation coding schemes. William Coplin, Stephen Mills, and Michael O'Leary argue that by controlling for "issue areas" the influence attempts aimed at one country by another change rather drastically. For example, calculating the mean value of influence attempts between two countries (on a positive-negative or cooperative-hostile scale), they then compared that score to the mean value of such influence attempts between countries for several different issue areas, such as Vietnam, territorial rights, economic aid and military aid and arms sales. They found, for example, that while the overall mean score of influence attempts from the United States to North Korea was −2.1, on the issue of Vietnam the mean value was −5.8, and that of territorial rights was −3.1. For Israel-Egypt, the overall mean score was −7.9; broken down, however, the Vietnam issue was −8.3 and territorial rights was −1.0. [89] While Coplin and his associates admit that these findings do not automatically mean gross indexes are going to provide inaccurate results, that suggestion is nonetheless very plausible.

These essentially methodological comments have a great bearing on theory development, for one reason research on bargaining has been confined for the most part to historical case studies and illustrations or to simple stimulus-response models is that bargaining implies "dynamic" models. And dynamic models are both difficult to conceptualize for interaction sequences, and extremely difficult to operationalize. Figures 7-3 through 7-6 illustrated some of those conceptual difficulties. An even more far-reaching problem is illustrated by Kenneth Boulding's distinction between "large" and "small" social systems. Social systems "in the small" do not contain the stability that social systems "in the large" do.[90] Examples from economics are perhaps the easiest to use. Stock market prices change constantly, and hourly or daily plottings of the changes may appear random or unstable: they oscillate back and forth frequently. But plotted on a longer term basis—say weekly or monthly—they take on a pattern that cannot be recognized in the smaller segments. There are so many forces acting on stock prices that they often cancel each other out "in the small." But over the long run the large-scale forces in the nation's economic, business, and social life have systematic impacts. The same holds true for many other series of an economic as well as political nature. Data from Charles McClelland's WEIS project show drastic fluctuations in state behavior on a daily or weekly basis, but when plotted across longer periods of time—"in the large"—definite patterns can be discerned. We have also pointed out that the same long-run patterns can be seen in data for presidential rhetoric.

The question here, of course, is: Where does the cutting point occur between large and small? Where does enough stability exist so that it can be analyzed? The answer is judgmental, but the distinction at least is helpful for understanding the difficulty encountered in dealing with international behavioral systems. The distinction also delineates two different philosophical outlooks: one that views each international action as a function of the decision-maker involved (understandable in itself),

[89] William D. Coplin, Stephen L. Mills, and Michael K. O'Leary, "The PRINCE Concepts and the Study of Foreign Policy," in *Sage International Yearbook of Foreign Policy Studies*, ed. Patrick McGowan, Vol. 1 (Beverly Hills: Sage, 1973), p. 90.

[90] Kenneth E. Boulding, *Conflict and Defense: A General Theory* (New York: Harper & Row, 1962), pp. 23–24.

and a second that views decisions as part of a larger trend (understand-able only as it fits into that larger component). The second perspective is present in many of the system-level theories considered in the last several chapters and also in the three models considered here. It differs slightly in focus from traditional diplomatic analysis, which pays greater attention to specific, isolated actions.

Bargaining theory contains many common-sense propositions on de-terrence, brinkmanship, and influence in general. It is concerned with what situations should produce the compliance of another party, what situations should result in successful deterrence. But a careful analysis of bargaining theory shows that it is of a very general and only suggestive nature. Few propositions are particular and specific. McClelland's re-search on the relationship between verbal and physical conflict reflects this problem. He observes that the "theory of influence" suggests gen-erally that verbal acts—threats—should be mixed with physical acts of punishment in order to obtain the desired result, and that the threat-punishment sequence should be accompanied by a promise-reward sequence.[91] "The would-be influencer," says McClelland, "benefits from the theory in knowing that he should mix two streams of deprivation and indulgence and that he should use both verbal and physical acts in explicit sequences." But unfortunately, as we suggested at the beginning of our conclusion above:

His problem is in knowing how to arrange the combinations. The theory tends to be silent on the details of managing the mixes and the sequences. In fact, traditional writings usually consign these details to the the realm of art. The effective diplomat or statesman is said simply to "know" when and how to initiate which moves according to the requirements of the situation.[92]

Systematic empirical studies of influence attempts are rare. Case studies and illustrations showing influence attempts abound but the sampling problem is momentous. The studies presented in this chapter illustrate this difficulty of systematically researching propositions involving in-fluence.

POLICY IMPLICATIONS

Because it is dealing with everyday diplomatic actions, the bargaining approach might conceivably be of greatest importance to decision-makers

[91] Charles McClelland, "Verbal and Physical Conflict in the Contemporary Inter-national System," mimeographed (Los Angeles: University of Southern California, 1970), p. 5.
[92] Ibid., p. 6.

in terms of policy advice. But so often advice to policy-makers concerning bargaining strategies is based on intuitive hunches with little empirical backing, and presented within a very parochial framework. For instance, proponents of deterrence strategies assume that a strong threat, backed up by actions of a "credibility-building" sort, will cause the opponent to back down. The parochial nature of this assumption is apparent when decision-makers ask themselves whether *they* would back down under similar action by an opponent. Were such a question asked of Dulles, or other strategic planners throughout most of the Cold War, the answer would certainly have been no. For the theoretician—as opposed to the policy-maker often concerned with the baggage of ideological concerns—the question then arises: "But if we would not back down faced with a threat and credible action going along with it, what does that say about the proposition that such behavior will result in the opponent backing down?" In other words, such "truths" seem to apply, so often, only to one side.

Furthermore, advice to policy-makers concerning bargaining strategies is unlikely to be helpful until it can be put in more particular terms. It is easy to offer general advice for policy-makers: be cautious, be sure threats are credible, show how urgent the situation is for you, convince your opponent that you have a great deal at stake, and so on. But to go beyond that general level is much more difficult. How can a situation be structured so that the threat becomes more credible? If a threat is not acceded to immediately, what further moves should one follow to create further credibility? If one threatens and the other side does not back down, how can one get out of that situation if one was bluffing in the first place? Such questions relate to one's own attempts to influence. But that game works two ways, and an equally important question relates to one's own response to the actions by the other side. How does one distinguish realistic from unrealistic threats? What different interpretations can one give to military moves by the other side? How should one respond to what appears to be very serious action in such a way as to gather more information about the other's intentions and yet not risk provoking him?

All of these particular questions are more crucial to policy-makers than the general kind. Because bargaining propositions have remained at the general level, saying little about the sequences of moves and interactions and the meaning of different kinds of sequences, advice can only be general and, in many cases, tautological. Some would retort that such a cookbook or laundry list of pointers on what to do in an influence relationship fails to recognize the differences from situation to situation, and that advice cannot be provided for each specific situation. The answer to that objection is two-fold. First, the objection implies that if we leave the level of broad generalizations, then we must provide very specific advice of a very minute nature; that is, that we either say "be credible," or that we provide the very words and actions that will lend credibility to a threat. A theory of bargaining, however, of use to the policy-maker, would fall somewhere in between. Second, to agree that each situation is different does not equate with saying that each situation is completely different. At some level, bargaining situations do possess similarities.

Despite the fact that no specific advice can be garnered from research reviewed here, propositions midway between the general and the particular do emerge. Russett's research—even given its methodological problems—suggests that the structural situation does carry a great deal of weight in terms of the outcome. Decision-makers, furthermore, operating under the simplistic theory that acquiescence can be gained merely by increasing hostility toward another power do not find much support in the numerous studies on the stimulus-response model. That is, states tend to respond "in kind," although not always. Blechman showed that Israeli reprisals resulted in a lower probability of Arab hostility—but only over the short term. Moreover, the hypothesis that punishment should produce cooperative behavior was clearly not upheld in the Middle East.

This type of advice does not set out clear-cut alternatives with exact details of bargaining moves to be made. It does, however, focus attention on the dynamics of the situation. It should, therefore, force an evaluation of bargaining situations that goes beyond reliance on "pet" theories of influence that do not always withstand empirical test. It also reinforces the conclusion that bargaining is an ongoing matter, which means that the underlying theories or models related to it must be capable of encompassing dynamic activity.

To explain international behavior as a function of bargaining between nations is probably the most complex of the many single approaches considered in this book. Because of that complexity, the explanations are low level and tend further to be general. Though it is not possible to set out a complete and comprehensive bargaining theory, this chapter nonetheless has established the types of explanations, following Patchen, that can be used in connection with the bargaining approach—and it has reviewed several different methods to test those explanations. As such, it should be able to serve as a guide rather than an end-product in understanding international relations as bargaining.

chapter 8   Multivariate Approaches

With some exceptions, the preceding chapters have concentrated on single theoretical approaches. Each chapter has isolated one perspective and demonstrated how researchers have investigated international behavior. Each approach was considered separately, and evaluated in terms of how it could singly account for international behavior. As a consequence, we have been able to contrast the various approaches with one another in terms of their respective potency, *assuming* that no other variables are involved. However, it would be hopelessly naïve to think that individual variables influence international behavior all by themselves, that they are unaffected by other variables. The fact is that no one theory or framework can account for either (1) all the variation in one type of behavior, or (2) the variation across a broad range of behavior.

We must, therefore, attempt some consideration of multivariate explanations. We cannot, however, respond to this task simply by asserting that *all* variables must be considered and therefore that *all* approaches are important. Such an assertion sounds fine and logical—as if even a fool would have known that—but in spite of its seeming validity, it says nothing about the *way* in which all the variables are to be combined. Nor does it address the problem of the relative importance of each of the theories. Moreover, such an assertion does not address the question of whether all the theories combined are capable of explaining all types of behavior, or whether some theories can account for only certain ranges or types of behavior.

Two different approaches can be used to analyze multivariate explanations. The first is to use multiple variables on the same level of analysis. The second approach, much more difficult to operationalize but also much more productive, combines several different levels (individual, state, international system) for the purpose of analysis. Because of the difficulties inherent in the second method, we shall offer only suggestions for the most part about *how* research could be carried out on that level.

Multivariate: Single Level

MAN AND THE STATE

Few systematic studies have been carried out combining more than one approach on the individual level of analysis. Reference has been made earlier (Chapter 2) to possibilities for carrying out this kind of analysis, perhaps combining personality variables with image analyses, but these remain only possibilities. This is not to say that there are no individual level studies that consider such numerous individual-level variables, but these for the most part fall into what we will term shortly ad hoc analyses, in which approaches such as belief systems, perceptions, personality, and images are only very loosely and unsystematically combined. Further, they are conceived as one unit—or one approach—as opposed to potentially competing approaches.

The state level of analysis encompasses primarily national-attribute theory, although certainly theories and models of decision-making might also be included if we were to assume that different types of nations would go about making decisions in different ways. Of the numerous studies assessing the impact of multiple national attributes, most found that only a small number of attributes turned out to be important. Even in combination with one another, they provided little more explanation than attributes considered singly.[1]

---

[1] These studies would include Michael Skrein, "National Attributes and Foreign Policy Output: Tests for a Relationship," Mimeographed: Support Study No. 4, World Event/Interaction Survey (Los Angeles: University of Southern California, 1970); Rudolph Rummel, "The Relationship Between National Attributes and Foreign Conflict Behavior," in *Quantitative International Politics: Insights and Evidence,* ed. J. David Singer (New York: The Free Press, 1968); Steven Salmore and Charles Hermann, "The Effect of Size, Development, and Accountability on Foreign Policy," *Peace Research Society Papers* 14 (1969), pp. 15–30; James Kean and Patrick McGowan, "National Attributes and Foreign Policy Participation: A Path Analysis," in *Sage International Yearbook of Foreign Policy Studies,* ed. Patrick McGowan, Vol. 1 (Beverly Hills: Sage, 1973); Jonathan Wilkenfeld, "Domestic and Foreign Behavior of Nations," *Journal of Peace Research* 5, No. 1 (1968), pp. 56–70; and Jonathan Wilkenfeld, "Some Further Findings Regarding the Domestic and Foreign Conflict Behavior of Nations," *Journal of Peace Research* 6 (No. 2, 1969), pp. 147–56.

Thus, if we consider the role of images, perceptions, belief systems, and personality, along with decision-making and national attributes as covering the primary foci on the level below the international system, it must be concluded that with the exception of the use of multiple attributes, and ad hoc analyses combining different approaches, systematic multivariate research on this level remains limited. It is quite possible that, with important variables discovered and research designs becoming more sophisticated, more effort will be put into this type of approach.

SYSTEM LEVEL

Michael Wallace tested a complex multivariate design on the systemic level centered around the variable of status inconsistency (Chapter 5).[2] He suggested that status inconsistency might be related to rates of change along both the capability and the status dimensions, and that the question becomes whether it is the large rates of capability change in the system or ·status inconsistency that causes system-level conflict. Status inconsistency, however, may produce greater alliance activity in an attempt to change the status quo of the system, and alliance activity itself has been linked to war.[3] It may also increase the level of stress in the system, reducing cooperative activities such as the formation of international organizations, which are also moderately related (negatively) to war. Finally, the tension that results from status inconsistentcy might further stimulate armed forces development, increases in which are also related to the onset of war. Figure 8-1 illustrates these relations.

Wallace's many findings can only be summarized here. First, the direct link between status inconsistency and war, as reported earlier, remains, although weak. Systemic change in capability affects war *only* through status inconsistency, perhaps suggesting why the focus on that systemic variable alone in Chapter 5 failed to produce many significant relations.[4] Furthermore, status inconsistency does relate to alliance aggregation, which in turn relates to change in arms level, which in turn affects the level of war. These last two steps are quite strong, though when adding status inconsistency at the beginning it becomes a less potent predictor of war. In fact, the direct link between status inconsistency and war is stronger in almost all cases than when adding in the two intervening variables.

[2] Michael Wallace, "Status, Formal Organization, and Arms Levels as Factors Leading to the Onset of War, 1820–1964," in *Peace, War, and Numbers,* ed. Bruce Russett (Beverly Hills: Sage, 1972).

[3] J. David Singer and Melvin Small, "Alliance Aggregation and the Onset of War, 1815–1945," in *Quantitative International Politics: Insights and Evidence,* ed. J. David Singer (New York: The Free Press, 1968).

[4] Wallace, "Status, Formal Organization, and Arms Levels," p. 63.

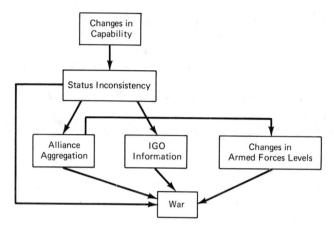

Figure 8-1. Potential model on system level for explanation of level of war.

Thus, in terms of a multivariate model, large discrepancies in capabilities do relate to status inconsistency, which in turn relates to the likelihood of war, both directly as well as through its effect on alliance aggregation and IGO formation. However, because in every case status inconsistency as well as the change in armament levels influenced war singly and independently, one might focus much more easily on these two variables—especially the latter—rather than modeling the system in a more complex way.

A somewhat more parsimonious and comprehensive illustration on the system level is "field" theory. Not a new theory in terms of the concepts involved, the notion of field nonetheless does add a new twist to some of the ideas we have already discussed. Most of the basic postulates and the variables of field theories are the same as those in Chapters 5 through 7. The variables involved—power, status, rank, integration, and similarity—are at the center of field theory and are now well-known to us. The most basic postulate of field theory, distance, is also well-known. Field theory combines several variables to create numerous distances between countries, and those distances represent the "field" within which states exist. Their position in that multidimensional field theoretically should account for their behavior.

To use an illustration from the individual level, we view people within "fields" all the time. A teen-age boy eating dinner with his parents is operating within a field. His behavior in that field is going to be quite different from what it is when he is eating a meal with his peer group or doing something else with that peer group, such as going to a movie or to a dance. The individual's behavior, in other words, is affected by the framework or field within which he is operating; change the field and the behavior changes. Another illustration of a field is the distance or relationship between student and teacher. Because the teacher has more power and greater status, the student's behavior toward him will be quite different from his behavior toward a friend or peer. Add in other variables—such as whether the teacher and the student hold similar political beliefs, and the behavior again is likely to change. Here the great differential in status combined with the very different political beliefs would produce interpersonal relations quite different from a situation of equal status levels and a very close similarity on belief. The important point in field theory is that behavior is a function of a multitude of forces all conceived in terms of distance.

Because the notion of a field appeals to our common sense, we use it to explain behavior all the time, although certainly without gracing it with the technical jargon of "field" or "distance." Quincy Wright was one of the first to formally suggest that field theoretic notions be used to understand international behavior, and he divided the fields into the geographical and the analytical fields. Wright's analytical field is most relevant here. The analytical approach to international relations, he says,

implies that each international organization, national government, association, individual or other "system of action," or "decision-maker," may be located in a multidimensional field. Such a field may be defined by co-ordinates, each of which measures a political, economic, psychological, sociological, ethical, or other continuum influencing choices, decisions, and actions important for international relations.[5]

He suggested several coordinates: material factors, such as military strength or technological advancement; moral factors, such as degree of reputability or reliability; and psychic factors, such as degree of satisfaction or anxiety. And he proposed several hypotheses reminiscent of power and social distance theories. For instance, he suggested that nations vulnerable to attack will become more and more hostile toward each other if they are "in psychic relations of opposition. If, on the other hand, geographic relations and technological conditions are such that each is relatively invulnerable to attack, psychic relations of opposition are not likely to lead to conflict." [6] Similarly, Wright contends that if the "psychic distances are diminishing more rapidly than strategic distances, peace becomes increasingly probable. But if strategic distances are diminishing more rapidly than psychic distances, war is probable." [7]

[5] Quincy Wright, "The Form of a Discipline of International Relations," in *International Politics and Foreign Policy: A Reader in Research and Theory*, rev. ed., ed. James Rosenau (New York: Free Press, 1969), p. 445.

[6] Ibid., p. 453.

[7] Ibid.

The empirical, systematic research on field theory, begun in the mid-1960s by R. J. Rummel and others, focused at first on international conflict behavior. The explanations offered for conflict were grounded in long-standing, traditional hypotheses about international behavior. However, because of Rummel's extensive use of the data-reduction technique of factor analysis,[8] with its assumption that empirically produced dimensions should have theoretical import, later research also included non-conflict dimensions, these being generated by the factor analysis technique. Another result of this reliance on factor analysis has been that the linkages between independent and dependent variables is less and less logically based on a prior verbal theory and more empirically grounded.

Much of the work of Rummel and others was highly mathematical, but it is not necessary for our purposes to dwell on that aspect. Basically, Rummel suggested that international relations consisted of a field comprised of *attribute* "space" and *behavior* "space." Attributes we are familiar with already (Chapter 4); nations possess numerous attributes and they differ from one another on attributes. These differences are central to field theory. Behavior space consists of the actions that pass between two nations, which can run the gamut from trade, mail, state visits, conferences, and tourist traffic to threats, accusations, military maneuvers, and war.

Attributes and behavior are brought together by the familiar concept of distance, for it is the distance between nations with regard to their attributes (or, more accurately, their attribute dimensions) that should predict their behavior. Put simply, the distance that exists between nations on their many attribute dimensions (as distinct from the single dimensions considered in Chapters 5 and 6) works as a "force" on their behavior.

Field theory is often confused with national attribute theory because similar data are used, but the manner of accounting for behavior in the two approaches is quite different. National attribute theory argues that behavior results solely from the properties of the nation. Field theory asserts that behavior is a function of the distance between countries on their attributes. Although attributes are used as the basic measure in each case, attribute theory continues to be founded on basic attribute data. Field theory, on the other hand, relies not on the basic attribute data as such but on the differences between countries on these attributes. As Rummel puts it:

Foreign conflict behavior . . . is not internally derived. Its genesis lies outside the nation. It is a *relational* phenomenon depending on the degree of economic,

[8] See appendix, paragraph C.

social, and political similarity between nations, the geographic distance between them, and their power parity. Participation in the system may increase the potentiality for conflict only. Whether conflict actually occurs depends in part on the social and value *distances* between the nations in contact and their relative power.[9]

To put it another way, it is hypothetically possible for two nations high on GNP to be more "distant" or "dissimilar" from one another than two nations that may be low on GNP and yet very close to one another. In spite of the fact that the first two have high GNPs and the second two low, the behavior—according to field theory—can be different between the two top countries not because their respective GNPs are high but because of the distance between them.

As the quote above from Rummel implies, field theory in his preliminary analyses was heavily grounded in the traditional concepts of values, rank, power, and geographic proximity. Distance on values clearly sets the stage for a conflict, for values include basic philosophical or ideological beliefs about political and economic systems. Power is considered as part of the rank dimension. Distance on power, therefore, acts in two ways: for rank, it is positive, for power alone it is negative. Power and rank may, therefore, cancel each other out. Power alone—absolutely, not in distance terms—may also operate as a force leading to conflict, for powerful nations are simply more capable of contact with other countries, even those geographically distant.[10] The sum of both nations' absolute power is called "joint power," and it acts as a force favoring conflict. Rummel's final variable was geographic proximity: the closer together two countries are physically, the more likely they are to engage in conflict behavior.

Rummel claimed that his first heuristic, preliminary test—on 91 dyads for the years 1955-1957—was heartening.[11] The most consistently significant variables were economic distance (rank), geographic distance, and value distance (vote in the U.N. on feminine rights). Slightly less significant were joint power and the value distance of self-government. The specific conflict dimensions (such as "communication" or "diplomatic" conflict) were slightly more strongly related than the calculated conflict magnitude—the summation of all four specific conflict dimensions—or the

[9] R. J. Rummel, "Some Dimensions in the Foreign Behavior of Nations," in *International Politics and Foreign Policy: A Reader in Research and Theory,* rev. ed., ed. James N. Rosenau (New York: Free Press, 1969), p. 612.

[10] In this case, Rummel's theory is not entirely on the systemic level, for power here is considered merely as an attribute. However, because the majority of the measures and the theory rest on the systemic level, the entire theory will be considered on that level.

[11] Rudolph Rummel, "A Social Field Theory of Foreign Conflict Behavior," *Peace Research Society Papers* 4 (1966), 131-50.

ordinal ranking assigned by Rummel. Though the vast majority of the variation of conflict was not accounted for, Rummel's findings did suggest some quite clear patterns, which were unlikely "chance" relationships.

Rummel's analysis of the largest errors—those dyads with the largest "residuals" showed that the least predicted dyads in every case were the most conflictual, such as the dyads involved in the Arab-Israeli War of 1956. Rummel contends that "the nature of the conflict between these nations suggests that there is a set of value-laden attributes that has not been tapped by the sub-analyses." [12]

That may be true, which may account for the inability of others, likewise, to account for the more violent types of conflict.[13] However, it may also be true that completely different variables are needed—and not just better measures of the value variable—implying that field theoretic notions cannot account for a certain range of behavior. A much more realistic view would see field theory as perhaps accounting for only some of the variation in conflict behavior, and that the remaining variation is going to be due to idiosyncracies, personalities, decision-making processes, or systemic variables such as bargaining that cannot be included within field theory.

In another test of field theory, Tong-Whan Park analyzed 342 dyads in the Asian subsystem for 1955 and 1963. He added the element of cooperation, constructing an index of "net conflict behavior"—the difference between conflict behavior and cooperation. Park's variables corresponded closely to Rummel's, although there were some differences.[14] For 1955, power parity accounted for most of the fairly small correlation (with fifteen independent variables, the multiple correlation was .16): the greater the parity, the greater the conflict. Almost the same results occurred for 1963, although the relationship was somewhat smaller. Analysis of Park's specific results also shows that in almost every case power parity emerged as the most important variable.

Moderately encouraging as these findings are—given the broad level on which field theory operates—they are nonetheless unsatisfactory in predicting much of the variation in foreign conflict behavior. Not surprisingly, the more recent testing of field theory, by Rummel as well as others, took a different turn on several points. First, the traditionally important variables of international politics—power, rank, values, geographic distance—were played down in favor of much more empirically

12 Ibid., p. 145.

13 Michael P. Sullivan, "Escalatory and Nonescalatory Conflict 'Systems,'" *American Journal of Political Science* 18 (August, 1974), pp. 549–58.

14 Tong-Whan Park, "Asian Conflict in Systemic Perspective: Application of Field Theory (1955 and 1963)," Mimeographed Research Report 35, Dimensionality of Nations Project (Honolulu: University of Hawaii, 1969).

derived dimensions produced from factor analysis. Many of these dimensions do correspond to traditional variables, but there is less *explicit* concern with the traditional variables as such. Factor analysis also produced less conflict-specific dimensions. Of thirteen measures of behavior, only two—negative sanctions and deterrence (military violence)—were explicitly conflict dimensions. Rather, Rummel came to focus largely on nonconflict dimensions such as salience (the number of translations of scholarly works done in another country), common IGO membership, and various other intercountry relations (students, emigrants, trade, and mail). This decision is sound, *if* we assume that the dimensions produced by the factor analyses are meaningful, both empirically and conceptually.

The best-predicted behaviors [15] are a combination of salience (relative number of translations) and international organization (common membership in IGOs); 63 percent of the variation on salience and international organization behavior for 182 dyads can be accounted for by differences on rank and power dimensions.[16] But none of the other behavior dimensions is at all accounted for, and when taken all together only 13 percent of their variation is accounted for by distances on attributes. It is of perhaps special note that none of the conflict dimensions were accounted for, including U.N. voting positions or actual conflict behavior.

Data considered separately in earlier chapters also support a field notion, but of a more limited nature. Sullivan, it will be recalled, investigated social distance and power distance in two sets of conflict dyads. He found that 60 and 71 percent of verbal and cooperative interactions in fifteen dyads were accounted for by social and power distance combined, and 40 percent of a scaled conflict index was accounted for. Social and power distances were unable to account for variation in the second set of conflicts.[17] North and Choucri found that for the major European nations from the late 1800s through 1914, changing levels of violence could be accounted for by distances on alliance commitments and defense allocations.[18]

Field theoretic approaches, therefore, appear to be able to account

[15] Because Rummel's interest in this case was accounting for a series of dependent variables rather than a single one, he used canonical regression analysis, which finds the best "fit" between a series of independent and a series of dependent variables. When this method is used subsequently, therefore, we must speak of the variables (plural) that are best explained by other variables.

[16] R. J. Rummel, "Field Theory and Indicators of International Behavior," Research Report 29 (Paper delivered before the Sixty-fifth Annual Meeting of the American Political Science Association, New York, September, 1969), p. 30.

[17] Sullivan, "Escalatory and Nonescalatory Conflict 'Systems.' "

[18] Nazli Choucri and Robert North, "Background Conditions to the Outbreak of the First World War," *Peace Research Society Papers* 9 (1968), pp. 125–37.

for international conflict behavior more readily when we consider the levels of violence rather than predicting to a range of cooperative to con-flictual behavior; or when confining oneself to geographical domains rather than the entire international system. Rummel later reduced the generality of his field theory—what he called Model I—by introducing a second Model which attempted to take into account cultural and his-torical differences between countries. Whereas Model I assumed that *general* field forces—distances—operated on all nations in the same way, Model II suggested these forces might change from country to country. An individual-level illustration might clarify this modification. Under the first model, we might hypothesize that individuals with a great dif-ferential in status between them and who differ drastically on their personality make-up will be hostile toward one another. This prediction would apply to all two-person situations. Under the revised model, each individual's behavior to other people must be considered separately; for John, for instance, the greater the status differential and the greater the personality differential, the greater the conflict, but for someone else—Jane—it may be that the greater the status and personality differential, the *less* the conflict. Although the theory is individual-specific, it still should predict one's behavior towards many other individuals, but predictions derived for one person may not apply to someone else.

In the international sphere, economic development (rank distance), for instance, would under Model I affect all dyads in the same way; countries with a higher rank will receive more conflict behavior. Under Model II, however, "differences in attributes are general forces all right, but their impact on the behavior of each nation is modified by forces within each nation." [19] To put it another way, the same general forces should work, but must be mediated by the nation itself. As Rummel explains:

Both China and Indonesia are affected by their attribute differences from other nations (that is, their socio-economic and political distances), but how these differences work themselves out in foreign policy outcomes toward other nations will differ for Indonesia and China due to their unique domestic policy environ-ments.[20]

Model II never deals with the entire sample of dyads under consideration. Rather, each nation must be taken separately in terms of its behavior to the other nations. For example, the importance of economic development may vary from country to country. United States behavior toward other nations might well be in line with that hypothesis, but another

---

[19] Rummel, "Field Theory and Indicators," p. 31.
[20] Ibid.

actor may respond completely differently to economic distances. While such a drastic difference is unlikely, the relative importance of variables is likely to change. Economic development distance may be the most important for the United States, but for Great Britain it may be geographic proximity and for China the most important may be value distance.

This variation is given great emphasis here because of its implications for the construction of theories. Quite obviously, Model II is a step down from a general theory. As such, it opens the way for the next logical question: If the variables and their relative importance depend on the actor, could not that apply also to the object? If the behavior of United States $\longrightarrow$ n countries is predicted and explained differently from the behavior of Great Britain $\longrightarrow$ n countries, then why shouldn't the behavior of United States $\longrightarrow$ India be explained differently than the behavior of the United States $\longrightarrow$ Israel? Such a theory no longer relies on general forces; in fact, it is no longer a theory because each case must be considered differently. Although Rummel certainly did not propose that step, no logical reason exists why it should not take place, *if* Model II likewise turned out to be a poor predictor.

The results of Model II on the 1955 data, not surprisingly, produced much higher relationships than Model I. Model II deals with each nations' foreign behavior to the other thirteen nations in the sample and therefore produces fourteen samples of thirteen dyads each. While the average correlations for the fourteen subsamples was high, nonetheless the number of observations is relatively small and the extreme values of the United States on many variables (such as GNP) might affect the correlation coefficients (see appendix, paragraph A and A.1). In fact, in generating four "distances" for each dyad simply from random numbers, Rummel noted that the correlations with the random numbers "are still uncomfortably high," [21] suggesting that one could achieve fairly high correlations merely by using random numbers, raising questions about the "significance" of the correlations he did uncover.

However, Models I and II are the extreme points running from the very broad-gauge theory to the very narrow theory. A middle ground would assume that in place of a separate model (actor $\longrightarrow$ n countries) for each actor, groups of actors with a similar foreign policy pattern might also be similar in other ways and therefore have similar weightings on the variables. Rummel arrived at eight different nation groups, in which the actors in each group shared similar attribute distances.[22] The

[21] Ibid., p. 36.

[22] The eight groupings are: U.K., Cuba, Israel, Brazil, and Poland; U.S.S.R., India, China, and Indonesia; U.S., Netherlands, Egypt; Jordan and Burma; China and U.S.S.R.; U.K. and Brazil; Burma and Indonesia; Poland and Israel.

average correlations for the groups dropped, although the respective random number correlations also decreased. The two groups with the best predictions were China-U.S.S.R. and U.K.-Brazil.

It is not surprising that Model II performs better but it is a much less general theory. Furthermore, comparing results of Model I in 1955 to 1963 illustrates an even further loss in generality. For 1955 the most consistently important variables were national income (power) and territorial distance (followed by rank and value), while for 1963, power and value distance were strongest, followed by rank and geographical distance. Relationships for specific actors also changed. For instance, power distance most strongly predicted China's conflict behavior in 1955, while in 1963 value distance was most important. For Brazil and Jordan the importance of geographical and power distance in 1955 gave way to value distance in 1963. For Cuba, geographic and economic development distance in 1955 was replaced by power distance as an important predictor in 1963. On the whole, the value dimension became much more important in 1963 in accounting especially for conflict behavior, while the importance of geographical proximity decreased. Perhaps most interesting, however, is that across both time periods the power dimension (measured by national income) is consistently important in predicting conflict behavior.

Sang-Woo Rhee replicated Model II with China as the acting country toward eighty-one object nations.[23] Power disparity was the most important variable, highly related to both China's trade and negative communications behavior. The values of the United States and the Soviet Union severely affected the results, however. After reducing these values to take out their extreme effect, Rhee found one pattern in which the more powerful the object nation and the more it was oriented toward the non-Communist bloc, the more China would trade with it and direct negative communication toward it. A second pattern was that socialist camp countries receiving aid from the U.S.S.R. would receive more trade and more diplomats and less negative communication from China, not a particularly surprising relationship. The third pattern, not as strong as the first, was even less surprising: Asian neighbors identifying with China and the Communist bloc in the Cold War would receive more diplomats, trade, aid, and have more common NGO memberships with China.

Vincent and his associates found that significant relationships emerged in a Model II test primarily on a cooperation dimension but not on the

[23] Sang-Woo Rhee, "Communist China's Foreign Behavior: An Application of Field Theory, Model II," mimeographed; Research Report 57, Dimensionality of Nations Project (Honolulu: University of Hawaii, 1971).

conflict dimensions.[24] This finding confirms at least one of Rummel's already related—that the best-predicted dependent variable was a cooperation dimension.

Don Munton found Canada's foreign behavior toward fifty-one countries related to distances on status, affinity, similarity, and proximity dimensions.[25] His behavior dimensions were commitment (basically a word-deeds continuum), and conflict-cooperation. Forty-five percent of Canada's commitment to other nations and 39 percent of its conflict-cooperation behavior could be accounted for by these four variables. Without a doubt the most important in each case was the status differential between Canada and the object nation—measured by energy consumption per capita, gross national income, and the number of embassies and legations in the nation's capital. The more status a country has over Canada, the more committed Canada will be toward that country, *and* the more conflictual. The second most important variable, affinity—measured by IGO memberships, U.N. vote agreement, and press freedom—indicated that the greater the affinity between Canada and the object nation, the greater Canada's commitment toward the other nation and the *less* the conflict.[26]

Rummel's Model II is clearly a better representation of the world, though, as we have pointed out, it has three major flaws. First, it views each actor (or group of actors) differently. Second, its findings show that while some patterns exist across actors, and some dimensions—notably power—are consistently important, relationships and best predictors change from actor to actor. Third, its findings indicate that relationships change even with one actor when moving from one time period to another. Such findings are certainly a long way from the deterministic laws—supposedly applicable to all nations—that a general field theory implies. Such a theory, therefore, has not been well supported, even though it is still possible that its problems are of an operational nature and not theoretical.

Thus, field theory can be considered from two perspectives: as a general theory applicable to all states at all times, which implies a very deterministic state of affairs, or as a less general theory, which means

[24] Jack Vincent, Roger Baker, Susan Gagnon, Keith Hamm, and Scott Reilly, "Empirical Tests of Attribute, Social Field, and Status Field Theories on International Relations Data," *International Studies Quarterly* 17 (December, 1973), p. 434.

[25] Don Munton, "Waiting for Kepler: Event Data and Relational Model Explanations of Canadian Foreign Policy Behavior" (Paper presented at the International Studies Association meeting, New York, March, 1973).

[26] Similarity and proximity were almost unrelated to the commitment behavior, but similarity was slightly related to conflict: the greater the similarity, the less the conflict.

that in addition to being more nation-specific it is also probabilistic rather than deterministic. Even if the majority of variation in any given behavior is not accounted for by field theory, the approach is in no way invalidated as *one* way in which to account for state behavior. Unaccounted variation is due to factors that cannot be tapped by such systemic approaches.

Despite the intuitive and parsimonious appeal of the field theory, several drawbacks must be pointed out. One drawback is that it is difficult to consider triads (as, for instance, in balance theory). In other words, the theory cannot truly reflect certain complexities in international politics, because behavior is sometimes a function of the existence, goals, threats, or distance of a third or fourth party.

Second, as Vincent has pointed out, attributes change very little over the short-term, say five to ten years, and yet there are numerous instances where dyadic behavior changes drastically during such short periods. Thus, concerning the domain of international behavior that field theory can account for, it may be much more applicable cross-sectionally than longitudinally, which means that it is much better at accounting for variation in behavior at one point in time rather than variation through time. Figure 8-2 illustrates China's behavior toward numerous other countries along a cooperative dimension, as predicted by a bloc affiliation score. Each set of connected lines indicates China's score on the two variables for the five years. Toward the Soviet Union as an object country, for instance, China was least cooperative in the years 1963 and 1965, and most cooperative in 1955 and 1960. Note that countries tend to line themselves up on the perfect prediction line in the way we would expect, with Taiwan receiving the least cooperation, followed by the United Kingdom, India, the United States, Poland, North Korea, and the U.S.S.R. The bloc affiliation score makes a fairly good prediction to the formal cooperation score (i.e., U.S.S.R. is higher in every year than the United States in bloc affiliation with China, and Sino-Soviet formal cooperation is higher than Sino-American).

The important point in Figure 8-2, however, is that with the exception of the United Kingdom, the United States (for three of the five years), and possibly North Korea, the changes in formal cooperation from year to year *for each actor* are not related to changes in bloc affiliation score. This ability to predict cross-sectionally at one point in time but not longitudinally across time is illustrated further by comparing Figures 8-3 and 8-4. Figure 8-3 shows the data for each country from Figure 8-2 for the year 1960. Note that the countries line up along the prediction line fairly well, which means that knowing the bloc affiliation score for that year gives a pretty good idea of where the country would be in terms of China's formal cooperation with it.

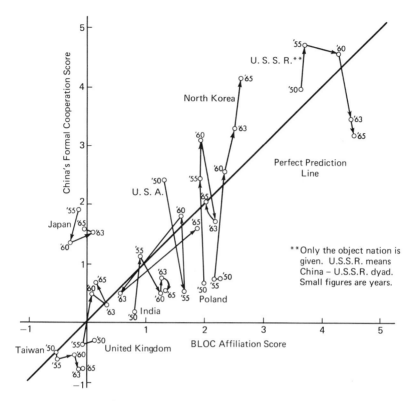

Source: Sang-Woo Rhee, "China's Cooperation, Conflict, and Interaction Behavior, Viewed from Rummel's Field Theoretical Perspective," Research Project No. 64, Dimensionality of Nations Project, University of Hawaii, January, 1973.

Figure 8-2.   China's bloc politics: formal cooperation pattern.

Figure 8-4, however, shows China's formal cooperative behavior toward the United States and North Korea for five years. From 1950 to 1955 the U.S.'s bloc affiliation score with China hardly changed, and yet China's cooperation with it did change. However, the years 1960, 1963, and 1965 show that the higher the bloc affiliation score (1960, 1965) the higher the cooperation. For North Korea, however, the bloc affiliation score is almost constant throughout the full five years and yet the formal cooperation changes more drastically than any other country; in other words, we can explain why North Korea has a higher cooperation score with China than Taiwan, for instance, but knowledge of bloc affiliation does not allow us to explain that drastic shift in China's cooperation with North Korea.

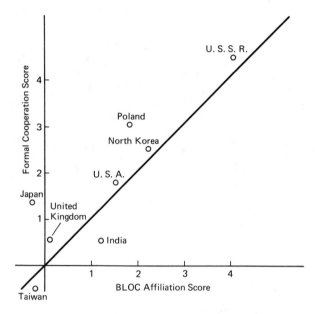

Source: This figure is adapted from Sang-Woo Rhee,
"China's Cooperation, Conflict, and Interaction Behavior,
Viewed from Rummel's Field Theoretical Perspective,"
mimeographed (Honolulu, Hawaii: University of Hawaii,
1973), p. 93.

Figure 8-3. China's formal cooperation and bloc affiliation score, 1960, with eight object countries.

These data suggest, then, that despite the strength that field theory
may have at one point in time to account for foreign behavior variation
across countries, it breaks down when trying to account for variation in
countries *across time.* Although not true for all of the countries in Figure
8-2, the pattern holds for most of them.

In almost every study surveyed, some variant of power was either the
most important of many variables or the only significant one. Even
Munton, although labeling it "status," was in a sense talking about power.
Two of the three measures loading high on his status dimension, national
income and energy consumption, have very commonly been equated with
power. It is possible, therefore, that what may emerge with future testing
is a field theoretic approach concentrating heavily on the variable of
power, and that position in a field will be found to be not as important
as position or distance on an extremely small number of dimensions.

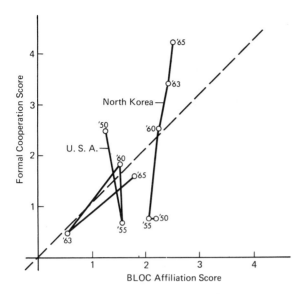

Source: This figure is adapted from Sang-Woo Rhee, "China's Cooperation, Conflict, and Interaction Behavior, Viewed from Rummel's Field Theoretical Perspective," mimeographed (Honolulu, Hawaii: University of Hawaii, 1973), p. 93.

Figure 8-4. China's formal cooperation and bloc affiliation score with U.S.A. and North Korea, 1950–1965.

Cross-Level Analysis

A much more difficult approach to utilize systematically in trying to understand international behavior is one that combines variables from several different levels of analysis. Experimental gaming provides the easiest opportunity to combine levels of analysis, such as the simulation of counterattack situations set up by Charles Hermann and his associates.[27] In using variables from the individual, decision-making, national, and systemic levels, they were able to account for roughly one-half of the variation in the decision to counterattack on warning. Of all the variables, basic capabilities (referring to productive resources of a nation,

27 Charles Hermann, Margaret Hermann, and Robert A. Cantor, "Counterattack or Delay: Characteristics Influencing Decision Makers' Responses to the Simulation of an Unidentified Attack," *Journal of Conflict Resolution* 18 (March, 1974), pp. 75–106.

and measured by the national attribute of GNP) was the strongest predictor, followed by the perception (by the simulation decision-makers) that the situation was ambiguous. Next in importance were the personality variable of self-esteem, and force capabilities. The final two significant variables were decision-making style and perceived tensions. Variables that appeared to be insignificant in accounting for the decision to counterattack or delay counterattack were the personality variable of cognitive complexity, the perception of the situation as accidental, and the perceived number of alternatives, as well as the systemic variable of the nation's isolation. In sum, no one level seemed to be completely excluded in accounting for this singular type of decision in a simulation experiment; at the same time both national attribute and individual-level variables seemed to be the most important.

Testing multiple variables from different levels in the real world, of course, is much more difficult. Wilkenfeld and his colleagues tested, on several Middle East countries, the hypothesis of national attribute theory which sees foreign conflict as a function of domestic conflict, against the stimulus-response model of bargaining theory (Chapters 4 and 7). They found that stimulus-response was a better predictor of a nation's foreign conflict behavior than was domestic strife. North and Choucri also compared state-level attributes against distances between attributes, and concluded that "only under certain circumstances are domestic pressures direct contributors to international conflict, and . . . these are clearly secondary to tension variables—defense preparedness and alignments." In a later, much more expanded version of their work, they combined the organizational variable of *past* military expenditure in a nation, the nation-level variables of density, technological advances, number of alliances and military expenditures, along with the system-level variables of other nations' military expenditure and violence to try to account for such behaviors as present levels of colonial expansion (during the 1870–1914 period), military expenditure, and violence. While they found that the important variables differed somewhat from country to country, as well as from one time period to another (not unlike earlier findings for field theories), nonetheless they did find some general patterns. The national attribute variable of density tended to affect expansion (extent of colonial area), and while a nation's violence was affected by such domestic factors as military expenditures, nonetheless the systemic factors of non-allies' military expenditures and the violence of others (stimulus-response) "generally predominate." They suggest a rather complicated cross-level model in which military expenditures and alliance behaviors are generated by domestic growth, but those two behaviors in turn foster violence in other nations, which in turn produces increases in one's own violence. However, it did appear that in terms of *direct* effects, the stimulus-response variables of military expenditures of non-allies and the violence of other nations seemed to be the strongest variables leading to a nation's violence.[28]

In a somewhat similar test, East and Gregg found that behavior was more a function of a country's international situation than of domestic sources (although admittedly some of their measures differ from what has been defined here as international distance).[29] Tanter also attempted a combination of levels by testing stimulus-response against the state-level variable of "organization process." [30] In his case, the findings were not very clear-cut, but that may have been as much a function of the problems with the research design as with the original theoretical underpinnings.

Rosenau and Hoggard compared the potency of national attributes (size, development, and accountability) to the systemic variables of proximity, socio-political similarity, and equal-unequal power relationships.[31] Their hypotheses for attribute theory were that large, developed, closed systems would have the least amount of cooperative behavior, and the most amount of conflict. Similarly, small, underdeveloped, and open systems would have the most amount of cooperative behavior and the least amount of conflictual behavior. For the systemic variables, they hypothesized that remote, similar, equal dyads would have the most amount of cooperative behavior and the least amount of conflict, and that the proximate, dissimilar, and unequal would have the smallest amount of cooperation and the highest amount of conflict.

Though they conclude that neither the national attributes nor the systemic approach is patently more potent than the other, there are "tendencies that are worth noting" and that "national attributes are somewhat more potent sources of both foreign conflict and cooperative behavior than are relational attributes." [32] They come to this conclusion in investigating the relationship between attributes and behavior controlling for the effect of the systemic variable; the average correlation

[28] Nazli Choucri and Robert C. North, "The Determinants of International Violence," *Peace Research Society Papers* 12 (1969), p. 56; Nazli Choucri and Robert North, *Nations in Conflict: National Growth and International Violence* (San Francisco: Freeman, 1975), especially p. 249.

[29] Maurice East and Phillip Gregg, "Factors Influencing Cooperation and Conflict in the International System," *International Studies Quarterly* 11 (September, 1967), pp. 244–69.

[30] Raymond Tanter, "International System and Foreign Policy Approaches: Implications for Conflict Modelling and Management," *World Politics* 24 (Spring, 1972, Supplement), pp. 7–39.

[31] James N. Rosenau and Gary D. Hoggard, "Foreign Policy Behavior in Dyadic Relationships: Testing a Pre-Theoretical Extension," in *Comparing Foreign Policies, Theories, Findings, and Methods,* ed. James N. Rosenau (New York: Wiley, 1974).

[32] Ibid., p. 141.

is .69. When they take out the effect of the attribute variables, however, and correlate the systemic variables with conflict, the average correlation is only .45. Two factors raise serious doubt as to the validity of that conclusion. The first is theoretical: their hypotheses linking attributes to levels of conflict and cooperation are much more plausible than linking distance variables to such levels. It is much more conceivable that large and wealthy countries are going to be more active in the system—of any type of behavior—than it is to expect equal or similar nations to interact more with each other.

The second factor flows from the first, and it is a problem that Rosenau and Hoggard note.[33] As has been reiterated at numerous points, it is crucial to understand what the dependent variable is. For Rosenau and Hoggard, that behavior is merely gross levels of action. If we form a ratio of conflict to cooperative acts, however, the relations between the predicted and actual rankings for conflict they suggested for the systemic variables are actually higher than for the national attribute variables (r_s = .45 for the systematic and .24 for attributes, compared to the .36 and .93 correlations reported by Rosenau and Hoggard). Furthermore, the average correlation reported by Rosenau and Hoggard between attributes and gross level of conflict, controlling for the systemic variables, is .69; taking conflict as a ratio to cooperative behavior, however, this drops to an average of .22. Even so, the systemic variables, when related to conflict controlling for the effect of attributes remains low: the average .45 reported by Rosenau-Hoggard drops drastically to .007.

In sum, the Rosenau-Hoggard finding that attributes are more potent predictors to levels of conflict and cooperation than are systemic variables is not particularly startling because it was unlikely that systemic variables would predict levels in the first place. In fact, it would appear on reanalysis that systemic relations do carry at least as much weight as attribute variables in accounting for ratios of conflict to cooperation.

Unfortunately, it is very difficult at the present point in time to go beyond these preliminary analyses. There are, quite simply, few systematic, empirical studies attempting to test complex models using multiple variables. While complex, multivariate, cross-level models have always been done verbally, there are serious disadvantages to such a strategy. First, variables are not always explicitly tied into larger theoretical concerns, such as those outlined here. Second, though the explanations are plausible they rarely include systematic attempts to measure the variables. Third, as presented, there is really no way to allow for nonconfirmation of the hypotheses. Finally, there is no way of assessing the

33 Ibid., p. 142.

strength of competing explanations. We therefore end up with complex verbal models, which, as has been apparent throughout, have severe shortcomings. Ad hoc, verbal models, therefore, combine multiple variables in little more than a plausible fashion, as illustrated in Kal Holsti's explanation of Soviet foreign policy:

> during the 1930s the structure of the [international] system (as interpreted in Marxist terms), national needs, traditional policies, and Stalin's personality and political role were the most important aspects of reality considered by Soviet policy makers in selecting goals and diplomatic strategies.[34]

Holsti quite easily moves through several different levels—the international system, "national needs" on the state level, and Stalin's personality and role on the individual level—to account for Soviet foreign policy, a fact which was not lost on him. "In the absence of systematic, comparative analysis of foreign policies in different countries," he concluded, it was very difficult for the analyst to make an assessment about which of the many variables, and under which circumstances, carries the greatest weight. His assessments, therefore, remain only propositions until tested.

Nowhere does ad hoc analysis show up more frequently than in government studies of international political questions. Michael O'Leary and his colleagues, in addressing the question of the "relevance" of social science research to foreign policy operatives, call attention to the "most demanding" types of analyses done by the State Department's Bureau of Intelligence and Research. Indeed, most of the bureau's analyses "represent such complexity that no single quantitative work in the social sciences could even begin to test their validity." [35] They cite several governmental studies in which there are a multitude of variables, several different levels of analysis and all showing relationships between variables and levels quite frequently and quite plausibly. Such multivariate models present numerous problems, however. If seen as a beginning and not as the final explanation, though, they can be helpful for constructing more complex descriptions and explanations of international behavior.

Several illustrations show how complex multivariate models might be tested. One possibility, for example, would be to combine the system-level variable of power distribution with the state-level variable of

---

34 Kal Holsti, *International Politics: A Framework for Analysis*, 2d ed. (Englewood Cliffs, N.J.: Prentice-Hall, 1972), p. 393.

35 Michael K. O'Leary, William D. Coplin, Howard B. Shapiro, and Dale Dean, "The Quest for Relevance: Quantitative International Relations Research and Government Foreign Affairs Analysis," *International Studies Quarterly* 18 (June, 1974), p. 228.

decision-making trends and the effect of organizational processes on decisional outcomes. A power distribution of high and stable concentration may produce a tendency toward greater reliance on organizational processes within the larger developed states, which means that foreign policies are likely to remain stable and undergo change only slowly, and that the level of conflict within the system—because of the combination of these two "stabilizing" agents—is likely to be low.

As the international power structure changes to *less* concentration and less stability, however, decision-making processes on the state level undergo changes away from reliance on organizational procedures and more on ad hoc decision-making. When that occurs, foreign policies will not remain as stable and—again because of the confluence of the two *de*stabilizing agents—the level of instability and conflict in the international system is likely to rise.

The behavior to be explained here is the level or probability of a given state's engaging in foreign conflict. The biggest problem in testing the model would be how to assess the level of "organizational processes." One suggestion might be to use the percent of expenditures by federal governments going directly into the entire bureaucratic system; as that percentage rises, there should be a great reliance on organizational process. Yet another model might combine the power distribution with the individual level variable of perception. International systems with power distributed widely are likely to cause a greater disparity between the decision-makers' perception of reality and actual reality (the S-r link in Chapter 2). Although we presented evidence earlier that the S-R link seemed to be stronger than the r-R link across more cases, nonetheless it may be that if data on a large number of cases were available, that certain nations—or nations in certain situations, such as the high involved-low involved category used in Chapter 2—might exhibit a stronger link between the perception of the incoming stimulus and the resultant response to the stimulus. Thus, as power becomes more and more distributed, that S-r link would become more tenuous—which might lead in some states to a situation where the link between stimulus and response becomes more tenuous, thus leading to more unpredictable foreign policy outputs.

Then, moving one step further by using the definition of crisis outlined by McClelland earlier, we would find more unpredictable foreign policy on the part of some states leading to a wider array of response on the part of responding states, resulting in more crises in the system. Thus, through this rather circuitous route, we move from power distribution on the system level through perceptual data on the individual level to result in a greater number of crises.

Combining power distance with state-level attribute variables could be even more complicated by including variation in personality types.[36] Although extremely difficult to operationalize across a large number of states, nonetheless, if personality "profile-typing" is at all reliable, several groups of dyads could be isolated for separate analysis, such as those with a small number, and those with a large number of deviant personalities. If personality affects behavior, even in combination with the other variables, then the results in the separate groups must be different. If they are not different, then either the measures of personality are bad, or personality has little or no impact. Further complications would, of course, control for situation, especially "crisis-noncrisis."

Personality could also be included in a multivariate design in other ways. Hypothesizing that deviant personalities are less likely to perceive accurately what is happening in the world, and that their responses are less likely to be in line with the stimuli they receive, one could combine a "deviant personality" control with investigations of the stimulus-response theory of bargaining. The assumption here would be that stimulus-response predictions would be more "accurate" under nondeviant personality situations than otherwise. Predictions from stimulus to response (Chapter 7) in control situations of deviant personalities would be much less accurate.

The real complexities emerge, of course, when combining many variables and levels and including feedbacks within the model. Figure 8-5

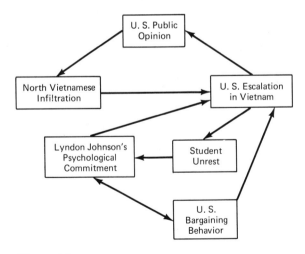

Figure 8-5.

36 Margaret Hermann, "Leader Personality and Foreign Policy Behavior," in *Comparing Foreign Policies, Theories, Findings, and Methods*, ed. James N. Rosenau (New York: Wiley, 1974).

illustrates one possibility having to do with the escalation of an ongoing conflict, in this case Vietnam. Two variables operate directly on the escalation in Vietnam: North Vietnamese infiltration (functioning as the stimulus to the United States response of escalating), and the symbolic commitment of the decision-maker to the conflict. A third variable might also instigate further U.S. escalation, namely, the verbal bargaining behavior the decision-maker uses in an attempt to influence the other side. His behavior is correlated with the escalation because he must escalate in order to make his bargaining "credible."

Yet the escalation itself also has a feedback effect on numerous variables that ultimately can work their way back on the escalatory behavior. U.S. public opinion in favor of intervention in Vietnam dropped, for instance, as U.S. military escalation continued. Those two factors in turn may have spurred the North Vietnamese to infiltrate, assuming they sensed that the United States was "giving in." Another internal variable strongly affected by the escalation was student unrest, which in turn may have affected President Johnson's further symbolic commitment to the war. Another complication, this one systemic, might be introduced: the long-term cyclical trend in violence in the international system.[37] The dependent variable of "U.S. escalation in Vietnam," therefore, might also be responsive to the level of the exogenous variable, "violence in the system." As violence increased, the likelihood of a leveling and gradual decline in the dependent variable in Figure 8-5 becomes greater. "Violence in the system" is also influenced, of course, by the dependent variable itself.

Model-building exercises such as these are far from useless as long as they are only viewed as *postulated* models and are not equated—as they so often are—with the actual *explanation* of international behavior. They remain ad hoc verbal descriptions until the variables have been specified so they can be measured and the different variations of the model tried out. The advantage of going beyond mere verbal models to their graphical specification and empirical testing is the possibility of eliminating one or more variables contained in the model. Several instances were cited, for example, where systemic variables seemed to be more powerful than state-level variables. This circumstance suggests that all variables do not have "some" or "equal" impact, but rather that systemic ones carry more weight, at least in some domains. While the primary problem in testing multivariate models has been methodological, the

[37] J. David Singer and Melvin Small, *The Wages of War, 1816–1965: A Statistical Handbook* (New York: Wiley, 1972); Frank Denton, "Some Regularities in International Conflict, 1820–1949," *Background* 9 (February, 1966), pp. 283–96; and Frank Denton and Warren Phillips, "Some Patterns in the History of Violence," *Journal of Conflict Resolution* 12 (June, 1968), pp. 182–95.

move from simple bivariate to multivariate analysis also carries a greater theoretical burden. It requires specifying linkages between the variables, including possible feedback loops—as Figure 8-5 illustrates.

This section, therefore, has only been able to suggest ways in which multivariate, cross-level tests might or should be done. Time could have been spent spinning numerous additional models, but without empiral tests these would be little more than possibilities. And certainly the testing of the almost infinite number of models that could be generated would be far beyond the scope of this book.

Conclusion

This chapter has presented two broad perspectives on how to bring single variables together into a multivariate analysis. In a sense, it pulled together the discussions in the previous chapters, which treated approaches to the study of international relations in isolation from one another. Perhaps the most important point to emerge here is that solving the "puzzles" of international behavior is drastically complex, and systematically modeling that complex behavior is extremely difficult. Plausible verbal models are quite easy to formulate, but without much question one direction of future research will be toward expanding and testing complex models. Though the elaboration and testing of such models of international behavior are the ultimate goal, the building blocks of these models will be the theories and research reviewed in the preceding chapters.

part III *Conclusion*

Final chapters in general books on international relations often discuss such general topics as "the future of mankind," "the possibility and promises of world government," "the future of international politics," "the problems and prospects of peace," or issues that are very time-specific such as arms control and disarmament in the 1960s or international pollution and energy problems in the 1970s. We shall not consider these topics in the usual way. This is not to say that "the future of mankind," for instance, is uninteresting or unimportant. Rather, it is to suggest that these subjects can be approached from a different perspective. Normally they are considered as appendages, as afterthoughts to a finished text, with little clear linkage to what has gone before. We shall attempt to avoid that pitfall and show how these topics are an integral part of the theories of international behavior reviewed throughout the preceding chapters.

The final subject of this conclusion will focus on several issues that concern both scholars and policy-makers, and will try to illustrate the linkages between these substantive topics and the theoretical issues of the past seven chapters. First, however, let us reiterate some of the points made in the introductory chapter, but from the perspective of having considered the several theories in the intervening chapters. With these chapters in mind, we will again discuss some of the premises of our approach to international politics, and the problems inherent with that approach. Second, we will discuss the importance, advantages, and handicaps of the different methods. Third, we will compare the different theories in terms of the domain of behavior to which they are most applicable.

PREMISES AND PROBLEMS

We have been primarily concerned in this book with accounting for the variation in the behavior of states, international systems and individuals acting, usually, in the name of the state. Something is causing the differences we see. If a nation's diplomacy is changing, then something is causing that change; if states move toward a world community, then something is causing it to move in that direction; if national actors become cooperative, then something is causing them to shift their stance.

Our basic premise is that individuals, states, or international systems will always *behave*, and it is that behavior that is of central concern to the scholar of international politics. Some may feel that the emphasis given to the nation-state reflects a narrow (and outmoded) bias. With the rise in importance in recent years of multinational organizations, terrorist and guerrilla groups, and international organizations, there has risen a concomitant interest in them as international "actors." Yet, as recent evidence suggests, the vast majority of research on international behavior—especially of a quantitative nature—focuses on the behavior either of national leaders or of the state itself, either singly or aggregated into larger international systems.[1] The perspectives presented here reflect that research. Furthermore, a content analysis of almost any daily newspaper would almost certainly show that the public's chief interest in international politics relates to the types of behavior investigated in this book.

A subsidiary premise pertains to one of the general problems in discussing international relations. Although there is great dispute regarding this premise, we have assumed that conflict is one type of international behavior that will be with us for a long time; as a consequence, we have given no attention to schemes or ideas thought to be capable of producing the millennium of "world peace." This does not mean that we like or want war, only that our premise is the result of a logical and empirical analysis of contemporary research into international politics, and a scanning of the daily newspapers. It is helpful to keep that assumption in the forefront of our thinking for it is too easy to get sidetracked into unsolvable issues and utopian schemes.

[1] John R. Handelman, John A. Vasquez, Michael K. O'Leary, and William D. Coplin, "Color It Morgenthau: A Data-Based Assessment of Quantitative International Relations Research," Prince Research Studies 11, mimeographed (Syracuse: Syracuse University, 1973) pp. 15a–15b.

Arend Lijphart's analysis of changes in international relations theory illustrates this problem. Many traditional theories of international relations, such as balance of power and collective security, are not really theories at all. Lijphart, citing T. S. Kuhn, observes that "research guided by a paradigm resembles puzzle-solving." [2] He adds: "Puzzles must have assured solutions, but the solutions need not be intrinsically important." [3] Then, citing Kuhn again, he suggests: "On the contrary, the really pressing problems, i.e., . . . the design of a lasting peace, are often not puzzles at all, largely because they may not have any solution." [4]

"Theories" such as collective security, Lijphart notes, were predicated on the assumption that final peace was in fact possible, and that only the details needed to be worked out, the specific "methods" or "techniques" figured out, or the "right" people convinced on the "right" ideas. Each one of these schemes however, contains a series of "if only" propositions: "if only" states would act in a certain way; "if only" the great powers would band together; "if only" those allied would abide by their agreement; "if only" large powers would not sell arms to small powers. Those who view these schemes as central to "peace" and therefore central to international politics research fail to recognize that the underlying propositions may be incorrect. Things don't work out the way the schemes say they do, just as the football team's plays don't work out on the field as they do on the coach's chalkboard. It is not the scholar's role to lament that fact but to find out why, which means solving "puzzles."

Thus, explaining behavior is really solving a puzzle. Yet another premise, therefore, has been that these puzzles can be solved. But we have warned throughout that answering questions about international behavior systematically—that is, truly solving the puzzles or finding out what really causes what—often goes much beyond common-sense, everyday explanations. We have not argued they are completely *different,* only that they sometimes go beyond the common sense. The previous chapter illustrated the problem by showing that common, ad hoc, multivariate explanations are extremely easy to verbalize, but very difficult to operationalize and test, especially when they involve different levels of analysis. The presentation of the numerous theories in the earlier chapters did not have as its goal the solving of explicit issues or puzzles. They were presented in order to provide the reader with some of the basic

---

[2] Arend Lijphart, "The Structure of the Theoretical Revolution in International Relations," *International Studies Quarterly* 18 (March, 1974), p. 55; citing T. S. Kuhn, *The Structure of Scientific Revolutions* (Chicago: University of Chicago Press, 1970), pp. 36–37.

[3] Lijphart, "Structure of Theoretical Revolution," p. 55.

[4] Ibid.

theoretical perspectives needed to solve these puzzles. It would take an entirely different volume to carry out that larger chore.

Because these are complex puzzles, the only way in which to really solve them is through continual research. Many scholars, however, are reluctant to research someone else's ideas, or to replicate a study already done. It is partly for this reason that evidence confirming or disconfirming many of the theories of international behavior is slim indeed. While part of the problem of replication may be a failure of original research- ers to spell out their own techniques, more likely it is a result of the lowly status that replication holds in the social sciences. As Karl Deutsch laments:

> We suffer from the curse of enforced originality which makes it a crime for a graduate student to replicate somebody else's experiment and forces the unhappy man to think up a new wrinkle on every experiment. I wish we could get an inter-university agreement that we expect everybody who earns a degree to do two things: first, to replicate honestly one experiment in social science and then, if he must, invent a new one. If physicists and chemists had not replicated each other's experiments, they would still be in the age of alchemy.[5]

Many will no doubt dispute the comparison with physics and chemistry —and the dispute could go on forever—but the suggestion is an intriguing one.

The systematic use of theories to solve puzzles is a quite different task, then, from the use of them only as verbal descriptions of plausible ex- planations. The acquisition of information necessary to solve the puzzles is often very difficult, and the complex data analysis and model building needed to reflect the world add even further burdens. Nonetheless, the analyst's goal should be the solution of the problem rather than the con- stant reiteration of the theme that they are insolvable.

METHODOLOGY

The term "methodology" has taken on a rather narrow meaning in recent years. It usually implies a certain statistical or quantifiable "method" of doing research. We use the term here, however, much more broadly to indicate an entire outlook on how to do research in a very general sense. To understand differences in behavior, we have used the

[5] Karl Deutsch, "Recent Trends in Research Methods in Political Science," in *A Design for Political Science*, ed. J. S. Charlesworth (Philadelphia: American Academy of Political and Social Science, 1966), p. 42; cited in Patrick J. McGowan and Howard B. Shapiro, *The Comparative Study of Foreign Policy: A Survey of Scientific Findings* (Beverly Hills: Sage, 1973), p. 219.

broad methodological perspective of proposing theories and then testing them, which as pointed out above, goes beyond presenting plausible possibilities.

As also noted, however, there are drawbacks in using the criterion of testability for evaluating theories. Empirical data can often be inaccurate and "loose," and it takes time and energy to do more than a simple statistical analysis of data. Despite these reservations, there are real advantages to using testability as a criterion because it necessitates at least *some* modicum of objectivity, some need to replicate, and some effort to achieve accuracy in measurement.

Even so, the methodology of the empirical test is methodology only in the most general sense. We have also given great attention to what many may feel are small methodological differences in research. What may appear at first glance to be a very minor difference, however, can have profound effects on the results and the interpretation of those results. The way in which a question is answered is often dependent on the way in which the evidence is handled, both in traditional as well as contemporary research. In traditional research evidence is sometimes handled selectively, consideration is not often given to "sampling" effect, and implicit models are often imposed on evidence and not often scrutinized for their reliability. In contemporary research, the problem is often the choice of a statistical test or model. Holsti and his associates, for example, imply on the basis of one statistical test that the perceptions of national leaders in 1914 were important for understanding an alliance's later behavior.[6] Yet we saw in Chapter 2 that on the basis of another test that in both the Dual Alliance and the Triple Entente perceptions were no more important in explaining the alliances' later level of response than the external stimulus.

Other illustrations also come to mind. Rosenau and Hoggard's conclusion that internal sources of foreign policy appeared more potent than systemic variables was true because their hypotheses more plausibly linked internal attributes to a higher level of foreign conflict and cooperative actions, behavior that is not as plausibly related to systemic, dyadic variables.[7] Another example would be Harf's analysis showing that the relationship between IGO membership and war differs, depending on whether IGO membership is aggregated for the whole inter-

[6] Ole Holsti, Robert North, and Richard Brody, "Perception and Action in the 1914 Crisis," in *Quantitative International Politics: Insights and Evidence,* ed. J. David Singer (New York: Free Press, 1968), pp. 152–57.

[7] James N. Rosenau and Gary Hoggard, "Foreign Policy Behavior in Dyadic Relationships: Testing a Pre-Theoretical Extension," in *Comparing Foreign Policies: Theories, Findings, and Methods,* ed. James N. Rosenau (New York: Wiley, 1974).

national system or aggregated by country.[8] Harf found that across thirteen five-year periods between 1900 and 1964 the level of war decreased as the average number of nations in international governmental organizations increased. However, taking the nation as the unit of analysis rather than the system, during the same period the more IGOs a nation was a member of, compared with all other nations, the greater its involvement in wars. Despite Harf's conclusion—that relationships at one level of analysis are not necessarily present at another level—his analysis in a sense has not tested the same relationship, although it appears to have done so. If one sees IGO membership as a cooperative and tension-reducing device, then we find confirmation of that on the systemic level, with negative correlations. However, when positive correlations show up on the state level of analysis, Harf concludes the relationship is not confirmed. However, IGO membership is related to size and development —large, economically developed states will join more IGOs—and evidence from national attribute theory suggests that large and developed states participate in a greater number of warlike acts. What Harf may have been testing in using the state rather than the system as the unit of analysis was the relationship between size and war, which of course turns out to be, as expected, a positive one.

These problems do not mean that research is useless, but only that methodology is important in framing the exact research question and in utilizing the means for achieving an accurate and valid answer to the question. An orientation toward stricter testing often results in a specific research question, which forces an explicit delineation of how the test of the question is to be done. We have tried at several points in each chapter to point out methodological decisions that may have influenced the results, and parts of the appendix are devoted to an elaboration of these problems.

A final general theme relating to the testing of theories, as already suggested in Chapter 1, is that scholars and students should not be interested merely in "proving one's point," of searching for and utilizing only that evidence that appears to support their own position or theory. Such tactics may be suitable for the debating class or the courtroom, but they are not suitable for solving the puzzles of how international politics operates. Just as one would not be satisfied with a jet pilot who disregarded all the empirical evidence that his plane would not fly and only concentrated on the evidence showing it would fly, we should be

---

[8] James E. Harf, David G. Hoovler, and Thomas E. James, Jr., "Systemic and External Attributes in Foreign Policy Analysis," in *Comparing Foreign Policies: Theories, Findings, and Methods,* ed. James N. Rosenau (New York: Wiley, 1974), p. 240.

dissatisfied with the ideologue interested only in supporting his pet theories.

BEHAVIOR

Understanding what the research question is means that we can talk clearly and explicitly about the puzzle we want to solve. A key element in solving puzzles is specifying as clearly as possible what behavior we are trying to understand. We have tried to be clear throughout concerning the exact type of behavior being considered in any given study, and in summary here we present a behavior matrix (Table III-1), which serves as an index for the book—numbers referring to pages—bringing together the various theoretical approaches with the behavior they have been applied to. In addition to serving as an index, however, the matrix, cumbersome as it is, has two advantages: It lessens conceptual or definitional confusion and it helps in the comparison of theories on international behavior. It reduces the confusion by outlining explicitly what behavior is to be explained in any given case. A great deal of the misunderstandings about theories of international politics—and what they can and cannot account for—flows from a failure to establish what behavior is under discussion. The presence or absence of war involves quite different behaviors from those that pertain during the escalation of a specific war, which in turn are quite different from those manifested during verbal hostility. It is entirely plausible that the explanations of each of these behaviors will be different. It might be misleading, therefore, to treat all of these conflict behaviors as equivalent, and try to apply the same theory to all of them. Each chapter has talked about different theories and the behavior they can explain. The matrix pulls these together.

The matrix, as we have said, also helps in making comparisons because it shows what theories of international relations seem more capable of explaining which behaviors, and what behaviors have received the greatest research attention. The corollary of the last point, of course, is that the matrix may also show areas that have been disregarded, either from lack of interest, lack of importance, or an inability to deal with the behavior.

The table is meant only as a heuristic, comparative device to bring together the disparate approaches covered in earlier chapters. Any implications clearly rest on the validity of the categorization of both theories and behavior. However, while the categories of behavior were constructed primarily *a priori* based on the analyses of behavior presented in this book, Peter Flora, in reviewing Singer and Small's compilation

Table III-1. A Matrix of Theories and Behavior (Numbers refer to page numbers in this volume.)

Chapters	Theories	Trends or Levels of Conflict								Trends or Levels of Cooperation						Trends or Levels of Perceptions				Specific Decisions		
		War or No War	Level of War	Conflict (Composite Index)	Escalation of Violence	Arms expenditure Military Buildup	Physical	Verbal	Diplomatic	Cooperation	Alliance Behavior	Treaty Activity	I.G.O., U.N., or Legal	General Participation	Community Formation	General Attitudes	Hostile	Positive or Negative	Mailing Process in Decision-	Large Shifts	Continuing Process	Single Decisions
Individual	Personality	28; 31		32; 34-37				23		32						30; 39	37-38	39			31	28; 31-33
Decision Making	Images	44	50	43-46; 55-58	50-51; 55-58			56-57								42; 46-49		45-46			43-44	42-43
Decision Making	Models	69		88	76; 80	88														78	74-80	69-74; 76-80
Decision Making	Theories			85; 88	85; 88	88										86			83-85		89-90	87; 90-91
National Attribute	Size-Development	110	110	112-113			110-113	110-113	110	112	116		114-116	109-110; 112		114-115						114
National Attribute	Government	118	118; 129	32; 118			124-126; 127	118-119	119; 129	32; 118		119	120	118								
National Attribute	Stability	129-131	122-126; 129; 131	126-127		131	124-127; 124-126	130	129-130	127												
National Attribute	Multiple Attributes		133-134	133-134			134-135	133-135	133-135	133												
Power	Distance	182-184	179; 181; 182; 184	179; 180; 189	186-187		179	179-181; 189	179; 189	180; 188	118-119	180		188								
Power	System	189; 190; 197	191-200			198-199				194	190			194								
Social Distance and Balance	Distance	233; 234; 237; 238	235; 236; 239	235-237	235; 237	237; 239; 240		235-236		231; 232; 235	237	232	231-233		230-232	86; 232-233		242-243		236		
Social Distance and Balance	Balance			242-243; 245-247							241					241-242						
Bargaining	Cognitive	279		285-291	284-285																	279-285
Bargaining	Stimulus-Response				284; 291	286	292-293	290		292-293												
Bargaining	Learning				292-293					302; 309; 311-314			309									
Multivariate	Single level		303-304	302; 308-309; 311-313	309	303	302; 307	302; 307; 304-312	302; 307													317-318
Multivariate	Cross level			318-320	309	318				319-320												

334

of war data, arrived at categories similar to those presented here, at least for war.[9] The matrix, finally, rests on the literature under review, and therefore is of necessity going to be less than completely exhaustive.

If the literature reviewed in this book is any indicator, scholars have focused their research to a large degree on conflict behavior; of those categories under conflict, it would appear at first glance that war/no war, conflict-cooperation, escalation of violence, and verbal violence have been given greater attention across the range of theories down the left hand side. Moving on to the cooperation category, we must conclude that, comparatively, cooperation per se has received much less attention. Likewise perceptions and decisions as dependent variables appear to have been relatively slighted compared to conflict. While no doubt potentially due to the bias of the author, the matrix seems to reflect the traditional international relations concern with refractory as opposed to conciliatory behavior.

What is of greater interest, of course, is the domain of each of the theories. In this case, it would appear that attribute theory has been applied to a larger domain of behavior than any other approach, focusing primarily in the conflict area and to a lesser degree on cooperation. Note, however, that attribute theory barely touches the area of perceptions, and does nothing with "decisions." The same general conclusion applies to the power and social-distance approaches. Balance theory has one of the most limited domains in the research reviewed, concentrating on conflict-cooperation and positive-negative attitudes. Bargaining theory seems almost exclusively to be limited to conflict behavior in its applications, not a surprising finding given its emphasis on influence and the potential use of force.

Most of the systematic research has been devoted primarily to areas that can be effectively measured, such as various forms of conflict, perceptions, and attitudes. That specific decisions have not been given as much attention in the research reviewed here is no doubt a function of the difficulty of measuring the dependent variable of a decision as well as systematically modeling the decision process. However, two other aspects of international behavior, namely, the various forms of alliance behavior and the numerous types of behavior called "cooperative," have also received less attention on the whole. One could argue persuasively that such omissions probably reflect less interest in cooperative behavior than in conflict behavior.

A further breakdown of the types of conflict shows that the categories of war, conflict-cooperation, and verbal conflict have received the greatest

[9] Peter Flora, "A New Stage of Political Arithmetic," *Journal of Conflict Resolution* 18 (March, 1974), pp. 150–51.

attention, whereas categories of escalation, tension, and military expenditures have received less. (The more specific kinds of conflict, such as physical, verbal, belligerent, and diplomatic, all tend very closely toward the cooperation-conflict or level-of-war continuum). Not surprisingly, more attention has been given to static behavior than to dynamic behavior. It is also not particularly surprising that system-level theories seem to cover a greater span of behavior, both in terms of different kinds of conflict as well as different kinds of cooperation. Individual, decision-making, and national-attribute theories almost completely ignore that aspect of international politics.

It is of course true that the decision-making models (Chapter 3) could be applied across the board to the entire range of behaviors—because all involve some decisions. Yet the serious problems of research and replication in connection with the decision models would still remain. Most serious is the problem of parsimony; the models require many more variables and types of data than other potential explanations. The same contention applies to the individual-level approaches of images and perceptions. Though the range of explanations plausible at the individual level could cover the entire range of behaviors, there would be somewhat lower reliability in such explanations because much of this research is not of a highly systematic nature.

In terms of conjunctions of bringing theories together with the behaviors they can explain, national attribute, power, and social distance theories appear heavily in the conflict categories. This most likely reflects the focus on the nation-state, on power, and on the desire for integration in the international system. There is no other portion of the matrix that appears to be so "active."

One central thrust of this book has been that there is no "one" approach to understanding international behavior, the primary reason being that there are so many kinds of behaviors. Table III-1 illustrates that point, and therefore helps to lessen our conceptual confusion concerning what—exactly—we mean when we say "international relations."

THE POLICY QUESTION

As we noted in Chapter 1, a great deal of interest in recent years has focused on how scholarly research might be useful for the policy-maker, and we have attempted in the concluding section of each chapter to address that question in general terms. Some will no doubt find this attention to policy somewhat narrow because no explicit policy advice has been offered. Nor has specific attention been given to what many have come to think of as the current policy questions of interest in international politics, such as the population explosion, the international environment, and the role, function, and activities of multinational corporations. Furthermore, as observed at the beginning of this concluding chapter, we are not discoursing here on questions normally reserved for the finale of a survey on international relations, such as the future of mankind or diplomacy, peace, world government, and so on. To have done so would have opened up a Pandora's box of potential policy questions. Dougherty and Pfaltzgraff, for instance, consider numerous possible "policy" issues, including the control of nuclear weapons; promoting tourism to the United States from nations with whom America is having balance-of-payments difficulties; improving U. S. relations with NATO allies; improving the image of the United States at the United Nations.[10] Others, of course, might include the "meaning" of recent "detente," whether the Cold War has "ended," the likely outcome of a "nuclear blackmail" policy, or current global resource problems.[11] In other words, there are a multitude of policy questions, many of them reflecting only the most recent or current "hot" topics in international affairs. There is the pitfall, however, of focusing on current headline topics that are frequently superseded in short order by other headline topics. It is probably safe to say that prior to October, 1973—the date the Arab nations imposed an oil boycott on the Western states—few scholars viewed global oil politics as a policy issue.

Another reason for not considering these policy questions separately is that to do so would perpetuate the notion that policy can somehow be considered apart from theory or theoretical perspectives. It isn't. Policy questions can almost without exception be considered within one or more of the frameworks that have been presented in this book. Once again, it all depends on how the question on international relations is asked.

No truly interesting question—or puzzle—about international politics can be approached without a theory, proposition, or hypothesis. In recent years, however, in reaction to the concentration on theory and empirical testing of hypotheses, the argument has been raised that scholars of international politics have lost sight of many important areas and problems, such as the role of international organizations, problems of the environment, multi-national corporations, the split between the "have" and the "have-not" nations, and so on. But in each case, the scholar must first isolate the specific behavior or set of behaviors of interest, and then his role is to go about explaining that behavior.

[10] James Dougherty and Robert Pfaltzgraff, *Contending Theories of International Relations* (Philadelphia: Lippincott, 1971), pp. 24–25.

[11] William D. Coplin and Michael K. O'Leary, "A Policy Analysis Framework for Research, Education, and Policy-Making in International Relations" (Paper prepared for delivery at the 15th Annual International Studies Association, Saint Louis, Mo., March 21, 1974), p. 27.

To illustrate this point somewhat more systematically, Table III-2 presents three policy issues—the environment, population, and multinational corporations—and links them with theories of international behavior previously considered. This linkage is accomplished in three steps: first, by showing that the issues can be viewed as a kind of behavior; second, by viewing these behaviors on different levels; and third, by showing that these behaviors might be accounted for by theories drawn from each of the pertinent levels. It is beyond the scope of the present volume to actually do that research; we aim only to illustrate the connection between policy issues and theories of international behavior.

Consider, for example, the issue of the international environment. The first question is: What interest does this have? For the international-relations scholar the interest should go beyond the ideological or value concerns of the effects of pollution, and should also go beyond mechanical considerations of how pollution occurs, how much pollution there is, and whether a threshold exists between safe and unsafe pollution levels.

Table III-2.   Theoretical Consideration of Three Policy Issues

Issue	Behavior	Level of Behavior	Theories
Environment	1. Nation-states polluting	1a. Nation-state b. System	1. National attribute
	2. Agreement on antipollution statutes	2a. Nation-state b. System	2a. National attribute b. Power distribution c. Stimulus-response
	3. Increased tension	3a. Dyadic b. System	3a. Power distance b. Stimulus-response
	4. War	4a. Dyadic b. System	4a. Power distance b. Power distribution
Population	1. State-level increases in population	1a. Individual b. State	1a. Goals and values b. National attributes
	2. System-level changes	2. System	2. Same as above
	3. Tension	3a. Dyadic b. System	3a. Same as above b. Power distance
	4. War	4a. Dyadic b. System	4. Same as above
Multinational Corporations	1. Economic business expansion	1a. State b. Dyadic	1a. National attribute b. Power distance
	2. Economic business competition	2. Dyadic	2. Power distance
	3. Internation Tension	3a. Dyadic b. Systemic	3a. National attribute b. Power distance

Rather, the scholar of international relations should be concerned with the *behavior* of the states or other international actors that are polluting, with how to account for that behavior, with the effect of more pollution on individual, state, or international behavior. Table III-2 suggests that we might be interested in *which* states are doing the greatest amount of polluting and which states are likely to agree to antipollution treaties. Just which states would be more amenable to international agreements, of course, is the much more interesting political question. Other behaviors open to analysis might include increased tension between nation-states resulting from the pollution or the warlike activity generated because of an incipient "world breakdown" from overpollution.

The next consideration for the analyst is to isolate the level of behavior that pertains to the situation under study—and to link theories to that behavior. In terms of environmental pollution, the first two behaviors can be viewed as either state-level action (namely some states are going to pollute more and some less, just as some states will be more apt to agree to antipollution statutes than others), or system-level action. If it is viewed as systemic, is the level of pollution system-wide—with no consideration to be given to which states are guilty of polluting most—likely to be higher at certain times than at others, and is the observance of antipollution statutes, if they exist, likely to be more strict at certain times than at others? The third and fourth behaviors are more likely to be dyadic or systemic because both tension and war usually involve more than one state.

The final and most important step is to determine which theories can account for the various behaviors. Certainly the national-attribute theory may account for which states are more likely to pollute simply because large, developed states are logically going to be the biggest polluters. A more difficult puzzle would be to explain higher or lower levels of pollution on the systemic level. Power distribution might be one approach. Or, in conjunction with the description of competing models by Singer and his colleagues,[12] we might hypothesize that the uncertainty present in a system of low concentration (equal power distribution) might result in more active development economically and militarily by all major countries in an effort to keep equal or get ahead of one another, which, to be sure, would result in greater worldwide pollution. Stable, highly concentrated systems, however, are less likely to produce uncertainty, and states might be less likely to move so vigorously into the different pollution-producing phases of development.

Still other important international behavioral questions related to

12 J. David Singer, Stuart Bremer, and John Stuckey, "Capability Distribution, Uncertainty, and Major Power War, 1820–1965," in *Peace, War, and Numbers*, ed. Bruce Russett (Beverly Hills: Sage, 1972).

pollution are these: Are states likely to agree to and abide by anti-pollution treaties on an international level? What is likely to bring about high agreement and high obedience to pollution agreements? Power distribution might again provide a cue, for low uncertainty would mean less interest in economic and military development and therefore greater agreement and closer adherence to antipollution statutes. Stimulus-response might also explain this behavior, if we assume that hostility will produce greater conflict reaction by the responding power (Chapter 7). If it does, then strategies of verbally attacking the major polluting powers and calling into play their "humanity" would not likely result in acquiescence to control policies. Other bargaining propositions—such as showing the other party the action he should follow is in his own best interests—immediately come to mind, but as remarked on earlier, the operational linkages in these propositions have not been worked out at all well.

The last two behaviors on the environment issue can also be viewed from either the dyadic or system level. If we conceptualize polluting behavior of states as an aggressive act (admittedly not considered as such thus far) then stimulus-response would suggest that it will result in hostile reactions, especially on a dyadic level. Combining stimulus-response with power distance on a dyadic level might explain why some dyads are headed for higher tension or increased conflict over coopera-tion in their interactions. Finally, power distance and power distribution might help in assessing which dyads or systems are likely to move into the war category.

The foregoing discussion merely scratches the surface of linking theories of international behavior to current policy issues. The same procedure could be applied to the other two issues listed in Table III-2, questions on population and multinational corporations. In terms of population, the suggestion under the theory category is that individual goals and values might be the dominant explanatory variables, as the changes in values concerning population planning and birth control have indicated. A leveling off of population growth has occurred where these values have changed. On the other hand, that relation may be spurious, because value changes in birth control have taken place almost without exception in countries with attributes of high wealth and de-velopment. As for the problems associated with the multinationals, Jack Behrman's study [13] suggests that one urgent reason for focusing on them is that their presence and growth may foster tensions among nations both

---

[13] Jack N. Behrman, *National Interests and the Multi-National Enterprise: Tensions among the North Atlantic Countries* (Englewood Cliffs, N.J.: Prentice-Hall, 1970), chap. 1, and by the same author *U.S. International Business and Governments* (New York: McGraw-Hill, 1971), chap. 3.

dyadically and system-wide. Furthermore, states may act differently out of a "fear of dominance" by the multinational corporations of the developed countries.

Figure III-2 is not presented, obviously, as a final analysis of any of these issues, but rather as a suggestion on how to begin handling them in terms of international relations theories. Ultimately, complex model-building will have to be carried out. The scholar of international relations must couple any value concerns on these questions with an earnest effort to deal empirically with the behaviors involved, trying always to find out what brings about different kinds of behavior.

This book has not offered *one* theory on or *one* approach to or *one* framework within which to study international behavior. Nor has it argued that there are many different approaches and that, like canapes on a tray, one simply takes one's pick. International behavior is simply too complex for that. Only a theory or approach so broad as to be almost completely unoperational and meaningless could be called *the* theory of international behavior. Rather, the point here has been that because of the complexity of the subject, different theories or approaches probably account better for certain behavior than other theories do. It is not then a question of picking and choosing but of assessing which theories are applicable to which behaviors.

We have tried to be as comprehensive as humanly possible, but no one book could possibly consider all research, especially when the subject is so broad and when scholars remain so productive. The categories and perspectives outlined here, however, should serve as guides for the analysis of international behavior and for the placement of research on that behavior into the proper perspective. Thus, what might appear to be a small, minor, even insignificant study into an obscure question takes on greater meaning if it can be placed in a larger theoretical framework or be compared with other studies in the same or related fields. Findings can be compared and contrasted, and when differences occur, reasons for those differences must be uncovered. By investigating many different perspectives on international relations, we can highlight what each approach implies and what kinds and ranges of behavior each is capable of explaining.

Systematic studies on international behavior have thus far, however, not been exceptionally successful in accounting for much of the variation in that behavior. One reason for this rather lackluster result is no doubt due to the inability of scholars to construct the complex models needed to represent international behavior and then to test them accurately. Yet it is also a function of the inability or unwillingness of scholars to submit a given set of data to alternative models. Linear relationships are only one of many possibilities of the way in which two variables may interact.

Simple additive or simple time models are the easiest to think of, but much more complex ones may be needed to model international behavior. Ad hoc verbal explanations are very attractive; they carry a good deal of plausibility because they can present a complex picture of the world. But the ad hoc-ness of such explanations means that while their plausibility is high, their applicability and generality are low.

International behavior continues to occur in many forms every day, and it will always be a challenge to explain it. The chapters presented here have not produced any automatic understanding or quick or easy solution to understanding that behavior. They have, however, set out the major explanations that have historically been utilized, and they have illustrated the kinds of evidence used to test them. If nothing else, the diversity of the theories and the methods offered here should suggest that international behavior is a dynamic process and the study of it cannot cease with this book.

appendix   Methodological
Problems and Issues

Introduction

One theme stressed throughout this book has been that the methods one uses to study international behavior will have a crucial effect on the results. Even what may appear to be only slightly different methods or methodological assumptions can affect, indeed completely change, research findings. A second theme has been that *methods* cannot be separated from the *substantive* research question. No empirical questions can be answered without reliance on some method.

This appendix contains material that might have been placed in the chapters themselves but would have impeded their flow. We shall focus here on a small number of methodological matters, including a brief description of statistical testing, the legitimacy of certain operational measures, and the things to watch for in analyzing research findings. The preceding chapters should have been understandable without this appendix, but the points made here should clarify observations made in the body of the text. The reader should be cautioned that what follows is very abbreviated and selective; excellent further treatments can be found for basic statistics, advanced statistics, and extended analyses of many of the questions that we can only touch on briefly.[1]

[1] Hubert M. Blalock, Jr., *Social Statistics*, 2d ed. (New York: McGraw-Hill, 1972); N. R. Draper and H. Smith, *Applied Regression Analysis* (New York: Wiley, 1966);

A. Statistical Analysis

The central goal of statistical analysis for our purposes has been to find out whether two or more variables are "related" to one another, and whether that relationship is "significant." One method of determining that significance is to estimate what the probability is that the relationship was merely a "chance" one. Could the relationship between variables that we actually find in our data have occurred, in other words, simply by using random data? To find out whether two variables are related, there must be—as Chapter 1 noted—some *variation* in each. The occurrence of variable A (Chinese détente with the United States) and the occurrence of variable B (Soviet hostility toward China) at the same time does not necessarily mean that these two variables are related. With no other information available, there is no way of knowing whether there had always been détente between the United States and China, nor whether there had always been Soviet hostility toward China. If, however, the period between 1946 and 1957 exhibited less hostility by the Soviets toward the Chinese than the 1958-1970 period, then there is variation on that variable. Similarly, we know there has not always been a state of détente between China and the United States.

But the discussion in Chapter 1 is simple: détente or no détente, Soviet hostility or no Soviet hostility. If we had a score for every year, we would have a more accurate estimate of the variation for each variable; perhaps events, such as diplomatic meetings, verbal exchanges, military maneuvers, and so on could be used to produce that score, and then, at a minimum, we could talk about "high," "medium," and "low" détente. This scoring could result then in a more informative table placing each of the twenty-two years in one of the categories for both variables, such as in Table A1.

These hypothetical data suggest a rather good relationship, insofar as the variation in détente is accounted for by variation in hostility: we need only know the level of Soviet-Chinese hostility to know the level of détente.

This example is an extremely simplified one, of course, and numerous complications could be introduced. For instance, by placing each one of the twenty-two years into only one of three categories, we lose information. If 1956 falls into the "high" category on both variables, and 1963 also falls into the "high" category, does that mean they have the exact same

J. Johnston, *Econometric Methods*, 2d ed. (New York: McGraw-Hill, 1972); W. Phillips Shively, *The Craft of Political Research: A Primer* (Englewood Cliffs, N.J.: Prentice-Hall, 1974); Ted Robert Gurr, *Polimetrics: An Introduction to Quantitative Macropolitics* (Englewood Cliffs, N.J.: Prentice-Hall, 1972).

Table A1. Hypothetical Data on Soviet-Chinese Hostility and U.S.-Chinese Détente

Soviet-Chinese Hostility	United States-Chinese Détente			
	High	*Medium*	*Low*	*Total*
High	4	0	0	4
Medium	0	12	0	12
Low	0	0	6	6
Total	4	12	6	6

score on each variable? Not necessarily, and therefore a refinement might be to treat each year separately, and plot the variables against each other in a scattergram: Figure A1 presents how this might hypothetically work out.

Figure A1 "plots" each of the twenty-two years according to its score on USSR-Chinese hostility and China-U.S. détente. Like Table A1, it shows a remarkably strong relationship: the lowest year in hostility is also the lowest in détente, the second lowest in hostility is the second lowest in détente, and so on. Each year, therefore, is treated as a separate unit rather than being lumped into general categories of high, medium, and low.

Extending this complication, it may be that by looking at *years* as the unit of analysis we cannot tell what happened within that year. We might then score each of the 264 months from 1950 to 1971. These data

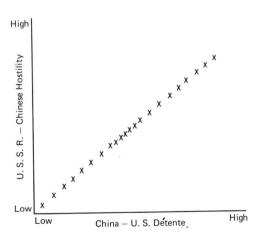

Figure A1. Scatterplot of hypothetical data on U.S.S.R.-Chinese hostility and China-U.S. détente, indicating very strong relationship.

could then either be set up as in Table A1 as illustrated above—the only difference being that the total in the table would be 264 rather than 22— or the 264 data points could be scatterplotted.

These hypothetical data are presented only as an extension of what was suggested in Chapter 1, and the main point at this juncture is that by using such data we actually have variation in both variables, variation that may or may not be related. To discuss that relationship, we utilize statistical analysis, for the fatal flaw with these data is that things never work out in reality the way professors say they do in books. Rare is the occasion when we would uncover data such as those in Table A1 and Figure A1. More likely would be the following:

Table A2.

Soviet-Chinese Hostility	United States-Chinese Détente		
	High	*Medium*	*Low*
High	4	3	1
Medium	2	5	1
Low	1	2	3

Or, even worse than that, the theory might hold no water at all and the result would be something like Table A3:

Table A3.

Soviet-Chinese Hostility	United States-Chinese Détente		
	High	*Medium*	*Low*
High	2	3	2
Medium	3	2	3
Low	2	3	2

In this last case we can't explain détente by hostility, for the variation in one does not match the variation in the other. Figures A2 and A3 illustrate this point further.

When assessing the data in Tables A1 to A3 and Figures A1 to A3, the most immediate question is where do we establish the cutting points between a "meaningful" or "significant" relationship and a mere random one? The data in Figure A1 would certainly suggest that we could account for the variation in Chinese-U.S. détente by the level of USSR-Chinese hostility. Figure A3, on the other hand, certainly appears to be random. Moreover, while the data in Figure A2 would appear to be

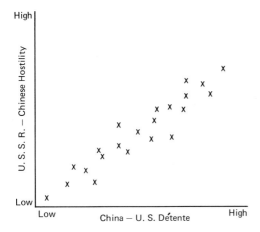

Figure A2. Scatterplot of hypothetical data on U.S.S.R.-Chinese hostility and China-U.S. détente, indicating moderately strong relationship.

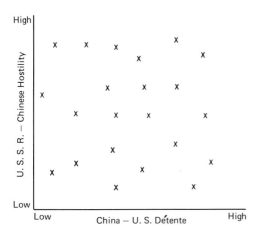

Figure A3. Scatterplot of hypothetical data on U.S.S.R.-Chinese hostility and China-U.S. détente, indicating no relationship.

strong, we could easily visualize many other such scatterplots which would approach randomness. How do we know where significance trails off into randomness? Statistical analysis provides a numerical gauge to assess (1) whether the relation is or is not a chance one, and (2), with some tests, exactly how much of the variation in one variable is accounted for by variation in another. Brief illustrations of these functions of statistical tests will be given here. The first is called a "rank order" correlation, the second a "product moment correlation." Using the hypothetical example of Soviet-Chinese hostility and United States-Chinese détente, we could give a *rank* to each year on hostility and on détente with 1 being low hostility and low détente, and 22 being high hostility and détente; in most cases some years will tie with one another, but in this case let us assume there are no ties. Table A4 presents three different hypothetical possibilities, or cases, for these ranks. A simple inspection of the three examples visually says something. Case A shows that the ranks on the variables for each year are exactly the same: years ranked high in hostility (high scores) also ranked high in détente. Case B shows the exact opposite relation, whereas case C is rather difficult to interpret.

The "rank order" and "product moment" correlations are computed differently, and they each have their advantages and disadvantages. The rank correlation uses the *differences* between the ranks for each year,

Table A4. Rank Scores in Three Hypothetical Cases of U.S.S.R.-Chinese Hostility and Chinese-U.S. Détente

Years	Case A		Case B		Case C	
	Hostility	Détente	Hostility	Détente	Hostility	Détente
1950	1	1	1	22	1	8
1951	2	2	2	21	6	19
1952	3	3	3	20	8	4
1953	4	4	4	19	22	3
1954	5	5	5	18	10	1
1955	6	6	6	17	14	21
1956	7	7	7	16	2	18
1957	8	8	8	15	7	16
1958	9	9	9	14	9	10
1959	10	10	10	13	15	12
1960	11	11	11	12	18	22
1961	12	12	12	11	20	13
1962	13	13	13	10	16	14
1963	14	14	14	9	3	9
1964	15	15	15	8	4	11
1965	16	16	16	7	5	5
1966	17	17	17	6	11	15
1967	18	18	18	5	12	2
1968	19	19	19	4	13	6
1969	20	20	20	3	17	7
1970	21	21	21	2	19	17
1971	22	22	22	1	21	20

whereas the product moment correlation uses the actual *scores*.[2] The rank method, therefore, uses less accurate information, but its assumptions are far less restrictive.[3] For present purposes we will focus on the rank correlation. For the three case examples, these correlations are 1.00, −1.00, and .13 (see footnote 2). As a rough rule, the closer to 1.00 or −1.00, the stronger the relationship; the closer to .00, the weaker the relationship between the two variables. There is little trouble with correlations approaching either extreme +1.00 or −1.00, though there are some problems, one of which is noted in paragraph A.1. (These problems need be of no concern here.) But what does a correlation of .90 mean? .85? .60? .30? .21? What is meaningful and nonmeaningful? It is at this juncture that the question of chance arises. If we take a list of ten random numbers and correlate them with another list of ten, we would probably get a low correlation (e.g., .10). But if you drew a second, third, fourth, etc., list of ten numbers and continued correlating them to the first list, eventually we would get a high correlation (e.g., .95, −.90) *simply by chance*.

We need a method of assessing whether the correlation we have found with real-world variables could in fact have very likely been produced by chance. Here we must turn to what the statisticians call the "law of large numbers," which simply means that if there are large numbers of a particular phenomenon, they tend to distribute themselves in what we all know as the "normal" or bell-shaped distribution. In the current example, if we generated a very large number of correlations between variables made up of random data, the average of those correlations would be very close to zero (because there can be positive and negative correlations), and most of these correlations would hover close to zero. Some would deviate from that zero figure, however, both to the positive and negative side, and these would form the tails of that normal distribution. The further we move out on that distribution, on each side,

---

[2] The rank formula is

$$r_s = 1.0 - \frac{6 \, \Sigma \, d^2}{N \, (N^2 - 1)} \, . \qquad \begin{array}{l} d = \text{difference on ranks} \\ N = \text{number of observations.} \end{array}$$

See Blalock, *Social Statistics*, p. 416; see also his p. 380 for the formula and analysis of the product moment correlation.

The computation of the rank correlation under consideration (called Spearman's rank correlation) is straightforward, as the formula indicates. We take the difference between the rank scores for each observation, one at a time, and square that difference. Summing all those squared differences (the squaring is done to get rid of negative numbers), we multiply the sum by 6, and divide the result by the number of observations (in this case 22) multiplied by the same number squared, minus 1 ($22^2 - 1 = 483$). The overall result is then subtracted from 1.00.

[3] See Blalock, *Social Statistics*, pp. 415–426.

toward the larger correlation, the smaller the number of correlations there would be. This phenomenon applies to larger areas of social and physical reality. If we were to stop the next fifty individuals on the street corner and ascertain their height, we would probably find those data to be normally distributed also, with the height of most of those fifty hovering around the mean or average, and fewer and fewer individuals falling further and further from that mean or average.

Once we have the idea of the normal curve in mind, we can then think of the idea of probability. Just as we know that if we were to stop the next twenty individuals on any street corner, probably very few of them would be taller than seven feet, likewise, we know that if we were to correlate random numbers probably very few of them would produce "high" correlations. If by some chance we were to find sixteen of the next twenty people on the street corner to be taller than seven feet, we would know something was amiss: we would most likely find out that we were near a tall-person's store. Similarly, if in correlating two variables we were to find an unnaturally high one—namely one that was unlikely to have occurred by chance—we would know that something was amiss. Possibly, the trouble is measurement error (our statistical "wrong corner"), but barring that we can attribute "meaning" or "significance" to the high correlation.

An important consideration, however, is the number of observations we utilize. Very simply, the chance of getting a correlation of 1.00 with five observations of random numbers is much greater than with 100 random observations. To revert to the example above, if we were to ascertain the height of the first five people we encountered on a given street corner, and four of those five turned out to be taller than seven feet, our common sense would contend that something was amiss. Most likely candidate, as noted, would be the fact that we had chosen a corner near a tall-person's store. If we then sampled another five, and found that of the total of ten only seven were over seven feet, our hunch would be given further confirmation. Ultimately, however, if we continued to sample and from a total of a hundred people found only ten that were above seven feet, our hunch would be almost completely disconfirmed. In such an event, of course, the early sampling error had been overcome by the fact that, in the long run, enough people had passed that street corner to give us a much more accurate accounting of height.

But what if our hypothesis to begin with was that people in that given city were taller than the average? Sampling five and finding four above seven feet would begin to confirm the hypothesis. But such a finding would be subject—as the earlier case was—to charges of sampling error. To continue the sample to a total of 100, and find 80 above seven feet would be much stronger confirmation, for the probability of that occurring merely by chance—such as careless sampling—would be enormously reduced.

For the example of Sino-Soviet hostility and Sino-American détente, if the scholar looked only at the 1950–1955 period and found a covariance between the two variables, he would have made an interesting discovery. But the skeptic might challenge him and say that the relationship might not apply to a later period (1956–1960), and therefore his theory was severely limited. The original scholar then takes the chance that his relationship will in fact be disconfirmed by adding in more years; if he increases the number of observations—from six to eleven—and the correlation remains the same, however, then his theory becomes more potent (applying to eleven rather than to just six years), and therefore more significant. Every time an observation is added, we run the risk that it will disconfirm the hypothesis; if it does not, then the hypothesis becomes more meaningful. A statistic is called significant if the probability of its occurring by chance is very low. In normal research we talk of significance levels of .05, .01, and .001, meaning that a given correlation could have occurred by chance, respectively, 5 times and 1 time out of 100, and 1 time out of 1,000. A rank correlation of, for instance, .20 with twenty observations could have occurred more than 50 times out of 100 simply by chance. On the other hand, the same .20 correlation calculated with eighty observations would have occurred by chance only once in 100 times.[4]

One use for statistical techniques, therefore, is that they allow us to make an assessment of the "significance" of the relationship between variables in terms of the probability of its having occurred simply by chance. To report a correlation of .40 between two variables may be relatively meaningless if we can achieve correlations of .50 or better with random numbers. A second use of statistical techniques, however, and the more common one traditionally, concerns the relationship between one's sample of observations and the larger "population" from which they were drawn. A researcher may desire some estimation that what he found to be true in a sample of observations is true also of the population from which the sample was drawn. A statistically significant correlation in this respect means that the researcher can safely generalize back to the population from his sample, without concerning himself with the possibility that his sample does not represent that population.

A significant correlation in either sense, however, does not necessarily mean that it is *important* in terms of accounting for variation in one variable by variation in another variable. For instance, in the example earlier, we were interested in accounting for the variation in the

[4] Ibid. pp. 159–65 and 292–294.

dependent variable of Sino-U.S. détente by the independent variable of Soviet hostility to China. If we had 284 observations, then a product moment correlation of .20 would normally have occurred only 5 out of 100 times by chance, and is therefore "significant" at the .05 (5 percent) level of significance. That may be important for certain reasons—the correlation is unlikely to be a chance one—but nonetheless we could not make very accurate predictions on the basis of that correlation. We can assess exactly how much of the variation in the dependent variable is accounted for by the independent variable by *squaring* the correlation coefficient: thus a correlation of .20, if squared, is equivalent to .04; a larger correlation, such as .84, is equivalent—when squared—to .71. In statistical terms, this means that the first correlation would have accounted for four percent of the variation in the dependent variable, and the second would have accounted for 71 percent. Why is this so?

Assume again the example of Soviet-Chinese hostility and Chinese-U.S. détente, but now let us assume for simplicity of presentation that we are only dealing with five years. Figure A4 shows the hypothetical scores for five years on détente. We want to know why some years show détente to be very low (i.e., 2), and other years reveal a very high détente relationship (i.e., 10 or 12). If the only information available was that contained in Figure A4, then we obviously don't know why one year is higher than another. Moreover, if someone asked, "What was the score of détente in 1968?" we could only guess, and the best guess would be to choose the mean score for all the years (the broken vertical line in the figure). If the score for 1968 had actually been 2, and we have chosen the average of 7, then we would have been off by 5. We would have been off by 5 also if we had chosen the score of 12. However, if the actual score for 1968 had been 7, we would have been correct in our guess. The point here is that we *could* cite the average score in answer to the question about 1968, but as noted there would very likely be a great deal of error in doing so.

The other way to tackle this problem is to find some independent variable that fluctuates with détente and use that to predict to the score on détente. If Soviet-Chinese hostility fluctuated with détente, then the scatterplot of the two variables might be represented by the X's in

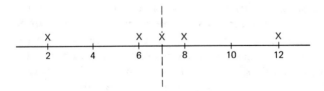

Figure A4. China-U.S. detente scores. Xs refer to hypothetical scores on détente for five different years.

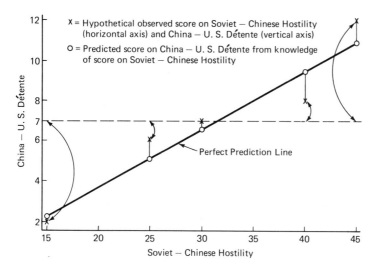

Figure A5. Hypothetical observed and predicted scores for five years on Soviet-Chinese hostility plotted against the scores for those same five years on U.S.-Chinese détente.

Figure A5: as Soviet-Chinese hostility increases, détente increases. The two will surely correlate statistically, but our concern here is more specifically with the notion of *how much* of the variation in détente can be explained by the variation in Soviet-Chinese hostility. What we would like to do here is reduce the errors we made using the mean score as our prediction. The *curved* lines in the figure A-5 represent the amount we would have been in error had we chosen that method. A regression equation,[5] however, will produce the straight line in Figure A5, representing the linear pattern of the two variables as they covary. If hostility were able to account for détente perfectly, then all the observations (Xs) would fall exactly where all the predictions are (Os). That is not the case, however, and the *straight* lines between each of the observations and the predicted score represent the error using the regression line as our prediction. Note that on the whole these lines are much smaller than the curved lines. In fact, subtracting each of the observations from the mean and squaring the difference (to get rid of negatives), we can think of the summation of these differences as the total variation around the mean. In this case, it amounts to roughly 52 "units" of variation around the mean that we want to account for (the scale is unimportant). Subtracting each *predicted* score from the mean and squaring would in this

[5] Ibid., p. 374. A regression equation shows the exact linear, mathematical relationship between the two variables.

case present us with roughly 47.77 "units"; these are units of variation that have been accounted for because those predicted scores have been derived by knowing the score on Soviet-Chinese hostility. Thus we have "accounted" for 47.77 out of 52 units of variation around the mean, or roughly 92%, leaving 8% unaccounted for—which consists of the observations subtracted from the predicted scores, or our error. The correlation coefficient between the two variables, computed using standard formulae,[6] is .965. Recall the observation above that the square of the correlation coefficient represents the amount of variation explained; squaring .965 equals 93 percent, which—given certain computational and rounding errors—is the equivalent of 47.77/52.00 or 92 percent. We can make much better predictions to a given year's score on détente if we know that year's score on Soviet-Chinese hostility than we could simply by guessing, using the mean score on détente. We have also thereby "accounted for" the largest part—roughly 92 percent—of the variation in détente.

In sum, statistical techniques can provide answers to several questions: whether there is more than simply a random relationship between two or more variables, whether the observed relationship in a sample is true of the population, and—with some tests—exactly how much of the variation in the dependent variable can be accounted for by the independent variables. While it would be too extensive to go into other tests here at any great length, two might be mentioned. One is the "difference of means" test, used to compare the average scores of two different groups, and the second is "analysis of variance," used with more than two groups.[7] In Chapter two, for instance, reference was made to a study of presidential rhetoric, in which Presidents Kennedy, Johnson, and Nixon's speeches on Vietnam were analyzed in terms of how many "symbols" they used. One thing to do with such data is to compute an average monthly score for each president and compare the averages. The assumption once again is that a comparison of the mean scores of any two sets of *random* numbers will show a very small difference. Just as correlations computed on random data will distribute themselves in a bell-shaped curve, the differences of means computed between sets of random numbers would form a bell-shaped curve, with only a small number being either very large negative or very large positive differences. In comparing Kennedy, Johnson, and Nixon on their average symbolic score we wanted to know what the probability would be of reproducing the differences we did find simply with random data. If we could produce differences that large or larger simply with *any* two sets of random numbers, then

[6] Ibid., p. 380.
[7] Ibid., pp. 220ff and pp. 317–360.

the observed difference is what we would expect and therefore it is not very significant. In that specific case the difference between Kennedy and Nixon was so small that we could have achieved it with random data, and therefore we did not attach much significance to it. Likewise, the difference between Kennedy and Johnson was not much different from what we would expect from chance. However, it is unlikely that simply comparing the means of random numbers would produce a difference larger than that found between Johnson and Nixon, and therefore that difference becomes "significant."

The second test, "analysis of variance," can be viewed as an extension of the difference of means test because it can be used with more than two groups. In this case, the means of each group are not compared directly, but rather the variation within each group is compared to the variation of the group means around the average for the whole data set. In the example just used, analysis of variance could have been utilized to compare the three presidents as a group, not merely two at a time.

Statistical tests are used because they provide a guide or anchoring point for making judgments about empirical data. If someone were to point to the differences between Kennedy and Nixon for instance—mean scores of 5.72 and 5.01 respectively—and conclude therefore that Kennedy was more symbolic in his rhetoric, the statistician would respond that the difference was not significant in that he could get that much of a difference simply by comparing the means of two groups of random numbers. One could still contend that Kennedy *was more symbolic* because his score was higher, but that difference may involve a measurement error or it may mean that despite the higher score, the *impact* of the higher level of rhetoric—on the public, or as a reflection of Kennedy's style—was in fact negligible. The statistical test provides only a gauge or a rule. The numerical gauge, though in no way inviolate, does provide some rough estimate of the importance and strength of research findings. The following paragraphs will now point out some common pitfalls and problems in utilizing statistical analysis.

A1. Data Distributions: Outliers

It was noted above that the product moment correlation requires much more restrictive assumptions about the data being used. One central assumption is that the data are "normally distributed" into the well-known bell-shaped curve, with most observations lumped around the mean, and fewer observations attached to the "tails" or extreme ends.

Figures A6a and A6b show two different data distributions: on energy

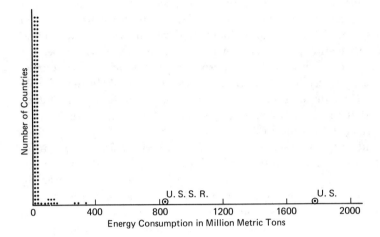

Source: This figure has been calculated from data presented in Charles Lewis Taylor and Michael C. Hudson, *World Handbook of Political and Social Indicators,* 2d ed. (New Haven, Conn.: Yale University Press, 1972), pp. 326–28.

Figure A6a. National energy consumption in million metric tons.

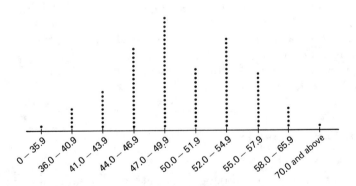

Source: This figure has been calculated from data presented in Robert C. Angell, "National Support for World Order: A Research Report," *Journal of Conflict Resolution* 17 (September, 1973), pp. 438–39.

Figure A6b. Scores of 114 nations on index of "national support for world order."

consumption and on support for world order.[8] The world order index does have a normal distribution, but the United States and a few other large countries quite clearly distort or "skew" the variable of energy consumption. If we were to scatterplot these variables against each other, the United States would be an extreme outlier; Figure A7 shows what might happen in a hypothetical illustration with only four observations. The product moment correlation for the relation between those two hypothetical variables is .99. But variables A and B are quite obviously not normally distributed, since three out of four of the observations are lumped below the score of 5, and one observation out at 10, not unlike Figure A6a. The rank correlation does not assume a normal, bell-shaped distribution, and using the formula presented earlier, we find the rank correlation is .20. Merely inspecting the figure tells us, however, that if for some reason our sample had not included that one outlying observation, the relationship between the three other observations in fact would be negative, in which observations with high scores on one variable would have low scores on the second variable.

An outlier, therefore, has a great effect on the product moment correlation. In addition to ranking the data and computing a rank correlation,

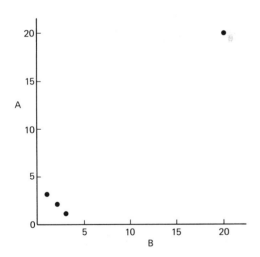

Figure A7. Scatterplot of four observations between two hypothetical variables (A and B). The numbers are also hypothetical.

8 The first set of data comes from Charles Lewis Taylor and Michael C. Hudson, *World Handbook of Political and Social Indicators*, 2d ed. (New Haven: Yale University Press, 1972), pp. 326ff; the second comes from Robert C. Angell, "National Support for World Order," *Journal of Conflict Resolution* 17 (September, 1973), pp. 438–439.

one could simply plot the data as in Figure A7 and see that the outlier is distorting the data: the correlation does not truly describe the relation between the variables.

A2. Aggregation

One of the goals of theory-building is to generalize about a relationship so that it applies to a broad range of cases. Research designs, therefore, attempt to include as many cases or observations as possible. The more cases that continue to support the theory, the broader the theory. But at some point we must aggregate the data, which means that we will not have information on what is happening inside the specific aggregated unit. With time series data aggregated by year, for instance, there is no way of knowing how variables relate *within each year*. A theory would become much stronger if instead of aggregating by year over a twenty-year period we aggregated by month and found that for 240 months the relationship still remained strong. And, of course, stretching the argument further, aggregating the data into 1,040 weeks would strengthen the theory even more—if, that is, it were to hold up.

Aggregation becomes an issue in terms of what the level of aggregation says about the theory involved. A theory confirmed at the year level of aggregation but not supported at the monthly level does not mean that it is no good. It simply says that different theories may be accounting for the dependent variable at different levels. In the case of Sorokin's study (Chapter 4), internal disturbances and external conflict may be related over long periods of time (aggregated into centuries), but the fluctuations in both variables do not covary within centuries. It is possible that long-range forces are causing the two to be related, but that does not occur in the short range. It would be inaccurate to say that the theory is "confirmed" if it only applies to behavior across centuries. The parameters of the theory must point that out.

A3. Nonrandomness and Strength of Relationship

As noted in paragraph A, statistical tests tell us the probability that the relation we have uncovered is merely a chance one, and, if it is not a random one, how *strong* that relation is. The two sets of information are quite distinct.

Statistically significant correlations may be unable to account for large portions of the variation in the dependent variable. One of the studies in Chapter 5, for instance, showed a correlation of .15; with more than 300 observations, that means that less than 1 out of 100 times would we get a correlation that large or larger simply by chance. But the amount of variation explained is just over 2 percent (squaring the .15 correlation), and thus the underlying hypothesis is not a particularly strong one, and predictions to the dependent variable would not be very good.

Another example illustrates the same problem with more roughly aggregated data. Holsti's study of the 1914 crisis (Chapter three) showed that the Dual Alliance perceived more alternatives in the "necessity" than in the "choice" category, while its enemies, in its mind, had more "choices." The same relation occurred with Germany taken separately; finally, communication patterns differed between high and low stress periods, with more communication occurring between alliances than within alliances in the low-stress period, and the reverse taking place during the high-stress period. Statistical analysis showed the relations in the three cases to be significant (at .005, .001 and .001 levels, respectively).[9] A nonstatistical analysis of Tables 5a, 5b, and 5c, however, shows that predictions made in Table 5b are much better than the other two. In each case, though the pattern of the data is nonrandom, meaningfulness differs. Predicting an interalliance communication from low stress (Table A5c) would mean one would be wrong 46 percent of the time. On the other hand, predicting that a German decision-maker would perceive that he had a "choice" in his alternatives (Table A5b) would produce a correct result only 8 percent of the time. Ideally, one wants situations that not only produce statistically significant correlations but also are able to account for large portions of the variation in the dependent variable. These illustrations show that even when the latter situation applies, it may not be significantly different from what we would expect from chance, and when the former situation is the case we must not necessarily equate the statistically significant relation with a strong and meaningful one.

A4. Errors in Prediction: Residuals

The goal of any science is prediction. In the example used earlier we wanted to predict from U.S.S.R.-Chinese hostility the level of Chinese-

---

[9] However, using the C statistic, which normalizes the original Chi Square statistic, taking into account the number of observations, and which can be read as a correlation coefficient ranging from .00 to 1.00, shows that the relations in the tables ranged from .35 to .85; Blalock, *Social Statistics*, p. 297.

Table A5a. Perception by Decision-Makers in Dual Alliance of Own and Enemies Alternatives

	Choice	Necessity	
Allies	39%	61%	C = .51
Enemies	78	22	

Table A5b. Perception by German Decision-Makers of Own and Enemies Alternatives

	Choice	Necessity	
Self	8%	92%	C = .82
Enemies	87	13	

Table A5c. Communication Patterns between and within Alliances in Low and High Stress Periods

	Communication Patterns		
	Intra-Alliance	*Interalliance*	
Low Stress	46%	54%	C = .35
High Stress	54	46	

Holsti, 1965.

American détente (technically this is not *pre*diction but *post*diction because the events have already occurred, but we will retain the traditional nomenclature). In that hypothetical example, the prediction that intense Soviet hostility to China would cause high levels of U.S.-China détente, was fairly accurate. There was, however, about 7 or 8 percent of the variation in détente still unaccounted for. This variation may have been the result of an error in measuring some of the variables, or, more likely, of having left out an important variable.

Analysis of these errors in prediction—or residuals—can be very helpful. One of the findings of Rummel's early test of field theory was that the worst-predicted dyads on the variable of physical conflict were primarily those involved in the Middle East War of 1956. Analysis of these residuals, then, suggests that the independent variables (power, rank, values, and geographical proximity) were unable to account for high levels of physical conflict. That information can then help to build on the original theory. In that case, as Rummel noted, the fault may have been the exclusion of a "value" variable taking effect in an intense situation like the Middle East.

Another illustration is Rummel's study of United States foreign relations for 1955.[10] Figure A8 shows the plot of power parity against the two behaviors of Western European cooperation and deterrence. In general there is a slight tendency for the U.S. to be more cooperative and exercise less deterrence than is predicted toward West Germany, Canada, Italy, Israel, and the Soviet Union. On the other hand, it is less cooperative and more deterrent-minded than it should be toward China, India, Japan, Egypt, and the United Kingdom. With the exceptions of the United Kingdom and the Soviet Union, the first group

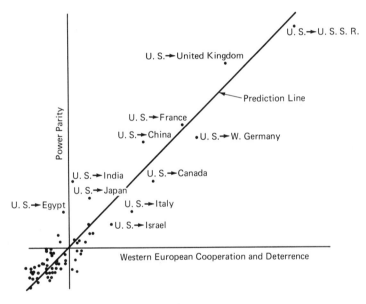

Source: This figure from Chapter 3, "U.S. Foreign Relations: Conflict, Cooperation, and Attribute Distances," by R. J. Rummel in *Peace, War, and Numbers*, Bruce M. Russett, editor, © 1972, pp. 71–113 by permission of the author and publisher, Sage Publications, Inc.

Figure A8. Scatterplot of dyadic power parity and the behavior dimensions of Western European cooperation and deterrence.

[10] Rudolph Rummel, "U.S. Foreign Relations: Conflict, Cooperation, and Attribute Distances," in *Peace, War, and Numbers,* ed. Bruce Russett (Beverly Hills: Sage, 1972).

of countries are much more western-oriented than the second group. Although Rummel suggests the addition of a variable measuring the "Europeanness of a nation" [11] to account for those systematic errors, it might be more helpful to construct a "western-leaning" variable to account for why the United States is overcooperative to the first group and undercooperative toward the second.

A final illustration of what inspection of residuals can do is found in the data on stimulus and response in Chapter 2 on the 1914 crisis. The correlations between stimulus and response were moderately strong. Yet a plot of the residuals against the response variable shows that for both the Triple Entente and the Dual Alliance the errors were not random. Rather, cases of low levels of hostile responses are consistently *under*predicted, whereas those of high levels of hostile responses are overpredicted. Hence, there is *systematic* error in the prediction of the response.[12] This finding takes on greater importance here because the low levels of hostile responses are usually at the beginning of the six-week crisis whereas the high levels of hostility occur later on. Therefore, the simple linear model does not fit the data as well as a model involving a time factor.

A great deal of information is sometimes contained in the pattern of the errors. Residuals can often be as enlightening in terms of building theory as the actual relationship itself, especially if this relationship turns out pretty much as expected.

B. Operational Indicators

In order to rigorously test hypotheses, variables must be as carefully defined and measured as possible. We have tried throughout the chapters to give a sense of what kinds of operational measures have been used. In this section, a small number are investigated in somewhat more detail, not only to show what kinds of operational measures have and can be used, but also to illustrate certain pitfalls.

Kissinger's analysis of leadership structures illustrates the problem of loose operational measures. It will be recalled that the bureaucratic leadership structure was epitomized by the American system, in which decision-making becomes

a series of adjustments among special interests. . . . Problems tend to be slighted until some agency or department is made responsible for them. . . . The out-

[11] Ibid., p. 102.
[12] Draper and Smith, *Applied Regression Analysis*, p. 89.

come usually depends more on the pressure or the persuasiveness of the contending advocates than on a concept of over-all purpose.[13]

This description approximates closely the bureaucratic-incremental decision-making model described in Chapter 3. No distinctions were made there, however, between different countries; the model, if correct, would apply to many nations. Kissinger admits that "while these tendencies exist to some extent in all bureaucracies they are particularly pronounced in the American system of government." [14] But there is no evidence confirming that statement, and Allison's organizational model suggested that all governments possess this attribute to some degree, and it is not at all clear that the American government has any particular monopoly on it.

The distinctions become somewhat more tenuous when Kissinger observes that "a Communist bureaucratic structure, *however pragmatic,* will have different priorities than ours; it will give greater weight to doctrinal considerations and conceptual problems." [15] Leadership structures in Communist countries, then, apparently do become bureaucratic, and perhaps extensively so. If true, then the distinction between bureaucratic governments and other governments breaks down. Second, he argues that it is something more than mere ritual when the speeches of the top Soviet officials "begin with hour-long recitals of Communist ideology. *Even if it were ritual,* it must affect the definition of what is considered reasonable in internal arguments." [16] Again, striking similarities can be seen between that behavior and behavior in the American political system, where the politicians' propensity for slogans, symbols, ideological arguments, and "recitals"—especially during campaign periods —is well known. References to "democracy," "freedom," "liberty," "way of life," are part and parcel of the American political rhetoric and ritual. Revolutionary structures, therefore, do contain bureaucratic elements, and nonrevolutionary ones do rely on ideological arguments.

The fact that these supposedly diverse leadership structures contain numerous similarities constitutes serious problems for any study that purports to explain different foreign policy "styles" as a function of different types of "leadership structures." Though the three categories of leadership isolated by Kissinger—bureaucratic, ideological, and charismatic—may differ not so much in terms of type as in degree, certainly

---

13 Henry Kissinger, "Domestic Structure and Foreign Policy," in *International Politics and Foreign Policy, A Reader in Research and Theory,* rev. ed. James N. Rosenau (New York: Free Press, 1969), p. 268.

14 Ibid.

15 Ibid., p. 271; emphasis added.

16 Ibid., emphasis added.

the above argument raises questions about even that possibility because other theories, particularly those involving organizational and bureaucratic processes, carry as a basic assumption that structures are very similar. To show that Kissinger's categories exhibit similarities does not imply that they are completely *un*differentiated, but it does suggest that to establish the distinctions between the types it might be worthwhile to work with potential operational indicators rather than merely nominal categories assigned by the researcher.

The advantage of such operational indicators could be demonstrated by any number of studies, but McGowan's on African alignment during the cold war will illustrate it well.[17] He constructed an index labeled "bloc interaction" that measured how strongly thirty-two states were aligned with the Soviet bloc, or how high their interaction was with the bloc. He used measures such as subscriptions to Communist state press services, students in Communist countries, Communist technicians in African states, foreign trade with Communist states, and economic assistance from Communist states. Inspecting the index illustrates that it has very strong validity. The U.A.R., Algeria, Guinea, Mali, and Ghana lead the list of high interactors with the Soviet Union, certainly reflecting an intuitive judgment that such countries would interact highly with the Eastern bloc. Of the top sixteen interactors with the East, only three had military security treaties with NATO powers in 1965, while ten of the bottom sixteen had such treaties. In other words, the index differentiates well among the thirty-two African states with respect to their Eastern bloc interaction.

The point of these two illustrations, therefore, is that operational indicators are very helpful for making sure that the concept under discussion actually distinguishes among the units we are using. If leadership structures are more similar than they are different, then it is unrealistic to expect them to produce different foreign policies. Likewise, if we could not predict to "interaction with the Soviet bloc" by African countries with the interaction index, such failure would most likely not be a function of the invalidity of the index, which appears—on the face, at least—to have very high validity. Similarly, if we were interested in the intensity of threat during the six week crisis leading up to World War I, we would be surprised if our measure showed the number of threatened actions, and their intensity, declining during those six weeks. Holsti's measures show that this was not the case, and that the number of actions, relatively flat for the first three weeks, showed a drastic increase for the remainder of the crisis. The intensity of those threats, very slightly de-

---

[17] Patrick McGowan, "Africa and Non-Alignment: A Comparative Study of Foreign Policy," *International Studies Quarterly* 12 (September, 1968), 262–95.

creasing for the first three weeks after the assassination of Archduke Ferdinand, then show a rather marked increase in the last six weeks.[18] Likewise, we would have been taken slightly aback had an operational indicator of polarity throughout the Cold War shown that the world was becoming more polarized; Wallace, to the contrary, reports that his data show a drop—although not "precipitous"—in polarization from 1945 to 1970.[19]

All operational indicators possess drawbacks and involve at times very rigid assumptions. Their utility is in making sure that we are clearly distinguishing among the units of analysis under observation. For if there is no variation in an "independent" variable, then it would be futile to expect it to account for variation in international behavior.

C. Factor Analysis

Because the number of variables susceptible to empirical measurement has increased drastically in the past generation, scholars have begun relying more and more on techniques to reduce them to a manageable number. In addition to the problem of manageable variables has been the assumption that there are meaningful dimensions—both of attributes and behavior—in the world, and that these dimensions are complex and can only be represented by combining a large number of variables. The most popular of the data-reduction techniques is factor analysis. More extensive analyses of this technique can be consulted for a sophisticated understanding.[20] What we have done here is provide a simple nontechnical understanding of what the technique is supposed to do.

Factor analysis assumes that there are large-scale dimensions in the world, and that these dimensions may not necessarily correspond with our immediate, intuitive judgment. Nations, for instance, do many things in their foreign behavior. They make agreements, join organizations, request information from other countries, protest other countries' actions, go to war with them, and so on. Scholars have *normally* viewed these numerous behaviors along the simple conflict-to-cooperation continuum,

18 Ole R. Holsti, *Crisis, Escalation, War* (Montreal: McGill-Queens University Press, 1972), p. 36.

19 Michael D. Wallace, "Alliance Polarization, Cross-Cutting, and International War, 1815–1964: A Measurement Procedure and Some Preliminary Evidence," *Journal of Conflict Resolution* 17 (December, 1973), p. 602.

20 R. J. Rummel, "Understanding Factor Analysis," *Journal of Conflict Resolution* 11 (December, 1967), pp. 444–80; R. J. Rummel, *Applied Factor Analysis* (Evanston, Ill.: Northwestern University Press, 1970); Harry Harmon, *Modern Factor Analysis*, rev. ed. (Chicago: University of Chicago Press, 1967).

and the trend in most studies utilizing "events" data is still to use that continuum or to use the number of acts falling into either the conflict or the cooperation categories. It may be, however, that states that do a lot of protesting and accusing—which are conflict acts—engage in very little warlike behavior—which is also a conflict act. Therefore, protests and accusations on the one hand and bombing on the other become two quite distinct phenomena, and may be caused by quite distinct independent variables. Nations high in fulminations may be low in gunsmoke; to lump together all such acts for each country tends to cancel out the true differentiation among countries.

Table A6 illustrates what might happen in an actual test. If we assume that the scores represent the number of conflict acts in each country, and also assume that all the conflict acts constitute one entity, then if we sum them, we would end up with the grand total on the far right of the table, showing country D with the most conflict and the other three with much lower but similar levels. Clearly this does not represent the reality in Table A6, where D is very high on verbal conflict acts, but third on physical acts. Even if we were to give a weighted score to each of the acts, such as 1 for deny, 2 for accuse and protest, 4 for mobilizations and 10 for war-like acts, the resultant grand total would show the four respective countries with scores of 68, 97, 125, and 126. This scoring procedure would indicate that countries C and D were about equal on "conflict," followed by B and finally by A. But quite clearly this also misrepresents what we know to be the case, namely that D is very high on one type of conflict—verbal—and relatively low on physical conflict, while country C is relatively high on the latter but low on verbal. Distinguishing between different kinds of conflict might be essential, therefore, for different theories might account for different kinds of conflict; to mesh quite distinctive behaviors into one would not uncover that. We have used the single example here of conflict

Table A-6. Hypothetical Conflict Data

Countries	Verbal				Physical			Grand Total
	Accuse	Protest	Deny	(total)	Mobilization	War-acts	(total)	
A	10	6	2	(18)	1	3	(4)	22
B	8	2	1	(11)	4	6	(10)	21
C	6	4	1	(11)	6	8	(14)	25
D	15	20	4	(39)	3	4	(7)	46

behavior, but quite clearly the technique can be used in almost any area where there are multiple measures and in which the investigator believes the measures may form distinctive dimensions.

A more technical description would be to say that factor analysis correlates all of the variables under consideration with one another, and that those variables *correlating highly with one another* form one dimension. In Table A6, verbal and physical conflict correlate negatively with each other and therefore result in different dimensions of conflict.

Factor analysis can then be used in at least two ways. All the variables in a factor analysis will correlate (or "load") on all factors, but the very assumption of factor analysis is that variables will load "heavily" (or correlate highly) with only one factor. For instance, in factor analyses of national attributes, we learned in Chapter 4 that population and gross national product correlated highly—or loaded heavily—on the factor of size, which means that those two variables probably best represent the "size" of nations. The first use of factor analysis, therefore, is to take the two or three variables loading most highly on a factor such as population and GNP for size and use them as the index of the factor in question. A second way to use factor analysis is to utilize the entire list of variables, and then in essence use the correlation of the variable with the factor as a "weight" for assigning the variable importance on the factor. This way we build an index using all the variables, which is more precise but a little more cumbersome than the first usage. For instance, in Chapter 4, we showed that population correlated at 1.00 with size, while GNP correlated at only .82 with that factor. Therefore population would be given a greater weight than GNP but both variables would be taken into account. Were we to use *all* variables, then we would more precisely reflect the underlying factor.

Thus the goal is to develop an index representing reality in not only an empirical sense but in an intuitive and logical sense as well. To combine verbal and physical conflict acts makes sense intuitively—and for certain reasons we may want to do just that. But to do so may hide actual, real-world distinctions, which raises the issue of drawbacks to factor analysis. Two can be mentioned here. The first is that one can pump any set of numbers into a computer factor analysis program, and "factors" will be produced. The vast majority of factor analyses produce dimensions that are intuitively meaningful, but from time to time factors do appear that make no immediate sense. What, then, is done with such dimensions? If there is no theoretically sound label that can be given to them, are they discarded? If so, what does that say concerning the other dimensions that at least on the surface appear meaningful?

A second problem with factor analysis is that dimensions may still be of interest to the scholar for theoretical reasons even though they may not show up in the analysis. This problem is especially acute when considering international conflict behavior, for instance, where the concern may still be the amount of conflict in a dyad or a system relative to all action in the dyad or system. When that concern persists, the scholar must opt for substantive interest over methodological rigor. Nonetheless, factor analysis—and other data reduction techniques—are often a necessity when the researcher is faced with an exceedingly large number of variables.

D. Time Series Analysis

Many phenomena in international politics have a "time series" nature, which means they must be analyzed in units of time (day, week, month, year) instead of through cross-sectional analysis where the units are other entities—nations, international systems, regions of the world. Two issues crop up in dealing with time series data. One concerns the *trend* in a time series (as distinct from the fluctuations within the trend) and the other deals with the *lagging* of one time series behind another. And these two issues relate to the ways in which any time series can be considered: by investigating the *trend* of the data (is it going up or down?) and by investigating the fluctuations within that trend.

Figure A9 shows the trend in the number of international govern-

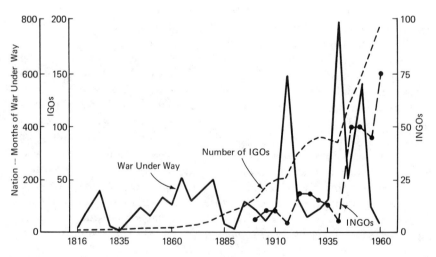

Figure A9.

mental organizations (IGOs) per five-year period and the number of nation-months of war under way per five-year period. A correlation of these two trends would very likely show a moderate positive relationship, yet it is clear in this instance that war is in no way related to the number of organizations, for the abrupt fluctuations in war do not have corresponding fluctuations in organizations. However, included in Figure A9 is the formation rate of international *non*governmental organizations (INGOs)[21] for the last half of the period; the fluctuations in the latter appear to coincide with the amount of war, but in an *inverse* direction, suggesting that there may be a relation between these two variables in that they fluctuate with each other.

The central issue in dealing with time series data is determining which questions we want answered. If our theory is concerned only with trends—*and* there is no other trend variable plausibly causing our dependent variable—then the theory may still be on solid ground. But if someone were to come along with another variable (for example, INGO formation rate) and show that its fluctuations correlated with the fluctuations in the dependent variable (war under way), then that variable takes precedence.

Time series analysis is not, therefore, an either-or situation. Its results depend on the question being asked and the way in which the data are handled. But we should be aware of the difference between the two types of questions and be wary of time series data treated only as trend, for very often there is a third variable that secularly increases over time and that in turn causes the increasing trend in *both* the independent and dependent variables.

The second issue that comes into play in dealing with time series data has to do with the lagging of variables. In theories involving time as a parameter, two variables may often be related not during the same period but only after a certain "lag" takes place. Low relationships that occur when no lag is introduced, therefore, do not necessarily imply that the original hypothesis was unconfirmed. Moreover, social theory is far from the point where we know what kinds of lags should be introduced, and consequently there is a great deal of "fishing"—numerous attempts at lagging the variables. Awareness of both problems might not only reduce the confusion about possibly contradictory findings in time series data, but sensitize the analyst to the necessity of asking clearly thought-out questions of his data.

[21] The data on INGOs have been approximated from Paul Smoker, "Nation-State Escalation and International Integration," *Journal of Peace Research* 4 (No. 1, 1967), p. 66; see Figure 6–5 for raw data as presented by Smoker.

E. Research Design

The design of a given research project has a considerable effect on the results produced and on the validity of those results. We shall here present a very brief review of seven different design problems that have been noted throughout the text. We shall also illustrate where decisions in the design had a bearing on the reasearch, how a design might have been done differently to alleviate possible problems, or how the analysts should think in terms of setting up competing designs in order to test competing theories. The seven research-design problems are as follows:

1. The Singer-Deutsch and Singer-Small studies in Chapter 5 concerned the polarity of the international system. The theory as originally proposed implied that free and uncommitted nations would produce a situation of "cross pressures," which in turn would lead to a lessening in warlike activity. The hypothesis they actually test involves using alliances as a measure of "cross pressures" and the index they use to measure cross pressures is equal to the number of nations that are in at least one alliance divided by the total number of nations in the system. Using that measure, the two following systems, with the letters representing countries, would both produce an interaction opportunity ratio of 1.0.[22]

1. ABC-DE
2. ABC-BCD-CDE-DEA

In both cases there are five countries, and all five are in alliance. Yet, as Zinnes argues, greater interaction opportunities exist in the second case because the alliances are overlapping. The same problem plagues the Singer-Small measure of bipolarity: it is unable to distinguish between systems having no overlapping alliance memberships from those that do. Thus, a mathematical manipulation of data that may at first appear to be perfectly logical often contains flaws that emerge only after very extensive analysis (which is, of course, the reason why a complete description of the data manipulation should be presented). In this case, while Zinnes's critique of the Singer-Small measure remains valid, nonetheless she re-tested the hypothesis using only years in which nations in alliance had only *one* alliance, which applies to 22 out of the 130-year period. The hypothesis was confirmed, thus lending some further credence to it, but full confirmation would of course have to await a re-testing on the entire 130-year period using a measure taking her critique into account.

2. Many times we are confronted with a hypothesis that receives con-

---

[22] Dina Zinnes, "An Analytical Study of the Balance of Power Theories," *Journal of Peace Research* 4 (No. 4, 1967), pp. 270–88.

firmation using a given set of data, but we suspect it may be spurious because of the operation of another variable. A case in point is Smoker's data, cited in Chapter 5, concerning the shift in U.S. and U.S.S.R. defense spending during the Cold War.[23] At that point it was argued that the shift may have been a function of the shifting alliance pattern (thus indirectly supporting the Singer-Small polarity theory); it may also have been, however, a function of stimulus-response: the admission of West Germany to NATO and the signing of the East European pact may each have been perceived as "aggressive" acts, to which the other side responded with increased defense expenditures. To eliminate one of the explanations, we would have to collect data on interstate behavior (such as events data) to see whether in each case the bloc that increased its alliance membership was also becoming more hostile to the other bloc outside of the increased alliance formation; if not, then the stimulus-response theory would not be supported. If investigation of a series of cases showed that the alliance-forming side was *not* hostile in other ways, then the interaction opportunities hypothesis would be more strongly supported (although not totally since one might still argue that formation of the new alliance was in fact a hostile gesture). Yet another crucial test might be to determine if the responding bloc, seeing the alliance being formed on the other side, *perceived* greater hostility or threat. If it did *not* (we must assume here that it would manifest its perception in some way, and Chapter 2 did indicate that perceived hostility would result in expressed hostility), but still responded by increasing its defense budgets, then the interaction opportunities hypothesis becomes more valid as the explanatory variable. If in each case increased defense budgets were accompanied by greater perception of hostility, however, then stimulus-response would be the more probable causal agent. Thus, there are two competing propositions, and the designs we have just suggested might be able to eliminate one or the other. If both propositions were valid, however, then we would find confirmation of both, and rather sophisticated statistical analysis might help to show which was the more potent proposition.

3. Healy and Stein's reworking of the Singer-Small study (Chapter 5) illustrates how the manner in which the question is asked, as well as how the variables are measured, can change the results. Singer and Small focused on alliances and war over long periods of time, whereas Healy and Stein focused on only one decade. By looking at what happened in that decade after the formation of alliances, they raised doubt about the

[23] Paul Smoker, "Fear in the Arms Race: A Mathematical Study," in *International Politics and Foreign Policy: A Reader in Research and Theory,* rev. ed., ed. James Rosenau (New York: Free Press, 1969).

Singer-Small proposition, but only for one decade isolated from the rest. Healy and Stein equate the formation of two important alliances in one decade with Singer and Small's *differences in* alliance aggregation across time; the twelve years prior to the fourteen-year period studied by Healy and Stein, however, had the same number of countries in alliances and the same number of alliances as the Healy-Stein period. The different results do not necessarily refute the Singer-Small findings; they are the function of different research questions.

4. Very often a research design will investigate a question that stops just short of the one we are interested in. Such was the case, for instance, with Holsti's study of Dulles's belief system (Chapter 2). Holsti's interest was in illustrating the presence of Dulles's belief system and its impact on Dulles's general evaluation, but we took that research one step further and related that evaluation to actual foreign policy. To do so, we utilized another set of data—not used by Holsti—that measured events between the United States and the Soviet Union along a conflict-cooperation continuum. It turned out that Dulles's general evaluation of the Soviet Union was only moderately correlated with actions directed by the United States toward the Soviet Union. Thus, in spite of the fact that Dulles's belief system filtered, and may have discounted, Soviet actions, his general evaluation was only moderately related to United States actions.

5. Raymond Tanter investigated the stimulus-response and "organizational process" models to explain NATO and WTO behavior in one Berlin crisis. The first model argues that one alliance's behavior is a function of the other alliance's behavior aimed toward it; the second model—from Allison's study of the Cuban Missile Crisis (Chapter 3)—argues that both alliance's behaviors are part of standard operating procedures, and therefore the behavior during any time period is going to be a function of its behavior during the previous time period. Davis Bobrow has raised interesting questions about the design of Tanter's research.[24] Tanter's organization model posits that nation-states will function under standard operating procedures, but Bobrow questions the assumption that alliances are similar organizations. Tanter's data— because they concern only events between the two alliances *about Berlin*— implicitly suggest that the organization model says behavior in a given arena is a function of previous behavior *in that arena,* clearly an inference not contained in the original Allison formulation.

In addition to Bobrow's general critique, the lack of significant find-

---

[24] Raymond Tanter, "International System and Foreign Policy Approaches: Implications for Conflict Modelling and Management," *World Politics* 24 (Spring, 1972, Supplement), 7–39; Davis B. Bobrow, "The Relevance Potential of Different Products," *World Politics* 24 (Spring, 1972, Supplement), pp. 204–228.

ings for the organizational model may be a function of the simplicity of the model used. To assume that organizations will behave at $t + 1$ in the exact same fashion as they behave at t is oversimplifying, for to do so implies a completely static entity. A more realistic model would assert that given an action X by the enemy, the organization will respond to that action every time in an identical fashion; once that action changes, however, the response will change and the behavior will change. By using this model, however, we insert rather craftily some elements of the stimulus-response model, for then an alliances' actions are due, at least partially, to the actions of the other bloc. What appears on the surface to be a simple, easily understood model, therefore, may contain hidden complexities.

6. In any social research, decisions must often be made that may distort the data. Rummel's study provides an illustration. In the early stages of his research, he restricted his data collection to the 1955–1957 period. Several reasons dictated his decision: no major wars occurred during that period except for the Middle East War of 1956 (a limited war by comparison with World Wars I and II, Korea, and later Vietnam); the world had recovered from most of the devastation of World War II, especially the economic; and, given the fact that he was collecting his data in the early 1960s, most of the information he was searching for would be available. Yet one serious problem *might* occur restricting data collection to a three-year period, particularly when using data on conflict acts. By cutting off data collection at a specific time, the researcher assumes that no great change would have occurred had the data collection extended back in time one, two, three, or six months, and likewise no great changes would have occurred in the distribution of the data had they been extended forward in time. That no change would occur remains only an assumption, however, until the data for those periods might be collected. If we think of conflicts as "systems," however, one parameter of these systems might be time itself, and it might be advisable (but much more expensive and time-consuming) to intuitively isolate the time parameters of a conflict and collect the conflict data throughout the time span of the conflict. Much aggregate data (GNP, population, telephones per capita and so on) do not change much during a one- or two-year time period, and therefore these problems do not apply. But with social action data, substantial changes can occur.

It is not a simple issue, however, and the researcher involved in such data collection can argue (1) that the time spent in bringing in these "judgmental" decisions does not warrant the amount of more accurate data acquired, and (2) that in studies where the number of observations is high (e.g., seventy-seven or more in Rummel's case), idiosyncracies will tend to cancel out one another in the average. There are in fact data

Table A7a. Number of Protests during Different Time Periods

	A	B	C
	1955-1957	1954-1957	1954-1958
United States	13 (12.)	21 (13.)	42 (13.)
France	57 (15.)	59 (15.)	67 (15.)
India	39 (14.)	40 (14.)	44 (14.)
South Vietnam	2 (8.)	3 (8.5)	3 (7.5)
West Germany	6 (10.)	19 (12.)	20 (12.)
Brazil	0 (3.5)	0 (3.5)	3 (7.5)
Canada	2 (8.)	2 (7.)	3 (7.5)
Iraq	0 (3.5)	0 (3.5)	1 (5.)
Peru	10 (11.)	10 (10.)	12 (10.)
U.S.S.R.	16 (13.)	16 (11.)	16 (11.)
Upper Volta	0 (3.5)	0 (3.5)	0 (2.5)
Honduras	2 (8.0)	3 (8.5)	3 (7.5)
Tanzania	0 (3.5)	0 (3.5)	0 (2.5)
Nicaragua	0 (3.5)	0 (3.5)	0 (2.5)
Senegal	0 (3.5)	0 (3.5)	0 (2.5)

r_s A - B .98
     B - C .96
     A - C .94

Table A7b. Number of Riots during Different Time Periods

	A	B	C
	1955-1957	1954-1957	1954-1958
United States	21 (12.)	22 (11.)	29 (10.)
India	98 (14.)	105 (14.)	111 (14.)
Italy	17 (11.)	28 (12.)	34 (11.)
Morocco	117 (15.)	143 (15.)	149 (15.)
South Africa	39 (13.)	41 (13.)	43 (12.5)
Chile	16 (9.5)	16 (9.5)	23 (9.)
South Yemen	1 (3.5)	1 (3.5)	6 (4.5)
Sri Lanka (Ceylon)	16 (9.5)	16 (9.5)	43 (12.5)
Israel	8 (6.)	8 (6.)	11 (6.5)
Belgium	11 (7.)	11 (7.)	11 (6.5)
Gabon	0 (1.5)	0 (1.5)	0 (1.)
Guinea	1 (3.5)	1 (3.5)	6 (4.5)
Tanzania	0 (1.5)	0 (1.5)	1 (2.)
Trinidad-Tobago	13 (8.)	13 (8.)	13 (8.)
Afghanistan	2 (5.)	2 (5.)	2 (3.)

r_s A - B .99
     B - C .97
     A - C .97

Mean r_s .97

These data have been extracted from Charles Lewis Taylor and Michael C. Hudson, *World Handbook of Political and Social Indicators.* 2d ed. (New Haven: Yale University Press, 1972), pp. 88-101. Under each row the first figure is the frequency of action for that country during the time period; the figures in parentheses are the ranks for the countries on those actions for the time period.

that support that contention. Table A7a and A7b show the number of protests and riots occurring in fifteen different countries; these were selected from the entire universe of countries by taking five with high, five with medium, and five with low numbers of protests and riots. Row A in both tables contains data from 1955-1957, while Row B adds in the data for 1954, and row C adds to that data for 1958. The raw frequencies for each country are followed by the rank of that country for the given time period. Though the numbers change when additional data is added, nonetheless the relative rankings are almost identical (average Spearman rank correlation of .97). In other words, the number of protests and riots does appear to be rather stable over time.

7. The same concept can often be measured in many different ways. Status inconsistency is one case in point. Wallace, for instance, in chapter eight, takes the average sum of the differences for each country on its ranks and then adds each of these together for each time period to get a measure of the amount of status inconsistency in the system for that time period. If for the 1820–1825 period, for instance, all countries in the sample occupied the same rank for each of the measures, then there would be no rank inconsistency: however, if for the years 1826–1830, France was ranked second on population, fifth on military force, and third on diplomatic status, then the average of its rank differences would be 2. That score would be added to all other such average differences to compute the inconsistency score for the system as a whole.

East, however, correlates each rank measure for each year with the others, and ends up with several correlations among the ranks for each year. A very high correlation indicates that countries high on one measure are high on others; a low correlation would mean there is great discrepancy on the ranks for each year.

It is hoped, of course, that two different measures of the same concept will produce equivalent data if done for the same period of time. If that did not occur, however, a logical analysis sometimes helps decide which is the best measure. In the present case, it is probable that East's measure would not change abruptly from year to year whereas Wallace's would, thus providing a greater amount of variation in the variable. If France shifted—in the above example—from second on population to fifteenth, the resultant discrepancy score for France at that time would be 8, which might drastically change the score of the system also. It is unlikely, however, that such a drop in rank when using a large number of countries is going to affect the rank correlation. In that sense, Wallace's measure may be more sensitive.

Name Index

Abravanel, Martin, 215, 232
Alcock, Norman, 178
Alker, Hayward, 15, 116, 216, 217, 218, 221
Allison, Graham, 71, 72, 73, 76, 77, 79, 80, 88, 98, 100, 363, 372
Angell, Robert C., 210
Azar, Edward, 278, 279

Banks, Arthur, 108, 126
Barber, James D., 30
Barnett, A. Doak, 205
Behrman, Jack N., 340
Benjamin, Roger, 92
Bernstein, Robert A., 47, 215
Blechman, Barry, 292, 293, 294, 300
Bobrow, Davis, 372
Boulding, Kenneth, 40
Brady, Linda, 85, 88
Brams, Steven, 15, 152
Bremer, Stuart, 138, 192, 193
Bronfenbrenner, Urie, 44
Bull, Hedley, 14
Burns, Arthur, 173, 228
Burrowes, Robert, 127, 128, 137
Burton, J. W., 157

Calhoun, Herbert, 246
Caporaso, James, 5, 212, 215, 219, 220, 249
Carleton, William, 252, 253

Cattell, Raymond, 27, 110
Chadwick, Richard, 113
Choucri, Nazli, 39, 43, 131, 137, 309, 318
Clark, Cal, 238
Clark, J. F., 116
Clark, W., 212
Claude, Inis, 164, 165, 166, 189, 190
Cobb, Roger W., 211, 229, 231, 232, 249
Coleman, James, 225, 237
Collins, John, 130, 131, 132, 139, 140
Coplin, William, 115, 119, 296
Coser, Lewis, 122, 226
Crow, Wayman, 283, 284

Dahl, Robert, 254
D'Amato, Anthony, 30
Dennis, Michael, 88
Denton, Frank, 146
De Rivera, Joseph, 27, 33, 42, 63, 86, 89, 90, 93
Deutsch, Karl, 157, 159, 170, 171, 209, 210, 214, 216-19, 221, 226, 230, 231, 233, 249, 330, 370
Dougherty, James, 59, 118
Druckman, Daniel, 33, 34, 50

East, Maurice, 109, 113, 136, 188, 199, 319, 375
Eckhardt, William, 39

377

Edinger, Lewis, 92
Elder, Charles, 211, 229, 231, 232, 249
Ellsberg, Daniel, 78, 79, 94, 96-98
Etzioni, Amitai, 213, 286

Feierabend, Ivo, 137, 138, 291
Feierabend, Rosalind, 137, 138, 291
Ferris, Wayne, 181, 183-85, 187, 193, 201
Fink, Clinton, 282
Fisher, R., 270
Fisher, W., 215, 218-19, 221
Fitzsimmons, Barbara, 112, 179
Franck, Thomas M., 40, 44

Galtung, Johan, 152, 176, 188
Gamson, William, 34, 46, 287
Gelb, Leslie, 75
George, A., 28-30, 33, 45, 49, 71, 263, 268, 284, 285
George, M., 28, 29, 33
German, C., 157
Gleditsch, Nils, 188
Goldmann, Kjell, 46, 205
Gregg, P., 113, 126, 319
Gregg, R. W., 115, 136

Haas, Ernst, 122, 164, 165, 210, 248
Haas, Michael, 113, 118, 130, 131, 196, 197, 201, 204, 205, 208, 237
Halberstam, David, 58, 75, 78
Halperin, Morton, 99, 100
Handelman, John, 328
Hanreider, Wolfram, 110
Harf, James, 239, 331
Harsanyi, J. C., 256, 273
Hazelwood, Leo, 134-35
Healy, Brian, 170, 173, 193, 194, 196, 200, 228, 243, 245, 371
Hermann, Charles, 31, 32, 43, 83, 90, 93, 109, 113, 114, 118, 133, 278, 284, 317
Hermann, Margaret, 31, 32, 60, 83
Herz, John, 189, 190
Hill, G., 151, 279
Hilsman, Roger, 74
Hilton, G., 57, 61
Hirschman, Albert, 7
Hoggard, Gary, 112, 139, 279, 319, 320, 331
Holsti, K. J., 14, 50, 138, 160, 181-84, 255, 321
Holsti, Ole, 37-39, 45-46, 49, 54-55, 60, 83-84, 86, 93, 119, 138, 160, 181-84, 225, 242, 243, 255, 294, 331, 359, 372
Hoopes, Townsend, 89
Hopmann, Terrence, 46, 152, 226, 227, 241, 243

Hughes, Barry, 152, 214, 215, 218, 232, 233, 236, 249

Ikle, Fred, 270, 273
Inglehart, Ronald, 217, 218, 221

Jenson, Lloyd, 254
Jervis, Robert, 41, 42

Kahn, Herman, 259, 260, 262
Kaplan, Morton, 152, 169, 170, 173
Kean, James, 110, 134
Kelman, Herbert C., 31, 40, 41, 66
Kennedy, Robert, 253
Kissinger, Henry, 104, 105, 190, 362, 363, 364
Knorr, Klaus, 14, 42
Kuhn, T. S., 328

Lambton, David, 42, 43, 60
Lasswell, Harold, 28, 165
Lauren, Paul, 261, 262
Leites, Nathan, 273
Lijphart, Arend, 329
Lindberg, Leon, 215
Lindblom, Charles, 70, 71, 72, 77
Loomba, Joann, 47-49, 62

McClelland, Charles, 112, 139, 144, 145, 147, 148, 152, 257, 297, 298, 322
McGowan, Patrick, 39, 110, 120, 121, 134, 137, 237, 279, 364
MacKinder, Halford, 103
MacMillan, Harold, 190
Mahan, Alfred, 103
Martin, Wayne, 12, 278
Midlarsky, Manus, 191, 197, 198
Milstein, Jeffrey, 185-87, 290, 292, 294
Modigliani, Andre, 34, 46, 287
Mogdis, Franz, 57, 289, 294
Moore, David, 133
Morgan, Patrick, 13
Morgenthau, Hans, 24, 50, 155, 156, 159-63, 165, 173-76, 190
Munton, Don, 313, 316

Newcombe, Alan, 178
North, Robert, 54, 55, 61, 131, 137, 166, 309, 318
Nye, J. S., 210, 215, 238

O'Leary, Michael, 116, 321
Onate, Andres, 127, 136
Organski, A. F. K., 139, 156, 167, 178
Osgood, Charles, 41, 61, 285

Paige, Glenn, 69, 85, 93
Park, Tong-Whan, 180, 308
Patchen, Martin, 272, 277
Pelowski, Alan, 5, 216, 219, 220, 249
Pfaltzgraff, Robert, 59, 118
Phillips, Warren, 126, 146, 291
Pool, Ithiel de Sola, 11, 52, 60
Puchala, Donald, 14, 217, 218, 221

Quistgard, Jon, 116

Rapaport, Anatol, 274
Raser, John, 275, 276, 283, 284
Rhee, Sang-Woo, 10, 11, 180, 181, 188, 312
Richardson, Lewis F., 145, 196, 237, 276
Riggs, R. E., 115
Riker, Williams, 174, 175
Robinson, James, 31, 66, 82, 83, 86-88, 93
Rochester, J. Martin, 115, 119
Ropp, Steve, 238
Rosenau, James N., 14, 15, 32, 46, 47, 50, 102, 105, 106, 120, 319, 320, 331
Rummel, R. J., 106, 107, 110, 112-14, 117, 124, 126, 128, 133, 152, 179, 180, 184, 189, 237, 306-11, 313, 360, 361, 373
Russett, Bruce, 15, 106, 107, 116, 132, 145, 146, 152, 174, 175, 233-36, 249, 272, 273, 280, 282, 283, 285, 300

Salmore, Steven, 113, 118, 133
Sawyer, Jack, 106, 107
Schelling, Thomas, 256, 257, 262, 266, 268
Schwarz, John E., 152, 214, 215, 232, 233, 249
Scott, William, 30, 31, 60
Sensenig, B., 115
Shapiro, Howard, 39, 137, 237
Simon, Herbert, 69, 70, 71, 73, 77
Singer, J. David, 14, 15, 25, 47, 138, 146, 147, 152, 170-73, 181, 182, 185, 191-94, 196, 197, 199, 200, 201, 225, 238, 265, 266, 271, 272, 339, 370 371
Singer, M. R., 115
Siverson, Randolph, 37, 38, 39
Skrein, Michael, 112, 113, 114, 133
Small, Melvin, 25, 146, 147, 170, 172, 173, 181, 182, 185, 191, 193, 194, 196, 197, 199, 200, 201, 225, 370, 371

Smoke, Richard, 263, 264
Smoker, Paul, 198, 199, 237, 239, 249, 286, 371
Snyder, Glenn, 263
Snyder, Richard, 31, 66, 68, 69, 81-83, 86-88, 93
Sondermann, Fred, 74
Sorokin, Pitirim, 122, 124, 146, 358
Spector, Bertram, 127, 128, 137
Stassen, Glen H., 46, 47, 49
Stein, Arthur, 170, 173, 193, 194, 196, 200, 228, 243, 245, 371
Stuckey, John, 192, 193
Sullivan John, 116, 118, 119, 140, 201
Sullivan, Michael, 15, 16, 39, 51, 60, 74, 179, 184, 185, 249, 309

Tanter, Raymond, 88, 126, 131, 291, 319, 372
Terrel, Louis, 131, 132
Thompson, W. R., 188
Todd, James E., 115

Verba, Sidney, 67
Vincent, Jack, 112, 114, 115, 116, 189, 312, 313, 314
Volgy, Thomas, 116, 152, 236

Wallace, Michael, 197, 199, 200, 204, 238, 239, 249, 303, 375
Waltz, Kenneth, 23, 104, 105, 122, 170, 173
Weede, Erich, 112
Weigert, K. M., 115
Weisband, Edward, 40, 44
Welch, Susan, 212
White, Ralph, 39, 44
Whiting, Allen, 10, 11, 122
Wicker, Tom, 58, 74, 77
Wilkenfeld, Jonathan, 110, 117, 127, 128, 129, 130, 132, 136, 290, 294, 318
Wilkinson, David, 137
Wittkopf, E. R., 116
Wright, Quincy, 50, 118, 122, 146, 182, 184, 196, 202, 211, 305

Young, Oran, 260-62, 268, 269, 273, 276, 278
Young, Roland, 68, 112, 278

Zinnes, Dina, 56, 57, 61, 110, 117, 129, 132, 136, 152, 166, 171, 172, 174, 175, 197, 370

Subject Index

Acheson, Dean, 46, 47
Africa, 130-32, 139, 140
Albania, 236, 243
Alliances. *See also* Balance of power; International behavior, types of; Power
as behavior, 2
behavior between, 225-26, 237, 241-42
behavior within, 116, 118, 225-26, 237, 241-42
causes of, 105, 173-75, 303, 371-72
effects of, 170, 191-94, 195 (*table*), 196, 200, 303, 309, 318
measurement of polarity, 191, 370-72
Alternatives, 71-72, 79, 84. *See also* Crisis; Decision-making; Perception
Arms races, 239, 250, 276, 286
Arms reductions, 228, 327
Attitudes, 30-31, 232-33
Austria, 44, 84, 194, 243
Austrian State Treaty, 46
Austro-German Alliance (1879), 245

Balance, 226, 227, 228 (*figure*), 229, 246 (*figure*), 335
Balance of power. *See also* Balance; Power
and alliances, 190
cessation of, 175
critique as a theory, 329

Balance of power (*cont.*)
definitions of, 164-65, 170, 172, 201
equated with power distance, 164
important questions concerning, 164
link with behavior, 166-67, 170, 175, 190
measures of, 172
normative aspects of, 164, 170
as polarity, 191
and prediction, 172
rules of, 169-70
in Southeast Asia, 74
Ball, George, 79
Bargaining
assumptions of, 255-57
data needed, 277
definition of, 259
difficulty in predicting effects, 260
difficulty in theorizing about, 261
domain of, 335
as a game, 252, 253, 259
as influence, 161, 265 (*table*), 271
in non-crisis, 254
and perceptions, 259
strategies of, 256-57, 259, 274-75
Bargaining theory, 262
Belief systems, 45-49, 60-61, 64, 153
Berlin crisis, 88, 148, 291, 372
Bipolarity, 169-71, 173, 191, 196-97, 250, 273. *See also* Balance of power; Multipolarity; Power
Brazil, 176, 312

Capabilities, 231, 303-4, 317
Capitalism, 104, 118
Causality, 5, 51, 122, 124, 231, 237, 240, 280. *See also* Correlations; Lagged variables
Central Intelligence Agency (CIA), 77, 80
"Character." *See* National attributes, non-measurable; Power
China, 57, 80
  admission to United Nations, 140
  aid to Ho Chi Minh, 43
  attitudes toward Soviet bloc, 58, 119
  attitudes toward West, 242
  behavior as function of rank, 188-89
  behavior toward Eastern bloc, 118-19, 243
  conflict behavior of, 312
  cooperative behavior of, 314, 315 (*figure*), 316 (*figure*), 317 (*figure*)
  Cultural Revolution, 7, 10
  domestic and external conflict, 127, 136
  in Indochina, 11, 279
  invasion of India, 6
  leadership effect on foreign policy, 10
  operational code, 42
  perception of Soviet Union, 58
  power distance and foreign policy, 180-81, 312
  relations with Soviet bloc, 119
  relations with Soviet Union, 120 (*figure*), 247
  relations with United States, 7, 10, 246, 275
  revolutionary leadership in, 104
  status of, 176
Clifford, Clark, 143
Coalition behavior, 174-75
Coercive diplomacy, 284-85
Cold War, 34-36, 147
Collective goods, 116
Collective security, 329
Commitment, 78, 267-71, 280, 313
Communications, 31, 89, 211-12, 214, 222, 225-26, 231, 237, 249, 359. *See also* Alliances; Crisis; Distance
Communication theory, 210, 248
Community formation, 215, 229, 230, 232
Conflict, 122, 179, 236, 257, 328, 366. *See also* International behavior, types of; War
Conflict resolution, 92, 257
Content analysis, 41-42, 51, 138
Correlates of War Project, 146, 181
Correlations, 344, 348-49, 355. *See also* Causality
Credibility, 299. *See also* Bargaining; Commitment; Deterrence

Crisis
  causes of, 322-23
  effect of, 61, 82-86, 88, 90, 257, 323
  elements of, 257, 261
  orientation of news media, 2, 154
  perceptions during, 37, 61
  policy advice for, 99
  prediction of, 152
Cuba, 104, 312
Cuban Missile Crisis, 64, 76, 284, 288
  air strike option, 93
  as bargaining game, 253
  decision-making models, 98
  evidence on, 73
  explanation of, using power, 161
  perception during, 55, 84-85
  symbolic rhetoric in, 51. *See also* symbols
  as type of behavior, 2-3
  watershed in Cold War, 37
Culture, and perception, 37

Decision-making
  collective, 90
  determinants of, 68, 71, 83, 91 (*table*)
  elements of, 82
  important questions concerning, 20
  individual's effect on, 86-87
  isolation of alternatives, 90-91
  lack of data on, 18, 99, 100
  models
    organizational process, 72, 77-81, 92, 319
    problems with, 67
    rational process, 69, 70, 72, 74-77
  progress in analysis of, 93
  theories of, 66, 81ff
  trends in, 321
  types of decisions in, 96, 98
Definition of the situation. *See* National interest
deGaulle, Charles, 32, 87, 118-19
Democracy. *See* National attributes, types of; Symbols
Density, 138, 318
Détente, 10-13, 204, 246, 344-46
Deterrence, 189, 262-64, 266-70, 280 (*table*), 281 (*table*), 282-84, 299. *See also* Bargaining
Diplomacy, 124, 152, 193, 255, 259, 278, 294, 298
Diplomatic bonds, 188. *See also* Distance
Distance
  communication as, 222-26, 237
  domain of theory, 120, 335
  in field theory, 304-6

Distance *(cont.)*
  link to behavior, 208, 223-25, 234-38, 242-45 *(tables, figures)*
  manner of explaining behavior, 207
  measures of, 222-24, 229, 233, 236, 242
  types of, 234, 241-42, 305, 309
Dual Alliance, 55, 57, 84, 194, 359
Dulles, John Foster, 45-46, 49, 54, 60, 205, 266-67, 279-80, 282, 299, 372

Economic development, 132-33, 134-35, 178, 310-11, 319-29, 322, 340. *See also* National attributes, types of; Power
Eisenhower, Dwight D., 34, 42, 76, 98
Equilibrium, 166, 190. *See also* Balance of power
Escalation, 236, 260-61, 284, 323 *(figure)*, 324
EUROATOM, 215, 219
European Economic Community (EEC), 215-16, 219-21, 232
Events, 11, 145, 147, 149, 366. *See also* Explanation; International behavior, as flow of events; World Event Interaction Survey
Evidence, 2, 11-15, 94, 119
Explanation, 10-13, 17, 28, 59, 68, 98, 320-21, 342. *See also* Theory

Factor Analysis, 106, 126-27, 234, 306, 309
Field theory, 304-16
France, 52, 77, 118-19, 120 *(figure)*, 194, 216, 218, 243
Frustration, 23, 131, 177

Game theory, 252, 259, 274, 317
Geography, 103, 178, 234-35, 307, 312, 319, 360, 361. *See also* National attributes
Germany, 52, 159, 194, 198, 216, 218, 220, 243, 371
Goals, 78, 314. *See also* Models, decision-making
Gross National Product, 178, 367. *See also* National attributes; Power

Hitler, Adolph, 29, 44, 59, 63
Ho Chi Minh, 43-44
Hungary, 235, 236

Ideology, 48 *(table)*, 121, 156, 170, 307. *See also* Values

Images
  conscious use of, 44
  effect of, compared to role, 48-49
  of India, 47
  link to attitudes, 48, 63
  link to behavior, 40, 42, 53
  manipulation of, 41
  role in U.S. response in Korea, 42
  "true" meaning of, 41
  types of, 42-43, 60, 64
Image theories, 41, 49, 60, 62, 336
Imperialism, 104, 118. *See also* National attributes
India, 11, 125, 149, 176, 314
Individual level of analysis, 23, 58, 65
Industrialization, 105, 108, 167. *See also* National attributes
Influence, 41, 157, 160-61, 254, 296-97. *See also* Bargaining; Power
Integration
  as cause and effect, 214, 221, 224, 248
  communication and, 209
  decision-making and, 213
  definitions of, 209, 214-15
  domain of, 209
  as explanation, 208-10, 213
  in field theory, 304
  institutional approach, 209
  perception of, 217 *(table)*
  problems with, 221, 224, 248, 249
  regional, 209, 216-18, 220, 221 *(figure)*, 222 *(figure)*, 223 *(figure)*, 249
  transactions as, 221
  types of, 215, 219, 220, 224, 240
Interaction opportunities, 171-72, 191, 193, 194, 200, 205, 371. *See also* Balance of power; Bipolarity; Multipolarity
International behavior
  assumption of regularities, 15, 144
  cooperative, 335
  different manifestations of, 2, 333-35, 339
  as "flow of events," 147, 148 *(figure)*, 149-50, 278. *See also* Events; World Event Interaction Survey
  as focus of research, 1-4
  as issues, 338
  laws of, 15, 17
  link to theory, 334 *(table)*
  as quasi-experiment, 5
  stability of, 145-46
  static vs. dynamic, 336
  on system level, 152-53
  types of, 2, 3, 59, 68-69, 110, 112-13, 124, 126-27, 132, 150, 151 *(figure)*, 156, 158, 201-2, 320
  unpredictability of, 144

International behavior *(cont.)*
  variation in, 20
International organizations
  and arms races, 240 *(figure)*
  causes of, 211
  and conflict, 210, 235-36, 238-39, 331,
    368 *(figure)*, 369 *(figure)*
  as cooperative behavior, 112, 309, 313
  effects of, 304
  as experiments, 5
  function of transactions, 229
  governmental, 145-46, 198, 304, 309, 317
  non-governmental, 198, 312
  as non-state actors, 328
  and United Nations voting, 233-34
International system
  anarchistic elements of, 157
  assumptions of, 144
  described by event flows, 149-50
  organized, 147
  stability of, 170-71
  types of, 169-70
  violence in, 324
Involvement, 54, 64, 322
Israel, 37, 128, 186, 292-93

Japan, 146, 204, 282-83
Johnson, Lyndon B., 32, 39, 51-52, 74-75,
    77-78, 89-90, 97, 284

Kennedy, John F., 34, 39, 43, 90, 253, 284,
    286
  decision in Cuban Missile crisis, 77, 80-
    81, 143
  and Vietnam war, 51, 74, 77-78, 95-98
Khrushchev, Nikita, 32, 34, 39, 49, 80, 242,
    253, 254, 270
Korea, 2, 11, 33, 37, 42, 59, 69, 77, 314

Lagged variables, 127, 200, 219, 221, 233,
    291, 368-69
Laws. *See* International behavior, laws of
League of Nations, 115, 120, 208
Lenin, V. I., 29, 104, 118
Limited wars, 170. *See also* War

MacArthur, Douglas, 33, 59
McNamara, Robert, 75-76, 78, 81, 96
Mao Tse-tung, 118, 119
Marxism, 109, 118
Memory, in perception, 56-57
Methodology. *See* Research design
Middle East, 37, 127, 149, 308, 360

Military expenditures, 318
Military strategists, 166, 252, 267. *See also*
    Bargaining; Deterrence; Game the-
    ory
Model-building, 324, 330, 341
Models, 134, 222-24
  additive, 133, 342
  bargaining, 265, 272, 295 *(figure)*, 296.
    See also Bargaining
  decision-making, 67-81, 263-64, 321-22,
    372
    assumptions of, 73
    compared to theories, 67
    comparison of, 70 *(figure)*, 72-73
    domain of, 336
    evidence for, 73, 93
    measurement of, 73
    types of, 70-72, 76-77, 79, 94-98
    utility of, 100
  definition of, 67
  descriptive, 68
  dynamic, 257, 297
  evaluation of, 73, 93, 96
  general, 226
  implicit, 331
  mediated stimulus-response, 54
  multivariate, 321, 324
  necessity in research, 8
  perceptual, 61
  simple, 132, 342
  static, 257
  statistical, 331
  types of, 56-57, 88
Morale, 139, 159, 178. *See also* National
    attributes; Power
Motivation, 69, 156, 256, 258, 259, 268-69,
    284
Multi-national corporations, 328, 340-41
Multipolarity, 171, 173, 196, 250. *See also*
    Balance of power; Bipolarity
Multivariate analysis, 60-61, 135

Nasser, Gamel Abdul, 39, 43
National attributes
  combined effect of, 132
  definition of, 103
  lack of change in, 139, 314
  link to behavior, 109-10, 111 *(table)*, 137,
    318
  non-measurable types of, 108, 137
  relations among, 139
  types of
    capabilities, 91
    domestic conflict, 103, 105, 107, 122,
      123 *(figure)*, 125 *(table)*, 324

National attributes (*cont.*)
  types of (*cont.*)
    economic development, 103, 105-6, 112-16
    leadership structure, 103-4
    morale, 108, 159
    needs, 134
    political development, 103, 105-6, 114, 178, 219
    political system, 20, 32, 105, 117-21, 128, 132-33, 136, 319
    resources, 134
    size, 103, 105-6, 112, 116-17, 133-35, 319-20, 322, 332
    societal stress, 108, 122, 130, 237, 303, 359
National attribute theory
  compared to other theories, 102-3, 306, 319-20
  decision-making and, 102, 335
  domain of, 335
  and environmental issues, 339
  and perception, 335
  premises of, 102
  simplicity of, 137
National interest, 49, 50, 60, 64, 213
Nationalism, 30, 32. *See also* Personality, types of
Negotiations, 34, 258, 260, 272-73. *See also* Bargaining
Neofunctionalism, 208, 212, 248
Netherlands, 77, 131, 218
Nixon, Richard, 9, 28, 39, 51, 87, 143, 254
North Atlantic Treaty Organization (NATO), 88, 116, 286, 291

Outliers, 181, 311, 357-58

Permanent Court of International Justice (PCIJ), 115, 120
Pentagon Papers, 74, 75, 94
Perception
  of alternatives, 84 (*table*), 318
  in bargaining, 276
  in decision-making, 72, 92
  differences in, 37
  domain of, 336
  importance of, 55
  of influence attempts, 254
  as intervening variable, 54, 64, 322-23
  links with behavior, 56-58, 61-62
  types of, 39, 43, 55-57, 61-62, 318, 371
  in United States foreign policy, 49. *See also* Images
  of war, 191

Personality, 27-32, 63, 318
  aberrant, 59, 63, 323
  in Cold War, 34
  crises and, 63
  debate on effect of, 40, 153
  domain of theory, 29, 33, 37, 60, 86
  indirect tests, 59, 62-63
  lack of effect on foreign policy, 34-39
  link to attitudes, 30, 60
  link to behavior, 26, 32, 39, 60-61, 63, 86
  measurement of, 59, 63
  problems as explanation, 27, 28, 30, 59
  psychoanalytic approach, 28-29
  role in negotiations, 34
  theories of, 27f
  types of, 30, 32, 33, 60. *See also* Belief systems
Poland, 236, 314
Polarity, 196-97, 201, 370. *See also* Balance of power; Polarization
Polarization, 84, 196, 197 (*table*), 198 (*figure*), 204-5, 225-26, 237, 365
Policy. *See* Relevance
Political development. *See* National attributes, types of; Power
Population. *See* Power, measurement of
Power
  assumptions of power theory, 157-58
  complexity of, 158, 162-63
  domain of power theory, 163, 335
  as drive, 155, 200
  in field theory, 304-5, 307, 309, 312-13, 316
  as influence, 157, 160-61, 178
  and integration, 213
  lack of explanatory focus, 200
  lack of immediate relevance, 203
  link to behavior, 112, 156-57, 160, 167, 168, 173, 181 (*table*), 182 (*table*), 183-86 (*figures*), 187, 192-93, 202-3, 309, 360-61. *See also* National attributes, types of
  link to status, 316
  measurement of, 131, 172, 178, 340, 367
  national attributes of, 107, 109, 158-59, 169-70, 172, 178, 254
  perceptions of, 178
  poles, 169-72
  relations of equality, 166-68
Power distribution, 160, 167-68, 192-93, 204, 308, 321-22, 339-40
Prediction, 359-60
Prisoner's Dilemma, 274 (*table*)

"Random-ness," 145, 344, 346

Rank, 176-77, 180, 189-90, 199-200, 303-5, 307, 310, 312-13, 316, 360-61, 375
Rationality, 67, 69, 71, 104, 174, 264, 269
Relevance, 15-16, 62, 99-100, 336-37, 338 (*table*)
Research design, 200-201, 331-32, 343
Role, 37, 46-48, 138. *See also* Belief systems
Rostow, Walt, 75, 89, 97
Russia, 52, 159, 194, 243, 245. *See also* Soviet Union

Salience, 309
Sampling, 13, 331, 350-51
"Significance," 344, 346, 350-52
Simulation, 31, 90, 114, 252, 284, 317
"Size" principle, 174-75
Social distance theory. *See* Distance
Soviet Union. *See also* Russia
  alliance with Eastern Europe, 199
  attitudes toward West, 242
  in Cuban Missile Crisis, 55, 76, 80
  defense spending, 199, 371
  foreign policy, general, 321
  organizational procedures, 79
  relations with China, 57-58, 205, 247, 314
  relations with United States, 56, 87, 247
Spillover, 212
Stalin, Joseph, 28, 34, 59, 63, 321
Statistics, 13, 134, 347, 351
Status. *See* Rank
Stimulus-Response, 6, 53, 56 (*figure*), 126, 287-90 (*figures, tables*), 318-19, 323-24, 362, 371-72. *See also* Bargaining; Models
Stratification. *See* Rank
Symbols, 39, 50-53, 64, 269, 270, 324
Syria, 127-28, 186-88

Taylor, Maxwell, 75, 78, 96, 97
Technology, 131, 318
Theory
  assumptions of, 7
  descriptions as, 92
  different uses of, 330
  domain of, 3, 6, 324, 334 (*table*), 335-36
  elements of, 4-9
  evaluation of, 9, 93, 331
  formalized, 16
  necessity in research, 8
  plausible, 331
  as puzzle-solving, 62, 329
  relation to policy issues, 327, 337, 338 (*table*)
  types of, 4-5
Trade, 112, 145-46, 235-37. *See also* Distance

Transactions, 208-11, 229, 231-32, 248. *See also* Distance; Integration
Triple Entente, 55, 57, 84, 288
Truman, Harry S., 34, 74, 76, 89, 90

Uncertainty, 191-93, 258, 266, 271, 339-40
United Kingdom, 159, 314
United Nations, 91, 116, 120
  as experiment, 5
  office-holding in, 115
  perception of delegates, 38, 114
  role of, 140, 208, 282
  voting in, 2, 114, 145-46, 233-34, 307, 309, 313
  and war, 238
United States
  attitude to United Nations, 140
  aversion to standing army, 159
  behavior as function of rank, 189
  behavior toward Communist bloc, 53
  bureaucratic structure of, 104
  and Cuban Missile Crisis, 55, 80
  decision in Korea, 69, 91
  defense spending, 199, 371
  deterrent behavior of, 180
  foreign aid, 140-41
  foreign relations (general), 361 (*figure*)
  power distance and foreign policy, 180
  relations with China, 246, 275, 279, 314
  relations with Soviet Union, 3, 247
  State Department, 62, 321
  and Vietnam war, 42, 74-75, 94, 96
Urbanization, 113, 138, 167

Values, 83, 87, 105, 231, 307-8, 312, 340-41, 360-61. *See also* Decision-making; National attributes
Variation, 344-48, 353-54
Vietnam war, 2, 9, 16, 39, 44, 51-53, 74, 89, 94, 95 (*figure*), 205, 270, 324

War
  causes of, 104, 130, 136, 167-68, 234, 304. *See also* Balance of power
  factor dimension of, 124
  as international behavior, 1, 3
  and morality, 26
  periodicity of, 146
  trends in, 25 (*figure*), 368 (*figure*)
  "will," 53, 137, 178, 267. *See also* Power
Wilson, Woodrow, 28-29, 33
World Event Interaction Survey (WEIS), 113, 114, 297
World War I, 51, 83